Quiet Time

one year daily devotional with commentary

QuietTime

one year daily devotional with commentary

Word of Life Local Church Ministries
A division of Word of Life Fellowship, Inc.
  Joe Jordan – Executive Director
  Don Lough – Director
  Jack Wyrtzen & Harry Bollback – Founders
  Mike Calhoun – VP of Local Church Ministries

USA
P.O. Box 600
Schroon Lake, NY 12870
talk@wol.org
1-888-932-5827

Canada
RR#8/Owen Sound
ON, Canada N4K 5W4
LCM@wol.ca
1-800-461-3503

Web Address: www.wol.org

Publisher's Acknowledgements
Writers and Contributors:
  Bill Boulet
  Dr. Tom Davis
  Don Kelso
  Dr. Chuck Sheide
  Dr. Charles Wagner

  1 Corinthians
  John, Revelation, Zechariah
  Psalms, Proverbs, Hebrews
  Ephesians, Titus, Philemon, 2 Timothy
  Joshua, Judges, Amos, Obadiah,
  Jonah, Micah

Editor: Dr. Tom Davis
Curriculum Manager: Don Reichard
Cover and page design: Boire Design

ISBN - 978-1-931235-94-5
Printed in the United States of America

helpful hints for a daily quiet time

The purpose of this Quiet Time is to meet the needs of spiritual growth in the life of the Christian in such a way that they learn the art of conducting their own personal investigation into the Bible. Consider the following helpful hints:

1 Give priority in choosing your quiet time. This will vary with each individual in accordance with his own circumstances. The time you choose must:

■ have top priority over everything else

■ be the quietest time possible.

■ be a convenient time of the day or night.

■ be consistently observed each day.

2 Give attention to the procedure suggested for you to follow. Include the following items.

■ Read God's Word.

■ Mark your Bible as you read. Here are some suggestions that might be helpful:

    a.   After you read the passage put an exclamation mark next to the verses you completely understand.

    b.   Put a question mark next to verses you do not understand.

    c.   Put an arrow pointing upward next to encouraging verses.

    d.   Put an arrow pointing downward next to verses which weigh us down in our spiritual race.

    e.   Put a star next to verses containing important truths or major points.

■ Meditate on what you have read (In one sentence, write the main thought). Here are some suggestions as guidelines for meditating on God's Word:

a. Look at the selected passage from God's point of view.
b. Though we encourage quiet time in the morning, some people arrange to have their quiet time at the end of their day. God emphasizes that we need to go to sleep meditating on His Word. "My soul shall be satisfied and my mouth shall praise thee with joyful lips: when I remember thee upon my bed, and meditating on thee in the night watches" (Psalm 63:5,6).
c. Deuteronomy 6:7 lists routine things you do each day during which you should concentrate on the portion of Scripture for that day:
— when you sit in your house (meals and relaxation)
— when you walk in the way (to and from school or work)
— when you lie down (before going to sleep at night)
— when you rise up (getting ready for the day)

■ Apply some truth to your life. (Use first person pronouns I, me, my, mine). If you have difficulty in finding an application for your life, think of yourself as a Bible SPECTator and ask yourself the following questions.

S – is there any sin for me to forsake?

P – is there any promise for me to claim?

E – is there any example for me to follow?

C – is there any command for me to obey?

T – is there anything to be thankful for today?

■ Pray for specific things (Use the prayer sheets found in the My Prayer Journal section).

3 Be sure to fill out your quiet time sheets. This will really help you remember the things the Lord brings to your mind.

4 Purpose to share with someone else each day something you gained from your quiet time. This can be a real blessing for them as well as for you.

my personal
prayer journal

daily prayer list

date | request   date | answer

daily prayer list

daily prayer list

date | request   date | answer

daily prayer list

date | request   date | answer

sunday

family

date	request	date	answer

Christian friends

date	request	date	answer

Unsaved friends

date | request   date | answer

Missionaries

date | request   date | answer

monday

family

date	request	date	answer

Christian friends

date	request	date	answer

Unsaved friends

date | request   date | answer

Missionaries

date | request   date | answer

tuesday

family

date	request	date	answer

Christian friends

date	request	date	answer

tuesday

Unsaved friends

date | request   date | answer

Missionaries

date | request   date | answer

15

wednesday

family

date	request	date	answer

Christian friends

date	request	date	answer

Unsaved friends

date | request   date | answer

Missionaries

date | request   date | answer

thursday

family

date | request   date | answer

Christian friends

date | request   date | answer

Unsaved friends

date | request   date | answer

Missionaries

date | request   date | answer

friday

family

date | request   date | answer

Christian friends

date | request   date | answer

Unsaved friends

date	request		date	answer

Missionaries

date	request		date	answer

saturday

family

date	request	date	answer

Christian friends

date	request	date	answer

Unsaved friends

date | request   date | answer

Missionaries

date | request   date | answer

daily praise list

date | I'm praising God for...

daily praise list

date \ I'm praising God for...

daily praise list

date | I'm praising God for...

something for everyone

Some people just can't get enough! That is why we have several dimensions in the Word of Life Quiet Time. Along with the daily reading, content and application questions for each day, two reading programs are given to help you understand the Bible better. Choose one or both.

Reading Through the New Testament Four Times In One Year

Turn the page and discover a schedule that takes you through the New Testament four times in one year. This is a great method to help you see the correlation of the Gospels and other New Testament books.

Reading Through the Whole Bible In One Year

Turn another page and find a program of several pages that will guide you through a chronological reading of the entire Bible. Follow this schedule and you will move from Genesis through Revelation in one year.

The Choice is Up to You

Whether you have a short quiet time, a quiet time with more scripture reading or one with a mini-Bible study each day, we trust your time with God will draw you closer to Him in every area of your life.

Read through the new testament four times in one year

Weeks 1-13

- [ ] Matthew 1-3
- [ ] Matthew 4-6
- [ ] Matthew 7-9
- [ ] Matt. 10-12
- [ ] Matt. 13-15
- [ ] Matt. 16-18
- [ ] Matt. 19-21
- [ ] Matt. 22-24
- [ ] Matt. 25-26
- [ ] Matt. 27-28
- [ ] Mark 1-3
- [ ] Mark 4-5
- [ ] Mark 6-8
- [ ] Mark 9-11
- [ ] Mark 12-14
- [ ] Mark 15-16
- [ ] Luke 1-2
- [ ] Luke 3-5
- [ ] Luke 6-7
- [ ] Luke 8-9
- [ ] Luke 10-11
- [ ] Luke 12-14
- [ ] Luke 15-17
- [ ] Luke 18-20
- [ ] Luke 21-22
- [ ] Luke 23-24
- [ ] John 1-3
- [ ] John 4-5
- [ ] John 6-7
- [ ] John 8-10
- [ ] John 11-12
- [ ] John 13-15
- [ ] John 16-18
- [ ] John 19-21
- [ ] Acts 1-3
- [ ] Acts 4-6
- [ ] Acts 7-8
- [ ] Acts 9-11
- [ ] Acts 12-15
- [ ] Acts 16-18
- [ ] Acts 19-21
- [ ] Acts 22-24
- [ ] Acts 25-26
- [ ] Acts 27-28
- [ ] Romans 1-3

- [ ] Romans 4-6
- [ ] Romans 7-9
- [ ] Romans 10-12
- [ ] Romans 13-16
- [ ] 1 Cor. 1-4
- [ ] 1 Cor. 5-9
- [ ] 1 Cor. 10-12
- [ ] 1 Cor. 13-16
- [ ] 2 Cor. 1-4
- [ ] 2 Cor. 5-8
- [ ] 2 Cor. 9-13
- [ ] Galatians 1-3
- [ ] Galatians 4-6
- [ ] Ephesians 1-3
- [ ] Ephesians 4-6
- [ ] Philippians 1-4
- [ ] Colossians 1-4
- [ ] 1 Thes. 1-3
- [ ] 1 Thes. 4-5
- [ ] 2 Thes. 1-3
- [ ] 1 Timothy 1-3
- [ ] 1 Timothy 4-6
- [ ] 2 Timothy 1-4
- [ ] Titus 1-3
- [ ] Philemon
- [ ] Hebrews 1
- [ ] Hebrews 2-4
- [ ] Hebrews 5-7
- [ ] Hebrews 8-10
- [ ] Hebrews 11-13
- [ ] James 1-3
- [ ] James 4-5
- [ ] 1 Peter 1-3
- [ ] 1 Peter 4-5
- [ ] 2 Peter 1-3
- [ ] 1 John 1-3
- [ ] 1 John 4-5
- [ ] 2 Jn, 3 Jn, Jude
- [ ] Revelation 1-3
- [ ] Revelation 4-6
- [ ] Revelation 7-9
- [ ] Rev. 10-12
- [ ] Rev. 13-15
- [ ] Rev. 16-18
- [ ] Rev. 19-22

Weeks 14-26

- [ ] Matthew 1-3
- [ ] Matthew 4-6
- [ ] Matthew 7-9
- [ ] Matt. 10-12
- [ ] Matt. 13-15
- [ ] Matt. 16-18
- [ ] Matt. 19-21
- [ ] Matt. 22-24
- [ ] Matt. 25-26
- [ ] Matt. 27-28
- [ ] Mark 1-3
- [ ] Mark 4-5
- [ ] Mark 6-8
- [ ] Mark 9-11
- [ ] Mark 12-14
- [ ] Mark 15-16
- [ ] Luke 1-2
- [ ] Luke 3-5
- [ ] Luke 6-7
- [ ] Luke 8-9
- [ ] Luke 10-11
- [ ] Luke 12-14
- [ ] Luke 15-17
- [ ] Luke 18-20
- [ ] Luke 21-22
- [ ] Luke 23-24
- [ ] John 1-3
- [ ] John 4-5
- [ ] John 6-7
- [ ] John 8-10
- [ ] John 11-12
- [ ] John 13-15
- [ ] John 16-18
- [ ] John 19-21
- [ ] Acts 1-3
- [ ] Acts 4-6
- [ ] Acts 7-8
- [ ] Acts 9-11
- [ ] Acts 12-15
- [ ] Acts 16-18
- [ ] Acts 19-21
- [ ] Acts 22-24
- [ ] Acts 25-26
- [ ] Acts 27-28
- [ ] Romans 1-3

- [ ] Romans 4-6
- [ ] Romans 7-9
- [ ] Romans 10-12
- [ ] Romans 13-16
- [ ] 1 Cor. 1-4
- [ ] 1 Cor. 5-9
- [ ] 1 Cor. 10-12
- [ ] 1 Cor. 13-16
- [ ] 2 Cor. 1-4
- [ ] 2 Cor. 5-8
- [ ] 2 Cor. 9-13
- [ ] Galatians 1-3
- [ ] Galatians 4-6
- [ ] Ephesians 1-3
- [ ] Ephesians 4-6
- [ ] Philippians 1-4
- [ ] Colossians 1-4
- [ ] 1 Thes. 1-3
- [ ] 1 Thes. 4-5
- [ ] 2 Thes. 1-3
- [ ] 1 Timothy 1-3
- [ ] 1 Timothy 4-6
- [ ] 2 Timothy 1-4
- [ ] Titus 1-3
- [ ] Philemon
- [ ] Hebrews 1
- [ ] Hebrews 2-4
- [ ] Hebrews 5-7
- [ ] Hebrews 8-10
- [ ] Hebrews 11-13
- [ ] James 1-3
- [ ] James 4-5
- [ ] 1 Peter 1-3
- [ ] 1 Peter 4-5
- [ ] 2 Peter 1-3
- [ ] 1 John 1-3
- [ ] 1 John 4-5
- [ ] 2 Jn, 3 Jn, Jude
- [ ] Revelation 1-3
- [ ] Revelation 4-6
- [ ] Revelation 7-9
- [ ] Rev. 10-12
- [ ] Rev. 13-15
- [ ] Rev. 16-18
- [ ] Rev. 19-22

Read through the new testament four times in one year

Weeks 27–39

- [ ] Matthew 1-3
- [ ] Matthew 4-6
- [ ] Matthew 7-9
- [ ] Matt. 10-12
- [ ] Matt. 13-15
- [ ] Matt. 16-18
- [ ] Matt. 19-21
- [ ] Matt. 22-24
- [ ] Matt. 25-26
- [ ] Matt. 27-28
- [ ] Mark 1-3
- [ ] Mark 4-5
- [ ] Mark 6-8
- [ ] Mark 9-11
- [ ] Mark 12-14
- [ ] Mark 15-16
- [ ] Luke 1-2
- [ ] Luke 3-5
- [ ] Luke 6-7
- [ ] Luke 8-9
- [ ] Luke 10-11
- [ ] Luke 12-14
- [ ] Luke 15-17
- [ ] Luke 18-20
- [ ] Luke 21-22
- [ ] Luke 23-24
- [ ] John 1-3
- [ ] John 4-5
- [ ] John 6-7
- [ ] John 8-10
- [ ] John 11-12
- [ ] John 13-15
- [ ] John 16-18
- [ ] John 19-21
- [ ] Acts 1-3
- [ ] Acts 4-6
- [ ] Acts 7-8
- [ ] Acts 9-11
- [ ] Acts 12-15
- [ ] Acts 16-18
- [ ] Acts 19-21
- [ ] Acts 22-24
- [ ] Acts 25-26
- [ ] Acts 27-28
- [ ] Romans 1-3

- [ ] Romans 4-6
- [ ] Romans 7-9
- [ ] Romans 10-12
- [ ] Romans 13-16
- [ ] 1 Cor. 1-4
- [ ] 1 Cor. 5-9
- [ ] 1 Cor. 10-12
- [ ] 1 Cor. 13-16
- [ ] 2 Cor. 1-4
- [ ] 2 Cor. 5-8
- [ ] 2 Cor. 9-13
- [ ] Galatians 1-3
- [ ] Galatians 4-6
- [ ] Ephesians 1-3
- [ ] Ephesians 4-6
- [ ] Phil. 1-4
- [ ] Colossians 1-4
- [ ] 1 Thes. 1-3
- [ ] 1 Thes. 4-5
- [ ] 2 Thes. 1-3
- [ ] 1 Timothy 1-3
- [ ] 1 Timothy 4-6
- [ ] 2 Timothy 1-4
- [ ] Titus 1-3
- [ ] Philemon
- [ ] Hebrews 1
- [ ] Hebrews 2-4
- [ ] Hebrews 5-7
- [ ] Hebrews 8-10
- [ ] Hebrews 11-13
- [ ] James 1-3
- [ ] James 4-5
- [ ] 1 Peter 1-3
- [ ] 1 Peter 4-5
- [ ] 2 Peter 1-3
- [ ] 1 John 1-3
- [ ] 1 John 4-5
- [ ] 2 Jn, 3 Jn, Jude
- [ ] Revelation 1-3
- [ ] Revelation 4-6
- [ ] Revelation 7-9
- [ ] Rev. 10-12
- [ ] Rev. 13-15
- [ ] Rev. 16-18
- [ ] Rev. 19-22

Weeks 40–52

- [ ] Matthew 1-3
- [ ] Matthew 4-6
- [ ] Matthew 7-9
- [ ] Matt. 10-12
- [ ] Matt. 13-15
- [ ] Matt. 16-18
- [ ] Matt. 19-21
- [ ] Matt. 22-24
- [ ] Matt. 25-26
- [ ] Matt. 27-28
- [ ] Mark 1-3
- [ ] Mark 4-5
- [ ] Mark 6-8
- [ ] Mark 9-11
- [ ] Mark 12-14
- [ ] Mark 15-16
- [ ] Luke 1-2
- [ ] Luke 3-5
- [ ] Luke 6-7
- [ ] Luke 8-9
- [ ] Luke 10-11
- [ ] Luke 12-14
- [ ] Luke 15-17
- [ ] Luke 18-20
- [ ] Luke 21-22
- [ ] Luke 23-24
- [ ] John 1-3
- [ ] John 4-5
- [ ] John 6-7
- [ ] John 8-10
- [ ] John 11-12
- [ ] John 13-15
- [ ] John 16-18
- [ ] John 19-21
- [ ] Acts 1-3
- [ ] Acts 4-6
- [ ] Acts 7-8
- [ ] Acts 9-11
- [ ] Acts 12-15
- [ ] Acts 16-18
- [ ] Acts 19-21
- [ ] Acts 22-24
- [ ] Acts 25-26
- [ ] Acts 27-28
- [ ] Romans 1-3

- [ ] Romans 4-6
- [ ] Romans 7-9
- [ ] Romans 10-12
- [ ] Romans 13-16
- [ ] 1 Cor. 1-4
- [ ] 1 Cor. 5-9
- [ ] 1 Cor. 10-12
- [ ] 1 Cor. 13-16
- [ ] 2 Cor. 1-4
- [ ] 2 Cor. 5-8
- [ ] 2 Cor. 9-13
- [ ] Galatians 1-3
- [ ] Galatians 4-6
- [ ] Ephesians 1-3
- [ ] Ephesians 4-6
- [ ] Phil. 1-4
- [ ] Colossians 1-4
- [ ] 1 Thes. 1-3
- [ ] 1 Thes. 4-5
- [ ] 2 Thes. 1-3
- [ ] 1 Timothy 1-3
- [ ] 1 Timothy 4-6
- [ ] 2 Timothy 1-4
- [ ] Titus 1-3
- [ ] Philemon
- [ ] Hebrews 1
- [ ] Hebrews 2-4
- [ ] Hebrews 5-7
- [ ] Hebrews 8-10
- [ ] Hebrews 11-13
- [ ] James 1-3
- [ ] James 4-5
- [ ] 1 Peter 1-3
- [ ] 1 Peter 4-5
- [ ] 2 Peter 1-3
- [ ] 1 John 1-3
- [ ] 1 John 4-5
- [ ] 2 Jn, 3 Jn, Jude
- [ ] Revelation 1-3
- [ ] Revelation 4-6
- [ ] Revelation 7-9
- [ ] Rev. 10-12
- [ ] Rev. 13-15
- [ ] Rev. 16-18
- [ ] Rev. 19-22

Bible reading schedule

Read through the Bible in one year! As you complete each daily reading, simply place a check in the appropriate box.

☐ 1 Genesis 1-3
☐ 2 Genesis 4:1-6:8
☐ 3 Genesis 6:9-9:29
☐ 4 Genesis 10-11
☐ 5 Genesis 12-14
☐ 6 Genesis 15-17
☐ 7 Genesis 18-19
☐ 8 Genesis 20-22
☐ 9 Genesis 23-24
☐ 10 Genesis 25-26
☐ 11 Genesis 27-28
☐ 12 Genesis 29-30
☐ 13 Genesis 31-32
☐ 14 Genesis 33-35
☐ 15 Genesis 36-37
☐ 16 Genesis 38-40
☐ 17 Genesis 41-42
☐ 18 Genesis 43-45
☐ 19 Genesis 46-47
☐ 20 Genesis 48-50
☐ 21 Job 1-3
☐ 22 Job 4-7
☐ 23 Job 8-11
☐ 24 Job 12-15
☐ 25 Job 16-19
☐ 26 Job 20-22
☐ 27 Job 23-28
☐ 28 Job 29-31
☐ 29 Job 32-34
☐ 30 Job 35-37
☐ 31 Job 38-42
☐ 32 Exodus 1-4
☐ 33 Exodus 5-8
☐ 34 Exodus 9-11
☐ 35 Exodus 12-13
☐ 36 Exodus 14-15
☐ 37 Exodus 16-18
☐ 38 Exodus 19-21
☐ 39 Exodus 22-24
☐ 40 Exodus 25-27
☐ 41 Exodus 28-29
☐ 42 Exodus 30-31
☐ 43 Exodus 32-34
☐ 44 Exodus 35-36
☐ 45 Exodus 37-38
☐ 46 Exodus 39-40
☐ 47 Leviticus 1:1-5:13
☐ 48 Leviticus 5:14-7:38
☐ 49 Leviticus 8-10
☐ 50 Leviticus 11-12
☐ 51 Leviticus 13-14
☐ 52 Leviticus 15-17

☐ 53 Leviticus 18-20
☐ 54 Leviticus 21-23
☐ 55 Leviticus 24-25
☐ 56 Leviticus 26-27
☐ 57 Numbers 1-2
☐ 58 Numbers 3-4
☐ 59 Numbers 5-6
☐ 60 Numbers 7
☐ 61 Numbers 8-10
☐ 62 Numbers 11-13
☐ 63 Numbers 14-15
☐ 64 Numbers 16-18
☐ 65 Numbers 19-21
☐ 66 Numbers 22-24
☐ 67 Numbers 25-26
☐ 68 Numbers 27-29
☐ 69 Numbers 30-31
☐ 70 Numbers 32-33
☐ 71 Numbers 34-36
☐ 72 Deuteronomy 1-2
☐ 73 Deuteronomy 3-4
☐ 74 Deuteronomy 5-7
☐ 75 Deuteronomy 8-10
☐ 76 Deuteronomy 11-13
☐ 77 Deuteronomy 14-17
☐ 78 Deuteronomy 18-21
☐ 79 Deuteronomy 22-25
☐ 80 Deuteronomy 26-28
☐ 81 Deuteronomy 29:1-31:29
☐ 82 Deuteronomy 31:30-34:12
☐ 83 Joshua 1-4
☐ 84 Joshua 5-8
☐ 85 Joshua 9-11
☐ 86 Joshua 12-14
☐ 87 Joshua 15-17
☐ 88 Joshua 18-19
☐ 89 Joshua 20-22
☐ 90 Joshua 23 - Judges 1
☐ 91 Judges 2-5
☐ 92 Judges 6-8
☐ 93 Judges 9
☐ 94 Judges 10-12
☐ 95 Judges 13-16
☐ 96 Judges 17-19
☐ 97 Judges 20-21
☐ 98 Ruth
☐ 99 1 Samuel 1-3
☐ 100 1 Samuel 4-7
☐ 101 1 Samuel 8-10
☐ 102 1 Samuel 11-13
☐ 103 1 Samuel 14-15
☐ 104 1 Samuel 16-17

Bible reading schedule
Day 105 - 199

- [ ] 105 1 Samuel 18-19; Psalm 59
- [ ] 106 1 Samuel 20-21; Psalm 56; 34
- [ ] 107 1 Samuel 22-23; 1 Chronicles 12:8-18; Psalm 52; 54; 63; 142
- [ ] 108 1 Samuel 24; Psalm 57; 1 Samuel 25
- [ ] 109 1 Samuel 26-29; 1 Chronicles 12:1-7, 19-22
- [ ] 110 1 Samuel 30-31; 1 Chronicles 10; 2 Samuel 1
- [ ] 111 2 Samuel 2-4
- [ ] 112 2 Samuel 5:1-6:11; 1 Chronicles 11:1-9; 2:23-40; 13:1-14:17
- [ ] 113 2 Samuel 22; Psalm 18
- [ ] 114 1 Chronicles 15-16; 2 Samuel 6:12-23; Psalm 96
- [ ] 115 Psalm 105; 2 Samuel 7; 1 Chronicles 17
- [ ] 116 2 Samuel 8-10; 1 Chronicles 18-19; Psalm 60
- [ ] 117 2 Samuel 11-12; 1 Chronicles 20:1-3; Psalm 51
- [ ] 118 2 Samuel 13-14
- [ ] 119 2 Samuel 15-17
- [ ] 120 Psalm 3; 2 Samuel 18-19
- [ ] 121 2 Samuel 20-21; 23:8-23; 1 Chronicles 20:4-8; 11:10-25
- [ ] 122 2 Samuel 23:24-24:25;
- [x] 123 1 Chronicles 11:26-47; 21:1-30, 1 Chronicles 22-24
- [ ] 124 Psalm 30; 1 Chronicles 25-26
- [ ] 125 1 Chronicles 27-29
- [ ] 126 Psalms 5-7; 10; 11; 13; 17
- [ ] 127 Psalms 23; 26; 28; 31; 35
- [ ] 128 Psalms 41; 43; 46; 55; 61; 62; 64
- [ ] 129 Psalms 69-71; 77
- [ ] 130 Psalms 83; 86; 88; 91; 95
- [ ] 131 Psalms 108-9; 120-21; 140; 143-44
- [ ] 132 Psalms 1; 14-15; 36-37; 39
- [ ] 133 Psalms 40; 49-50; 73
- [ ] 134 Psalms 76; 82; 84; 90; 92; 112; 115
- [ ] 135 Psalms 8-9; 16; 19; 21; 24; 29
- [ ] 136 Psalms 33; 65-68
- [ ] 137 Psalms 75; 93-94; 97-100
- [ ] 138 Psalms 103-4; 113-14; 117
- [ ] 139 Psalm 119:1-88
- [ ] 140 Psalm 119:89-176
- [ ] 141 Psalms 122; 124; 133-36
- [ ] 142 Psalms 138-39; 145; 148; 150
- [ ] 143 Psalms 4; 12; 20; 25; 32; 38
- [ ] 144 Psalms 42; 53; 58; 81; 101; 111; 130-31; 141; 146
- [ ] 145 Psalms 2; 22; 27
- [ ] 146 Psalms 45; 47-48; 87; 110
- [ ] 147 1 Kings 1:1-2:12; 2 Samuel 23:1-7
- [ ] 148 1 Kings 2:13-3:28; 2 Chronicles 1:1-13
- [ ] 149 1 Kings 5-6; 2 Chronicles 2-3
- [ ] 150 1 Kings 7; 2 Chronicles 4
- [ ] 151 1 Kings 8; 2 Chronicles 5:1-7:10
- [ ] 152 1 Kings 9:1-10:13; 2 Chronicles 7:11-9:12
- [ ] 153 1 Kings 4; 10:14-29; 2 Chronicles 1:14-17; 9:13-28; Psalm 72
- [ ] 154 Proverbs 1-3
- [ ] 155 Proverbs 4-6
- [ ] 156 Proverbs 7-9
- [ ] 157 Proverbs 10-12
- [ ] 158 Proverbs 13-15
- [ ] 159 Proverbs 16-18
- [ ] 160 Proverbs 19-21
- [ ] 161 Proverbs 22-24
- [ ] 162 Proverbs 25-27
- [ ] 163 Proverbs 28-29
- [ ] 164 Proverbs 30-31; Psalm 127
- [ ] 165 Song of Solomon
- [ ] 166 1 Kings 11:1-40; Ecclesiastes 1-2
- [ ] 167 Ecclesiastes 3-7
- [ ] 168 Ecclesiastes 8-12; 1 Kings 11:41-43; 2 Chronicles 9:29-31
- [ ] 169 1 Kings 12; 2 Chronicles 10:1-11:17
- [ ] 170 1 Kings 13-14; 2 Chronicles 11:18-12:16
- [ ] 171 1 Kings 15:1-24; 2 Chronicles 13-16
- [ ] 172 1 Kings 15:25-16:34; 2 Chronicles 17; 1 Kings 17
- [ ] 173 1 Kings 18-19
- [ ] 174 1 Kings 20-21
- [ ] 175 1 Kings 22:1-40; 2 Chronicles 18
- [ ] 176 1 Kings 22:41-53; 2 Kings 1; 2 Chronicles 19:1-21:3
- [ ] 177 2 Kings 2-4
- [ ] 178 2 Kings 5-7
- [ ] 179 2 Kings 8-9; 2 Chronicles 21:4-22:9
- [ ] 180 2 Kings 10-11; 2 Chronicles 22:10-23:21
- [ ] 181 Joel
- [ ] 182 2 Kings 12-13; 2 Chronicles 24
- [ ] 183 2 Kings 14; 2 Chronicles 25; Jonah
- [ ] 184 Hosea 1-7
- [ ] 185 Hosea 8-14
- [ ] 186 2 Kings 15:1-7; 2 Chronicles 26; Amos 1-4
- [ ] 187 Amos 5-9; 2 Kings 15:8-18
- [ ] 188 Isaiah 1-4
- [ ] 189 2 Kings 15:19-38; 2 Chronicles 27; Isaiah 5-6
- [ ] 190 Micah
- [ ] 191 2 Kings 16; 2 Chronicles 28; Isaiah 7-8
- [ ] 192 Isaiah 9-12
- [ ] 193 Isaiah 13-16
- [ ] 194 Isaiah 17-22
- [ ] 195 Isaiah 23-27
- [ ] 196 Isaiah 28-30
- [ ] 197 Isaiah 31-35
- [ ] 198 2 Kings 18:1-8; 2 Chronicles 29-31
- [ ] 199 2 Kings 17; 18:9-37; 2 Chronicles 32:1-19; Isaiah 36

Bible reading schedule

- [ ] 200 2 Kings 19; 2 Chronicles 32:20-23; Isaiah 37
- [ ] 201 2 Kings 20; 2 Chronicles 32:24-33; Isaiah 38-39
- [ ] 202 2 Kings 21:1-18; 2 Chronicles 33:1-20; Isaiah 40
- [ ] 203 Isaiah 41-43
- [ ] 204 Isaiah 44-47
- [ ] 205 Isaiah 48-51
- [ ] 206 Isaiah 52-57
- [ ] 207 Isaiah 58-62
- [ ] 208 Isaiah 63-66
- [ ] 209 2 Kings 21:19-26; 2 Chronicles 33:21-34:7; Zephaniah
- [ ] 210 Jeremiah 1-3
- [ ] 211 Jeremiah 4-6
- [ ] 212 Jeremiah 7-9
- [ ] 213 Jeremiah 10-13
- [ ] 214 Jeremiah 14-16
- [ ] 215 Jeremiah 17-20
- [ ] 216 2 Kings 22:1-23:28; 2 Chronicles 34:8-35:19
- [ ] 217 Nahum; 2 Kings 23:29-37; 2 Chronicles 35:20-36:5; Jeremiah 22:10-17
- [ ] 218 Jeremiah 26; Habakkuk
- [ ] 219 Jeremiah 46-47; 2 Kings 24:1-4, 7; 2 Chronicles 36:6-7; Jeremiah 25, 35
- [ ] 220 Jeremiah 36, 45, 48
- [ ] 221 Jeremiah 49:1-33; Daniel 1-2
- [ ] 222 Jeremiah 22:18-30; 2 Kings 24:5-20; 2 Chronicles 36:8-12; Jeremiah 37:1-2; 52:1-3; 24; 29
- [ ] 223 Jeremiah 27-28, 23
- [ ] 224 Jeremiah 50-51
- [ ] 225 Jeremiah 49:34-39; 34:1-22; Ezekiel 1-3
- [ ] 226 Ezekiel 4-7
- [ ] 227 Ezekiel 8-11
- [ ] 228 Ezekiel 12-14
- [ ] 229 Ezekiel 15-17
- [ ] 230 Ezekiel 18-20
- [ ] 231 Ezekiel 21-23
- [ ] 232 2 Kings 25:1; 2 Chronicles 36:13-16; Jeremiah 39:1; 52:4; Ezekiel 24; Jeremiah 21:1-22:9; 32:1-44
- [ ] 233 Jeremiah 30-31, 33
- [ ] 234 Ezekiel 25; 29:1-16; 30; 31
- [ ] 235 Ezekiel 26-28
- [ ] 236 Jeremiah 37:3-39:10; 52:5-30; 2 Kings 25:2-21; 2 Chronicles 36:17-21
- [ ] 237 2 Kings 25:22; Jeremiah 39:11-40:6; Lamentations 1-3
- [ ] 238 Lamentations 4-5; Obadiah
- [ ] 239 Jeremiah 40:7-44:30; 2 Kings 25:23-26
- [ ] 240 Ezekiel 33:21-36:38
- [ ] 241 Ezekiel 37-39
- [ ] 242 Ezekiel 32:1-33:20; Daniel 3
- [ ] 243 Ezekiel 40-42
- [ ] 244 Ezekiel 43-45
- [ ] 245 Ezekiel 46-48
- [ ] 246 Ezekiel 29:17-21; Daniel 4; Jeremiah 52:31-34; 2 Kings 25:27-30; Psalm 44
- [ ] 247 Psalms 74; 79-80; 89
- [ ] 248 Psalms 85; 102; 106; 123; 137
- [ ] 249 Daniel 7-8; 5
- [ ] 250 Daniel 9; 6
- [ ] 251 2 Chronicles 36:22-23; Ezra 1:1-4:5
- [ ] 252 Daniel 10-12
- [ ] 253 Ezra 4:6-6:13; Haggai
- [ ] 254 Zechariah 1-6
- [ ] 255 Zechariah 7-8; Ezra 6:14-22; Psalm 78
- [ ] 256 Psalms 107; 116; 118
- [ ] 257 Psalms 125-26; 128-29; 132; 147; 149
- [ ] 258 Zechariah 9-14
- [ ] 259 Esther 1-4
- [ ] 260 Esther 5-10
- [ ] 261 Ezra 7-8
- [ ] 262 Ezra 9-10
- [ ] 263 Nehemiah 1-5
- [ ] 264 Nehemiah 6-7
- [ ] 265 Nehemiah 8-10
- [ ] 266 Nehemiah 11-13
- [ ] 267 Malachi
- [ ] 268 1 Chronicles 1-2
- [ ] 269 1 Chronicles 3-5
- [ ] 270 1 Chronicles 6
- [ ] 271 1 Chronicles 7:1-8:27
- [ ] 272 1 Chronicles 8:28-9:44
- [ ] 273 John 1:1-18; Mark 1:1; Luke 1:1-4; 3:23-38; Matthew 1:1-17
- [ ] 274 Luke 1:5-80
- [ ] 275 Matthew 1:18-2:23; Luke 2
- [ ] 276 Matthew 3:1-4:11; Mark 1:2-13; Luke 3:1-23; 4:1-13; John 1:19-34
- [ ] 277 John 1:35-3:36
- [ ] 278 John 4; Matthew 4:12-17; Mark 1:14-15; Luke 4:14-30
- [ ] 279 Mark 1:16-45; Matthew 4:18-25; 8:2-4, 14-17; Luke 4:31-5:16
- [ ] 280 Matthew 9:1-17; Mark 2:1-22; Luke 5:17-39
- [ ] 281 John 5; Matthew 12:1-21; Mark 2:23-3:12; Luke 6:1-11
- [ ] 282 Matthew 5; Mark 3:13-19; Luke 6:12-36
- [ ] 283 Matthew 6-7; Luke 6:37-49
- [ ] 284 Luke 7; Matthew 8:1, 5-13; 11:2-30
- [ ] 285 Matthew 12:22-50; Mark 3:20-35; Luke 8:1-21
- [ ] 286 Mark 4:1-34; Matthew 13:1-53
- [ ] 287 Mark 4:35-5:43; Matthew 8:18, 23-34; 9:18-34; Luke 8:22-56
- [ ] 288 Mark 6:1-30; Matthew 13:54-58; 9:35-11:1; 14:1-12; Luke 9:1-10

Bible reading schedule

Day 289 - 365

- ☐ 289 Matthew 14:13-36; Mark 6:31-56; Luke 9:11-17; John 6:1-21
- ☐ 290 John 6:22-7:1; Matthew 15:1-20; Mark 7:1-23
- ☐ 291 Matthew 15:21-16:20; Mark 7:24-8:30; Luke 9:18-21
- ☐ 292 Matthew 16:21-17:27; Mark 8:31-9:32; Luke 9:22-45
- ☐ 293 Matthew 18; 8:19-22; Mark 9:33-50; Luke 9:46-62; John 7:2-10
- ☐ 294 John 7:11-8:59
- ☐ 295 Luke 10:1-11:36
- ☐ 296 Luke 11:37-13:21
- ☐ 297 John 9-10
- ☐ 298 Luke 13:22-15:32
- ☐ 299 Luke 16:1-17:10; John 11:1-54
- ☐ 300 Luke 17:11-18:17; Matthew 19:1-15; Mark 10:1-16
- ☐ 301 Matthew 19:16-20:28; Mark 10:17-45; Luke 18:18-34
- ☐ 302 Matthew 20:29-34; 26:6-13; Mark 10:46-52; 14:3-9; Luke 18:35-19:28; John 11:55-12:11
- ☐ 303 Matthew 21:1-22; Mark 11:1-26; Luke 19:29-48; John 12:12-50
- ☐ 304 Matthew 21:23-22:14; Mark 11:27-12:12; Luke 20:1-19
- ☐ 305 Matthew 22:15-46; Mark 12:13-37; Luke 20:20-44
- ☐ 306 Matthew 23; Mark 12:38-44; Luke 20:45-21:4
- ☐ 307 Matthew 24:1-31; Mark 13:1-27; Luke 21:5-27
- ☐ 308 Matthew 24:32-26:5, 14-16; Mark 13:28-14:2, 10-11; Luke 21:28-22:6
- ☐ 309 Matthew 26:17-29; Mark 14:12-25; Luke 22:7-38; John 13
- ☐ 310 John 14-16
- ☐ 311 John 17:1-18:1; Matthew 26:30-46; Mark 14:26-42; Luke 22:39-46
- ☐ 312 Matthew 26:47-75; Mark 14:43-72; Luke 22:47-65; John 18:2-27
- ☐ 313 Matthew 27:1-26; Mark 15:1-15; Luke 22:66-23:25; John 18:28-19:16
- ☐ 314 Matthew 27:27-56; Mark 15:16-41; Luke 23:26-49; John 19:17-30
- ☐ 315 Matthew 27:57-28:8; Mark 15:42-16:8; Luke 23:50-24:12; John 19:31-20:10
- ☐ 316 Matthew 28:9-20; Mark 16:9-20; Luke 24:13-53; John 20:11-21:25
- ☐ 317 Acts 1-2
- ☐ 318 Acts 3-5
- ☐ 319 Acts 6:1-8:1
- ☐ 320 Acts 8:2-9:43
- ☐ 321 Acts 10-11
- ☐ 322 Acts 12-13
- ☐ 323 Acts 14-15
- ☐ 324 Galatians 1-3
- ☐ 325 Galatians 4-6
- ☐ 326 James
- ☐ 327 Acts 16:1-18:11
- ☐ 328 1 Thessalonians
- ☐ 329 2 Thessalonians; Acts 18:12-19:22
- ☐ 330 1 Corinthians 1-4
- ☐ 331 1 Corinthians 5-8
- ☐ 332 1 Corinthians 9-11
- ☐ 333 1 Corinthians 12-14
- ☐ 334 1 Corinthians 15-16
- ☐ 335 Acts 19:23-20:1; 2 Corinthians 1-4
- ☐ 336 2 Corinthians 5-9
- ☐ 337 2 Corinthians 10-13
- ☐ 338 Romans 1-3
- ☐ 339 Romans 4-6
- ☐ 340 Romans 7-8
- ☐ 341 Romans 9-11
- ☐ 342 Romans 12-15
- ☐ 343 Romans 16; Acts 20:2-21:16
- ☐ 344 Acts 21:17-23:35
- ☐ 345 Acts 24-26
- ☐ 346 Acts 27-28
- ☐ 347 Ephesians 1-3
- ☐ 348 Ephesians 4-6
- ☐ 349 Colossians
- ☐ 350 Philippians
- ☐ 351 Philemon; 1 Timothy 1-3
- ☐ 352 1 Timothy 4-6; Titus
- ☐ 353 2 Timothy
- ☐ 354 1 Peter
- ☐ 355 Jude; 2 Peter
- ☐ 356 Hebrews 1:1-5:10
- ☐ 357 Hebrews 5:11-9:28
- ☐ 358 Hebrews 10-11
- ☐ 359 Hebrews 12-13; 2 John; 3 John
- ☐ 360 1 John
- ☐ 361 Revelation 1-3
- ☐ 362 Revelation 4-9
- ☐ 363 Revelation 10-14
- ☐ 364 Revelation 15-18
- ☐ 365 Revelation 19-22

From the Liberty Bible, King James Version. Copyright ©1975, Thomas Nelson, Inc. Publishers. Used by permission.

Our English word *Psalms* is derived from a Greek word denoting *poems sung to the accompaniment of string instruments.* The English translation of the Hebrew title is Book of Praises. The book of the Psalms is actually an artistic arrangement of five collections of psalms, each collection ending with a "doxology" psalm (a psalm of praise). The superscriptions in the Hebrew text ascribe authorship of 73 psalms to David and 27 to various other writers. 50 psalms are anonymous. However, New Testament references and textual content indicate that some of the 50 were authored by David. Truly, David was "raised up on high and anointed of God" not only to be king, but also as "the sweet psalmist of Israel" (2 Samuel 23:1).

Several Scriptures let us know that the human authors of Psalms, as well as other Old Testament books, were aware that they were writing under the power and in the wisdom of God, the Divine Author. See 2 Samuel 23:2, Psalm 102:18, 19 and 1 Peter 1:10-12.

The Psalms contain praise, petition, prophecy and perspective on the history of God's people. A number of them are songs about the creation, glorifying the Creator. Others extol the veracity and the power of God's Word. The prophetic psalms are especially intriguing. Sixteen of these are designated "Messianic" psalms because, in whole or in part, they foretell events concerning either the first or the second coming of the Messiah, which in Greek is "the Christ." The words of the risen Christ Himself in Luke 24:27 and 24:44 should alert us to search for our Lord in many of the Psalms.

If you will find time to meditate on the words of the Psalms, here are some promises for you: You will be fruitful and prosperous in all that you do (1:2, 3). You will sleep well (4:4, 8). Your soul will be satisfied (63:5-6). You will be glad in the Lord (104:34). You will not sin against your God (119:11) but will have respect unto His ways (119:15). You will be wiser than your enemies and understand more than your teachers and your elders (119:97-100).

Please note that each year, in the Word of Life Quiet Time, we cover a different portion of the Book of Psalms, which means that this year we break into the Psalms at Psalm 77 and will study through to Psalm 103. Be patient: in 6 years you will have worked your way through all 150 psalms!

Psalm 77:1-20

What is the writer saying?

How can I apply this to my life?

pray   *Angola – For committed translators to bring the scriptures to the 20 language groups that have none.*

The psalmist Asaph tells of a time of deep despair over which he has had victory: "I…was troubled, I complained, and my spirit was overwhelmed" (v. 3). This psalm (vv. 1-9) first presents a "complaint" to God, saying, "I don't know what to do about my troubles and there is no one to help me!" In the second half of the psalm (vv. 10-20), the psalmist gives great comfort to readers who also have troubled souls, as he recounts past triumphs of God for His "flock" (v. 20).

In his despair, the psalmist asks six questions (vv. 7-9). These questions can be summarized as, "Has God changed? Is God unreliable? Has God just stopped caring?" The psalmist can't sleep, for he is communing with his "own heart" (v. 6) instead of with God.

In verse 10, Asaph recognizes his error as he turns his eyes from his circumstances to the Lord. Instead of complaining and questioning God's faithfulness and goodness, he begins praising God and extolling His greatness. Notice the key was his "remembering" (vv. 10-11) God's past great works to "redeem" (v. 15) His people from their troubles. He starts "meditating" (v. 12) on God's Word which tells him of God's wondrous work on behalf of Israel.

The Word of God produced the faith necessary for Asaph to believe the promises that the Word proclaimed (Romans 10:17). Faith has the power to turn the direst of circumstances into eager expectancy of God's deliverance. Thereby the despair brought on by worrying about a seemingly hopeless situation is changed to the expectancy of faith in God's strength and wonders (v. 14).

Life stEP

As long as we are in this world we should expect difficult circumstances. So, are you facing overwhelming circumstances? How can you put things in a right perspective by *remembering all God's works* (vv. 11-12)? Will you stop worrying and take time to meditate upon God's faithfulness?

Psalm 78:1-16

What is the writer saying?

How can I apply this to my life?

Today we begin a look at a psalm entitled "Maschil of Asaph" which means the *Instructions of Asaph*. Asaph is going to teach much by means of the historical lessons presented. We are to reflect upon the experiences and conduct of believers in past ages so that these might influence us.

Today we read the psalm's introduction (vv. 1-8) and then the first lesson about the backsliding of Ephraim, a large tribe of Israel (vv. 9-16).

Let's look at the purpose of the psalm as spelled out in its introduction:

- Verses 4, 6: To teach the "generation to come the praises of the Lord."
- Verse 7: That the next generation "might set their hope in God."
- Verse 8a: So they will not be "stubborn and rebellious" as their fathers.
- Verse 8b: So their hearts will be "set... aright," being "steadfast with God."

Ephraim was one of the two sons of Joseph, and fathered the tribe that became first amongst the twelve tribes of Israel. Ephraim was the recipient of special blessings from God. For example, once Israel had entered the Promised Land, the tabernacle was set up at Shiloh, a city in Ephraim's allotted territory. This made Ephraim the political center of the confederation of tribes and keeper of the very symbol of the nation's existence, the Ark of God. Sadly Ephraim, the *first tribe* in weaponry (v. 9a) became the *least tribe* of Israel as it failed in faith and courage (v. 9b; Judges 12:1-3). Ephraim also fell into rebellion against the Law of God (v. 10) and then into idolatry (v. 11, Hosea 13:1-3), leading the other tribes as it went.

Life stEP   Since you too have been greatly blessed by God, how are you involved in carrying out God's plan of teaching Bible truth to the "generation to come"?

Psalm 78:17-31

What is the writer saying?

How can I apply this to my life?

pray — *Argentina – For the salvation of the president and the stabilization of this country's economic and judicial systems.*

The historical events of these verses are taken primarily from Israel's journey in the wilderness (Exodus 16 and Numbers 11). Our passage looks at how Israel responded to God's gracious care.

"Bread of heaven" (Psalm 105:40) is a term referring to the food God provided for Israel in the wilderness. The people called it *manna* (Exodus 16:15) which means, *What is it?* It was intended for a wilderness journey of only a few months. Upon entering the Promised Land they were to eat from vineyards already producing food (Deuteronomy 6:11) and from the "corn [grain] of the land" (Joshua 5:12). At first the manna tasted like wafers made with honey (Exodus 16:31). After eating God's manna for forty years, they asked, "[Why] have ye brought us up out of Egypt to die...?

For there is no bread" (Numbers 21:5). Remember that God had miraculously delivered Israel from slavery in Egypt, and then He met their every need in the wilderness. The people refused to trust Him to lead them to a victorious conquest of the Promised Land, yet they repeatedly blamed *God* for the discomfort of continuing their arduous wilderness trek! Notice the psalmist's remarks concerning their actions: By their questions, Israel displayed *unbelief* in God's ability to sustain (v. 22); they *complained* about God's provision and they *provoked* Him with their *skepticism* of God's goodness and their *insolence* towards their Provider (vv. 19-20). The result was God's judgment upon His own chosen people (v. 31).

Many Christians live like "Wilderness Christians," displaying *unbelief* in God's care, *complaining* about God's provision, and showing their *skepticism* and *insolence* towards their Lord! Are you a Wilderness Christian, wandering aimlessly through the hard places of life and questioning God's care for you? How can you believe God's promises of daily provision in your life and then act with confidence in His goodness?

Psalm 78:32-44

What is the writer saying?

How can I apply this to my life?

Notice the contrast in these verses between that which is said about the people and what is said about God. They sinned, believed not, flattered God, lied to God, failed to keep the covenant, provoked God, grieved God, turned back, tempted (tested) God, limited God, and did not remember God's deliverance. In contrast, God was their Rock, their High God, and Redeemer (v. 35). He was full of compassion, forgiving, forbearing (v. 38), and considerate (v. 39).

Israel's root problem was a heart problem: "their heart was not right with him" (v. 37, Psalm 95:10). This heart problem brought upon them a lifetime of futility and trouble (v. 33) and eventually their death in the wilderness (v. 34).

Their heart problem displayed itself when they "flattered Him with their mouth" while lying at the same time (v. 36). Somehow they thought that God was like a wealthy person or conceited king who loved to be lavished with praise and flattered with compliments. They figured, once distracted by their flattery, God would not notice that their hearts were false! Sadly they "remembered not" (v. 42) that God *hates* flattery. "For there is no faithfulness in their mouth...they flatter with their tongue" (Psalm 5:9). "The LORD shall cut off all flattering lips" (Psalm 12:3).

Their heart problem also "limited the Holy One of Israel" (v. 41). It was as if they, in their arrogance, were saying to God, "Your path is here; You must do this or that or we will not worship You!" Such impertinence, "limiting" God! In *Treasury of David*, Spurgeon pictures this by saying, "Not thus is the Eternal God to be led on a leash by his impotent creatures."

True praise comes from an overflowing heart of love that is truly repentant and in submission to God. Do you display an honest heart of a true believer?

Psalm 78:45-58

What is the writer saying?

How can I apply this to my life?

Today's passage continues the unmistakable contrast between the greatness and graciousness of God (vv. 43-55) with the fickleness and stubbornness of His people (vv. 40-42 and 56-58). The psalmist summarizes (vv. 43-53) Israel's early history, listing six of the ten plagues God used to bring Israel out of slavery in Egypt (Exodus 7 to 14), and then summarizes Israel's wilderness wanderings and their conquering and dividing of the Promised Land.

Notice the first several verses that begin with the pronoun *He*; God alone was the source of Israel's redemption from slavery and the source for gaining a homeland in Israel. The contrast between God's faithfulness and Israel's unfaithfulness is displayed when our passage switches from the *He's* to "Yet they...they...they" (vv. 56-58).

The description of Israel includes:

• *"Tempted and provoked"* God (v. 56): This phrase is a repeat of earlier charges against Israel (vv. 17-18, 40-41). Thus Israel still had the same unfaithful character as did their fathers!

• *"Turned back"* (v. 57a): This phrase pictures someone going back to his old ways and *repeating the same old offenses*—thus declaring that while this was a new generation of Israel, it was the same nation, and "their heart was [still] not right with" God (v. 37).

• *"Like a deceitful bow"* (v. 57b): This parallels the Hebrew word for *sin*, meaning to *miss the mark*. God is pictured as a hunter who fashions a high-quality arrow that will *hit his mark*. However, the bow is defective (a picture of Israel), so it deceives its owner by *turning aside*, causing the hunter to *miss his mark*.

Life stEp   Can you do the same as our psalmist and list all the things that *He* has faithfully done for you—first bringing you to salvation and then giving you a new life in Christ? Now, how can you avoid living a life that can be summarized with the statement, *Yet I turned back*?

Psalm 78:59-72

What is the writer saying?

How can I apply this to my life?

We saw that verses 10-54 contrasted a caring and faithful God and His "stubborn and rebellious" people (v. 8); from their deliverance out of Egypt until their settling in the Promised Land. Verses 55-72 highlight incidents from their settling in the Land until the rule of King David.

Joshua set up a center of worship and government at Shiloh in the territory of the tribe of Ephraim, the prominent tribe of the 12-tribe confederation. The *Ark of the Covenant*, which represented the presence of the LORD, was also housed there (Joshua 18:1). Later the Ark was captured by the Philistines. When it was returned to Israel, it came to the tribal lands of Benjamin and then to Mt. Zion in the land of Judah, where David established his new capital city, Jerusalem.

Since our psalm ends with a summary of God *choosing* David to be the shepherd of God's "sheepfolds" (v. 70), let's consider some of the other verses in the Bible that draw on this picture:

• "I have gone astray like a lost sheep" (Psalm 119:176).
• "All we like sheep have gone astray" (Isaiah 53:6).
• "My sheep hear my voice…and they follow me" (John 10:27).
• "For ye were as sheep going astray; but are now returned unto the Shepherd and Bishop of your souls" (1 Peter 2:25).

Notice that (1) David was obediently tending sheep when he was called to tend God's people (v. 70b). (2) He faithfully cared for his needy sheep (v. 71). (3) He skillfully guided his flocks and people (v. 72). God's people need a shepherd who has *integrity*! David's appointment as shepherd (vv. 70-72) points to Jesus Christ, the *Son of David* (Luke 1:32; Matthew 21:9), who would become our "Good Shepherd" forever!

Do you have responsibilities for the care of young or new Christians? How is your care of God's flock? How can you be a better servant of Jesus, the "Chief Shepherd"?

Psalm 79:1-13

What is the writer saying?

How can I apply this to my life?

The *sad lament* of verses 1-4 arises from the destruction brought upon Jerusalem by the Babylonians in the year 586 B.C. (2 Kings 25:8-10). Before Israel entered the Promised Land, the LORD warned that this very calamity would befall His people if they forsook Him and worshiped idols. (Compare verse 2 with Deuteronomy 28:26.)

"How long, LORD?" (v. 5) was Israel's *cry of suffering* after the destruction of Jerusalem. It also reflects other cries of suffering through the ages. This psalmist joins Job (Job 7:19), David (Psalm 6:3; 13:1-2; 35:17), Moses (Psalm 90:13), Jeremiah (Jer. 12:4, 47:6) and Habakkuk (Hab. 1:2) in this plea. It was the cry of the angel on behalf of Jerusalem (Zechariah 1:12). It continues to be the cry of suffering saints and will be in the future (Revelation 6:10). It is like saying, "Why doesn't God hurry and *do something!*" Yet in times of travail, it seems the Lord is slow to rebuke evil and relieve suffering.

In verses 9-13, the psalmist presents to God reasons why He should answer the petitions of verses 6-8. It is His holy name that is being reproached (v. 9). His great power needs to be manifested to the nations (v. 10). It is His character to show mercy to His sinful people (v. 11). They are His sheep and the ones who are called to offer thanks and praise unto Him (v. 13).

"For the glory of Thy name...for Thy name's sake" (v. 9). The name of the LORD is infinitely precious to Him, though it means so little to most men (Jeremiah 14:7; Ezekiel 36: 21, 22). Satan delights for men to profane the holy name of God.

Life stEP   It is our privilege and responsibility to *give thanks* to Him (v. 13) and glorify His name on earth (1 Peter 2:9). How then can you specifically *show forth praise* to God in your life today?

Psalm 80:1-19

What is the writer saying?

How can I apply this to my life?

This psalm was most likely written as the Assyrians were besieging the Northern Kingdom of Israel (2 Kings 17:5) just before it was destroyed and most of its surviving people deported to the far corners of Assyria.

This psalm is divided into three addresses to God by the repeating, closing refrain, "*Turn us again*" (vv. 3, 7, 19).

• The *first address* (vv. 1-3) begins with a prayer for restoration of Israel to their former status as recipients of God's special favor.

• The *second address* (vv. 4-7) presents the plight of the people of Israel and an appeal to God to again forgive and restore His people.

• The *third address* (vv. 8-19) describes the people of Israel as a "vine" which God, as a farmer, originally "planted." This image of *Israel the Vine* is itself divided into three parts:

1. *The Prosperous Vine* (vv. 8-11): God had caused His "vine" to grow into a great plant that covers the hills, stretching to the sea.

2. *The Ruined Vine* (vv. 12-13): The question is asked, why has God broken down the protective hedge around His vine so that the wild boars can "waste" [uproot & destroy] the once-prosperous vine?

3. *The Restored Vine* (vv. 14-19): The psalmist places his hope in God's future *visiting of the vine* (v. 14) when He will bring restoration.

Notice that the psalmist, who three times has asked for God to "turn" Israel, here asks for God to turn *Himself* to His people ("*return*," v. 14). The psalmist also asks for "the man of thy right hand...the son of man" (names that would later be given to Jesus Christ!) to lead God's people so that they will no longer *turn away* ("go back") from God (v. 18).

Life *stEP*   How are things in your life? Do you need to "call upon" God (v. 18) in repentance as you turn again to Him?

Psalm 81:1-16

What is the writer saying?

How can I apply this to my life?

This psalm was likely sung during the annual feasts of Israel. The psalm has two parts that review God's redemption of Israel:

• *A Call to Celebrate* (vv. 1-7) is given to "sing [joyfully] unto God our strength" accompanied by timbrel, harp and trumpet. Such rejoicing is based upon the historical deeds of God (vv. 6-7).

• *The Voice of God*, (vv. 8-16). "Hear, O my people" is heard as God uses history to "testify" (v. 8) as to His faithfulness and ability to supply Israel's needs. Notice the 20 times (vv. 5-16) where *I, my,* and *me* are used as God presents His pleadings for a right response.

The psalmist then uses powerful reasoning as he presents Israel with their obligation to their Redeemer:

▶ Verses 5-7 recall the deliverance from slavery in Egypt (Exodus 1:11) that God wrought for Israel.

▶ In view of that deliverance, God asks His people in verses 8-9 to "hearken unto me" and not worship "any strange god" (Ex 23:13).

▶ Verse 10, "I am the Lord thy God," is the foundational introduction to the Ten Commandments (Exodus 20:2). It is used here to remind Israel that they were bound by gratitude and duty to keep God's Laws.

▶ Yet Israel, upon hearing God's request (v. 11), refused to respond to God's Laws or be ruled by them, not wanting anything to do with Him.

▶ Thus we see that God was justified in His judgment; He let them follow their *scheming hearts* and *stubborn wills* (v. 12).

▶ Yet, if their hearts had been right towards Him, God would have preferred to *satisfy* all their needs (vv. 14-16)! *Satisfied* means *to be full* as when one has *eaten even more than enough.*

Psalm 82:1-8

What is the writer saying?

How can I apply this to my life?

pray *Netherlands Antilles – Praise God for faithful radio staff that keep the gospel accessible to many.*

A good title for this psalm would be *Judging the Judges.* God is pictured here as having assembled all the "mighty" rulers and judges at His meeting hall. God then declares that "all the *foundations* of the earth are *out of course*" (v. 5) which is to say: First, judges and powerful rulers are *foundational* to God's righteousness ruling in the world. But, secondly, they are *slipping off their intended path.* Why?

▶ They were judging "unjustly"; that is, *to leave what is right.*

▶ They were allowing "wicked" men in their *god-like* profession.

▶ They did not know God was watching them!

▶ They did not care or wish to hear about their true responsibilities.

▶ They were choosing not to see the wrongs that needed to be judged ("Walking on in darkness," v. 5)

The phrase "How long?" (v. 2) is a plea by God that they begin to dispense justice on earth as God would: "defend," "do justice," "deliver the poor and needy," and "rid them out of the hand of the wicked." If they fail to do so, God, the *Most High Judge,* will bring His judgment upon them (v. 7).

It is surprising that God calls these earthly judges "gods" (vv. 1 and 6). The idea here is that God has ordained many affairs on earth to be administered by human agency. Therefore when a person becomes a judge, he acts as God's agent exercising a divine or "God-like" privilege of judging between right and wrong. Thus a judge is like a "god."

Christians need to remember we too are "judges"—judging situations and people in our lives so as to guard our walk with God. For example, "Since I 'judge' that his actions are consistently evil, I will not go along with him."

Life stEP While only a few are appointed or elected as judges, we can all take a stand for those who are being wronged!

Psalm 83:1-18

What is the writer saying?

How can I apply this to my life?

There are a number of episodes that could be the historical basis for this psalm, such as when Gideon faced an alliance headed by the Midianites (Judges 7:12); or when God delivered Israel by arranging things so that their assailants destroyed each other (2 Chronicles 20:1-2, 22, 23).

The psalm can be divided into four parts:

1. A prayer for God's rescue from a terrible enemy (vv. 1-4)
2. A listing of the peoples who are "confederate against" them (vv. 5-8)
3. A prayer requesting God's judgment upon these enemies just as God had destroyed past enemies (vv. 9-12)
4. A prayer that their enemies learn, even the hard way, that God alone is the sovereign ruler over all the earth (vv. 13-18)

An interesting name for God's people appears here: "*Thy hidden ones*" (v. 3). It is from a verb meaning *to hide or keep secret a thing of value*. Here the emphasis is upon God's special protection for his people (Psalm 91:1, "dwelleth in the secret place"). What does this teach us?

• God's hiding is not normally to *conceal* but to *openly preserve* His people. God keeps us *secure* in the midst of life's storms.

• This provides an illustration for a New Testament lesson: Paul says, "Set your affection on things above... your life is *hid* with Christ in God" (Colossians 3:2-3). Again safety, not invisibility, is in view.

• Not only are we His "hidden ones," but we rejoice that God Himself is our "*hiding place*" (Psalm 32:7; 119:114). So then we know when God places us on *exhibit* before our enemies, like cities on a hill that cannot be hid, He is also our shield and wall of protection.

Life stEP · School, work, and your community are all places where you can come under attack by determined enemies of God. How can you be God's *lighted candle* so that others will see the Light of God in you (Luke 8:16), yet still trust Him to protect you as one of His "hidden ones"?

Psalm 84:1-12

What is the writer saying?

How can I apply this to my life?

pray Mexico – For Bible schools to be characterized by doctrinal accuracy, depth, and personal integrity.

This psalm was sung by pilgrims on their way to the Temple at Jerusalem. The three stanzas or poetic-paragraphs overflow with anticipation of renewed, sweet fellowship with the Lord:

• The *Pilgrim Anticipates* his renewed fellowship with God (vv. 1-4).
• The *Pilgrim Approaches* Jerusalem and is *strengthened* (vv. 5-8).
• The *Pilgrim Arrives* and seeks God's enablement (vv. 9-12).

"Tabernacles," "courts," "altars," and "house" are descriptive designations for God's dwelling place. "Tabernacles" and "courts" are plural since there were several rooms in the temple complex where people would gather for worship, in addition to the temple itself. Like the sparrow and swallow that dwell there (v. 3), the psalmist appreciates the place but His deepest desire is for the God of the place. "Soul," "heart," and "flesh" speak of the entire being and are the equivalent of "spirit and soul and body" (1 Thessalonians 5:23).

The "valley of Baca" (v. 6) means the *valley of weeping*. Those faithful worshipers who journeyed through the desert found a spiritual oasis at Zion, which was their designation for the Temple Mount. The psalmist is grateful for the privilege of living at the oasis. He prefers the lowliest assignment in the work and the presence of his God above anything the world has to offer.

It is proper for a dedicated believer to sense the special presence of the Lord when we gather at our places of worship (Hebrews 10:25). However, if our entire being is consumed with a desire for His presence, we may live every moment in the oasis of His provision because of that which Christ has done for us. If we truly believe that promise of verse 11, we live above the trials of this *vale* of tears.

friday 2

Psalm 85:1-13

What is the writer saying?

How can I apply this to my life?

pray *Netherlands Antilles – For the Papiamento Bible that was published in 1997 to be an impact on those who use it.*

The historical basis for this psalm is the return of Israel to their Promised Land after their exile in Babylon. Likely it was written at the time of the revival lead by Ezra and Nehemiah, recorded in Nehemiah 8. An outline for this psalm is as follows:

• *Praise for the Past* (vv. 1-3): The LORD is praised for bringing His people back to the land.

• *Petition for the Present* (vv. 4-7): A plea for the Lord to return the land to its former productivity.

• *The Promise of Peace* (vv. 8-13): These verses contain ten assuring promises in answer to the psalmist's petition.

The key to understanding this psalm is in the repeating words: *turn, turned*" (vv. 3, 4, 8); "*land, earth*" (vv. 1, 9, 11); "*peace*" (vv. 8, 10); and "*mercy*" (vv. 7, 1a).

Now let's assemble the picture: *First*, these Jews are *praising* the Lord, who has *blessed* them with His *mercy* (steadfast love), allowing them to *return* from their exile to their *land* in *peace*. This becomes the foundation for the *second* section of the psalm, as they boldly present their *petition* for their present need of the Lord's continued *mercy* to *return* their *land* to its former bountiful state. *Third*, the psalm turns to the Lord's steadfast work of making their hearts spiritually productive; thus, their hope in the promise of continued *peace* as God keeps His people from *turning again* away from Him. Notice their "*peace*" is a product of their "*salvation*" (v. 9) from sin, their "*righteous*" standing before the Lord (vv. 10, 11), their good life under God's blessing (v. 12), and their expectation of a continued walk in God's "*way*" (v. 13).

 You have a similar basis for your hope in God's promises. Since God, when He saved you, delivered you from a spiritual *exile* in the *land of sin*, you can now praise Him for bringing you home to the land of God.

Psalm 86:1-17

What is the writer saying?

How can I apply this to my life?

Some Bible prayers are primarily confession (Ezra 9, Psalm 51). Some are praise and adoration prayers (1 Samuel 2), while others are mostly thanksgiving (1 Chronicles 29). Many, including this psalm, are largely supplication. Confession, praise, and thanksgiving are sprinkled throughout the psalm, but the majority deals with petitioning God for His favor. There are six petitions in the first four verses, followed by nine more in verses 6-17.

Four times the psalmist calls upon Yahweh (LORD). That is the name of the great God, majestic in essence, as He descends to look upon lowly humans and act on their behalf. Seven times the psalmist invokes the name Adonai (Lord), which portrays God as the master of a large plantation who receives the plea of His servant.

David is beset by an enemy and waivers between distress (vv. 1, 14) and trust (vv. 2, 7). He begins (vv. 1-6) by reciting five reasons why Yahweh should respond favorably to his petitions. (Note the word *for* in vv. 1-5).

• Because he is "poor and needy" (v. 1), thus helpless and the pawn of "proud" and "violent" men (v. 14).

• Because he is "holy" (v. 2). In context, this means he is *set aside* for God's purposes; *a godly man*, one who is devoted to God. (The New Testament parallel is Romans 12:1-2).

• Because he has continually trusted in his Master (vv. 2-3).

• Because he has only sought help from the Lord (v. 4)

• Because of the fundamental character of his Lord (vv. 5-6) "Thou, Lord, art good...and plenteous in mercy!" Therefore the servant may expect the Lord to listen.

Since your master is a God of compassion, grace, patience, mercy, and truth, then which of these *for's* will you claim as your foundation for trusting Him to give you all "strength" necessary for your present hard situation?

Psalm 87:1-7

What is the writer saying?

How can I apply this to my life?

Pray for the elderly in your church and those who are shut-ins.

"The LORD loves the gates of Zion" (v. 2) is the theme of this psalm. Zion was the hill upon which Jerusalem was built; it was here that God would *set His foundation* above all other places on earth (v. 1), which is to say, *make His presence known.* This is a repeated theme in the Psalms; e.g., "For the LORD hath chosen Zion; He hath desired it for His habitation. ... here will I dwell; for I have desired it" (Psalm 132:13, 14). Six times in Deuteronomy 12 Moses told Israel the LORD would choose a particular place for *His name to dwell,* the place where Solomon was directed to build the Temple (2 Chronicles 7:12). Five nations surrounding Israel are mentioned in verse 4 ("Rahab" is another name for Egypt, Isaiah 51:9). The hope presented here is that these countries, which historically wanted Israel "cut off from being a nation" (Psalm 83:1-8), will desire to come to Zion to worship the Lord (Isaiah 2:2, 3; 56:7; Zechariah 8:22; 14:16). While many "glorious things" can be said about Jerusalem (v. 3), this psalm declares that the greatest thing will be these nations' change in attitude, that they will desire to be citizens of God's kingdom! These people will be like children born at Jerusalem (v. 5).

Notice God's response to this anticipated situation: He is presented as a king who will "*count*" (v. 6a) as born citizens those who have been liberated and added to His kingdom. He will also *write their names* (v. 6b) in His official register of those recognized as citizens with ensured places at Zion. These will come under His care, protection, and rule!

Finally, we have the response of the citizens of God's kingdom; they will be rejoicing and singing, declaring that the Lord has become the "springs" or fountain (v. 7) from which flow all their blessings.

Life stEP Is the Lord the *spring* from which blessings flow into your life? Make a list of those blessings today.

Psalm 88:1-18

What is the writer saying?

How can I apply this to my life?

pray   *Bolivia – For the Holy Spirit to bring about maturity in the lives of those studying for the ministry.*

Surely this is the most sorrowful of Psalms! Even in David's direst distress, he says, "For in Thee, O LORD, do I hope; Thou wilt hear, O Lord my God" (Psalm 38:15). Though Job was in deep despair, he proclaimed, "When He hath tried me, I shall come forth as gold" (Job 23:10). But in this psalm, not one ray of hope shines through.

Verses 8, 9, 15 and 18 suggest that the psalmist has suffered from leprosy and is going blind as he approaches death. His life has held no gladness and no respite from pain, loneliness, rejection and darkness.

Why did God include such a portion in His Word? First, it presents a graphic picture of the earthly plight of countless human sufferers. Second, it furnishes us with a needed contrast. Life might have some hard turns, but we can always find some causes for rejoicing!

Since no answers for the bitter life are presented, let's look at this pitiful being from an eternal perspective. What does the Bible say elsewhere about this sad situation?

• Since he has placed his trust in the one true God (vv. 1, 9, 13), we must conclude that his God is about to release him from his earthly bonds and bring him into eternal bliss (Job 14:14-15).

• From an eternal perspective, is he not better off than the most fortunate and comfortable unsaved person that ever lived?

• Every moment of "affliction" continues to produce some *glorious* benefit on his behalf (see 2 Corinthians 4:17). While this man's life has been hard, God has all of eternity to even things out for him.

• God does not always answer our questions about why life is hard. Sometimes, like the psalmist, we can only continue to place our hope in God's eternal plan for us.

Life STEP   How can you express your faith in God's care for you even when you do not know what God is doing or what He intends to accomplish?

Psalm 89:1-18

What is the writer saying?

How can I apply this to my life?

The theme of Psalm 89 is *God's faithfulness*. *Faithfulness* or *faithful* appears more times in this psalm than in any other (vv. 1, 2, 5, 8, 24, 33, 37). The psalmist chooses to spotlight God's faithfulness at a time when it appeared as though God had forgotten His chosen people. Because of their sin, rebellion, and idolatry, they had lost possession of their land and become captives in a foreign country. Still, God's *mercy* (v. 1), *strength* (vv. 6, 8-10, 13) and *justice* (v. 14) are extolled, in accompaniment with His *faithfulness*.

Verses 4 and 5 are confirmation from God's own covenant with David (2 Samuel 7:8-16). The point is being made that, even though they had lost possession of God's Promised Land, they should keep their confidence in the faithfulness of God to His promises.

The psalmist reminds us that the angelic beings in Heaven react with praise as they watch the faithfulness of God to His promises (vv. 5-6). During difficult circumstances, God's people should likewise maintain their confidence in God's faithfulness.

God is able to perform faithfully because He is omnipotent (*all powerful*, vv. 8, 13), sovereign (vv. 9-10, 18), and Creator (vv. 11-12). He is so marvelous that even the prominent mountains desire to rejoice in Him ("Tabor and Hermon," v. 12). *Justice, judgment, mercy* and *truth* are also personified as inhabitants of Heaven who sing before God (v. 14).

Notice the figurative use of *horn* (v. 17). When one had a significant advantage, he was said to have a *horn* (like a horned animal has advantage over a hornless one). Thus, a believer in the Lord has the *significant advantage* of being in *God's favor*. In Luke 1:69 Christ is the "horn of salvation." Christians have Christ as our *significant advantage*.

 How might you sing praises to God, who has given you a *significant advantage* in Christ?

wednesday 3

Psalm 89:19-37

What is the writer saying?

How can I apply this to my life?

pray — *North Korea – For the abandoned children on the streets to find a place of refuge.*

In this entire section of Psalm 89, the psalmist summarizes what the Lord Himself has said concerning the covenant He made with David (2 Samuel 7:8-16). Notice all the personal pronouns; *I, me,* and *my.* Back in verses 3 and 4 the Davidic Covenant was introduced; now (vv. 19-37) an exposition of the covenant's details is presented as follows:

- The *favored people* (vv. 15-18)
- David, the *favored king,* is anointed (vv. 19-21).
- David's *favored kingdom* shall be exalted (vv. 22-25).
- David's *favored "seed"* (future heir) will reign forever (vv. 26-29).
- A warning of judgment on the King's *favored children* (vv. 30-33). Remember this psalm was written after God's disciplinary judgment had come upon Israel.
- Yet, the *favored covenant* is to be "established for ever" (vv. 34-37).

The critical Messianic nature of these verses is seen when we look at other passages that refer back to it. For instance, while in a Jewish synagogue, Paul makes reference to verse 20 as he explains that Jesus was the Jewish Messiah (Acts 13:22). Hebrews 1:5-6 draws from verses 26-27 when it identifies Jesus as the promised Son of God the Father. "Higher than the kings of earth" (v. 27b) looks forward to David's greater son, the Messiah. The term *firstborn* (v. 27a) denotes position and preeminence that the Messiah will have among kings (Psalm 72:11; Isaiah 60:3). He is also "firstborn" in God's creation (Colossians 1:15), among God's many sons (Romans 8:29), in the resurrection from the dead (Colossians 1:18), and in the church (Hebrews 12:23).

The above references qualify Psalm 89 as one of the sixteen psalms designated as *Messianic.*

Life stEP — What eternal promises of God are especially precious to you? Is sin keeping you from claiming those promises?

thursday 3

Psalm 89:38-52

What is the writer saying?

How can I apply this to my life?

pray — *Japan – For this country's youth to turn from drugs and materialistic pleasures to the living God.*

The psalmist of Psalm 89 was a man named Ethan who had inherited the position of worship leader at the temple. In verses 1-37, he fulfills his office by leading the people in praise concerning God's faithfulness. Twice, God Himself spoke through the psalmist, confirming and expanding the covenant He had previously made with David.

Now, in verses 38-45, the psalmist presents the response of the people to Ethan's earlier effort to lead them in praise to God's faithfulness. In contrast, they measure God's faithfulness by their present, sad circumstances. Their king has been deposed and covered with shame (vv. 38-39, 44-45). His citadel is destroyed (v. 40). His city, Jerusalem, has been plundered (v. 41). His enemies are exalted and rejoicing (v. 42). His army is slaughtered (v. 43). Therefore, the people accuse God of violating His own Word. It is important for us to notice that there is not one word of *trust in God* or *confession of the sin* that led to all their problems!

Finally, in verses 46-51, the psalmist speaks for himself. He presents his own prayer to God to remember His promises and restore His people. Ethan gives two reasons why God should speedily restore His people: (1) Life is short and he wants deliverance before he dies (vv. 47-48). (2) Both God's people and their enemies are bringing reproach upon God (vv. 49-51), who appears to have forsaken His people and forgotten His promises to Israel.

Verse 52 is not an integral part of Psalm 89, but is rather a benediction to close out the Third Book for the Psalms (Psalm 73-89).

God uses adversities to strengthen and temper our lives. Is there adversity in your life? What does God desire to accomplish by allowing the adversity to come into your life?

Psalm 90:1-17

What is the writer saying?

How can I apply this to my life?

This psalm is one of three songs written by Moses. The first is a song of redemption for the deliverance of Israel from slavery (Exodus 15:1-19). The third is a song of instruction to Israel just prior to the death of Moses (Deuteronomy 32:1-44). The second song is this psalm by Moses, the weary leader, in need of help from above to finish his earthly sojourn.

The psalm consists of three stanzas, each presenting a contrast:

1. *God's Majesty* is compared with *Man's Frailty* (vv. 1-6). While God has been *"our dwelling place"* (i.e., a "protecting shelter" for needy people, v. 1) throughout history, man is limited by time. In God's sight, earthly time is like a 4-hour night watch or grass that withers.

2. *Man's Sins* are compared with *God's Wrath* upon sin (vv. 7-12).

3. *God's Servants Appeal* for the return of *God's Favor* (vv. 13-17). Since life is brief and the efforts of man cannot make progress without the blessings of God, Moses now prays for "wisdom" to realize that "our days" are limited (vv. 9-10, 12, 14, 15)

Notice the three lessons to be learned from this prayer of Moses:

1. Since life is short, we must make every day count. Only within our limited days (vv. 9-10) do we have opportunity to serve God!

2. Life is full of evil; only God's mercy can "satisfy us" and "make us glad" (vv. 14-15).

3. Moses establishes a *pattern of prayer* which we should follow: (a) express an understanding of the greatness and majesty of God (vv. 1-6); (b) confess sins (vv. 7-12); and (c) once a right perspective is established, present our personal petitions (vv. 13-17).

Life STEP

With what are you filling your days? Make a list of the five or six things that take up your time. Now ask: which of these are self-centered ambitions that amount to nothing of any significance, and which are deeds of substance that bring honor to God?

Psalm 91:1-16

What is the writer saying?

How can I apply this to my life?

pray   *Nigeria – Pray that the churches in Nigeria would be more committed to ministering to their children and youth.*

Verses 1 and 9 of this psalm tie it to Psalm 90. While anonymously composed long after Moses' psalm, it was arranged as a follow-up to Psalm 90.

The psalm begins with a declaration of trust: "He is my refuge and my fortress; my God, in Him will I trust" (v. 2). A *refuge* is a sheltered harbor where a ship may hide from a storm that threatens to destroy it. *Fortress* pictures an inaccessible nest protected in high cliffs of rock.

Verses 3-8 give three pairs of verses that detail the resultant blessings:
• The blessing of deliverance and protection (vv. 3-4);
• The blessing of knowing one is in God's care brings the removal of fear of both secret and open enemies (vv. 5-6);
• The blessing of being protected from judgment, even when that judgment

is falling upon thousands all around (vv. 7-8).

Before proceeding further, he repeats his declaration of trust (v. 9) and stresses that these promises are for those who trust in the Lord.

• No such disaster or judgment can befall a person who has, by faith, taken shelter in God as his harbor of refuge (v. 10).

• God provides guardian angels to protect us from demonic attack and other dangers that would hinder us from fulfilling God's purposes for us on earth (vv. 11-13; also Daniel 6:22; Acts 5:19; Hebrews 1:14).

In verses 14-16 the Lord declares His own seven-fold promise to those who trust Him; He promises to "deliver," "set...on high," "answer," "be with [us] in trouble," "honor," "satisfy," and "show...[His] salvation."

Life **stEP**   Obviously, the psalmist wants us to consider our own trust in God, especially during the storms of our lives! Ask yourself: is my "ship" anchored in God as my "harbor of refuge"? Like our psalmist, who twice gives us his *declaration of trust*; take a minute and write out your own *Declaration of Trust*!

Psalm 92:1-15

What is the writer saying?

How can I apply this to my life?

pray — Panama – For youth ministry workers to commit their time, creativity, and love to Christ's use.

Today's psalm is a hymn of thanksgiving for Sabbath Days. But it is also an artistically crafted piece of wisdom that builds concentric circles around the psalm's middle lesson (v. 8) which literally says, *Lord, you are exaltedness itself!* Around this central theme are three circles:

• The inner circle declares God's moral rule over the world (vv. 6-7, 9). This rule of God is not known by the "brutish man" (*a person with no sense of personal discipline*, v. 6a,), the "fool" (v. 6b), the "wicked" (v. 7a), "workers of iniquity" (vv. 7b, 9b), or "enemies" of the Lord (v. 9). These do not "understand" (v. 6b) the "great" and "deep" (v. 5) works of God that cause them to "perish" (v. 9).

• The middle circle presents a contrast of the psalmist himself (vv. 4-5, 10-11). He knows and trusts in the Lord's "works" and as a result he is "glad," and "will triumph" by God's hand (v. 4). He considers the deep thoughts of God (v. 5), and his "horn" will be "exalted" (v. 10). The Hebrew word "exalted" here is a word related to "most high" of verse 8 (literally, *exaltedness*). The psalmist understands one of the deep truths of God: that He grants to His people that very *stuff* that makes Him great.

• The outer circle calls all who know and trust the Lord to round-the-clock, life-long praise of the Lord (vv. 1-3 and 12-15). This outer circle also praises God as it identifies Him as our LORD, the Most High, and our Rock who is unfailing, loving, faithful, fruitful, and upright.

Verse 8 then is a high mountain above the valley of verse 7 where we live while the enemy flourishes. When our eyes are on the mountain, our horns are exalted above the horns of the wicked (Psalm 75:10) and we flourish because we are planted in the house of the LORD.

Life **stEP** — What are some ways God is causing you to "flourish"?

Psalm 93:1-5

What is the writer saying?

How can I apply this to my life?

The octet of Psalms 93 to 100 has a common theme: *The LORD reigns, therefore sing!* Our psalm begins the octet by highlighting four attributes of God which manifest His absolute sovereignty: His majesty, omnipotence, immovability and eternality. To be "clothed with majesty... [and] strength" (v. 1) is to possess those qualities to the fullest degree.

Verses 1-2 announce the LORD as the reigning and "established" King of the world. His *majesty* is a concept that exceeds our ability to adequately describe. Its Hebrew root means *to be raised up* and implies *glorious or exalted in triumph*. So here, *majesty* speaks of God's grandeur, splendor, authoritative aura, and awesome presence.

Verses 3-4 contrast the turbulence of the storms of life on earth with the stability and security of the LORD who is "on high" and "mightier" than all such "mighty waves." Clearly the intent of the descriptions of the physical storms is to picture the personal storms that rage in our lives.

Verse 5 brings us to the climax of the psalm. The LORD has declared His own "sure" witness which reveals His consistent, abiding character. His witness also declares His will concerning our conduct in life, i.e., "holiness." Finally, this Holy One who is higher than our troubles invites us to fellowship with Him. (For Israel, this fellowship was done through worship at the Temple, God's earthly "house.")

The LORD's testimonies are seen in many parts of Scripture which tell of His personality and His purposes. For instance, He is holy and therefore desires to see holiness exemplified in His household members. Since He is immutable, that desire for holiness will never cease. As children in His "house," we must desire to live in the realm of His purposes.

Let's use a 2-column chart to create a picture of this same contrast in your life: In the first column list several storms that are lifting up "mighty waves" in your life. Then in the second column, list the elements of God's care that bring stability, security, and calmness into your *stormy* life.

Psalm 94:1-11

What is the writer saying?

How can I apply this to my life?

A key to understanding today's psalm is its deliberate placement after Psalm 93 and second in a series of eight psalms (93 to 100) that deal with God's reign as King of the world. Today's psalm assumes that the reader knows its subject is the reign of our King and thus it does not declare, like Psalm 93:1, "The LORD reigns."

In the ancient world, a king occupied the throne, wore a crown on his head, and held a scepter in his hand. The crown speaks of the king's privilege and prerogative. The king's scepter speaks of his obligation and responsibility to judge.

The psalmist beseeches the LORD, his King-Judge, to fulfill His responsibility to condemn wickedness. He is saying: *We recognize your right to the crown, now use your scepter! The wicked boast, they oppress, they murder, and they are ignoring You, LORD God. How long before You bring judgment?*

At verse 8, the psalmist changes focus. Having finished his prayer, he now feels compelled to warn the wicked of God's sure judgment! So he says, *How foolish to think that the Creator of your ears cannot hear. If He made your eyes, don't you realize He can see everything you see? Since He knows everything, don't you know it is foolish* ["vanity," v. 11] *to ignore that He will bring you to judgment?*

Though many "brutish" people (*dull-minded; blinded by the smoke of one's own fire*, v. 8) do not want to think about God's sure judgment of wickedness, this does not keep God from seeing their deeds, nor does it keep God from judging their wickedness in His own time.

Are you living like one of the "brutish" people (v. 8) in this psalm? Since the Lord is your King, are you being mindful of the words you use (v. 9a), the things you do (v. 9b), and the thoughts you dwell on (v. 10)?

Psalm 94:12-23

What is the writer saying?

How can I apply this to my life?

The theme of this Psalm now changes from *concern* to *confidence*; from a prayer for *judgment* upon the wicked (v. 1) to praise for the *blessing* of being disciplined and instructed by the LORD (v. 12). The psalmist focuses on the favored status of the "upright in heart" (v. 15) that allows them to "rest" (v. 13) in God's care. Those who are "His people" (v. 14) are assured that God will not "forsake" (v. 14) His promises to them and that the Lord will be their "help" (v. 17).

The next section of the psalm, verses 16-19, begins with the psalmist asking two questions. This time the questions are not directed to God or to wicked men but to the psalmist himself. These questions begin a confident affirmation that the LORD is the psalmist's only source of help. Whenever he is at the point of being defeated by despair (v. 17) brought on by evildoers, the

LORD would be his help. The psalmist illustrates this by saying, *while my foot was slipping, when I was at the moment of falling, the LORD reached over and held me up*! This pictures two friends walking side-by-side when one steps on a slippery spot and begins to fall. The other friend, with his own feet on solid ground, is able to reach over and catch the first, carrying the weight of both.

Comparing verses 3 and 19, notice the marked change in perspective when one rests in God's promises (or we could say, leans on the arm of the one with solid footing). The psalmist continues, fully aware of the evil being perpetrated by godless people (vv. 20-21), but he sees it all from his safe refuge: the LORD, his Rock (v. 22).

Life stEP

Likely, your life also has its rough spots that cause your Christian walk to slip. What hard situations have come into your life bringing you to the point of falling into personal despair? To make matters worse, perhaps the *slippery patch* in which you are walking is deliberately-spilt oil! What hardships tend to cause you to forget that the Lord is on solid ground and is always there to *hold you up* (v. 18)?

Psalm 95:1-11

What is the writer saying?

How can I apply this to my life?

Pray for the President of the United States to submit to the wisdom and guidance of the Holy Spirit.

As noted earlier, Psalms 93 to 100 are a series of psalms that deal with God's reign as King over His world. The series was intended for use in worship services at the rebuilt Temple (516 BC) after the Jews had returned from their exile to Babylon (538 BC). These psalms are related mainly by their calls to praise and sing to the King who reigns.

Today's psalm has two parts. The first is an *invitation* for His people to come into God's presence and sing praises to Him (v. 1-7b). The second is an *exhortation* of the serious responsibility of God's people to hear and obey "His voice" (v. 7c-11).

Verses 1-5 were sung *antiphonally* (responsively), with half the choir singing verses 1, 3, and 5 and the other half singing 2 and 4. The psalm invites all believers to "sing," *to shout joyfully,* and to *sing while accompanied by instruments* (meaning of "with psalms," v. 2b). The reason for their singing was 3-fold:

1) God, as the "great King above all gods," is majestic (v. 3).
2) God is to be praised because of His great works of creation (vv. 4-5).
3) God as a Shepherd has made them "sheep" in His pasture (v. 7).

Following the *invitation to sing* is the *exhortation to hear and obey* God's words (vv. 7c to 11). The instructions here are a warning not to repeat the error of heart as the first generation of redeemed Israelites did. They had forgotten that God was caring for them as His sheep, so they missed enjoying the blessings God intended for them.

Since Hebrews 3:7-11 quotes verses 7c to 11 in their entirety, the psalmist's invitation and exhortation are made applicable to us Christians. The point is that we too can miss God's intended blessings for our lives. We too can waste our lives wandering in a spiritual wilderness by failing to trust Him, the Shepherd who will care for us.

Life stEP

How can you have an open heart that listens to "His voice"?

Psalm 96:1-13

What is the writer saying?

How can I apply this to my life?

In the Septuagint (early Greek translation of the Hebrew Scriptures), there are two superscriptions above Psalm 96: "A Psalm of David" and "When the house was being built after the captivity." These along with the following details provide the best explanation for this psalm.

1 Chronicles 15:25-16:6 describes a celebration when King David brought the Ark of the Covenant to Jerusalem. Verse 16:7 says "David delivered first this psalm to thank the LORD into the hand of Asaph." Verses 16:8-36 then recite his psalm. We note that verses 23-33 of David's psalm are repeated here in Psalm 96 with some additions. The additions were for liturgical purposes at a similar celebration by Jews who had returned from exile and were rebuilding the temple.

Psalm 96 may be divided into four stanzas (poetry's paragraphs):

• A call to all nations to praise and glorify the LORD (vv. 1-3).

• A declaration of His worthiness to be praised (vv. 4-6).

• A series of earnest pleas to acknowledge and worship the greatness of the LORD (VV. 7-9).

• A call to all nations, the heavens and all of creation to joyfully celebrate the coming One, Jesus Christ, who will judge the earth in righteousness and truth (vv. 10-13).

The answer to the calls of Psalm 96 will not come "until the times of the Gentiles be fulfilled" (Luke 21:24), nor until Israel as a nation says "Blessed is He that cometh in the name of the Lord" (Luke 13:35). Yet we can be very sure that "He that shall come will come, and will not tarry" (Hebrews 10:37). Notice that this hope of Christ's Second Coming is the closing prayer of the entire Bible; "Amen. Even so, come, Lord Jesus" (Revelation 22:20).

Life **STEP**   How can you show to others that He is your Master?

Psalm 97:1-12

What is the writer saying?

How can I apply this to my life?

There is considerable figurative language in Psalm 97. Here is our understanding of the imagery in verses 1-8:

• "Isles" (or coasts) is frequently used in the Old Testament to designate not islands, but the far-flung places on earth inhabited by Gentiles (Isaiah 41:5; Jeremiah 31:10).

• "Clouds," "darkness," "fire," and "lightnings," used together, indicate the manifestation of God toward earth in judgment of sin (Exodus 19:16; Hebrews 12:18; Revelation 8:5).

• "Hills" is figurative for *nations* (Isaiah 2:2, 40:4).

• "Zion" is Jerusalem, where God's true government rests (Isaiah 2:3).

• "Daughters of Judah" are the other cities around Jerusalem.

• The Hebrew word translated "gods" is found more than 250 times in the Old Testament and means any personages that receive the homage due the one true God.

In verse 1, the LORD is ready to manifest, as Messiah, His right to reign on earth. Verses 2-5 speak of the judgment upon the governments of this world preceding Messiah's enthronement at Jerusalem. Verses 6-9 describe the results of His appearance:

• All in Heaven and earth will see His glory.

• Those who serve false gods will be ashamed.

• Those who are God's people will be glad and rejoice.

Verses 10-12 conclude the psalm with a plea to those who "love the LORD." We are to "hate evil" by being committed to a conduct of life that reflects a faithful obedience to God's righteous standards. Such a commitment results in "gladness" and rejoicing with thankfulness.

Life **stEP**   Does your righteous conduct in life make it evident that you "hate evil"?

Psalm 98:1-9

What is the writer saying?

How can I apply this to my life?

Isaac Watt's song "Joy to the World" is from Psalm 98. We sing it to celebrate Christ's birth but it looks to His ultimate reign. The singing of "a new song" (v. 1) is mentioned nine times in the Bible. A new song is called for whenever the LORD does a new "marvelous thing" (v. 1). In Psalms 96, 98 and 149, that *marvelous thing* is the final "victory" of the Lord Jesus (v. 1b) when He is enthroned as Messiah. Three different aspects of the work of Messiah are highlighted in this psalm, each with an exhortation for His people to praise:

• *Sing to Messiah, our Deliverer*, who has "made known His salvation" and "righteousness" (vv. 1-3). We enjoy His salvation because, in His strength (implied by the symbols of power, His right hand and arm), He has acted upon His faithful and loyal love for us.

• *Shout joyfully to Messiah, our King* (vv. 4-6). He will be extolled as the world's King with singing, joyful shouts, rejoicing, praise and musical instruments.

• *Make a thunderous roar to Messiah, our Judge* (vv. 7-9). "Sea," "floods," and "hills" summarize the physical creation; they also symbolize the nations of the world (Revelation 17:15). Verse 9 is a summary of Isaiah 11:1-5 which describes the righteous rule of the Messiah in His future Millennial Kingdom, and underscores the Ruler's prerogative to also act as Judge.

This psalm ends with an unusual phrase, "[he shall judge] *the people with equity*" (v. 9b). "*Equity*" refers to the benevolent justice of ancient kings, who, in celebration of the completion of their first year of reign, would cancel the debts of their people and free prisoners and slaves (e.g., Cyrus, Ezra 1:1). In like manner the LORD our King has cancelled our spiritual debt to Him and has freed us from sin and death!

Life stEP How can you be gracious to forgive someone who has wronged you?

Psalm 99:1-9

What is the writer saying?

How can I apply this to my life?

pray Argentina – For church leaders to know the Word, live in the Spirit, and disciple others to replace them.

Psalm 99 consists of three stanzas of different lengths (vv. 1-3, 4-5, 6-9). Notice that each stanza ends with a declaration that *God is holy* (vv. 3b, 5b, 9b). In the Bible, "holy" is the most stressed of the attributes of God. The Hebrew word means *set apart* or *distinct from*.

Concerning God's holiness, the psalmist makes several observations:

1. *He sits on His throne "between the cherubim"* (v. 1; a reference to the Mercy Seat above the Arc of the Covenant). The Lord is always available to His people who come to Him with their needs. This was Israel's unique honor in the ancient world, that God had chosen to establish His special presence in their midst.

2. *"Let them praise thy great and terrible name; for it is holy"* (v. 3): This verse is not pointing to the *purity* of God's holiness, but rather focuses on His *fearsome majesty* and the *awe-inspiring respect* with which people may approach Him with their praise. This is an oft-forgotten aspect of our worship of God! We remember to praise God as our loving Father; yet we forget to reverence Him as our awesome and fearful Judge (which is picked up as the emphasis of verse 4).

3. *"You have established equity; You have executed justice and righteousness"* (v. 4). The Lord also oversaw the activities of Israel's kings who were themselves to rule with strength, love and righteous judgment. If the king supported any wrong or protected any criminal, then that king was not *exalting the Lord our God*.

Three Old Testament men—Moses, Aaron, and Samuel—are identified as examples of civil and religious leaders whose manner of service reflected God's holiness; "Be holy for I am holy" (Leviticus 11:45).

As a Christian you are called to declare His holiness in both your words and actions. What actions or words do you need to *choose* not to use today?

Psalm 100:1-5

What is the writer saying?

How can I apply this to my life?

pray   *New Zealand – To see many won to Christ through church–run food banks and counseling ministries.*

This short psalm of praise and thanksgiving closes a series of psalms (93 to 100) having a common theme: *The LORD reigns, therefore sing!* It also repeats the themes seen in the series.

Being a psalm entirely of praise, it is one of the most memorized psalms. No doubt it is the beautiful poetic balance of thoughts in this psalm that has made it a favorite to memorize. We suggest the following outline:

A 3-fold Invitation: Shout ("joyful noise"), *Serve,* and *Come* (vv. 1-2)

- *A 3-fold Assertion*: Our motivation for praise (v. 3)
  1. *"The LORD he is God."* This was a declaration that *Jehovah,* the God of Israel, and not one of the other "gods" of the ancient world, is the *Supreme One in Heaven.*
  2. *"He who has made us."* This establishes His right to divine sovereignty (He is our king) and thus His right to judge us.
  3. *"We are His people, and [His] sheep."* God had granted this right to Israel. They were His people under His special, watchful care. In a similar manner, Christians are the new people of God who can also claim these ancient promises.

A second 3-fold Invitation: Enter, Give thanks, and Praise (v. 4)

- *A second 3-fold Assertion:* Our motivation for trust (v. 5)
  1. God, in character, is *good.* Therefore, I know He will do what is best for me
  2. God, in character, is *unfailing in His love* ("mercy"). Therefore, I know He will be patient with me.
  3. God, in character, is *faithful.* (The psalmist denotes His *fidelity* "to all generations.") Therefore I know I can trust what He says!

Life **stEP**   This psalm challenges you to cultivate a thankful spirit. When life is hard, do you thankfully look for God's purpose in it?

Psalm 101:1-8

What is the writer saying?

How can I apply this to my life?

pray   *Pray for those who are persecuting believers around the world (Matthew 5:44).*

In Psalm 101, King David expresses the high purposes and noble aspirations of a ruler as he ascends to his throne. The psalm is divided into two stanzas, each with four verses. The first stanza presents the proper *heart purpose* of a leader regarding his own conduct. The second presents his *personal determination* for his realm.

In the first stanza, the psalmist's desire was to live a life that reflects the LORD's own *mercy and judgment* (v. 1) and to practice such before others (v. 2a). He wanted a constant *sense of God's presence* with him so that his way will be one of wisdom (v. 2b). He was concerned with *his walk* and that which he looked upon (vv. 2c, 3). He purposed to *avoid wickedness* and to separate himself from evil doers (v. 4).

In the second stanza, he resolves to seek faithful companions to serve in his government. His qualifications are

people who...
• Are free from *slanderous* gossip (v. 5a). *Slandering one's neighbor* refers to the practice of seeking to raise oneself up by spreading false or hurtful stories that discredit others.
• Are without a "*high look*" (v. 5b). A "high look" refers to a conceited, over-confident self assessment. Thus, one with *eyes above others*.
• Are without a "*proud heart*" (v. 5c). This refers to a *puffed-up* attitude that demands special attention and treatment. Such a privileged outlook brings out self-promoting ambition instead of a service-to-others outlook. Note that David wanted servants (v. 6)!
• Have no *works of deceit* or *telling of lies*. Neither wicked actions nor deceptive statements would be tolerated in David's government. People who would serve him had to act and speak truthfully!

Life stEP   Which of the qualities noted here need prayerful attention in your life?

Psalm 102:1-14

What is the writer saying?

How can I apply this to my life?

The title of our psalm is very helpful: "A prayer of the afflicted." The historical details hint at a time of writing when Jerusalem had suffered damage (notice "ashes," v. 9; "stones," and "dust," v. 14) and the writer was facing an untimely death ("shortened my days," v. 23).

Clark suggests a helpful outline that points out the psalm's *back-and-forth* reflections between his *prayer* concerning his *profound affliction* (vv. 1-11, 23-24a); and his *praise* to the LORD that gives him *perfect assurance* (vv. 12-22, 24b-28).

Verses 1-11 are the complaints of one overwhelmed by his situation:

• He complains that his life is being snuffed out like vanishing smoke or like wood being consumed by fire (v. 3).

• He is so heart sick that he forgets to eat and is wasting away (v. 4-5).

• He is like the desert owl that resides as a solitary creature, dwelling in the most remote and desolate places (v. 6).

• He feels all alone while being oppressed by his enemies (vv. 7-8).

In verses 12-14 the perspective changes when the psalmist centers upon the LORD's faithfulness and the coming "set time" when the LORD will no longer "hide His face" (Deuteronomy 31:18). Notice the following:

• While our lives are brief, the Lord "shall endure forever" (v. 12a).

• While our friends have abandoned us and forgotten their promises to us, the Lord remembers until the end of time (v. 12b).

• While our current situation is dire, we can take confidence that the Lord will "arise" and show "mercy" upon His people (v. 13).

• While our Holy City of Jerusalem is destroyed, we "take pleasure" in knowing that at Jerusalem God has promised to do great things (v. 14).

Life stEP How can you express your *assurance* in God's care for you?

friday 5

Psalm 102:15-28

What is the writer saying?

How can I apply this to my life?

pray   *Canada – Pray for Bible institute ministry teams to have a lasting impact in local churches.*

Our passage begins with a continuation of the psalmist's expression of perfect *assurance* in God's faithfulness to His promises (vv. 15-22).

▶ The psalmist knew the day will come when the "heathen [people from places where the LORD is not known] shall fear the name of the LORD"; i.e., *honor the character of the true God* (v. 15).

▶ The psalmist knew God would "build up Zion" (Jerusalem, v. 16).

▶ The psalmist knew he was writing for a "generation to come" (v. 18)

▶ The psalmist, while greatly troubled, knew that God was always *looking down* upon him (v. 19) and *hearing* his prayers (v. 20).

▶ The psalmist knew one day people would gather "together...to serve the LORD" (v. 22).

Despite these assurance, the psalmist somehow failed to maintain a divine perspective. Perhaps some time passed and his prayers went unanswered, resulting in a return of lingering fears. So he reverts to earlier complaints (vv. 23-24a): *You have taken away my strength at an age when I should be strong. Why are you shortening my life? You are forever; why are you doing this to me?*

Gladly, the psalmist's faith again steadies as he remembers the eternal and unchanging character of God (vv. 24b-28). It is important to note that verses 25-27 are quoted in Hebrews 1:10-12 and applied to Jesus, God the Son. They are among seven Old Testament passages cited in Hebrews 1:5-13 for the purpose of proclaiming the deity of Jesus Christ, our Great High Priest. This quotation presents the Son's pre-eminence as Creator (see also Colossians 1:16-19) as well as His eternality and immutability.

Life stEP   When you face life's harsh experiences, what aspect of God's strength, unchangeable character, or eternal care will see you through?

Psalm 103:1-22

What is the writer saying?

How can I apply this to my life?

pray *El Salvador – For those taking Bible correspondence courses to gain a passion for studying the Word.*

Here is a psalm of worship! Observe that David opens with a call to stir himself up, with his entire being, to "bless the LORD" and "bless His holy name" (vv. 1-2). To *"bless"* is to *sound out favorable words*; it suggests a *praising of God* while *bending one's knee* as a salute. In verses 3 to 5, he further admonishes himself not to forget *all the benefits* bestowed upon him by the LORD. Six benefits are listed: He has been spiritually forgiven; morally healed; redeemed from judgment of sin; lovingly crowned; satisfied with good; and renewed like an eagle that, after molting its old wings, acquires a completely new set of wings.

In verses 6 to 10, David tells how the LORD has dealt with His people in the past. Notice how he magnifies the attributes of God: righteousness, divine justice, mercy, grace, and long-suffering. In verses 11-14, David pictures the unbounded character of *God's mercy*: as high as Heaven, "as far as the east is from the west" (in ancient times, both directions reached beyond what was geographically known), like a father's care of his children, and as limitless as God's own knowledge.

In verses 15-18, David considers the *eternality of God* by comparing it to the brevity and frailty of a man's life. In verse 19, David presents the unending extent of the *sovereignty of God's kingdom*.

David began the psalm by urging himself to *"bless"* the LORD. In verses 20-22, he closes by urging a *universal blessing* of the LORD. He calls upon the angelic beings to join him in blessing the LORD. He then calls upon all the "works" of Creation everywhere to praise Him. He closes by going back to his own soul, in a repeat of the opening line of the psalm: "Bless the LORD, O my soul!"

Life **stEP** Follow David's example and make a list of the "benefits" which the LORD has graciously brought into your life.

Ephesians

The book of Acts records the history of the early church. Primarily Jewish in character, the church remained in Jerusalem after the Resurrection and Ascension of the Lord. Its adherents continued to worship in the temple and synagogues, as well as in their own assemblies. These early believers were not yet fully aware that in Christ all those Old Testament practices were done away with. Their belief in Christ as the Messiah, however, was sufficient to bring persecution that was so intense (Acts 8:4) that the believers fled Jerusalem and went everywhere preaching the Word.

Paul's part in the persecution of the church and his conversion to following Christ are both recorded in Acts 9, along with his commission to preach the gospel to both Jew and Gentile. The church confirmed his testimony and ministry, and he made three notable missionary journeys. The first (Acts 13-15:35) was to Asia Minor, accompanied by Barnabas and John Mark. The second (Acts 15:36-18:22) finds Paul and Silas crossing over into Europe after a brief visit to Syria. Timothy (at Derbe) and Luke (at Troas) join the team. In Greece, they visit Athens and Corinth, where Paul meets Aquila and Priscilla. He then visits Ephesus (Acts 18) and after a brief time of reasoning in the synagogue, he parts company with Aquila and Priscilla and continues on his way. The third journey (Acts 18:23-21:14) finds Paul returning to Ephesus (Acts 19), where he remains for nearly three years in a teaching ministry. He finally departs to visit Macedonia and Greece, planning to return to Jerusalem for Pentecost (Acts 20:16). A very touching scene is given to us in Acts 20 as he stops off at Miletus, some 40 miles south, and calls for the elders of the Ephesian church. His visit to Jerusalem ends in his being arrested and finally brought to Rome as a prisoner in bonds. It is from Rome, a prisoner under house arrest, that he writes the Ephesian epistle, and has it delivered by Tychicus, a "beloved brother" (Ephesians 6:21).

WHY THE EPISTLE WAS WRITTEN

The early church was not only persecuted (Acts 8:4), but was threatened by doctrinal heresies, including that of Gnosticism. This doctrine presumed to "know," and sought to thrust between the soul and God all sorts of human and celestial mediators. Paul's letter to the Colossians deals with this heresy and emphasizes the pre-eminence of Christ. In Him alone dwells "all the fullness of the Godhead bodily" (Colossians 2:9).

What Paul has to say to the Ephesian church is appropriate for all churches, both then and now. In fact, numerous scholars are of the opinion that Ephesians was "a circular letter," a doctrinal treatise in the form of a letter, to the churches in Asia Minor. Some reliable Greek manuscripts omit the words "at Ephesus" in 1:1. Since Paul had worked at Ephesus for about three years, and since he normally mentioned many friends in

Ephesians

the churches to whom he wrote, the absence of personal names in this letter strongly supports the idea of its encyclical character. It was likely sent first to Ephesus by Tychicus (Ephesians 6:21-22; Colossians 4:7-8) and is probably the same letter that is called "the epistle…from Laodicea" in Colossians 4:16 (Ryrie).

Harry Ironside offers this note: "There are very remarkable correspondences between certain Old Testament books and New Testament epistles. The Epistle to the Romans, for instance, answers to Exodus; the letter to the Hebrews is the counterpart of Leviticus; and this Epistle to the Ephesians is the New Testament parallel to Joshua. In Joshua we have the people of Israel entering upon the possession of their inheritance. In Ephesians believers are called upon to enter by faith now into the possession of that inheritance which we shall enjoy in all its fullness by-and-by. We are far richer than we realize. All things are ours, and yet how little we appropriate."

THE CONTENT OF THE EPISTLE

Some have called this epistle "the most profound book in existence." The epistle is divided into two sections: the first doctrinal and the second practical, each taking three chapters. The church is viewed as the body of Christ, in which God unites Jew and Gentile, and through which He will manifest His purposes to the universe. The epistle stresses the unity of the Church, the unity of Jew and Gentile in Christ, and the unity of its members within the body. The key words in the epistle are *in* (93 times), *grace* (13 times), *spiritual* (13 times), and *heavenlies* (5 times). Accompanying Paul's focus on unity in this letter is his great emphasis on love. He uses the verb form of *love* (*agapaō*) nine times, and the noun form (*agape*) ten times. Of the 107 times Paul uses the word *love* in all of his writings, 19 are here in Ephesians. Thus, more than one-sixth of Paul's references to *love* appear in this brief epistle to the Ephesians. This letter begins with love (1:4, 6), and ends with love (6:23-24). May Paul's encouragement in this vital area of interpersonal relationships permeate those churches, and people, that claim the name of Christ.

Ephesians 1:1-6

What is the writer saying?

How can I apply this to my life?

pray

France – For godly elected officials who will provide leadership to a government and a country at an important crossroads.

Paul's opening words are magnificent. He introduces himself as Paul (using his Gentile name: *small*) not Saul (his Hebrew name: *to ask or pray*), and identifies himself as an apostle (*one sent on a mission*, in this case as an official ambassador of Christ). He uses his position to give the letter official character, for his apostolic appointment was "by the will of God" (v. 1).

He writes to "saints" (*set-apart ones*, Greek = *Hagios*; i.e., set apart for God). From the same word comes the great doctrinal word *sanctification*. At salvation, the new believer becomes a "saint." This is *positional* sanctification, to be followed by *progressive* sanctification, which is to be a life-long process until *ultimate* sanctification takes place in glory.

Paul describes these "saints" as "the faithful in Christ Jesus." Here the term *faithful* does not refer to lifestyle (though a saint should be faithful), but to the fact that they had placed their faith in Christ. Others (pagans) were set apart to their gods; Paul's readers were set apart to Christ.

Other words of import in this passage: "grace" and "peace" (v. 2). Grace is God's steadfast love toward man, and peace refers to the relational state as a result of that grace. Verses 3-14 give us quite possibly "the longest sentence of connected discourse in existence" (Wuest). When Paul writes, "Blessed be the God," he uses the Greek word *eulogetos*, from where we get our word *eulogize: Let our God be well spoken of.* Other words to examine are "chosen," "predestinated," and "adoption." One should also not overlook the truth that all of the "spiritual blessings" the believer receives are found "in Christ" (a phrase or its equivalent that is used ten times in verses 3-13).

Life stEP

Can you list out ten reasons why you are thankful for the salvation God gives? Pray your thanks back to God.

monday 6

Verses 3-14 comprise one long and magnificent sentence in the original Greek text. In this passage, Paul continues his doctrinal dissertation of God's work on man's behalf. In verse 7, he directs our attention to our "redemption" (*to deliver by paying a price*); and "the forgiveness of [our] sins" (cf. Matthew 26:28), both secured "through His [Christ's] blood" (cf. Ephesians 2:13; 1 Peter 1:19) and "according to the riches of his grace" (cf. Ephesians 1:6; 2:7).

In verses 8-10 we find that in God's grace, the believer has the resources necessary to comprehend and understand God's will and purposes throughout the ages. Without God's gracious revelatory input, all of this would have remained a "mystery" (v. 9, cf. 3:3, 4, 9; 5:32); that is, not something mysterious, but rather a secret hidden with God and held in reserve until its proper time of revealing. That mystery, relative to this book, is that of the New Testament church as one body composed of both Jews and Gentiles (3:1-12); and the church as the bride of Christ (5:23-32).

The phrase beginning verse 11 can be read two ways: "we have obtained an inheritance," or *we were made His inheritance*. Both ideas are true: we, who were outcasts, are "heirs of God and joint-heirs with Christ" (Romans 8:17). And also, Christ, "for the joy that was set before Him [that's us: we're His inheritance] endured the cross" (Hebrews 12:2). Paul assures us that this inheritance is sure: God's will cannot be frustrated, nor will His purposes for His people be thwarted. Why not? Because once salvation has taken place, the believer is "sealed with the Holy Spirit" (v. 13), a mark of ownership and a pledge that our promised redemption will be completed.

Write a few sentences describing what you think heaven will be like. Tell God that you are looking forward to being in heaven with Him.

Ephesians 1:15-23

What is the writer saying?

How can I apply this to my life?

pray — Bulgaria – Outreach to Turk and Gypsy men who are largely unemployed and enslaved by alcohol.

Paul thanks God for the Ephesian saints' "faith in the Lord Jesus" (a vertical relationship), and their "love unto all the saints" (a horizontal relationship). The former is to lead to the latter. He was concerned that his readers fully comprehend what they had received in Christ, and that God would continue to bestow upon them "the spirit of wisdom and revelation in the knowledge of him" (v. 17). Only with the help of the Holy Spirit would that take place (cf. 1 Corinthians 2:14). Three areas of desired knowledge are addressed:

1. *The Past* — "The hope of His calling" (v. 18);
2. *The Future* — "The riches of the glory of his inheritance in the saints" (v. 18c). Here the emphasis is on *God's* inheritance: the believers He purchased at great price.

3. *The Present* — "The exceeding greatness of His power toward us who believe" (vv. 19-23). This power makes continued growth in the Lord possible.

Four words in the final verses of the chapter explain how much power is available to the believer: "power" (*dunamis*), inherent power; "working" (*energeia*), operative power; "mighty" (*krator*), demonstrated strength; and "power" (*ischus*), the possession of power. That power, available to the believer, was manifested in Christ's case through His resurrection (v. 20a), exaltation (v. 20b) and currently in His present position of absolute, universal authority and head of the church, His body (vv. 21-23).

Life **STEP** List three problems you might face this week. Now pick out statements from today's reading that address your problems.

Ephesians 2:1-7

What is the writer saying?

How can I apply this to my life?

pray — *India – Protection and boldness for believers facing persecution by Hindu extremists.*

Chapter 2 gives to us a spiritual "before and after" picture. It shows some of the changes the Gospel makes in men. Death here is spiritual death, separation from God. In that state the unsaved man (1) walks according to the *world*, his external enemy (v. 2a); (2) is controlled by *Satan*, his infernal enemy (v. 2b); and (3) dominated by the desires of the *flesh*, his internal enemy (v. 3). The result: as unbelievers we are the children of disobedience (v. 2c) and wrath (v. 3b).

God, however, has not left the believer at the mercy of these enemies. The very resurrection power of Christ is at our disposal. Because that is true, no longer do we have to live defeated in a devil-dominated world system, but we can live victoriously. In His "great love" (v. 4) and mercy, God intervened by (1) implanting spiritual life in all who believe, meaning they are no longer separated from God; (2) elevating them to a new level of life; and (3) permitting them to enjoy a continuous relationship with Christ in this present earthly life (v. 5). All of this takes place through the instrumentality of the "grace" of God (v. 7), (i.e., unmerited favor extended where wrath was deserved).

In verse 6 we see the marked contrast between the former lost condition of believers and their present situation in Christ. Though still in human bodies on earth, they also participate in the resurrection life of Christ, being seated with Him "in heavenly places" (cf. 1:3). The emphasis here is on the believer's identification with Christ in His death (v. 5), resurrection (v. 6) and ascension (v. 6). Throughout all eternity, believers will be a trophy of God's grace.

Life stEP — List three accomplishments in life that resulted in you receiving a reward, trophy, or public recognition. Now imagine God holding you up in joy as a trophy of His gracious work.

Ephesians 2:8-13

What is the writer saying?

How can I apply this to my life?

pray — Finland – For the hopelessness that pervades society to be replaced by the joy of salvation.

In verses 1-10, Paul gives three reasons behind God's desire to save people. His first reason is to show His love (vv. 1-6). Secondly He shows His grace, and third, He shows His workmanship by our good works. The salvation His love provides is "by *grace* . . . through *faith*." This is spelled out in verse 5: "By *grace* ye are saved"; and amplified in verse 8: "For by *grace* are ye saved through *faith*." Furthermore, "it is the gift of God." There are three key words to be noted: "*grace*"—the cause behind the plan of salvation; "*faith*"—the instrument by which it is received; and "*gift*"—the source of this grace is God Himself, and He gives it with no strings attached.

Noting the freeness of the *gift*, and its inability to be earned, Paul makes it clear that boasting is eliminated (v. 9). However, even though salvation cannot be earned, and works have no ability save, good works always follow salvation. Believers are God's "workmanship" (v. 10), His *work of art* that began at salvation and continues for a lifetime. "Ordained" to "good works" means we are to "walk in them." In fact, believers were "created in Christ Jesus" for that purpose. While works cannot bring salvation to a person, they are to always accompany salvation (cf. James 2:17).

Verses 1-10 have application to both Jews and Gentiles before conversion; verses 11-13 have special reference to Gentiles. Jews referred to them as the *uncircumcision*, those with no part in the Old Covenant. Even some Jewish believers were hesitant to treat them as equals in the faith. But now, says Paul, that great gulf that separated Jew and Gentile has been removed, and those Gentiles who "once were far off" and without "hope" have been "made nigh" (brought near) "by the blood of Christ" (vv. 12-13).

What three "good works" could you add to your life this week to bring honor to *your* savior?

Ephesians 2:14-18

What is the writer saying?

How can I apply this to my life?

Paul notes that Jew and Gentile, once alienated, are now one in Christ (v. 14). He now goes on to state what is involved. First, the "wall of partition" that once existed has been broken down (v. 14). The "enmity" or animosity that existed, which centered on the advantages God has given the Jew (which the Gentiles resented), was done away with in Christ (v. 15). Now reconciled, the two have been made "one new man" (a reference to the church, the body of Christ; 1 Corinthians 12:12-13; Ephesians 1:22-23).

That reconciliation (removal of enmity) was brought about by the death of Christ; for in His work on the cross, He rendered the Law inoperative, tearing it down so that it is no longer a separator. Wiersbe states the tearing down was three-fold: *Physically*, for in Christ we are all one (Galatians 3:28-29); *Spiritually*, the "far off" Gentiles were brought "nigh" (v. 13); and *Legally*, Christ fulfilling the Law in Himself (by meeting all of its requirements and ending its reign at the cross (v. 15).

Not only is there peace between Jew and Gentile (v. 14), but also between God and those who place their faith in Him (v. 16). (See also Romans 5:10; 2 Corinthians 5:18-20; and Colossians 1:20.) The bottom line is all believers, whether Jew or Gentile, have a common denominator: their new life in Christ. In it they find oneness that does away with that which had kept them apart. They have lost their separate identities in the church. Through His death on the cross (v. 16), Christ *proclaims* peace to all mankind (v. 17), and He *IS* peace; for through Him all men have access to God by way of the Holy Spirit (v. 18).

Life **stEP** Social "clicks" harm the fellowship of the believers. Are there any "outsiders" that you should reach out to and include in your group of friends?

Ephesians 2:19-22

What is the writer saying?

How can I apply this to my life?

Kenya – For the 500 Kenyans working as missionaries within sub-cultures and other countries.

Paul changes the imagery from that of a body to that of a temple. Here we find a graphic picture (v. 21) of what the work of Christ will result in: a living temple built out of people who are called "living stones" (1 Peter 2:4-8). Jews had their temple in Jerusalem and the Gentiles of Ephesus knew of the great Temple of Diana.

Paul begins (v. 18) by making it clear that Gentiles in Christ (just like Jews in Christ) are secure, no longer strangers to God as outsiders. They are now "fellow citizens," along with Jewish believers by birth, set apart as members of the household of God. Both Jew and Gentile are on equal footing in the Church of Jesus Christ. This temple is a securely built, solid structure. Christ is the foundation (1 Corinthians 3:11), laid by the New Testament apostles and prophets. Some have translated verse 20 to imply that the foundation *is* the apostles and prophets, but elevating them to this position destroys the imagery of the context. Like all other believers, they are part of the temple building, but Christ alone is the foundation. He is also the cornerstone, because every line in the temple building is justified only when aligned with Him.

This "building" (v. 21), this "habitation of God" (v. 22), is the place where God dwells while the church is in this world. In the Old Testament, God dwelt first in the tabernacle (Exodus 40:34) and then in Solomon's temple (2 Chronicles 7:1). In the Gospels, God dwelt in Christ Himself (John 1:14); and today He dwells in individuals (1 Corinthians 6:19-20) and the church (Ephesians 2:21).

If Christ called to say that He was going to visit your house tonight, what would you have to do to get ready for His visit? Anything need "cleaning up" for Christ to feel at home in your life?

Ephesians 3:1-7

What is the writer saying?

How can I apply this to my life?

pray   *Honduras – For godly businessmen to establish enterprises to employ and evangelize the poor.*

In 2:11-21, Paul briefly discussed the union of Jews and Gentiles in one body, called the church. Now, as he was about to offer a prayer for these united believers, he stopped right in the middle of a sentence (end of 3:1), and then returns to his prayer in verse 14. In between, Paul inserts one long sentence in which he felt compelled by the Holy Spirit to explain in some depth the equality of position Jews and Gentiles have in the church. Prior to this interruption, he reminds his readers who he is: "the prisoner of Jesus Christ" (not of Rome, though detained by them), and was such "for you Gentiles." Then he begins to develop for them the ministry to which he has been called, that of "the dispensation of the grace of God" (v. 2). He was to make known to the world the meaning of the mystery God had revealed to him (vv. 3-4): the no-distinction union of Jew and Gentile in the New Testament Church. "Mystery" here is not something mystical, but incomprehensible until God chooses to reveal it, first to and through Paul, and then others: "Holy (set apart) apostles and prophets" (v. 5).

In verse 6 Paul makes clear the meaning of the mystery in this context. It is not that Gentiles finally could be saved, for elsewhere Paul quotes Old Testament passages demonstrating God's past redemptive work among the Gentiles (Romans 9:24-33; 10:19-21; 15:9-12). It is that Gentile believers and Jewish believers are *together*: (1) "fellow heirs," (2) of the "same body," and (3) "partakers of His promise" (a messianic promise) found "in Christ [cf. 2:12, Galatians 3:29] by the Gospel." This joining together of Jew and Gentile into one was a revolutionary concept to both parties.

Do you remember your embarrassment, or the embarrassment of a friend when picked last for a baseball game? Imagine the joy of these First Century Gentiles after reading these encouraging verses.

Ephesians 3:8-13

What is the writer saying?

How can I apply this to my life?

pray *Cuba – For more Bibles, books, and teachers to train the leaders and pastors.*

Paul articulates his personal feeling of unworthiness for his task, saying he is "less than the least of all saints." No doubt his background of persecuting the church (Acts 9:5; 1 Timothy 1:13, etc.) contributed to that assessment, hence his genuine humility in being given the assignment of proclaiming to the world the "mystery" of the church. He was to "preach among the Gentiles the unsearchable riches of Christ," (v. 8) riches *past finding out* or *untraceable* (as in, *not capable of being tracked by footprints*). Reason: these riches had "from the beginning of the world... been hid in God" (v. 9). While just now being revealed, it had always been a part of God's eternal plan (cf. 1:4, 11). Paul's task was "to make all men see what is the fellowship of the mystery"; (v. 9) he is to *turn on the light* (from a word translated "photo" in English). He is to see to it that the entire world *gets the picture* that, because of the grace of God, Jew and Gentile are now one body in Christ, and through whom the world is to learn of the glories of the gospel. But the Lord will also use this new union, called the church, to reveal the wisdom of God to angelic beings ("principalities and powers" 6:12). Comparing verse 10 with 1 Peter 1:12, we find that even angels did not previously know what God had planned for the Church Age, and only learned it when God chose to reveal it through Paul.

Paul closes his interruption (begun in v. 1) by exhorting his readers to "faint not at my tribulations" (v. 13) incurred on their behalf. Instead, feel honored that in God's plan, their salvation was important enough for His servant to undergo such difficulties. While not glad he had to suffer, they could rejoice in its purpose and accomplishment.

Life stEP

Paul knew his mission in life. What is your mission in life? How could you find out? Who should you ask?

Ephesians 3:14-21

What is the writer saying?

How can I apply this to my life?

pray — Czech Republic – For continued and increased growth and depth within Bible-believing churches.

Paul's digression ends and he returns to the thought he had in mind as he began this chapter. "For this cause"—that is, God's wonderful work of bringing Jew and Gentile together as one body in Christ—the apostle humbles himself before God in a great prayer for the church. This is the second of Paul's two prayers in this letter. The first prayer (1:15-23) emphasized *knowledge,* while this second prayer emphasizes *lifestyle.* Paul wanted them to understand what they had and put it into practice. He prays for God's "whole family in heaven and earth" (v. 15). This is based on the fact that He created everyone in heaven and earth.

He then enumerates his requests for God's people. (1) That they would be "strengthened... in the inner man" by the power of the Holy Spirit (v. 16). (2) That Christ may dwell (feel at home) in their hearts by faith—that He would have the *run of the house* (v. 17). (3) That they "may be able to comprehend...and to know the love of Christ, which passeth knowledge" (vv. 18-19)—an appeal to an experiential knowledge of Christ's love which exceeds all theoretical and intellectual knowledge (for Christianity is far more than a series of doctrines, it is a life to be experienced). (4) That believers "might be filled with all the fullness of God," or better: *with respect to all the fullness of God.* No believer could possibly contain all the fullness of God, but He is the unlimited source from which we draw for all of our needed spiritual resources.

Verses 20-21 form a *doxology,* or praise to God, in which Paul notes that God can do "exceedingly abundantly ("superabundantly") above all that we ask or think." And He does it through the power of the Holy Spirit that works in us.

Life stEP — What is happening in your life this week that needs God's "exceedingly abundantly?" Talk to the Lord about these struggles often.

wednesday 7

Ephesians 4:1-10

What is the writer saying?

How can I apply this to my life?

pray — *Cayman Islands – For the strong percentage of Christians to step out and share the Gospel.*

Chapters 1-3 are doctrinal while chapters 4-6 are practical. Following his doctrinal dissertation, Paul now tells the Ephesians to "walk worthy of the vocation wherewith ye are called," i.e., the calling every believer has received and which brings to them the designation *saint*, or *one set apart to God*.

This profession of sainthood will be marked by three qualities listed in verse 2: (1) *"Lowliness"*—true, not false, humility: in Greek culture thought of as a vice to be practiced only by slaves. Christ demonstrated genuine humility (Philippians 2: 6-8). (2) *"Meekness"*—gentleness: not weakness, but ability to control one's emotions. Christ was meek (Matthew 11:29), but drove out the moneychangers from the temple (Matthew 21:12-13). (3) *"Longsuffering"*—the ability to be patient with the weakness of others. Unity will not take place without these three qualities.

Paul lists (vv. 4-6) the seven-fold oneness believers all share and the reason for a unified walk. (1) *One body*—all believers, from Pentecost to the Rapture (1:23; 2:16; 3:6); (2) *One Spirit*—the indwelling Holy Spirit (2:22); (3) *One hope*—an expectant attitude toward Christ's return and their personal future; (4) *One Lord*—Christ, the head of the church (1:22-23); (5) *One Faith*—demonstrated by trusting Christ for salvation and life; (6) *One baptism*—that of the Holy Spirit which all believers experience at salvation, making them one; (7) *One God and Father*—the relationship established when one trusts Christ.

Life stEP — Can you think of three people who have demonstrated humility in their lives even though they are truly great? Can you imagine yourself following their example?

82

Ephesians 4:11-16

What is the writer saying?

How can I apply this to my life?

pray — *Bolivia – For the continued spiritual hunger and salvation decisions taking place within the Bolivian army.*

For the church to accomplish its purposes, the Lord provides gifted men and places them providentially (Acts 11:23-26) through His Spirit (Acts 13:1-2).

Verse 11 lists four or five types of giftedness. The first two, *apostles* and *prophets*, are foundational gifts to the church. The former would include the Twelve Apostles, Paul and perhaps a handful of others, commissioned by the Lord to represent Him and deliver His message. The latter, strictly speaking, were those who were given direct revelation by God to communicate to man before the New Testament was written. Being foundational in nature, neither has existed since the first generation of believers. *Evangelists* are preachers of the gospel, helping to bring the lost into the body of Christ, while *pastors* and *teachers* are those who shepherd the flock and instruct them in their ministries.

The goal of the church is outlined in verses 12-16. These gifted men are to (a) "*perfect* [mature, prepare]...*the saints*" by using their gifts (b) so they, in turn, will be able to accomplish "*the work of the ministry*," (c) with the result of "*edifying* [building up] *the body of Christ*" (v. 12). Verse 13 makes it plain: spiritual unity and spiritual maturity are closely linked. The purpose of this linkage is described in verse 14, where the term *children* is applied to some believers. Spiritual children are often doctrinally insecure and can be "tossed to and fro," like a small boat in a storm, when false teaching comes along (v. 14). But when the *truth* is spoken "in love" (v. 15), "the whole body" (no insignificant parts; 1 Corinthians 12:14-17) is "joined together" (v. 16), resulting in an edified body, united to its head (Christ), that functions as designed.

Life **stEP** — What do you imagine your spiritual gift is? Have you had a chance to use it?

Ephesians 4:17-24

What is the writer saying?

How can I apply this to my life?

pray — Columbia – Pray for the safety and accuracy of those participating in Bible translation projects.

Paul begins a long passage ending at 6:9. He challenges believers to "walk not as other [unsaved] Gentiles walk, in the vanity of their mind." The challenge suggests two things: one, they *could* walk that way; two, they did not have to. Though one's fallen nature is not eradicated at salvation, the believer, by receiving a new nature and the indwelling Spirit, no longer needs to be governed by it, though internal warfare between the two will be constant (Romans 7; Galatians 2:20; 5:13-26).

Those "other Gentiles" have had their "understanding darkened" (v. 18) and are "past feeling" (v. 19). They have no sense of shame, the result of years of sin and debauchery, and "have given themselves over unto lasciviousness" (sensuality), which leads to all types of "uncleanness" that goes deeper and deeper because it is never satisfied. Three times in Romans 1 Paul says that God gave them over to something: *first*, to sinful desires (1:24);

second, to shameful lusts (1:26); *third*, to a depraved mind (1:28). Areas thereby perverted are (1) right living, (2) right loving, and (3) right thinking.

"But ye have not so learned Christ" (v. 20). These Ephesians no longer existed in this state of ignorance and separation from God. They had been taught the truth about Jesus and had received salvation; yet even so, they still had the responsibility of discarding their old way of life ("put off" – verse 22), denying the appetite of their old sinful nature. This responsibility is only accomplished by being "renewed in the spirit of your mind" (*continuously yielding to the Holy Spirit*, verse 23) while at the same time *putting on* (v. 24) the "new man"—allowing the Holy Spirit to be the controlling force in one's life. Doing so manifests itself in "righteousness and true holiness" (v. 24).

Life stEP — What dirty clothes (figuratively) do you need to take off? What aspect of Christ's life should you put on to keep clean in those areas?

Ephesians 4:25-32

What is the writer saying?

How can I apply this to my life?

Speaking of true and false teachers, Christ said, "by their fruits ye shall know them" (Matthew 7:20). A similar application may be made relative to believers, for the fruit that comes from a person's life and actions will prove whether the individual is yielding to his old sinful nature or to the Holy Spirit. To illustrate, Paul uses four representative examples of problems present in his day and in ours.

1. *Lack of Truthfulness* (v. 25). This was common among the heathen, but because Christians are "members one of another," lying among them is unthinkable. Would one's foot lie to one's hand?

2. *Anger* (v. 26), which is sometimes justified by its cause, must not be permitted to stay and fester and give the devil an opportunity to gain a foothold in one's life.

3. *Stealing* (v. 28) is clearly wrong, but was apparently being practiced by some believers who carried many of their old ways into their new lives. Paul says: Stop!

He then provides them with a practical antidote: Work! That will not only meet their needs, but also provide relief for others.

4. *Corrupt Communication* (foul speech) (v. 29), another *unthinkable* for the believer. The remedy is more positive than negative: speak only "that which is good to the use of edifying." Let your language always build up, ministering "grace unto the hearers."

Paul underscores these instructions with a stern command: "grieve not the holy Spirit of God" (v. 30). The Spirit is a person, not an influence, and can be hurt when the believer turns away from His leading and follows the promptings of his flesh (some mentioned in verse 31). Paul closes this chapter with a number of positive characteristics that should mark all believers: kindness, a tender heart and forgiveness (v. 32).

Pick two of Paul's challenges to work on in your own life this week.

Ephesians 5:1-7

What is the writer saying?

How can I apply this to my life?

pray   *Ecuador – For those in authority to deal honestly, to resist social bribery, and to receive Christ.*

The *therefores* in the second half of the book (4:1,17,25; 5:14,17) refer back to the first half of the book (chapters 1-3). The *practical* follows the *doctrinal*. Aware of who we are doctrinally (the church, the body of Christ), our lifestyle should be worthy of that relationship. Ephesus was home to the Temple of Diana, where all sorts of vile sexual immorality took place in the name of religion. In verses 3-5, Paul warns the believers to avoid the pitfalls of the pagans, including "fornication" (sexual immorality); "uncleanness" (any kind of impurity); "covetousness" (greed); "filthiness" (shameless, immoral conduct); "foolish talking" (characteristic of an empty head); and "jesting" (words with double meaning) —for those who practice such things give evidence of an unchanged life and will have no place in God's kingdom. Positively, however: Be *"followers [imitators] of God"* (v. 1). Throughout the New Testament, believers are told to imitate *good* (1 Peter 3:13); *Paul* (1 Corinthians 4:16; 11:1); *godly men* (Hebrews 6:11-12); and *Christ* (by implication, 1 Corinthians 11:1). But here, they are given direct instruction to imitate *God*. To do so may not be as unrealistic as supposed, for we are His "dear children" (v. 1), are partakers of His nature (2 Peter 1:4); have access to Him (Romans 5:2), and fellowship with Him (1 John 1:3). Such a relationship makes possible a higher kind of life than the unsaved can know; a life the behavior of which is ordered by "love" (*agape*, v. 2); and because "God is love" (1 John 4:8, 16), believers imitating Him will live a life that manifests that same love (1 Corinthians 13). The motivation for such a life is found in the sacrificial actions of Christ on the cross "for us" (for our benefit, v. 2).

Life stEP   What jokes, coarse words or sarcastic comments should we probably remove from our patterns of speech?

Ephesians 5:8-14

What is the writer saying?

How can I apply this to my life?

pray   *Costa Rica – For the growth and strengthening of Bible schools that train leadership.*

Paul again points out some contrasts between the conditions of the unbeliever with that of the believer. An unbeliever is dead; a believer has new life (v. 14). An unbeliever is asleep; the believer is awake to reality and truth (v. 14). An unbeliever is darkness (note: not *in* darkness, but darkness itself), while the believer is light. That darkness was once true of the believers (v. 8); now they are numbered among those who are lights in the world (Matthew 5:14), and as such are to "walk as children of light" (keep their lights on); living lives reflective of their new life.

The parenthetical ninth verse explains that "the fruit of the Spirit" (or, better, "fruit of the light"), is "goodness and righteousness and truth," all desperately needed in a world of sensuality, sin, and evil (vv. 3-5). "Light" comes from the Greek *photos* from which we get *photography*. It is a common biblical expression, normally depicting the drastic difference between "what is acceptable unto the Lord" (v. 10), and that which is characteristic of a sinful life.

Verse 11 places upon the believer two responsibilities with respect to sin. *First*, in no way is he to have "fellowship [*to become a partaker*] with the unfruitful works of darkness." *Second*, he is to reprove such behavior by letting his life show a superior way of living. By proper conduct, the believer living as a *child of light* will expose the deeds of those who are not walking in the light. Their deeds were so vile that Paul hesitated to even mention them (v. 12), but he notes that they would be "made manifest [revealed] by the light" (v. 13).

Life stEP   Can you anticipate some situations this week where you can be a light in the darkness of the world?

Ephesians 5:15-21

What is the writer saying?

How can I apply this to my life?

Paul urges the Ephesian believers to pay careful attention to their behavior, walking "circumspectly" (with respect to your position in Christ, v. 15). They are to walk "as wise, redeeming [buying back] the time, because the days are evil [morally corrupt]" (v. 15-16). In a once-born world, the twice-born Christian is to take every opportunity to shed light on the darkness.

"Wherefore" (noting the commands to walk in *light*, v. 8 and in *wisdom*, v.15), "be ye not unwise" (senseless), but conduct yourselves in a manner demonstrating an "understanding" of "the will of the Lord" (v. 17). The pagan cannot do so (1 Corinthians 2:14); believers can. They possess in Scripture the objective revelation of His will and the indwelling Holy Spirit to interpret it. The Spirit will aid the believer in the application of Scripture. "Be not drunk with wine" (v. 18) was a common sin among unbelievers. It

has no place among believers. Instead, the believer is to "be filled with the Spirit." Paul has already taught that *all believers are sealed*, once for all time, at the point of salvation (1:13-14; 4:30), but *not all believers are filled*. Filling is commanded in Scripture and is dependent upon one's yieldingness to God's will (v. 17), thus differing from God's instantaneous act of sealing. It can be repeated according to Acts 2:4 and 4:31. All believers have the Spirit; the command here is that the Spirit is to have the entire believer. Verses 19-21 advise how to carry out the command; *First*, through music (a) with other believers and (b) in your heart to the Lord (v. 19); *second*, through constant thanksgiving to God for all things (v. 20); and *third*, through voluntary and willing submission to one another.

Life stEP — Get in the habit of consciously asking for the filling of the Spirit every time you confess a sin or before performing a service for the Lord.

Ephesians 5:22-33

What is the writer saying?

How can I apply this to my life?

pray   *Chile – For the perseverance of Chilean saints as only 38% attend church regularly.*

The key word is "submit" (v. 22), from a Greek word of military origin, emphasizing the act of voluntary (not forced) submission to a proper authority. Paul uses it as a basis for the relationships between husbands/wives, parents/children and masters/servants.

He deals first with the *husband-wife relationship*, it being the most fundamental. "*Wives*, submit… unto your own husbands," for that is your service "to the Lord." God has made the husband the family's spiritual leader. His position is compared to Christ's headship over His church; Christ is the Savior of the body, the husband the protector of his wife. For her to fail in voluntary submission would be like the church usurping Christ's headship. She is to respond to his assigned position of authority. This is not a picture of superiority vs. inferiority, but simply a role assignment.

"*Husbands*, love your wives," doing so "as Christ…loved the church and gave Himself for it" (v. 25). This is self-sacrificial love, giving of oneself for another person. When the husband practices such Christ-like love, willing submission on the part of the wife should not be difficult. Christ's death (v. 26) was to *set-apart* His bride (the church) for Himself forever. He did so by cleansing her "with the washing of water by the word" (v. 26). Verses 28-30 apply the truths of verses 25-27. The church is the body of Christ, united to Him, its head. The wife is united to her husband, they become "one flesh" (v. 31), and men are to love their wives as their own bodies, a manner that precludes anything but the exceptional care Christ displayed for His body, the church.

Life stEP   Can you think of any relationships where you know you should submit but you have not done so, at least not with the proper attitude?

Ephesians 6:1-9

What is the writer saying?

How can I apply this to my life?

Paul's discussion of personal relationships continues with parents/children and masters/servants. All these relationships require Spirit-controlled lives (5:18), hence the instruction here is pointedly to believers.

Children and Parents (vv. 1-4): Even as wives are to be subject to their husbands, so children are to "obey" their parents, doing so "in the Lord." The *submission* of wives implies voluntary action, but "obey" is much stronger, implying that parental direction is to be carried out regardless of the children's wishes. "Honor" goes beyond obedience to the heart attitude. *Obedience* is the duty (external); *honor* the disposition (internal). Attached to such positive behavior is a promise (v. 2). (See the fourth commandment—Exodus 20:12—the only one of the ten with a promise.) As for the parents, they are to earn such obedience and honor, hence the instruction: "Provoke [exasperate] not your children to wrath"; i.e., don't be unreasonable in your expectations of your children; "but bring them up in the nurture [training] and admonition [instruction] of the Lord" (v. 4). Parents are to practice neither unlimited permissiveness nor spirit-breaking discipline (Colossians 3:21). Balance is the goal.

Masters and Servants (vv. 5-9): These instructions apply today to employer-employee relationships. Employees are to carry out the orders of their employers (v. 5), understanding that no matter whom they serve in "the flesh," they are really serving Christ (v. 6), and their ultimate reward comes from Him (v. 8). Employers are to have similar attitudes, treating their employees fairly, for their ultimate responsibility is also to Christ. Both are to understand that God is impartial; both master and servant are equal in His sight.

Life stEP

What are some common short cuts that people take at work, thereby cheating their employer? Do we need to repent of any poor work habits?

Ephesians 6:10-17

What is the writer saying?

How can I apply this to my life?

pray — *Joe Jordan, Executive Director of Word of Life, for a consistent pursuit of holiness and God's direction for the ministry.*

Paul often speaks of the Christian life in military terms. This is, however, more than analogous language. The battle is real and no true soldier (cf. 2 Timothy 2:3) of Jesus Christ can expect to be immune from enemy attacks. So Paul exhorts the believers to "be strong in the Lord and in the power of His might" (v. 10). Victory will not be achieved on one's own; the believer needs the strength only the Lord can supply.

The "whole armor of God" is to be "put on" (v. 11). Paul is writing from prison, in full view of fully armored Roman soldiers. That physical armor provides a picture of the spiritual battle facing the believer, a battle "not against flesh and blood," but against Satan, his strategies and his cohorts ("principalities...powers," etc., (v. 12). In God's armor, victory is assured (v. 13), for it meets every need.

Briefly, here is what the believer is to put on (all of which are found in Christ):

(1) *The Girdle of Truth*—tightened up, it keeps everything else in place. Integrity is vital; union with the truth makes integrity possible (John 14:6); (2) *The Breastplate of Righteousness*—to protect the heart, imputed to the believer (2 Corinthians 5:21), demonstrated in life; (3) *The Shoes of Peace*—feet carry the soldier to battle, and the good news of salvation provides "peace with God" (Romans 5:1), and calm for the conflict; (4) *The Shield of Faith*—to ward off the weapons of the enemy, rendering them ineffective (1 John 5:4); (5) *The Helmet of Salvation*—to protect one's head (intellect)—"take" it, says Paul; this salvation (all three tenses: *past*, from the penalty of sin; *future*, from the presence of sin; and *present*, from the power of sin) is a free gift. With it God provides victory. Finally, (6) *The Sword of the Spirit*—God's Word, to defend oneself against the thrusts of the enemy and attack his false teachings.

Life
stEP — What practical issue in your life is addressed by each piece of armor?

Ephesians 6:18-24

What is the writer saying?

How can I apply this to my life?

pray

Angola – For medical missionaries laboring in a nation where landmines outnumber people and famine is widespread.

Paul now deals with the importance of prayerfulness and watchfulness in this spiritual conflict. Two different words are used: "*prayer*" (prayers in general—the necessity of a consistent prayer life) and "*supplication*" (special requests), both to be offered "in the Spirit." "*Watching*" means to be sleepless, always awake, which is characteristic of a reliable soldier. Having the proper attitude in spiritual warfare cannot be overemphasized. The conflict is real, the enemies spiritual, but a proper attitude will lead to victory. Prayer is to be constant ("always") and for "all saints," for they are all in the same battle (v. 18). Paul's request for himself was more ministerial than personal. Even in prison his request was not for ease or prosperity, but that God would give him the ability to preach the Gospel with boldness (v. 19). That was always Paul's chief aim in life. He considered himself an "ambassador in bonds," representing his Lord at all times.

Verses 21-22 are similar to Colossians 4:7-9. Recognizing that Paul's readers would want to know how he and his associates were doing ("*our* affairs," v. 22), Paul sends them this letter by the hand of Tychicus to provide that information and to "comfort" their "hearts" (v. 22). He doesn't name his associates, perhaps indicating that this letter was to be circular in nature, intended for a number of churches around Ephesus.

Paul's closing benediction utilizes some of the same terms he used in beginning this letter, including "peace," "love," and "grace," all of which find their source in God, and which he desired for his brothers (and sisters) in Christ, for they are all "members one of another" (4:25).

Life STEP

List five believers, five unbelievers, and five issues that you should pray for regularly this week.

Joshua

The book of Joshua is a very practical book. It deals with God's people, Israel, claiming their inheritance or possessing their promises in the Promised Land. Moses has died, and Joshua is the new leader. God had prepared Joshua for this challenge.

Joshua's background is not that impressive. Some of his forefathers in the tribe of Ephraim were cattle rustlers. No one bragged about being from the tribe of Ephraim, but he was God's man for the job. His obedience and loyalty to Moses, God's appointed leader, was unquestioned (Exodus 17:8-14; Numbers 11:26-30). Remember, Joshua was one of two (Caleb being the other) who dared to take a minority position when they spied out the land forty years earlier. He dared to *reach for the grapes* when the rest were *looking at the giants*. He was aware of the challenge and felt that God was with them. Now, after a long wait, he is given another chance for the grapes as God's leader for the day.

Joshua was also a humble man. For years he was *number two*, and even after Moses dies Joshua is called Moses's *servant*. He is aware that *there will never be another Moses*, but goes on to serve God in his own way. So, now he is ready! Some of his greatest victories are recorded, helping us in our quest too, to possess our possessions.

Israel, led by Joshua, is a picture of the believer today who, already having been redeemed, is to take all that God has given and possess his inheritance. It is God's people no longer on the defensive; it is offensive warfare. So, as you read this book, look for yourself. Questions that should come to us are: Am I willing to apply the *two foot* rule and claim the victory the Lord has promised? Read the book and find God's spiritual road map for a life of victory. As you study the victories and defeats and as you observe the mountain peak experiences and the valley challenges, feel free to apply the passages to your own life.

Sunday 9

Joshua 1:1-11

What is the writer saying?

How can I apply this to my life?

pray *Pray for those who work with the youth of your church to have love, wisdom, and perseverance.*

In this chapter we have the *two-foot rule of faith* (v. 3). The Lord had already given them the land; they were to claim it – possess it by faith. The dimensions of the land are given in verse four. It was backed up by the promise of God that He would not fail or forsake them (v. 5).

In many ways, Joshua's account corresponds with the book of Ephesians. There we are told that we are "blessed ...with all spiritual blessings in heavenly places in Christ" (Ephesians 1:3). Note, we have been blessed, that is now (not when we get to heaven). We are seated with Christ, and we need to do what God commanded in Joshua; claim it by faith.

As Joshua stands at the river Jordan getting instructions from His commander, he is given a vital promise, he is assured of God's power and then he is given a vital provision from the Lord. He was to meditate day and night in the book –the law that was given them. How true this is for us as believers. However, our meditation is in the complete *book* of the Bible (how privileged we are).

There are 365 *fear nots* in the Bible. There is one here (v. 9). Do you think that Joshua was apprehensive about such a formidable task of taking the land? Indeed. But again, he is assured of the presence of the Lord (v. 9).

Life **stEP**   Do you believe the Lord is with you now? We need to *practice His presence.* Hudson Taylor's life was turned around when he discovered what he called his spiritual secret: "The Lord Jesus *received* is holiness begun; the Lord Jesus cherished is holiness advancing; the Lord Jesus counted on *as never absent* is holiness complete."

Joshua 2:1-11

What is the writer saying?

How can I apply this to my life?

Two spies are sent by Joshua to spy secretly and view the land (v. 1). They lodged in Rahab's house. When the king heard they were there, Rahab was approached. While she hid them, she told the enemy that she didn't know where they were. Was she right in lying? We don't believe that it is ever right to do wrong to do right. In other words, the end does not justify the means. Would the Lord have supplied another way of escape if she had not acted as she did? We believe so. However, we must look beyond this act by one outside the family of Israel and note that while she erred in judgment, she actually sought out the spies and desired to be on God's side. Read verses ten and eleven which show her desire to be a believer. This is corroborated by the mention of Rahab in several New Testament passages. We read, "By faith the harlot Rahab perished not with them that believed not, when she had received the spies with peace" (Hebrews 11:31). Also, we read that the reality of her faith is seen in her works (James 2:25). Rahab is the first convert in the Promised Land and her testimony of turning to the Lord is very special.

Life stEP

One commentator writes; "The salvation of Rahab, the harlot, illustrates that even in a doomed city a wicked individual could find grace by turning to God in faith" (Scofield). What an encouragement to us as we ask the Lord to lead us to others in this wicked world – who need to be saved. Yes, the world is depraved and wicked, but He is still saving the lost. Pray that you might be His instrument today.

Joshua 2:12-24

What is the writer saying?

How can I apply this to my life?

pray   *Ecuador – Pray for the protection of evangelical churches from prejudice, threats, and violence.*

In our present passage, we find the spies instructing Rahab about future deliverance and then returning to report to Joshua. The instructions were explicit. When Jericho was attacked, Rahab was to drop a scarlet thread in the window, where she had let them down. When the approaching armies saw the scarlet thread, they were to spare Rahab and her house. The Passover in Egypt was a picture of deliverance by blood. So too, when the scarlet thread was seen it meant deliverance for the family.

How thankful we should be that we have trusted Christ who is our Passover (1 Corinthians 5:7).

It is interesting that Rahab was one of the distinguished women included in the genealogy of Christ (Matthew 1:5). While she was a woman of ill repute, the grace of the Lord intervened and she was saved. Isn't that our testimony too? We are saved by grace (Ephesians 2:8-9). Works then follow that grace. (Ephesians 2:10). That's the way it was with Rahab, and that's the way it is with each of us.

Salvation is "faith in Christ plus—nothing"!
"Amazing grace how sweet the sound that saved a wretch like me."
The "wretch" was Rahab, and she was saved. That's our testimony too. Rejoice in it.

Joshua 3:1-17

What is the writer saying?

How can I apply this to my life?

Israel is getting ready to cross the Jordan River. Think of crossing the Jordan as a picture of moving into the area of an offensive Christian experience. While it is true that Jordan is often thought of as a picture of physical death (I won't have to cross Jordan alone), you should remember that once they crossed the river there was warfare. The message is simple: Canaan land is not a picture of heaven (no war there) but a life of daily victory. In this passage, Joshua is instructed to cross the Jordan. Every step was a step of faith. They were told that the Lord would do wonders among them.

One of the most important things to remember is the Ark of the Covenant. Clearly, they were to cross the Jordan, ever keeping an eye on the ark. Of course, the ark is a beautiful picture of the Lord Jesus. Within the ark was manna (Christ is the Bread of Life), the law of Moses (Christ kept it perfectly), and Aaron's rod that budded (resurrection of Christ). On the ark was the "mercy seat" where the blood was sprinkled once a year (Leviticus 16). Christ is our "mercy seat" and the meeting place with the Father. But note here that they were to march over the river with an eye on the Lord (vv. 3-11). How familiar are the words, "Behold, the ark…." (v. 11). Yes, beholding the Lamb saved us, and we are sustained and led by the Lord as we march *on to victory*!

Life stEP Today our walk is one of obedience and faith. Step by step we follow Him, assured that He will lead us in our warfare. It is a daily experience of expecting great things from God. As we approach the river in obedience, just in the nick of time we find Him intervening.

Joshua 4:1-14

What is the writer saying?

How can I apply this to my life?

pray *Costa Rica – For God to keep the school doors open for the Gospel to be preached .*

There are two memorials in our passage. The first one (vv. 1-8) involves stones, which were to be placed on the banks of Jordan at Gilgal. One man from each tribe was involved. It was to remind their children in days to come of what the Lord had done. The second memorial (vv. 9-24) included twelve stones placed in the midst of the Jordan (4:9).

This is a wonderful picture of the two memorials the Lord has left for his church. One is baptism, which is a sign to all that we have died with Christ and have been raised to walk in newness of life (Romans 6:4). The second memorial for the church is the Lord's Table.

While baptism speaks of positional union with Christ, the Lord's Table speaks of our daily communion with the Lord. Each of them speaks both to us and to the world. "For as often as ye eat this bread, and drink this cup, ye do show the Lord's death till He come" (1 Corinthians 11:26). The word "show" is the same Greek word translated "preach" in other places. Baptism and the Lord's Table, our memorials, preach the message of Christ's work and the way it has touched our lives. They are present-day memorials to God's work in our lives.

The purposes of the two memorials in the Old Testament and in the New Testament were designed as a reminder of what the Lord has done. Both our union and communion are very important in our lives. Union, of course, takes place once, when we trust the Lord. But communion is an on-going process. It is so vital that we commune with the Lord as *friend with friend*. Be sure and keep up that day–by-day relationship with the Lord.

Friday 9

Joshua 4:15-5:1

What is the writer saying?

How can I apply this to my life?

pray Czech Republic – Pray for the establishment and growth of Christian institutes and seminaries.

We have noted that there were two memorials established among Israel to remind them of what God had done. The river parted and, following the ark, they passed over on dry ground. Hundreds of years later, another Joshua—the Lord Jesus—was magnified as John the Baptist baptized him (Matthew 3:16). This event took place in Bethabara beyond Jordan (John 1:28). Could it be that it was the same place Israel crossed? This is very possible in that Bethabara means *the place of passage.*

Perhaps Israel's crossing the Red Sea typifies God's judgment on sin and crossing the Jordan typifies His judgment on self. The Believer is not an old self renovated, but rather crucified. He has had a new self imported and implanted. Our natural self was put to death on the cross, which must continually be regarded as the place of death – both Christ's and ours.

As a believer, I can and should refuse to serve Satan, the world, and the flesh. It is more than being saved from judgment (the Red Sea). It is being saved unto a new life of victory; it is an achievement and conquest available to me as a believer day by day (Jordan River). "The sea saw it, and fled; the Jordan was driven back. The mountains skipped like rams, and the little hills like lambs" (Psalm 114:3, 4).

Saturday 9

Joshua 5:2-15

What is the writer saying?

How can I apply this to my life?

Pray for those who teach in your church to be faithful to the word, enthusiastic in their presentation, and compassionate toward the lost.

The Lord now commands that the men be circumcised. Naturally, one wonders why the Israelites, of all people, were not circumcised. After all, it was the special mark that distinguished them as God's covenant people (Genesis 17:10-11). It was also necessary to partake of the Passover feast. The answer is found in Joshua 5:4-5. Their fathers had ceased to practice it while they wandered in the wilderness. They were disobedient. Now the whole new generation had to be circumcised. We are not surprised. Israel showed many signs of disobedience in their wanderings.

While physical circumcision is not required today, the New Testament speaks of "spiritual circumcision." "In whom also ye are circumcised with the circumcision made without hands, in putting off the body of the sins of the flesh by the circumcision of Christ" (Colossians 2:11). This means that we are to break with sin, and when there is sin in our lives, we need to deal with it immediately and forthrightly. Now, how can this be done? For one thing we need to stay in the word. "I remember the days of old; I meditate on all thy works; I muse on the work of thy hands" (Psalm 143:5).

Life step

Looking at this whole picture, it might seem unreasonable for a people who were getting ready to fight to be debilitated physically as they were. But obeying at all costs, even when it doesn't seem _reasonable_, is the only way. "Trust and obey, for there's no other way to be happy in Jesus, but to trust and obey."

Joshua 6:1-11

What is the writer saying?

How can I apply this to my life?

pray *Cuba – Increased freedom in the areas of Bible printing, importation, and distribution.*

"Joshua Fit the Battle of Jericho" is the title of the song many of us have sung with gusto (every morning we would sing it when I taught this book at Word of Life, N.Y. and Florida). The Bible gives instructions as to how the city was to be taken. They were to march around it every day for six days and seven times the seventh. Humanly speaking, this may have sounded senseless. But God had given such instructions and they were to act by faith. In the New Testament we read, "By faith the walls of Jericho fell down, after they were compassed about seven days" (Hebrews 11:30).Note that we are not told whether or not the people who were marching knew the full plan. We are told that the Lord spoke unto Joshua (v. 2). Could it be that they were just willing to obey and do as the Lord commanded?

Isn't that often true with us? We just keep marching with obedient feet in the direction given by the Lord. The city was about eight or nine acres large, not making it very difficult to march around. They were to follow the ark. We are told that as they marched, they did so "before the ark of the Lord" and "before the Lord" (vv. 7-8). They sensed the presence of the Lord.

Seven times around on the final day and the trumpets sounded. God had commanded, they exercised simple faith, and their faith was rewarded. This is the same kind of faith the Lord wants to see in us. Without faith "it is impossible to please God." Whatever your wall of conflict is—"God is able." We need to trust Him.

Monday 10

Joshua 6:12-27

What is the writer saying?

How can I apply this to my life?

pray Canada – For "fruit that remains" within the local churches where Bible institute ministry teams serve.

Considering the fall of Jericho, there were several conditions that were to be followed. First, the city was judged and it was "accursed." We should remember that Jericho is a picture of the world, as the king of the city is a picture of Satan. So, in a real sense we can see ourselves here. The world and its ruler, Satan, are judged. Christ said, "Now is the judgment of this world: now shall the prince of this world be cast out" (John 12:31). The world is condemned! Praise the Lord we have victory over it and are not identified with it. Paul said, "...by whom the world is crucified unto me, and I unto the world" (Galatians 6:14).

As promised, Rahab the harlot and all of her house are allowed to live (v. 17). The people shouted, the priests blew the trumpets, and the walls of the city collapsed. Every living thing – human beings and animals – was killed.

As we apply this passage, we recognize that the world is condemned. When Christ died, we died with Him and died to the world. We are to reckon this to be true in our lives personally. Then, just as Jericho's walls fell because of God's power, so we are assured of victory. "For whatsoever is born of God overcometh the world; and this is the victory that overcometh the world, even our faith. Who is he that overcometh the world, but he that believeth that Jesus is the Son of God" (1 John 5:4-5).

Can you think of a sin in your own life that has not been conquered successfully? Bow to the Lord now and ask His help to overcome this battle by exercising faith, obedience and trust in His power. Claim the promise of 1 Corinthians 10:13.

Joshua 7:1-13

What is the writer saying?

How can I apply this to my life?

pray   *Fiji – For the success of church planting ministries, as Mormons and Jehovah's Witnesses grow in numbers.*

Obedience is so vital to the Christian life. When we fail to obey, there are serious consequences. We see this in our chapter when Achan sinned against the Lord in refusing to obey the clear commandment of the Lord. God had said that no booty was to be taken from Jericho.

In the first nine verses of the chapter we see the danger of self-confidence when it is outside of the Lord and His will. *Heights are dangerous places.* We are most vulnerable to the attack of Satan when we develop an inflated view of ourselves (Proverbs 16:18). "Pride of life" is of the world (1 John 2:16). Israel had just enjoyed a great victory at Jericho. Joshua was famous (Joshua 6: 27). He normally consulted the Lord in uncertain times; there is no indication of such here. Riding on the crest of the wave of victory in Jericho, there seems to be self-confidence. So, when they move against the enemy at Ai they reason that *it was a snap.* Not many warriors were necessary. Defeat followed (vv. 4-5). Joshua is devastated and sounds very carnal in his response (vv. 7-9). He actually sounded like the men of unbelief in a past experience (Numbers 14). He is reprimanded by the Lord (v. 10). This is one of the few cases where the Lord told a man to stop praying and stop complaining. Sin had to be judged because sin is a very serious thing and has serious consequences (vv. 10-12).

When you experience a victory, be careful that you give all the glory to the Lord. Also, don't neglect your cherished time with the Lord. Satan knows that we are most vulnerable after victories, and we are tempted to take some credit for ourselves. Keep humble or you'll stumble.

Joshua 7:14-26

What is the writer saying?

How can I apply this to my life?

pray *Philippines – Safety of missionaries working within the reach of Muslim extremists in Mindanao.*

When we sin we generally affect others. This is demonstrated in this paragraph. Because of Achan's sin, the whole body of Israel was affected. Certainly, "A little leaven leaveneth..." (1 Corinthians 5:6). Unless the sin was purged from the camp, God would no longer bless them as a nation. When you hurt your thumb, the whole body hurts; one rotten potato affects the whole bag. This is also the case in the church. When there is sin in a person or in a group, God cannot bless. It is so important that we recognize this.

The remedy for the condition is clearly stated (vv. 13-26). They were to determine the tribe (it was Judah), the family or clan (Zarhite), the household (Zabdi), and the individual (Achan).

When it was discovered that Achan was the one who sinned against the Lord, he gives his *testimony* as to what happened. You might want to mark this in your Bible. He said, "When I saw among the spoils a beautiful Babylonian garment.....I coveted them and took them." It began with seeing and resulted in taking.

The Babylonian garment looked so good. It seemed so right to take it. On the surface it seemed so innocent, but it was contrary to the Word of God. Judgment followed (vv. 24-26).

Life stEP We need to be so circumspect and careful that we obey the Lord. When we don't, we touch others and hinder revival in our church or group. "A little leaven leaveneth the whole lump." Don't forget it.

Joshua 10:1-14

What is the writer saying?

How can I apply this to my life?

pray *Korea – For youth ministries working among South Koreans, as they disciple believers to maturity.*

When word got around of the defeat of Ai, it resulted in strong reaction from other kingdoms. Five kings formed a coalition to fight against Gibeon (who had made peace with Joshua and company). Gibeon asked for help. The Lord assured Joshua that the enemy would be delivered unto them (v. 8). The lesson here is clear: When a person is saved, there will be opposition. We need the Lord's help. He has assured it. The battle is recounted in verses 9-11. Joshua and his men traveled through the night marching twenty-six miles from Gilgal to Gibeon. This involved an ascent of four thousand feet. When the Israelites arrived, the Amorites fled in fear into the region of Beth-horon. The geography of the area is interesting. There were two adjacent villages with the same name Beth-horon, upper and lower. The upper was approached by a gradual ascent through a long and dangerous ravine. We see God intervening with both sword and hailstones (v. 11).

We even see the day lengthened in order to have more time to gain victory. The language used here of the sun standing still is simply using the language of human experiences. We use the terms "sunrise" and "sunset" in the same way today.

Life stEP We are at war with the world, the flesh, and the devil. But our "Joshua," the Lord Jesus, leads us on to victory. We have his assurance and blessing. We are reminded of another day when the *King of Righteousness* will prevail, when He comes in great power and glory. Then too will be supernatural changes in the heavens (Joel 2:10, 31; Amos 8:9; Matthew 24:29).

Joshua 11:16-33

What is the writer saying?

How can I apply this to my life?

The "long time" mentioned in verse 18 can be calculated in the life of Caleb. He was forty years old at Kadesh-Barnea (Joshua 14:7). He was eighty-five years old at the end of the conquests (14:10). This totals forty-five years. Subtract the 38 years of wandering and you have seven years – the years of conquest.

In this passage we have a recapping of God's faithfulness:

God and His enemies (11:20). Note the hardening in verse 20. When men harden their hearts against the Lord, He often will confirm them in their unbelief.

The giants (11:21, 22). Remember it was fear of the giants that caused the people to *pull back* when they were first challenged (Numbers 13). Someone has well said, *Giants are dwarfs to omnipotence*. If God's people had known and believed over forty years earlier, they would have had earlier victory.

A view of the future (11:23). While the conquests were coming to an end, there remained much land to be possessed (13:1). God was good to His Word in fulfilling His promises.

Life stEP

We should remember that our Joshua (Jesus) won the victory for us when He died and rose from the dead. He defeated the enemy, Satan. Now all the power we need to live a life of victory is available to us, but we must claim the power and reckon it to be true (Colossians 2:10; 2 Peter 1:3-4). We must possess what is already ours of heavenly blessings. Read the first three chapters of Ephesians.

Joshua 14:5-15

What is the writer saying?

How can I apply this to my life?

The Bible's most popular senior citizen is the subject of our passage: Caleb. What a delight he is to all of us. Remember, he was one of the two (Joshua and Caleb) that wanted to take the land forty years earlier, but because of unbelief the long wait ensued. Back then, Moses promised that he would posses the land and now it has finally become a reality. His testimony is challenging. He reviews the situation (vv. 6-12). Note that he "wholly followed the Lord" (v. 8). He gives God the credit for being alive, and at eighty-five years of age he states that, "I am as strong this day as I was in the day that Moses sent me…"(v. 11).

The following words are exciting, "Now, therefore, give me this mountain" (v. 12). Notice that it was the same mountain he wanted years ago, infested with giants (v. 12)! We admire Caleb for His faith in spite of obstacles. Do we have faith like that? We admire him for his perseverance. Are we able to *hang in there* when everything seems to be turned against us? We admire him for his ambition. Is it wrong to be ambitious?

Life **stEP**   Ask the Lord to help you be ambitious for Him even in dire circumstances. In faith, let us pray: "Give me this mountain"!

Joshua 20:1-9

What is the writer saying?

How can I apply this to my life?

pray · Dominican Republic – Pray for the more than 3,500 villages that have no evangelical witness.

The "cities of refuge" were designed for those who had accidentally killed another person. It was important for each person to know the cities' locations. Signs were posted along the roads to point the way. To be *near* the city was not sufficient; one had to be *in it* to be in the place of safety. Of course, the cities of refuge are a great picture of our refuge in the Lord. Can you recall verses with the word "refuge" in them?

"God is our refuge and strength" (Psalm 46:1). "In God is my salvation and my glory: the rock of my strength, and my refuge, is in God" (Psalm 62:7). "But the LORD is my defense; and my God is the rock of my refuge" (Psalm 94:22). "The eternal God is thy refuge, and underneath are the everlasting arms." (Deuteronomy 33:27). When we think of refuge we think of the Lord.

(Read Hebrews 6:18-19 where we learn He is our refuge and our anchor.) What was said about the refuge in the Old Testament can be said of our Lord and our relationship with Him today. It was always accessible and available. How true this is of Christ, who made provision for every person (2 Corinthians 5:14). Even the names of the cities remind us of the Lord. Secondly, the refuge was their only hope, which is true of Christ. How important it is to get out the message. Those in the cities of refuge were free from judgment. Indeed, this is true of those of us who are "in Christ" (Romans 8:1).

Life STEP — Remember our refuge is a "very present help in trouble" (Psalm 46:1). Just when we need Him most, He is there to help us and sustain us. God is with us, and we are "in Him." Praise the Lord for His mighty provision!

Monday 11

Joshua 21:43-22:9

What is the writer saying?

How can I apply this to my life?

Pray for your pastor and the leadership of your local church.

Now that the land was being divided, it was time to *settle* with the two and one half tribes that earlier demanded they be allowed to serve on the other side of Jordan (Read Numbers 32:16-32; Deuteronomy 3:12-20 and Joshua 1:11-15). Moses had promised them their request if they did their share in battle to possess the land. Now that the land has been taken they are given their portion.

While the two and one half tribes are to be commended for their being good to their word in their share of involvement in taking the land, we need to be aware that sometimes God allows us to have what we ask for in the hardness of our hearts, even if it is not His best for us.

Retracing the steps of Israel, the Psalmist wrote: "And he gave them their request; but sent leanness into their soul" (Psalm 106:15). Such was the case here. As a matter of fact, if you follow these tribes' history, you will find their choice was hardly God's best. They were the first to be taken in battle as enemies bordered them (1 Chronicles 5:25-26). What a lesson to us all. Their act of selfishness and lack of faith resulted in the loss of security, happiness, and blessing.

Life **stEP**

Are there desires in your heart that you would like fulfilled? Does your prayer life reflect some wants and preferences that may not be sin in themselves, but are not really God's best for you? Are you willing to look at those again, and be careful in praying for what may not be God's greatest choice? Remember Paul's prayer for the Philippians that they would "approve things that are excellent" (Philippians 1:10) – not simply what is good, but what is best. Be careful in your prayer life.

Joshua 23:1-8

What is the writer saying?

How can I apply this to my life?

In chapter thirteen we read that Joshua was old and stricken in years (v. 3). How much time had elapsed between this chapter and chapter thirteen we do not know. But he is over a hundred years old and still concerned about the future. He reviews what God has done and urges the people to be courageous in keeping and doing all that was written in the book of the law. Then he calls for a consistent, separated position (v. 7). There was a great difference between the patience the Israelites should have had with their brethren (Joshua 22) and the need to be separated from evil (Joshua 23). Not only were they to be set apart from the other nations, they were not to even mention the names of others gods.

Remember, it is easy *to walk in the counsel of the ungodly,* and then (another step down) *stand in the way of sinners,* and finally *sit in the seat of the scornful* (See Psalm 1).

Putting it all together, we are to *be courageous* in keeping the word (v. 6), separate from the ungodly (v. 7), and "cleave unto the Lord" (v. 8). Translating this into spiritual *shoe leather* is important. It is easy enough to *let down the bars* and *give in a little* when so much pressure is placed upon us to be civil, reasonable, and tolerant. We need to listen to the *old man* Joshua, who has experienced it all and gives us good advice.

Are there areas in our lives that need to be reassessed? Are we walking consistently in both separation from the world and separation unto the Lord? Let's pray that the Lord will help us to be faithful every day.

Joshua 23:9-16

What is the writer saying?

How can I apply this to my life?

Guatemala – Reconciliation between the Mayan and Spanish – speaking believers divided by past war.

It is one thing to state we need to have a balance between the patience we should show to our fellow brethren and strong stand we should take against the world, but how can this be achieved? The answer comes to us in verse eleven where we are told to take heed to ourselves and that we are to love the Lord. This reminds us of the advice of Paul to the elders of Ephesus where he said, "Take heed therefore unto yourselves, and to all the flock, over which the Holy Ghost hath made you overseers…" (Acts 20:28). There needs to be a spiritual introspection, (looking inwardly) as to our relationship with the Lord. Loving the Lord will help us hate evil (Psalm 97:10) and at the same time love the brethren (John 13:34-35).

Joshua's FINAL word, his valedictory address, is now given beginning with verse fourteen. His counsel reminds them of God's faithfulness to His Word (v. 14). There was a promising future (v. 15), but obedience was mandatory. The message is plain: God will not tolerate disobedience (vv. 15-16). Note the words "when" and "then" in verse sixteen. When you sin, God will deal with that sin appropriately.

Of course the bottom line here is to be aware of our spiritual state and be sure that we have not diminished in our love for the Lord.

Life stEP

Do we have the same love for the Lord as we did earlier in our Christian lives? To the Ephesian church Christ said, "You cannot bear those who are evil…" yet, He said, "Nevertheless, I have somewhat against thee because thou hast left thy first love" (Revelation 2:2, 4). Let's take heed to ourselves.

Joshua 24:1-13

What is the writer saying?

How can I apply this to my life?

pray — *Angola – Pray for churches to develop a unity in Christ that transcends tribal loyalty and politics.*

It is good to review God's faithfulness. That's exactly what is happening here in this passage. Continuing his valedictory, Joshua summarizes the work of God on their behalf. Only when we have a good understanding of what God has done, can we go on, believing what He is going to do. Note the words of Joshua as he recounts the work of God. Words like, "I took" (v. 3), "I gave" (v. 4), "I sent" (v. 5), and "I brought you out" (v. 5) are telling! It is the work of God, and His faithfulness that is clearly seen.

While God had been faithful, Israel had many lapses in their journey. It is significant that in verse seven we read, "and ye dwelt in the wilderness a long season." Joshua uses just eight words to summarize thirty-eight years of wandering and disobedience. Also, when we turn to the "faith chapter" (Hebrews 11), we find God skipping from the faith crossing of the Red Sea to the marching around the walls of Jericho – completely ignoring and passing over any reference to those thirty-eight years as though they didn't even exist. In God's mind, they resulted in *zero*. (See Hebrews 11:29-30.) How thankful we should be that God often blesses in spite of our unfaithfulness and shortcomings! Finally, God tells the people, "I delivered them (the enemy) into your hand" (v. 11). Great is His faithfulness! (Be sure and mark the words: "I gave, I took" etc. in your Bible. It presents quite a picture of the work of God.)

Life STEP — Pause for a few moments and review the faithfulness of the Lord in your own life. Do you see His hand? Hasn't He been wonderful in ordering your paths and directing your ways? Indeed! Stop and thank Him right now for being such a wonderful Lord.

Joshua 24:14-24

What is the writer saying?

How can I apply this to my life?

pray — *Cuba – Protection for those making undeclared mission trips into this country.*

There are three exhortations in this passage. Israel is told to: 1. Fear the Lord (v. 14a), 2. Serve the Lord (v. 14b), and 3. Make right choices (v. 15). Fearing God is approaching the Lord with a reverential awe. It isn't a dread or a trepidation, but an awareness of who He is. If we want to get to *serving the Lord*, we must first "fear the Lord." This is apparent as we study the Bible. It is only when we *sanctify the Lord God in our hearts* (that is, recognize Him as Lord in every area of life), that we can *give a reason for the hope that is within us— with meekness and fear* (1 Peter 3: 15). His Lordship is followed by service. Service is to be done "in sincerity and in truth" (v. 14).

All gods are to be put away – those gods whom their fathers served. Service is to be exclusively apart from any tinge of the world. Nothing of our past is to be included. Now, Joshua the elderly, makes a statement that is often quoted: "Choose you this day whom ye will serve, whether the gods which your fathers served that were on the other side of the flood, or the gods of the Amorites, in whose land ye dwell; but as for me and my house we will serve the Lord" (Joshua 24:15). Life is full of choices. When we make them we should do so resolutely and deliberately. Fear God, serve God, and let Him be Lord exclusively.

 Life stEP

Will you reaffirm your decision to follow the Lord and serve Him? Will you say, "In spite of what is going on around me, and in spite of the trends today of compromise and carnality, I will choose to fear the Lord and serve the Lord"?

Joshua 24:25-33

What is the writer saying?

How can I apply this to my life?

There are really three funerals in the last paragraph of the book (the book also begins with a funeral). Joshua died at 110 years of age. The bones of Joseph, which had been carried all this time, were buried in the land; and Eleazar, the son of Aaron, died. Three faithful men who served the Lord well were gone. Now it was up to a new generation to carry on the task of possessing its inheritance and obediently following God's commands.

Now that we have finished the book of Joshua, how do we stand in our faithfulness to the Lord? The famous English preacher Charles Haddon Spurgeon wrote: "We admire fidelity in Joshua, and we confess that he needed it; but we may, perhaps, forget that there never was an age in which decision for God was not equally required. It is well to admire this in another, but it is far better to possess it ourselves. In all times it is imperative upon men to take their stand for God and truth."

Let us remember that Joshua corresponds with Ephesians. God has given us so much, but we need to appropriate it. The "two foot rule of faith" we saw in Joshua chapter one, is true for us today. We need to claim and possess our inheritance.

Defensive warfare is good, but offensive warfare is better. We are to serve God affirmatively; it is not *holding the fort* but *storming the fort* for God. It is not *holding our own* but going on with God in a day by day walk of faith. So, go on today, by faith, claiming your inheritance!

Titus

The book of Titus, along with Paul's two letters to Timothy, make up that section of New Testament books known as the Pastoral Epistles. Separated from his two young protégés Titus and Timothy, the elder Paul provides them with written information – "how-to" books, if you will – to use in their respective ministries (Timothy in Ephesus; Titus on the island of Crete). The key verse for all three books is found in 1 Timothy 3:15, where Paul says, in effect, that since he cannot at the present time be with them, here is how they are to "behave (themselves) in the house of God... the church of the living God, the pillar and ground of the truth." Titus was written shortly after 1 Timothy, approximately A. D. 63, during that period of time between Paul's two imprisonments.

Helpful to an understanding of the books individually is to view them collectively. Three themes seem to resonate throughout all three letters: (1) church organization, (2) sound doctrine, and (3) consistent Christian living. While all three books touch on all three themes, each book has its particular emphasis. 1 Timothy emphasizes church organization; 2 Timothy, sound doctrine; and Titus, consistent Christian living. Charles Erdman, in writing about these three books early in the twentieth century, offered this summation of the three themes this way: "Church government is not an end in itself; it is of value only as it secures sound doctrine; and doctrine is of value only

as it issues in life." The point is this: you *organize* (1 Timothy) so that you can teach *sound doctrine* (2 Timothy), and you teach *sound doctrine* so that *consistent Christian living* (Titus) can result.

As to Titus himself, our knowledge concerning him is somewhat limited (in comparison to Timothy, for example). We meet him first in Galatians where we learn that he was a Gentile (Galatians 2:3) who had been with Paul as early as, or even prior to, the time when Barnabas went to Tarsus to bring Paul back to Antioch (Galatians 2:1; cf. Acts 11:25-30). Paul's reference to him as "a true son" or "mine own son after the common faith" (Titus 1:4) is an indication that Titus had come to Christ through Paul's ministry. Some scholars have speculated that Titus may have been the younger brother of Luke; and to avoid charges of nepotism, Luke never mentioned him when he authored the book of Acts. That he was a very capable and gifted young man can be deduced from the assignments that Paul gave him. He had been given the responsibility of reporting to Paul on the sad spiritual condition of the Corinthian Church (2 Corinthians 2:12-13; 7:2-16). He then returned to Corinth to deliver Paul's second letter to that church, a letter designed to correct the problems there. He also represented Paul in the matter of the collection for the saints in Jerusalem (2 Corinthians 2:3-4; 13; 7:6-16; 8:16-24). In light of his success in these assignments it is no surprise that

Paul left him on the island of Crete to strengthen, organize and correct the churches there. Paul offers a great compliment when he calls him his "partner and fellow-helper" (2 Corinthians 8:23).

As to Crete, the place of his assignment, our studies will show it was not an easy assignment. The people of Crete, by their own admission, were "liars, evil beasts, slow bellies" (Titus 1:12). Paul confirmed that evaluation (Titus 1:13). Crete itself is a rather large island, approximately 160 miles long and 35 miles wide. It is located in the Mediterranean Sea, about 100 miles southeast of Greece. We can only surmise when the church there actually began. It could have been the result of a missionary journey that Paul took between his imprisonments, or it may go all the way back to the Day of Pentecost, some thirty years earlier. (Acts 2:11 indicates that Cretans were there.) If the latter is the case, it is no wonder Paul placed him there to "set in order the things that are wanting" (v. 5). A church with apparently minimal direction for such an extended period of time would have many things "wanting."

The purpose(s) of the book can be summed up as follows:
(1) To remind Titus of his work of reorganizing the church and appointing elders.
(2) To warn him about false teachers.
(3) To encourage him in pastoring the different kinds of people in the church.
(4) To emphasize the true meaning of grace in the life of the Christian.
(5) To explain how to deal with church troublemakers.
(It is likely that the Cretan church suffered from two sources of trouble: (a) visiting Judaizers, who mixed law and grace; and (b) ignorant Christians who abused the grace of God, and turned their liberty into license.)

A major emphasis in the book is *consistent Christian living*. Paul wanted the Cretans to be both *hearers* and *doers* of the Word (James 1:22); hence there is a constant emphasis upon "good works" (1:16; 2:7, 14; 3:1,5,8,14). Those "good works" ought to be the natural result of one's salvation, something Paul made very clear in Ephesians 2:8-10. A key verse for the book would be Titus 3:8: "that they which have believed in God might be careful to maintain good works."

Titus 1:1-9

What is the writer saying?

How can I apply this to my life?

Paul introduces himself as a "servant of God" (*doulos* – one born into slavery, whose will is swallowed up in the will of another – this should be true of all believers) "and an apostle of Jesus Christ" (*apostolos* – one sent with proper credentials to represent someone else). His commission was to further "the faith of God's elect" leading to "godliness" (v. 1), a word which introduces the theme of "good works" (1:16; 2:7, 14; 3:1, 5, 8, 14). The addressee is Titus, though it is clear that like 1 and 2 Timothy, the letter was to be widely read. He is referred to as Paul's "own son after the common faith," similar to Timothy (1 Timothy 1:2), an indication both of these young men were products of Paul's ministry. Titus's assignment was two-fold: First, he was to preach the Word (v. 3). Second, he was to organize the church and "set in order" (like setting a broken bone) the church's deficiencies (v. 5). One possible reason for their disorganization may have been minimal apostolic instruction since its inception, which could have been as early as the Day of Pentecost some thirty years earlier (cf. Acts 2:11). Titus's task would involve dealing with false teachers (v. 9ff) who had stepped into the gap.

To correct the problems, Titus was to "ordain elders in every city" (v. 5); an ordination based on proper qualifications, some of which are listed in verses 6-9, and similar to 1 Timothy 3:1-7. Those qualifications fit into numerous categories, such as (1) General, verses 6-7; (2) Family, verse 6; (3) Personal, verses 7-8a; (4) Mental, verse 8b; and (5) Spiritual, verses 8c-9 (Homer Kent). Without biblically qualified leadership, a church courts disaster, for leadership sets the pace and establishes the standards. The leader ("elder" in verse 5, "bishop" in verse 7 – the terms are interchangeable; cf. Acts 20:17, 28; 1 Peter 5:1-2) is to hold "fast the faithful word" so that by "sound doctrine" (healthy teaching) he can both exhort believers and rebuke opposers.

Life **stEP**   A church's success, in God's eyes, is tied to its commitment to the Word of God. Is your church's ministry biblically-saturated, or simply biblically-scented? It does make a difference.

Titus 1:10-16

What is the writer saying?

How can I apply this to my life?

pray | *Bulgaria – For freedom from the media and local government's constant attempts to obstruct any form of evangelical outreach or growth.*

After mentioning the elders' responsibility to refute the false teachings of "gainsayers" (KJV), or *opposers*, Paul discusses their characteristics and how to deal with them. Men who oppose truth are just the opposite of the prescribed elder: "unruly" (demonstrated by a rebelliousness against both God's Word and God's messengers); "vain talkers" (their talk is useless, accomplishing nothing); and intentional "deceivers." This was especially true of those "of the circumcision" (cf. Galatians 2:12ff) – Jewish believers in the Cretan congregation who mistakenly taught that adherence to circumcision and Jewish ceremonial laws was necessary for salvation.

The description continues: they had an inordinate interest in money (v. 11), and held to unscriptural "Jewish fables, and commandments of men" (legalism and traditionalism) (v. 14). They were ascetics (practicing extreme self-denial

for supposed spiritual value), labeling certain foods and practices as defiled, even that which God considered good (vv. 14-15; cf. 1 Timothy 4:3-5; Acts 10:15). They did not understand that the blood of Christ sounded the death knell for legalism.

To effectively describe Cretan character, Paul quotes a sixth century Cretan poet – a philosopher named Epimenedes. His description is unbelievably harsh (v. 12), but accurate (v. 13). "To Cretanize" in Greek literature meant "to lie and cheat." To deal with such erroneous teaching, Paul told Titus to do the following: (1) *Stop their mouths* – silence them, for in failing to do so, "whole houses" (churches) would be subverted, or upset (v. 11); (2) *"Rebuke them sharply." Rebuke* here means *to convict, convince or point out.* The goal: "that they may be sound in the faith" (v. 13). Correction and restoration are to be Titus's goals.

Life **stEP** — Never compromise the truth. False doctrine (unhealthy teaching) will lead to sickness in the body of Christ. The emphasis must always be on "sound doctrine" (v. 9) and sound faith (v. 13).

Titus 2:1-10

What is the writer saying?

How can I apply this to my life?

Pray for the salvation and protection of those serving in the military around the world.

Paul now moves to positive exhortation. Certainly error must be dealt with, but there must be balance: truth must be taught and exhortations given. Otherwise, negativity will permeate a ministry. So Paul instructs Titus to "speak thou the things which become sound (healthy) doctrine" (v. 1) – a phrase familiar in all three pastoral epistles. Out of such teaching, good works such as faith, love, and patience (v. 2) are produced. He then addresses three categories of church members:

1. *The Aged Saints* (older, more mature Christians) (vv. 1-3). Paul deals first with the men, then the women. The point behind his instruction was that both are to serve as spiritual examples to the church. While all believers should possess the virtues noted, they should to an eminent degree be manifested by those of advancing years. And to older women a very pointed assignment: pass on their insight as wives and mothers to the next generation of women. If those lessons are not taught and practiced, God's Word will be blasphemed.

2. *The Younger Saints* (vv. 4-8). They were to listen to the older saints, and pursue the character qualities that should already be present in their parent's generation. As for Titus (vv. 7-8), he is to set the pattern. One's actions often speak louder than one's words, but both "good works" (v. 7) and "sound speech" (v. 8) are necessary.

3. *Servants/Slaves* (vv. 9-10) Upwards of 25% of the Roman Empire were slaves. Those who were believers, as with all other categories of believers, were to voluntarily submit to their masters in such a way that they beautified ("adorned") their beliefs by their behavior. Paul's advice to slaves and masters, which he amplifies in other passages (see Ephesians 6:5-9; Colossians 3:22-4:1; 1 Timothy 6:1-2), is good advice to employees and employers today.

Life stEP

There's a saying that matches today's passage: "Your talk talks, and your walk talks; but your walk talks louder than your talk talks." Read it again, and be sure to practice it. A consistent life gains a responsive audience.

Titus 2:11-3:3

What is the writer saying?

How can I apply this to my life?

pray   *Chile – For future church leaders to be called from among those saved at evangelistic activities.*

In verses 11-14 we have the first of two major doctrinal portions in the book. The second will follow a chapter later (3:4-7). These verses demonstrate the balance of doctrine with Christian living. They illustrate Paul's instruction (v. 10) to "adorn the doctrine of God" with a lifestyle that pictures a transformed life. This passage begins with the doctrine of the *incarnation of Christ* ("the grace of God ... hath appeared," v. 11), and then relates that doctrine to a life that: (a) negatively, denies "ungodliness and worldly lusts" and (b) positively, lives "soberly, righteously and godly" in the here and now: "the present age" (v. 12). It continues by seeing in the return of Christ the incentive for Christ-honoring conduct ("looking for that blessed hope..." v. 13), which ultimately expresses itself in personal holiness: purified "unto Himself (Christ)...people [who are] zealous of good works" (v. 14). This passage, much like Ephesians 2:8-10, teaches us that God's purpose in

redeeming us is not only to save us from hell; He also wants to free us so that we can produce good works that glorify Him. Certainly these two appearances of the grace of God -- the first of which (the incarnation) provided redemption, and the second of which (Christ's return) will result in rewards – should provide much motivation for *consistent Christian living* (a key theme in this book).

In the early verses of chapter 3, Paul addresses the Christian's obligation to earthly government (subjection to authority), not a particularly positive trait among the Cretans. (Remember the description of them in 1:12.) Paul reminds them to be good citizens ("ready to every good work," v. 1). In doing so, they would reflect positively on the power of the Gospel and bring glory to God. An additional motive for good works would be to remember that, but for the grace of God (2:11), they would still be lost in their sins and no different than the pagans they lived with (v. 3).

Look back: Christ came with redemption in mind. *Look ahead:* He will return with rewards in hand. *Look within:* Does your life demonstrate gratefulness for those two appearances of the grace of God?

Titus 3:4-15

What is the writer saying?

How can I apply this to my life?

This section begins with the word *But*, indicating the contrast between man's degenerative nature described in verse 3, and God's "kindness and love" (v. 4). In verses 4-7, we have the book's second major doctrinal portion. Paul writes that salvation is God's work, not the result of our own righteousness or works (v. 5). The two agents of our "regeneration," or new birth, are (1) *The Word of God* which *washes* (See John 15:3); and (2) *The Spirit of God* which *renews* (See John 3:5). The latter has been "shed" (poured out) upon believers from Pentecost (Acts 2) to the present, and the mediator of this wonderful outpouring is "Jesus Christ our Savior" (v. 6).

Paul then moves from the overall doctrine of salvation to two of its aspects. The first is *justification*: God's declaration that the believer has been vindicated in His sight by Christ's work on the cross (cf. Romans 3:24-25; 5:9); hence all charges have been dropped (Romans 8:1, 31-34). The second is *adoption*. Once justified, adoption takes place (Galatians 4:5) and the believers' lives are "hidden with Christ in God" (Colossians 3:3), and they become heirs "according to the hope [utmost confidence] of eternal life" (v. 7).

Verse 8 is transitional, with the "faithful saying" referring to the doctrinal statement of verses 4-7. Titus is to keep on affirming "these things." Doing so is to result in continued "good works." Verses 9-11 admonish Titus to avoid anything that would cause unacceptable behavior in the assembly, and to cut off ("reject," v. 10) divisive people after two warnings (cf. 2 Thessalonians 3:14-15). In the remaining verses (12-15) greetings are given, as well as a challenge to "maintain good works." As in his other letters, Paul closes with his favorite benediction: "Grace be with you all."

Life stEP

We are saved to serve a holy God with a holy life. How are you doing?

While he was under house arrest in Rome, the Apostle Paul wrote four letters which are thus referred to as his Prison Epistles (see Acts 28:16-31). Three of those letters are similar in nature and style to his other epistles: Ephesians, Philippians and Colossians. One, however, is very unusual. It is this little one-chapter letter from Paul to Philemon, a letter from one friend to another. Paul, we are well acquainted with; Philemon, however, is another story. He was a close friend of Paul's and had probably come to know Christ through Paul's ministry (vv. 19-20).

The story line is this: at the time of the writing, Philemon was a very wealthy Christian living in Colossae, and in keeping with the culture and economy of that day, was a slave owner. One of his slaves, a man by the name of Onesimus (v. 10), had stolen some money from Philemon and then run away. Under Roman law, this crime carried with it the possible penalty of execution, to be exacted at the discretion of the slave owner. In running away, he wound up in Rome, met Paul, and eventually came to know Christ as his Savior. Paul then mentored him in his early days as a believer, and an obviously strong bond was forged between the two men. Now that he was a believer, however, Onesimus was faced with a difficult problem. He had wronged his master and confession was necessary. Proper restitution required that he return to Philemon and place himself back under Philemon's mastership and accept whatever consequences his master deemed appropriate (including execution).

This letter from Paul, however, accompanied Onesimus's return to Philemon; a letter in which Paul would be Onesimus's intercessor and defender. In it, he asks Philemon to receive Onesimus as himself (v. 17), and should any stolen funds need to be replaced, Paul said to place them on his account (v. 18). What happened when Onesimus returned is not recorded in Scripture, but church history does provide us with some hints. Some forty years after the sending of this letter, a well-known early church leader by the name of Ignatius, arrested for his belief in Christ and sent to Rome to be executed, wrote a number of letters to various groups of believers to encourage them to stand firm in their faith. One was sent to the believers of Ephesus, and in it he sent a personal greeting to the bishop (or pastor) of the church in that city. His name was Onesimus. It is quite possible that this is the same man; and if so, what an amazing testimony to the saving grace of Jesus Christ and the power of the Gospel - to take a slave, free him and place him in the Gospel ministry!

This brief letter is a wonderful picture of that which Jesus Christ has done for those who place their faith in Him. Onesimus had the death penalty hanging over his head and needed someone to plead his cause. That someone would have to be familiar with both parties; in this case, Philemon and Onesimus. Furthermore, the only way that Onesimus could be justly restored would be for the debt to be paid. Paul stepped into the breech and did all of this and more. This is exactly what Christ has done for the condemned sinner (Romans 6:23), separated from God by sin and a fugitive on the run. Just as Paul intervened to restore Onesimus to Philemon, Jesus intervened to restore us to God. He took the sinner's deserved penalty on the cross of Calvary, and reconciliation (returning man to the place of perfect fellowship in which he was originally placed) becomes the sinner's lot once he accepts the gift offered in Christ (Acts 16:31). Paul says it this way in 2 Corinthians 5:21 "For he [God] hath made him [Christ] to be sin for us, who knew no sin; that we might be made the righteousness of God in him."

Friday 12

Philemon 1-9

Uhat is the writer saying?

How can I apply this to my life?

pray

Guatemala – For more willing hearts to join the 100 missionaries sent from Guatemala in the last 15 years.

Paul begins this letter as he normally does by introducing himself, but his following title is unique to this book. He calls himself "a prisoner of Jesus Christ" (not of Rome, though in their custody). He alludes to that status often (vv. 9-10,13,22-23). He forgoes the use of his official title of Apostle since this was to be a letter of request, not command. He wanted Philemon's response to be love-generated and not a response to authority. He adds Timothy as his associate in ministry (as he often did).

The addressee is Philemon, Paul's "dearly beloved...fellow laborer." Apphia may have been Philemon's wife and Archippus, his son, perhaps an elder in the Colossian Church (see Colossians 4:17). He also addresses "the church in thy house" (v. 2). (Until the third century, churches met in private homes and not separate buildings.) His greeting closes with his usual combination of the Greek idea of "grace" (favor displayed where wrath is deserved), and the Hebrew concept of "peace" (internal, not based on circumstances, a result of grace) (v. 3).

He continues (v. 4) with words of thanksgiving, and notes the reasoning behind them: Philemon's faith in Christ and his love for the saints (v. 5). He prays that Philemon's faith would continue to be an "effectual" (effective) faith, one that has already brought great refreshment in the "bowels [*splancha*—the innermost part of one's being; as deep as you can go] of the saints" (v. 7). (*Splancha* is sometimes translated "heart," but here Paul intentionally uses *splancha*=bowels and not *kardia*=heart.) Philemon was obviously an encouragement to others. Paul wanted that to continue.

In verses 8-9 Paul gets to the point: a passionate appeal to Philemon to accept his runaway slave, Onesimus, back into his household. His appeal was based upon matters about to be addressed, and not on "bold" authority (which he could have used as an apostle), but on the mutual love that they (Paul and Philemon) shared (v. 9).

Christ told His disciples that people would recognize them as Christians by their love for one another. Paul has the same idea. If hauled into court on the charge of being a Christian, would there be enough evidence to convict us?

Philemon 10-25

What is the writer saying?

How can I apply this to my life?

pray   *El Salvador – For effective discipling and motivation of believers for service, witness, and missions.*

Paul's appeal to accept Onesimus back into his household picks up steam. Having referred to himself in verse 9 as "aged," he pleads for his "son Onesimus." Paul often uses the picture of a father-son relationship when speaking of his converts (cf. 1 Timothy 1:2; Titus 1:4). "My son" literally means *my child*, and looks back to when Onesimus, under Paul's ministry (Acts 28:30-31), came to know Christ (v. 10).

Salvation changed Onesimus's life. He who was once "unprofitable" (useless) to Philemon, was now "profitable" (useful) to both Philemon and Paul (v. 11). Understanding that restitution was required for past behavior, Paul tells Philemon he is sending Onesimus back, though he would have preferred to keep him (v. 13). He uses the term "bowels" once again (v. 7) to express the positive emotional connection that existed between he and Onesimus (v. 12), and which had been cultivated as Onesimus ministered to Paul in prison. In fact, he had served Paul in Philemon's "stead," and Paul would like him to continue, but only with Philemon's consent (v. 14).

Verses 15-16 indicate that, whether by plan or by circumstance, Onesimus's departure was for a "season" (short time). While not for positive reasons, there were positive results: i.e., his salvation and service on Paul's behalf (cf. Romans 8:28). When Onesimus comes, "receive him…not now as a servant but above a servant, a brother beloved," for now a spiritual bond exists between all three: they are partners (v. 17). "If he…oweth thee ought [anything]," Paul says, "put that on mine account" (v. 18). To support his commitment legally, Paul notes he had used his own hand (not that of a scribe) to write the letter. He expresses "confidence" that Philemon will respond positively (v. 21), and in doing so refresh Paul's "bowels [that word again!] in the Lord" (v. 20). He closes with the anticipation of a soon release, a request for lodging and greetings from some friends (vv. 22-24).

Life **stEP**   Paul begins (v. 3) and ends (v. 25) with grace. Grace sent Christ to Calvary, compelled Paul to serve and is to motivate our lives. Thank God for its provision.

Revelation

John the Apostle wrote the book of Revelation around A.D. 95 during the reign of the Roman emperor Domitian (A.D. 81-96). John was in exile on the Isle of Patmos (a four by eight mile island that served as a penal mining colony located 60 miles southwest of Ephesus). Tradition states that John was released under Emperor Nerva who reigned A.D. 96-98.

In harmony with Christ's statement to Peter in John 21, and according to church history, John was the only apostle to live to an old age (although he also died a martyr's death). It is believed that the Gospel of John and the epistles of 1, 2, and 3 John were also written in the A.D. 90s, so we can't say dogmatically that Revelation was the last book written. It does, however, logically conclude the information given in both testaments. John was the "beloved disciple." He was a member of Jesus' inner circle of disciples along with Peter and James. He was with Christ on the Mount of Transfiguration. He took Peter to the high priest's home for Christ's first trial, as apparently John knew that influential family. He alone of all the disciples is mentioned at the crucifixion, as Christ asked him from the cross to take care of Mary. By A.D. 95 he would have been serving Jesus for almost 70 years. What memories would have enriched his mind as he received the amazing information contained in the Book of Revelation. Of all the New Testament authors, only Luke and Paul provide more written Scripture.

"Revelation" is the translation of the Greek word *apocalypse*. Both refer to an *unveiling*. While we normally associate the *unveiling* of future events (prophecy) with the book, actually the word is referring to the revelation of the person of Jesus Christ who is both the main subject and the *spirit* of future events. Revelation 1:19 provides a nice outline of the book in three tenses. John was told to write the things which "thou hast seen" (past tense—chapter 1), "the things which are" (present tense—chapters 2, 3), and "the things which shall be hereafter" (future tense—chapters 4-22). We could also consider the way in which the book presents Jesus. In chapters 1-3, He is pictured as the *Lord over the churches*. In chapters 4-20, He is presented as the *lion over the nations*. In chapters 21-22, He is viewed as the *lamb of eternity*.

The book is highly symbolic. Some of the symbols are explained in context. Most of the symbols have precedents in the Old Testament. We must be careful not to force statements introduced by "like" or "as." They indicate comparison, not identification.

Historically, there have been four ways to approach the book. In the *Preterist Theory*, the predictions are thought to apply to events surrounding the A.D. 70 destruction of Jerusalem by the Romans. In the *Historical Theory*, the predictions are thought to cover all of world history from John's day until the end of time.

Revelation

In the *Idealist Theory*, it is thought that the book teaches principles, not specific events. The fourth view, which is the view affirmed in this commentary, is the *Futurist Theory*. It holds that chapters 4 22 still lie in the future.

There is an amazing use of numbers in the book ("seven" appears 50 times!). Scholars have noted over 550 allusions to the Old Testament with 278 of the 404 verses containing references to Old Testament ideas. Daniel 2 is alluded to ten times and Daniel 7 has 30 parallels. The Greek text contains many irregularities in grammar that can only be explained by John's intense excitement as he received and recorded the information.

The book presents the final struggle of God the Father, Son, and Holy Spirit against Satan, the father, son (Antichrist), and unholy spirit (false prophet). Revelation concludes with *newness*: the new heaven and earth, new people, a new bride, a new home, a new temple, and a new light. It is the answer to the tragedy of Genesis 1-3 with paradise regained for redeemed humanity. Revelation is the only book in the Bible that promises a blessing for those who read it. (Yet for most of church history it has been ignored as being too hard to understand.) Perhaps Daniel 12:4 indicates that in the end times, Christians would become knowledgeable in prophecy ("But thou, O Daniel, shut up the words, and seal the book, *even* to the time of the end: many shall run to and fro, and knowledge shall be increased.").

Sunday 13

Revelation 1:1-8

What is the writer saying?

How can I apply this to my life?

"Revelation" means *unveiling*. It is an unveiling of future events and also the unveiling of a person, the person of Jesus Christ. Note the route of this revelation. It came from God the Father, to God the Son, to an angel, to John who then wrote it down for the rest of us. Angels ("messengers") appear in the chain of revelation over seventy times in the Bible.

God "signified" (v. 1) the information, which not only means *to indicate*, but also *to put into signs*. There are many signs and symbols in this book. The word "shortly" (v. 1) does not mean *soon* but rather that the events described can happen at any time (i.e., *imminent*). Later in the book there will be another word used for *soon*. God has both a living Word (Jesus Christ) and a written Word (the Bible). Both "he that readeth" and "they that hear" (v. 3) will be blessed, indicating a public reading of the material with many listeners. The three tenses of *to be* in verse 4

remind us of the meaning of *Jehovah* as explained in Exodus 3:13-14. The number seven is often associated with God, perhaps denoting completion and perfection. The seven "Spirits" (v. 4) may be seven angels or more likely, a reference to the fullness of the Holy Spirit (i.e., the sevenfold Spirit). The Greek word for "witness" (v. 5) is the word "martyr." So many of the early Christian witnesses lost their lives for the faith that we associate *death* with the word "martyr." "First begotten" (v. 5) refers to Christ's resurrection. The descriptive phrases concerning Christ in verse 5 are alluded to in Psalm 89, which is a commentary on the Davidic Covenant in 2 Samuel 7:1-16. "Amen" (v. 6) comes from the Hebrew word for *to believe* or *be firm*. Christ's return in the clouds is mentioned in Daniel 7:13 and every eye seeing Him in Zechariah 12:10. Both ideas are included in Matthew 24:30. Behold (v. 7) occurs 25 times in this book.

Life **StEP** Even so come Lord Jesus. Even so come today!

Monday 13

Revelation 1:9-16

What is the writer saying?

How can I apply this to my life?

pray   *Bolivia – For youth outreach activities to the 53% of the population that is 19 or under.*

John was exiled to the Isle of Patmos. It was the first day of the week, *Resurrection Day* as it is still called in the Russian language. As John meditated, a commanding voice ("trumpet") interrupted his thoughts. "Alpha" is the first letter in the Greek alphabet and "Omega" is the last. Since "books" as we know them were not invented yet, John would have recorded this information on a scroll that would have been about fifteen feet long unrolled. Apparently each of the seven churches would have then copied the information to keep for their use.

John saw Jesus walking among seven separate lamp stands (not the seven-branched Menorah of the Old Testament holy place). During the Church Age we do not have one place of religious observance (Jerusalem), but because of the indwelling Spirit of God we have worship centers around the globe. One day, apostasy will extinguish the light of the churches and God will re-ignite Israel as His nation of priests. Of all the titles that Jesus could use to describe Himself, He preferred "Son of Man" since it associates Him with us.

The golden girdle was part of the high priest's garments (Exodus 28:8). "White" was the color of God's hair in Daniel 7:9-10, speaking of holiness. "Brass" should be "bronze" since that is the modern technical name for what the ancients used (an alloy of copper and tin). Since the altar in the temple was covered with bronze, we associate judgment with that metal. "Waters" convey power and tranquility. In Daniel 10:5-6, a supernatural being has a similar appearance and there his voice is described as the "voice of a multitude." The "right hand" is the place of power, privilege or protection. "Stars" represent either the guardian angels of the seven churches or more likely the human pastors. The sword signifies the on-going power of Christ's Word.

Life stEP   Can you imagine the awe John felt as he viewed the resurrected, glorified, ascended Lord!

Tuesday 13

Revelation 1:17-20

What is the writer saying?

How can I apply this to my life?

pray   *Czech Republic – For godly public school teachers who will use their religious freedom to evangelize.*

"Fear not" is a trademark saying of Christ from the Gospels. If John didn't already recognize who He was, this phrase should have alerted him. "First and last" parallels the illustration of "Alpha and Omega." In the Book of Revelation, these designations are used of both God the Father and Jesus, implying their equality as deity. Christ's death, burial, and resurrection are the heart of the Gospel (cf. 1 Corinthians 15:3-5). It is because of His victory over death that we have the promise of our own salvation and the assurance that He (and not Satan) controls the after-life.

Verse 19 provides the past, present and future outline for the whole book. Chapter 1 represents the past tense ("things which thou hast seen"). Chapters 2 and 3 provide the present tense ("the things which are"). This refers to John's day of A.D. 95. In chapters 2-3 Christ has words for the seven churches of Asia Minor. These

were real, historic churches about fifty miles apart in a circle around Ephesus. We will discover that the Lord criticizes five of the seven churches and that the two not criticized are the only cities remaining today (Smyrna and Philadelphia). Laodicea is the only church of the seven with no commendation.

Some commentators feel that the seven churches represent successive ages of church history. While God certainly could encode such symbolism into His Scriptures, it is of little value since the saints of the first century could not have understood the material as prophetic and we cannot prove it even with hindsight. It is more important to understand that these churches are representative of seven types of churches found in any age or locality. As chapter 1 comes to a close, we can say that it functions as the *signature* of the author to the letter to the seven churches and to us as well.

Life stEP Jesus is the Lord over the churches, the lion over the nations, and the lamb of eternity.

Revelation 2:1-7

What is the writer saying?

How can I apply this to my life?

Costa Rica – For a new generation of godly, effective leaders for the churches that will commend the Gospel.

"Ephesus" means *desirable*. It was the mother church of the region. Paul spent three years, his longest stay, at Ephesus (Acts 19). Aquila and Priscilla were there (Acts 18:26). Timothy eventually became the pastor of the church where he received the challenge from Paul not to be timid. By tradition, John lived at Ephesus starting in A.D. 68. With all of these significant early church leaders, the church received a firm foundation in doctrine. The following letters were written to the church at Ephesus: Ephesians, 1 and 2 Timothy, and Revelation. While Paul ministered in Ephesus, he wrote 1 Corinthians. John probably wrote the Gospel of John and 1, 2, 3 John from there. Ephesus was important even later as in A.D. 431 the Third General Church Council was held there.

In the first century, the city was prominent because it was a port city and controlled a major route through Asia Minor. One of the seven wonders of the ancient world was there, the Temple of Diana, which was three times as big as the Parthenon with 120 columns 60' high plated with gold. The ancients also hosted famous athletic games there.

"Says this" is a phrase that Persian kings used to introduce decrees. Seven of the eight times that this phrase occurs in the New Testament are here in Revelation. By A.D. 95, the church would have been over forty years old. Despite their spiritual heritage, not all the members were truly saved as Christ anticipates that some might not be overcomers (the normal activity of saved individuals, cf. Romans 8:37). The Nicolaitans excused immorality and compromise with pagans. The "deeds" of the Nicolaitans of 2:6 become the "doctrine" by 2:15. Perhaps this group was started by the Nicolas of Acts 6:5 and had Hymenaeus and Philetus of 2 Timothy 2:17 as members.

Life stEP

How sad when the thrill of new love weakens into careless presumption. Make it a point to fall in love all over again every morning in your meditations on the Lord over the churches.

Revelation 2:8-11

What is the writer saying?

How can I apply this to my life?

"Smyrna" comes from the word *myrrh*. Myrrh was highly valued in the ancient world as an aromatic plant. It was used for burial and interestingly enough, only released its odor when crushed. Myrrh was one of the gifts presented to baby Jesus by the wise men and would have been used for His burial as well. Smyrna was famous for its natural beauty, famous as the birthplace of Homer, and was the Asian center for emperor worship. This would explain the tribulation that the believers faced. Later, around A.D. 150, the great church leader Polycarp was there. The word for "tribulation" is used elsewhere to refer to the pressure involved in the crushing of grapes. The word for "poverty" refers to abject poverty, probably produced by the persecution. Their enemies are Jewish, although Christ is careful to explain that such "Jews" are not true followers of Jehovah. "Blasphemy" refers to *injurious speech*. It probably refers to

the slander leveled against Christians such as cannibalism (because they ate the "body" of Jesus in communion) or immorality (because they practiced the holy kiss) or atheism (because they rejected the pagan gods) or subversion (because they refused to worship Caesar). In the Roman Empire prior to A.D. 325, Judaism was the only legal monotheistic religion. The "ten days" probably indicates that the persecution would be short-lived.

Notice that for each of these seven letters, Christ goes back to chapter 1 and picks one descriptive phrase to introduce Himself to that church. These are not random selections, but seem to be tailored to the situation at that church. Notice that here He is the resurrected Lord (v. 8) and that He promises resurrection to the overcomers (v. 11). Also notice that all of these letters are addressed, not just to the specific church, but also to all "the churches" (v. 11).

Life stEP   Life can be tough and seemingly unfair. God promises that it will be worth it all when we see Jesus.

Revelation 2:12-17

What is the writer saying?

How can I apply this to my life?

pray Cuba – For the persecuted Christians to be encouraged and continue their service for the Lord.

"Pergamos" is also spelled Pergamum. It means *citadel*. The name refers to an actual military stronghold on a hill towering 1000' above the city. It was a center for parchment and paper manufacturing. At one time it also had a large library with 200,000 books, which were eventually moved to the famous library in Alexandria, Egypt. The city was honored by the Roman government and given freedom in determining some of its affairs without first consulting Rome. This included "ius gladii," the Latin legal term *for the right of the sword*, which referred to capital punishment. The believers were therefore under immediate threat of death at the whim of the local courts. Notice that Christ is introduced as one who also possesses a mighty sword and that martyrdom is mentioned as a problem for the church. The city had several prominent religious expressions including an altar to Zeus, and a temple to a serpent god (the god of healing who was also called "savior.") Pergamos was the first Asian city to have a temple for emperor worship (29 B.C. for Caesar Augustus). The man's name, "Antipas" means, *against all*.

Balaam was that unusual prophet in Numbers 22-24, 31:16, who was hired by King Balak of the Moabites to curse the children of Israel, but every time he tried, God put a blessing in his mouth. He eventually encouraged Balak to seek Israel's destruction by *religious syncretism*, namely, that if the Jewish men fell in love with the Moabite women they would then worship the gods of the Moabites and Jehovah would judge them. Here it is called the "doctrine" of Balaam. In Jude 11 it mentions the "error" of Balaam (thinking that you can manipulate God) and in 2 Peter 2:15 we have the "way" of Balaam (religion for hire).

Life stEP Those who are faithful will eat heavenly food (manna), have a transformed life (new name), and free access into heaven (white stone, often used in ancient times as a ticket).

Revelation 2:18-29

What is the writer saying?

How can I apply this to my life?

pray Ecuador – For an end to anti-missionary propaganda from anthropologists, traders, jungle exploiters, and those with a political agenda.

"Thyatira" means castle of *Thya*, in honor of a regional goddess. It was a *religious* town with each trade guild supported by a patron religion. Lydia, the "seller of purple" (Acts 16), was from Thyatira. Scholars know the least about the church in this town, but this is the longest of the seven letters. Christ is presented as one who can see through phonies and is unmovable in judgment. The letter contains five compliments including even the "love" which Ephesus lacked! By ancient tradition, a woman founded the city. It was also the seat of a prophetess-established cult named *Sambatha*. If Lydia also founded the church here, we can understand the influence of women in this church. Christ criticizes the error of a female church member. "Sufferest" (v. 20) is worse than the "hast" of 2:14. Since this condemnation was read publicly before the whole church, can you imagine the reaction in the church the Sunday it was read?

The word "tribulation" is used for persecution or judgment in general and also that special time of future judgment first presented in Daniel 9:27 (the seven-year tribulation period). Christ's warning of impending judgment will also find fulfillment in the lives of the apostate Christians who miss the Rapture and enter the tribulation period. We don't know what particular heretical sect this woman promoted, but it is similar to one version of the ancient Gnostic error that claimed: *In order to defeat Satan you have to experience evil deeply.* Verse 27 contains the triumphant imagery of Psalm 2:9. This judgmental destruction and victorious ruling is further described in chapters 4-22. The "morning star" is the planet Venus, which is often visible just before dawn. It is used of Satan in Isaiah 14:12-14 ("Lucifer" means *morning star*) as the usurper and also of Jesus Christ who is the *true* morning star (Revelation 22:16).

Life **stEP** Attack from within is more dangerous than persecution from without.

Revelation 3:1-6

What is the writer saying?

How can I apply this to my life?

pray *El Salvador – For godly leadership training where war, lack of finances, and lack of staff have crippled efforts.*

Sardis derived its name from a gemstone that was a deep red color. The city also claimed to be the first to dye wool. These two physical facts plus the content of the letter has led some to refer to Sardis as the *stained church*. Christ is presented as the one who "hath" the seven Spirits of God. This implies His authoritative possession of the Holy Spirit and the fact that as the Lord of the churches, He bestows the Holy Spirit on whomever He wills. The plurality of "Spirits" simply indicates that the Spirit is available for all seven churches (not seven different Holy Spirits). The seven "stars" would be the seven *angels* (either guardian angels behind the scenes or the human pastors) of the seven churches.

Archaeologists have uncovered coins with the inscription: "Sardis, the First Metropolis of Asia and of Lydia and of Hellenism." This would not have been the case in A.D. 95, so it speaks of a past glorious heritage. Christ says that they had a "name" (reputation), but in actuality they were "dead" (time had passed them by). The patron goddess of Sardis, Artemas, supposedly could raise the dead. Christ implies that they shouldn't assume Artemas would be able to help them in this deadly spiritual state. They were stained by the world and becoming indistinguishable from the world. They practiced *inoffensive Christianity*.

Verse 3 warns the believers of the importance of vigilance. It is significant that even though Sardis was located on steep cliffs, twice in her history she was conquered in sneak attacks (by the Persians in 549 B.C. and by the Greeks in 214 B.C.). The word for "thief" ("kleptes" as in "kleptomaniac") refers to the furtive *cat burglar*, not the armed robber who strikes in broad daylight. The letter concludes with more color analogies. Their garments were "defiled" (*dyed* by dirt) but for the overcomer, garments *dyed* white were waiting in heaven.

Life STEP Our society is consumed by fashion. What is the color of heaven? It is white, trimmed in white with white accessories!

Monday 14

Revelation 3:7-13

What is the writer saying?

How can I apply this to my life?

pray Brazil – Pray for a stable financial climate so that inflation will not diminish missionary support.

"Philadelphia" means *City of Brotherly Love*. It was located at the end of a narrow valley and therefore was known as the *Gateway to the East*. The city was founded specifically to spread the Greek culture eastward. In the sequence of the seven churches, it is a rose between two thorns (Sardis the dying church and Laodicea the useless church). The "open door" (v. 8) in general refers to ministry opportunities, but specifically has the messianic kingdom in mind. While their Jewish adversaries (v. 9) prided themselves as the object of God's messianic plan, it was these faithful New Testament saints who would receive the "key of David" (v. 7). The true Jew is the one who believes in Jesus of Nazareth. The Jewish Messiah loves the Gentiles rejected by the Jews of Philadelphia.

Verse 10 is the strongest statement of the pretribulational timing of the Rapture of the church. Note that it is not only the judgments that the believers will escape but also specifically the time period during which the judgments occur. The exact same phrase ("keep … from") occurs in John 17:15 and a similar phrase ("save from") occurs in John 12:27. In both cases only total exclusion from the situation would make sense. Therefore, total separation from the period of judgment (not just protection through the time period) seems to be the promise. That this promise extends beyond the church at Philadelphia to all churches is assured by the repeated final challenge, "He that hath an ear, let him hear what the Spirit saith unto the churches."

The region around Philadelphia was subject to earthquake activity. They had a devastating earthquake in A.D. 17. An interesting feature of architecture, the laws of physics and earthquakes is that while roofs and walls fall down, many times pillars do not (e.g., "Weebles wobble but they don't fall down.").

Life **STEP** Believers will stay standing like pillars, will feel safe, and God will give them a threefold name, not "666."

Revelation 3:14-22

What is the writer saying?

How can I apply this to my life?

Laodicea was named for a king's wife, Laodice, but the word also means *justice of the people*. It was a wealthy city famous for many business enterprises. These included banking, black wool processing, medical schools, ear and eye medications, and hot spring resorts. Their wealth and self-sufficiency is noted in the fact that after an earthquake in A.D. 60, they rebuilt their city with no financial help from Rome. The city did not have safe drinking water. Drinking water was piped in from ten miles away, which meant they rarely enjoyed cold drinking. We know from Colossians 4:16 that this church would have received a copy of Ephesians and perhaps Colossians as well. Christ is introduced as the "Amen" or *truth personified* as contrasted with Satan, *the father of lies* (John 8:44). Jesus is also the "beginning" because he was the *Beginner*. Hot water and cold water are both desirable for drinking (e.g., hot coffee or iced tea). Room temperature beverages are undesirable or even nauseating. Despite their financial wealth, their famous black wool for clothing, their medicines and doctors, they were poor, unclothed, and sick. In place of their self-efforts for physical and spiritual wealth, God offers them His gold (genuine faith), His white garments (righteousness), and His eye salve (spiritual insight).

We often think of the "door" as the door to our life. Christ seeks entrance for fellowship with both unsaved and the saved. It also reminds us of the door to the messianic kingdom. Christ is ready to return to the planet and wants to have face-to-face fellowship with repentant believers. The *eating* would be the sharing of "the marriage supper of the Lamb" (Revelation 19:9). Overcomers then join the twelve apostles on the thrones of the kingdom (Luke 22:29-30).

In the world we see anarchy; in Christendom we see apostasy. Could it be that in the evangelical church we are in danger of apathy?

Revelation 4:1-11

What is the writer saying?

How can I apply this to my life?

pray

Fiji – Outreach among the 59,000 highly resistant Muslims and protection for persecuted new converts.

Chapters 4 and 5 form a unit that presents *throne room theology*. In chapter 4 we are introduced to the *Creator God*. In chapter 5 we view the *Redeemer God*. "After this" means *after the messages to the seven churches* and perhaps also implies after the Church Age. John is also taken up to heaven for this information, as the church will be at the Rapture. Notice that the first individual John sees in heaven is faceless and formless. Only His glory is described. He is God the Father, the Ancient of Days, the Universal Judge. Jasper is a clear gem like our diamond and perhaps speaks of God's holiness. Sardius (cf., the city "Sardis") is ruby-red, perhaps speaking of the righteousness supplied by Christ's blood. The green rainbow reminds us of God's mercy as shown to Noah, the first human to behold a rainbow. The twenty-four elders could parallel the twenty-four courses of priests in the temple service rotation or perhaps twelve representative Old Testament saints and twelve representative New Testament saints (as also appearing in the city of Jerusalem in Revelation 21). These elders wear the *victor's crown* (not a diadem or *kingly crown*). It indicates that they have run a race and have won. The reflecting pool magnified the light in the throne room and set God apart from creation by His purity. The word "beast" translates the word "zoa" which refers to *a living being* (and is also the root of the word "zoo"). These beasts are almost certainly the class of angel called Cherubim (*Watchers* of the holiness of God) or Seraphim (*burning ones*). The four faces also appear in the vision in Ezekiel 1. They represent the highest creature in their particular category of living creatures and also bear an uncanny resemblance to the theme of each of the four Gospels (e.g., "lion" for Christ the King in Matthew, etc.).

Life STEP This splendid vision of God in heaven leads to an outburst of praise that we have turned into a praise chorus, "Thou Art Worthy."

Revelation 5:1-7

What is the writer saying?

How can I apply this to my life?

pray   New Zealand – For support to be raised to send pastors and missionaries to Bible schools.

The right hand in biblical times was a place of authority, privilege, and advantage. Both the Romans and the Jewish people used multiple-sealed scrolls for legal documents such as wills and title deeds. In Jeremiah 32:11 we see Jeremiah receiving such a title deed for land he had purchased. That there would be writing on the outside does not necessarily mean that there was abundant information. These title deeds would consist of two copies. Inside, protected by the legal seals, was the official copy, while a second copy was outside the seals for reference sake. The sealed copy could only be opened in a court of law. Archaeologists have recovered title deeds where someone had altered the boundaries in the outer copy!

Notice the dynamic nature of this scene with a "strong" angel and a "loud" voice. Twenty times in Revelation something is described as being "loud." "Worthy" means of *proper weight*, referring to an intrinsic or earned quality. Initially, no one is found who can even look at the scroll, let alone open it. John is emotionally devastated by this problem. Some suggest that he was crying because he wanted to know the prophecies that the scroll contained. There are other times in Scripture when men are told that they cannot know something, and they don't respond by crying. It seems that the scroll signifies more than just information to John. His outburst is stemmed by the announcement that the Lion has prevailed to open the book. This statement is in the past tense, yet the scroll has not yet been opened. This illustrates that certain facts in Scripture are legally true before they are practically accomplished. When an entity steps forward to open the scroll, it is described as a lamb. In fact, not a strong adult ram, but rather a unique term used twenty nine times in Revelation that means *young lamb*.

Life STEP   When is the lamb a lion and the lion a lamb? When we are viewing the person of Jesus Christ!

Revelation 5:8-14

What is the writer saying?

How can I apply this to my life?

pray *El Salvador – For their Christian Institutes and media to continue the impact they have already brought to El Salvador.*

Notice that the twenty-four elders claimed that the Lamb had redeemed them, indicating that they were humans, not holy angels. Harps and gold are two of the standard items associated with heaven. The Greek word for "harp" is the same word from which we get *guitar*. In biblical times this stringed instrument had 10-20 strings.

Of all the prayers that saints have prayed over the last 1900 years, which one has probably been repeated the most? Would it be, "Our Father which art in heaven, Hallowed be thy name. Thy kingdom come. Thy will be done *in earth, as it is in heaven*"? If so, then here we have a very specific and practical application of those prayers. These saints revel in their current citizenship status as kings and priests while noting that their actual reign is still in the future. Despite the fact that the Jews were said to be a "kingdom of priests" (Exodus 19:6) here people of all ethnic backgrounds are included in the assembly of the redeemed. All rational creatures in every nook and cranny of the universe join voices to praise both the Father and the Son. These include both the angelic creatures and redeemed humanity. As in chapter 4, this heavenly vision in chapter 5 gives us a popular praise chorus, "Worthy is the Lamb." In verse 6 the lamb was described as a slain lamb. Now in verse 14 it is described as a lamb that will never die again.

Theologically, some conclude that because New Testament saints are described by some of the phrases used of Old Testament saints (e.g., "kingdom of priests") this means that the church has replaced Israel in God's program. We would argue that such analogies are not mutually exclusive. Both Israel and the church can be a "kingdom of priests" without contradiction or the subservience of the one to the other.

Life stEP God lives regardless of our existence, activities or thoughts; but He becomes alive to us in our praise. If you want to know God better, praise Him better.

Revelation 6:1-8

What is the writer saying?

How can I apply this to my life?

Revelation 6:1-8:1 describes the seven seal judgments. As each seal is opened on the scroll, John witnesses a prophetic event. The first four seal judgments are also known as the *four Horsemen of the Apocalypse*. Notice that the four living creatures of chapter 4 call these horsemen forth. The thunderous voice of the first living beast implies judgment. The color "white" speaks of victory and perhaps counterfeit purity. While the horse and bow are both instruments of ancient warfare, perhaps the absence of arrows implies a political conquest (cf. Daniel 7:8, 24). It says that the rider of the white horse "was given" his authority ("crown") indicating that these events are initiated from the throne of God and therefore, would be classified as God's wrath being poured out on the sinful earth as a judgment.

While no specific chronological markers are given here in chapter 6, both Daniel and Matthew associate war with the entire seven years of the tribulation period. Therefore, we could suggest that the opening of the seals begins shortly after the Rapture of the church and that the white horse represents the beginning of the Antichrist's rise to world dominance. The "red" horse speaks of the bloodshed of war. The "black" horse represents the famine that comes in the wake of war. The voice that describes the symbolism of the third horse is God's (from the midst of the four living creatures) indicating once again that this is God's judgment on sinful mankind. Wheat is more nutritious than barley. The prices mentioned indicate tenfold price inflation. Since olives and grapes grow wild, these items are not immediately affected. The famine is limited and the wealthy still have their food. The last horse is yellowish green (the word is "chlorine" in Greek). It represents death in general ("green around the gills"). "Hell" (actually "hades" representing the grave) is like the hearse, bringing up the rear.

If this happened tomorrow, 1.5 billion people would die. Are your friends safe?

Revelation 6:9-17

What is the writer saying?

How can I apply this to my life?

Cayman Islands – For the wealth of the island to be used to extend God's kingdom.

The four horsemen seem to be analogous to the "four severe judgments" predicted in several Old Testament passages (cf. Ezekiel 14:21). These are usually listed as sword, wild beast, famine, and plague. The fifth seal is not so much a judgment as it is a justification for judgment. Apparently enough time has transpired in the tribulation period for a significant number of people to have accepted Christ as their Savior and then be martyred for their faith. (The Greek word for "testimony" in verse 9 is the source of the English word "martyr" because so many of the early Christians lost their lives for their testimony). They address God with a special Greek word for Lord, the word "despotes" from which we get the English word "despot." It means *absolute master*. The concept *earth dwellers*, in the book of Revelation, refers to unsaved mankind, who is hostile toward God. God encourages the martyrs with pure clothing and the promise that it will only be a short time until their murder is avenged (at least we could say *less than seven years*).

The sixth seal involves catastrophic *cosmic signs*. Matthew 24 describes earthquake activity prior to the midpoint of the tribulation period (which is marked by the establishment of the *abomination of desolation* in the temple). These unusual events in the physical world are calculated to make men think that the universe is coming apart at the seams. All men, great and small, are unnerved and apparently think that they can escape God's wrath by dying. In Scripture, God's end-time wrath ("day of the Lord" wrath) is said to come upon sinners "as a thief" (1 Thessalonians 5:4). If that is the case, then the comments of these distraught humans form an announcement that the seal judgments are day of the Lord events, not that the seventh seal will be the start of the day of the Lord. "Who is able to stand?" may be a rhetorical question, but we will find an answer in chapter 7!

Life
STEP "It is a fearful thing to fall into the hands of the living God" (Hebrews 10:31).

Revelation 7:1-8

What is the writer saying?

How can I apply this to my life?

The seventh and final seal is not opened until 8:1. In chapter 7, we take a break from the chronological sequence and step back to fill in details of some of the other things that God is doing during the first half of the tribulation period. In 7:1-8 we are introduced to the 144,000 sealed Jews who are protected from the divine judgments, and apparently become the evangelists on the planet after the Rapture of the church. Ancient Jewish superstition claimed that winds blowing from the "corners" (east-northeast, etc.) of the compass were harmful. The direction of the rising sun (East, v. 2) is associated with the following positive concepts in Scripture: paradise; the direction that the Shekinah glory of God takes when returning to the temple; the Magi; and the messianic title, "Dayspring" (Luke 1:78). God is called the "living God" as contrasted with the *dead* gods of paganism.

The ancient world was familiar with tattoos and distinctive cuttings in the flesh for tribal, military, trade guild, or religious purposes. In Revelation 13 we will be introduced to the infamous "mark ...of the Beast," 666. Here, as in a parallel situation in Ezekiel 9, the individuals are marked on the forehead. In Ezekiel 9:4 the "mark" was actually the Hebrew letter "tav" or "t." At that time, the Hebrew letter even looked like a small cross!

In the Bible, there are many different arrangements of the *12 tribes of Israel*. In addition to the original twelve sons of Jacob, we have the two sons of Joseph, Ephraim and Manasseh. Levi is left out in some lists since as priests they were given cities throughout the country and not territory. Joseph is left out in many lists to make room for his sons. In this list, Dan and Ephraim are missing. Perhaps Dan is missing because that tribe left the original tribal allotment in the south, moved to the extreme north, apostatized, and was absorbed into Syrian paganism. Perhaps Ephraim is missing because that tribe opposed Judah and David.

Life stEP God does dangerous things, but always with great care for those who are part of His master plan.

Revelation 7:9-17

What is the writer saying?

How can I apply this to my life?

"After this" could mean *the next thing I saw*, but a tighter understanding would be *as a result of the sealing of the 144,000, many people came to know Christ as Savior.* We are not introduced to the "two witnesses" until Revelation 11; however, it is clear that they are mighty preachers during the first half of the tribulation period. We could suggest the following chronology. At the Rapture, for the first time in human history, there will not be one saved individual left on the planet. To provide a renewed witness, God sends the two witnesses. They help lead the 144,000 to Christ. The two witnesses are killed by the antichrist at the middle of the Tribulation, but the 144,000 continue preaching to the end. It is their converts from seven years of missionary work that we see here in chapter 7.

Palm branches (called "lulav" in Jewish ceremonies) were standard joyous decorations for both Jewish and Roman celebrations (cf. the Triumphal Entry on Palm Sunday). The Roman emperor claimed the title *Savior* (v. 10). Here God is the rightful bearer of that title. Verse 12 repeats the seven attributes from Revelation 5:12 with just the slight change of "thanksgiving" instead of "riches."

Note that these saved individuals come from the entire earth; every ethnic group is represented. The number is also significant. The number is so great that no man could count it. In Revelation there are many numbers. The largest is the number 200,000,000 (9:16). Therefore, we could conclude that even during the world's darkest hour, over 200,000,000 people will come to salvation by God's gracious intervention.

Life Step

God is great and God is good, but mostly He is good. He didn't have to offer salvation during the time of well-deserved judgment, but He does. As a believer, you are convinced of His eternal graciousness. He also wants to show you grace right now, today, as you trust Him.

Revelation 8:1-13

What is the writer saying?

How can I apply this to my life?

Chapter 8 begins with the opening of the seventh and final seal. All of heaven is shocked into adoring silence with the realization that the title deed to planet earth is now back in the hands of the rightful owner and the official copy is now open in the heavenly court with the breaking of the last seal. Satan, the usurper, is in the process of being defeated and expelled from his squatter claim. Adoring silence as a mode of worship is observed in other passages such as, "Be still and know that I am God" (Psalm 46:10). In biblical times, trumpets were used to get attention, call people together, and announce important events. Both metal and ram's horn trumpets (the *shofar*) were known and used. It is not clear here what type is being used. Earlier we noted that "Thy kingdom come" is probably the most frequently uttered prayer. The altar of incense symbolizes the prayers of the saints going up to God. Here, the coals from that altar are also symbolic of the judgment to fall upon the rebellious earth.

The accompanying physical traumas heighten the judgmental aspect of these trumpets. Note that the seventh seal is not a specific judgment, but rather contains all seven of the judgments in this next series of judgments. The first four trumpet judgments fall on nature and indirectly attack man. The first trumpet judgment attacks green vegetation. The second trumpet judgment affects the salty sea. The third trumpet judgment attacks fresh water. Wormwood is "absinth," a bitter chemical used to kill intestinal parasites. Amazingly, it is also the meaning of the name Chernobyl, the city in the Ukraine with the tragic nuclear reactor malfunction. The fourth trumpet judgment affects the heavenly light. A similar phenomenon took place in one of the ten judgments upon the Egyptians and also the day Christ died.

Revelation 9:1-12

What is the writer saying?

How can I apply this to my life?

At the end of chapter 8, John is told that there are three more trumpets to sound and that they will be the three (final) woes to fall upon mankind. Actually, this is a very accurate statement as the third woe, seventh trumpet, is in fact the final series of judgments, the vial (bowl) judgments. The devastation these judgments bring is cataclysmic. If you take one-fourth of a number (the fourth seal judgment) and then one-third of the remainder (the sixth trumpet judgment) the result is half of the original number. There are over six billion people on the planet today. This would represent a death toll of over three billion people!

The "star" (v. 1) represents a spirit being. He has authority to open the bottomless pit. Smoke comes out, darkening the sun and also mimicking the darkening of the sun produced by a great swarm of locusts. These are not normal locusts but demonic locusts. Instead of eating vegetation, their *diet* is human flesh. Their "sting" is like that of a scorpion.

Some scorpions have deadly stings but these do not. The sting of a scorpion has been described as the equivalent of being stung by two wasps at the same time. Torment for God-haters is the stated mission for these horror-film creatures. That they would do so for five months is significant because that is the length of the lifespan of a normal locust. It is not clear why these tormented men cannot commit suicide. Perhaps it means that they are in so much pain they wish and think they should die from the stings but don't. Some have speculated that the fanciful description of these demonic beings was the best John could do in describing weapons of modern warfare. While God can use modern equipment to produce such torment, it would not be surprising if this were a literal description of the fearful appearance of these bizarre creatures. Both "Abaddon" and "Apollyon" mean the same thing, *Destroyer.*

Life stEP

We have a choice. We can fear God now in reverential awe that leads to eternal salvation, or we can fear Him later in stark terror.

Revelation 9:13-21

What is the writer saying?

How can I apply this to my life?

The sixth trumpet or second woe is a precursor to Armageddon. The announcement comes from the altar of incense where the prayers of the martyred saints ascend to God. Since the four angels are bound, this would indicate that they are fallen angels (demons). The Euphrates River in the Bible is the border between Israel and the Gentile empires of Assyria, Babylon, and Persia. It runs for 1700 miles from the mountains of Turkey to the Persian Gulf. In Revelation 16:12-16 the River Euphrates is dried up to allow the kings of the East to come to the Valley of Armageddon in Israel. Some have noted the parallelism between the two passages and have suggested that the 200,000,000 demons of chapter 9 indwell the armies of chapter 16 to induce them to come to Armageddon. Some commentators have imagined some sort of modern weapon with guns belching fire from the front and tail. We can just as easily imagine God using the traditional and modern representations of demons and extraterrestrial monsters to scare and punish sinful mankind. They are colorful. "Fire" would be golden, "jacinth" can be reddish-orange, blue, or purple, and "brimstone" (sulfur) is yellow. They kill with fire (burning), smoke (asphyxiation), and brimstone (chemical poisoning?). These creatures and their weapons kill one-third of the remaining people. Those who survive amazingly do not recognize God's hand in the matter and continue in their sinful ways. Demonic activity on earth peaks when the Messiah is about to establish the kingdom (in both His first and second comings). The Greek word translated "sorceries" is "pharmakeia," from the same root as *pharmaceuticals*. The ancients used drugs to achieve an altered state of consciousness when worshiping. They would then become *in theos* (enthused) or *indwelt by the gods*.

Life stEP   You are possessed by what you value. Value Satan's things and he will claim you. Value God's characteristics and you will be His eternally.

Revelation 10:1-11

What is the writer saying?

How can I apply this to my life?

Saints feel inferior to and afflicted by the unsaved. However, God and His helpers are described in majestic language. Here the announcing angel is "mighty." He has the glory clouds of God (cf. Daniel 7:13-14). The beauty of the rainbow adorns his head (since Noah's day, a symbol of God's mercy). His face is radiant like the sun. His feet are burnished by fire as were Christ's in Revelation 1:15. He is large enough to straddle the land and sea. His voice is powerful like the kingly lion. The little book (actually a scroll, since *books* as we know them were not invented yet) represents the judgments. Apparently we could have had another series of seven judgments, the *Thunder Judgments*, but God wouldn't let John write that information down. This indicates that there is more to the story than we know and therefore, we have to trust God when certain elements don't seem to make sense,

because we do not have all the data. Notice the emphasis on God as the Creator God. His puny creatures are in big trouble because they have offended their Creator.

Verse 7 indicates that once the bowl judgments begin, events will run rapidly to the conclusion. "Ate" (v. 10) means to *internalize* or *read* (cf. Psalm 19:9). Ezekiel also had a similar experience (Ezekiel 3:1-4). The scroll was sweet to the taste because it was the very Word of God and His words are sweeter than the honeycomb (Psalm 19:10). However, since it contained judgments, it was bitter in John's stomach. Verse 11 indicates that while the bowl judgments lead quickly to the end, there are other details about the tribulation period that God wants John to include in his prophecy. These are covered in chapters 11-14.

Life STEP "For we walk by faith, not by sight" (2 Corinthians 5:7). It would be great if God told us everything, but then we would not be practicing a *faith walk* if we already knew everything.

Revelation 11:1-12

What is the writer saying?

How can I apply this to my life?

pray   *That the leadership of your church will live justly, love mercy, and walk humbly with God (Micah 6:8).*

Some theologians argue that the Book of Revelation was written prior to the A.D. 70 destruction of the temple and that most of the prophecies herein were fulfilled in A.D. 70. They see no future Jewish Temple. However, in 2 Thessalonians 2:4, Paul envisions worship of the antichrist in the temple. Since this did not happen in A.D. 70, it must be a future event. "Measure" implies ownership and authority. God lays claim to the temple even while predicting its desecration. It would seem that the "forty-two months" refers to the second half of the tribulation while the 1260 "days" refers to the first half. For the first 3½ years of the tribulation, the two witnesses will preach in Jerusalem. This is the same length of time as Jesus' public ministry. They will be invincible until it is God's time for their martyrdom by the Antichrist as he dominates Jerusalem for the second half of the tribulation. Verse 4 uses the imagery of Zechariah 4:1-14. Elijah announced a drought on Israel and called fire down from heaven. He is also the predicted forerunner of Christ (Malachi 4:5). Moses is also mentioned in Malachi 4:4 along with "Mt. Horeb" (Mt. Sinai) which both men visited in their ministries. Both men also appeared with Christ on the Mount of Transfiguration. They are good candidates for the two witnesses. The "beast" is defined as the Antichrist in Revelation 13:1-18. The abyss defines his satanic origins and perhaps a resurrection from a mortal wound. The whole world will know of the two witnesses' death and will rejoice. Today satellite TV makes this possible. In earlier times, ambassadors in Jerusalem from every nation would have made this possible. They do not rise until the fourth day proving that indeed they were dead and that this is a supernatural resurrection.

Life
stEP   Why does the world hate us so much? It is because their father, Satan, hates our Savior, Jesus Christ.

Revelation 11:13-19

What is the writer saying?

How can I apply this to my life?

pray   *Romania – For dynamic youth ministries that will inspire and teach teens how to live for Christ.*

An earthquake accompanies the resurrection of these martyrs, as was the case with the death of Christ and the resurrection of some Jerusalem believers (cf. Matthew 27:50-54). The resurrection of the two witnesses, like all miracles in the Bible, is a sign of God's existence, power, and authority. Even unbelievers are moved to worship. Verse 15 beautifully describes the majesty of God and rings in our ears as the "Hallelujah Chorus" in George Frederick Handel's oratorio, "The Messiah." Some ancient manuscripts do not contain the future tense "art to come" in verse 17. While His future existence is certain, to leave out the explicit statement might be a purposeful literary devise implying that this great person "which art" and "wast" will certainly exist into eternity. As the impending doom of sinners and the sin-cursed earth is announced, John sees into the inner sanctum, the Holy of Holies in heaven, where the *ark of the covenant* is kept. In the earthly tabernacle and temple, only one man, the high priest, could enter the Holy of Holies, and only on one day per year. Even then it took elaborate preparations and animal sacrifices to open the door to the presence of God. On the day that Christ died, that doorway curtain was ripped from top (heaven) to bottom indicating that man now has free access into God's presence through the death of Christ. Perhaps this is why so many priests believed (Acts 6:7). Here in Revelation 11:19, the Holy of Holies is open in judgment. The *ark of the covenant* (*testimony* and "testament" are equivalent to *covenant*) contained the Law of Moses. Mankind is about to be judged by the Law.

Life
sTEP

Gifted men can write amazing stories in moving detail, but the storyline and phrasing of these verses seem beyond mere mortal invention. Only a supreme being could create such an amazing description of the transition from the *age of sinful man* to the *age of God's absolute rule* on planet earth.

Revelation 12:1-9

What is the writer saying?

How can I apply this to my life?

pray *France – Passionate outreach to the nearly 50,000,000 people who have no real link with a Bible – believing church.*

Chapter 12 adds more actors and activities to the tribulation story. The man-child is obviously Jesus, so the woman would then represent the nation of Israel. This is affirmed by the twelve stars, which would represent the twelve tribes of Israel. In the Joseph story in Genesis, the sun and moon represented Joseph's father (Jacob) and mother (Rachel). The red dragon is obviously Satan (and so identified in verse 9). He appears as a serpent in Genesis. The color red may reflect Egyptian mythology that featured a fearsome red crocodile. The "stars" swept from heaven may refer to the angels that joined Satan's rebellion (cf. v. 9). If so, then we would have the added bit of information that 33% of the angels followed Satan becoming *demons*. Revelation 12 is the first of several passages that speaks of Satan's end-time kingdom as composed of ten or seven countries/kings. Daniel 7:7-8 teaches that ten confederated kings will be dominated by Satan's Antichrist, who eliminates three of them, leaving seven kings over ten territories. In a parallel description in Revelation 13:1 there are ten horns, seven heads, and ten crowns instead of the seven crowns mentioned here in Revelation 12.

Another important observation from this chapter is the freedom with which the prophecies jump around the timeline. For instance, from 5a to 5b we jump from Jesus' birth to His ascension (33 years). From 5b to 6 we jump over the entire Church Age (1970+ years) to the tribulation period. We can conclude that biblical prophecy does not have to be strictly chronological or inclusive. Verses 7-9 would seem to be a mid-tribulation event providing the reason why the second half is more intense than the first half of the tribulation. "Devil" means *slanderer*. "Satan" means "accuser." He is the original and master deceiver. Verse 6 describes what Israel does to escape the dragon, namely, hide in the wilderness for the last half of the tribulation.

Life **stEP** God has a master plan and He is in control of even His enemies.

Revelation 12:10-17

What is the writer saying?

How can I apply this to my life?

Satan has a number of "falls" in Scripture. First, he fell from holiness when he rebelled against God. Next, he fell when the disciples were ministering during the time of Christ (cf. Luke 10:18). He fell at the Cross and Resurrection. Here he falls as he is cast out of heaven and limited to the earth for the duration of the tribulation period. He is a false high priest as he accuses the saints before the heavenly throne, instead of interceding for them the way our Great High Priest does (cf. Hebrews 4:14). Zechariah 13:8 indicates that 66% of all the Jews, at least of those living in Israel, will be killed by the Antichrist. According to Daniel 11:41, the countries of Edom and Moab will not be conquered by the Antichrist, making this wilderness region around the Dead Sea a safe place for the Jews. Notice another way to refer to half of the tribulation period: "time" (1) + "times" (2) + "half a time" (½) = 3½ years. The region around the Dead Sea is very rugged with many valleys and mountains.

Edom was noted for trusting in her mountain fortress (Obadiah 3). Edom (now in the country of Jordan) has whole cities carved out of the side of the mountains such as Petra, the Rose City. The area geographically has been called the *back door* of Israel, the place to flee to when danger comes in the *front door* (from the Mediterranean). Herod the Great had several mountain retreats throughout this region. The wilderness is also a dry place, unable to support many citizens, so it is a place to get away and be alone. Many churches had monasteries in the wilderness during the Middle Ages. The locals were also afraid of the demons they thought lived in the wilderness. To this day, every year several people are killed in flash floods as they are trapped in steep ravines when a sudden rain comes.

Life Step There are four women in Revelation. Two are evil (Jezebel and the Harlot) and two are good (the woman and the bride). Which two appeal to you?

Revelation 13:1-10

What is the writer saying?

How can I apply this to my life?

The Greek word for "sea" is the same word translated "bottomless pit" in Revelation 11:7 and 17:8. In context, "bottomless pit" refers to the lower parts of Hades from which satanic evil emerges. Here it clearly refers to watery depths, but elsewhere the watery sea is a symbol of the Gentile nations in sinful turmoil (Luke 21:25). The beast is a symbol of both the kingdom of the antichrist and the Antichrist himself. That the beast comes out of the sea indicates its Gentile (European) roots. The ten horns and crowns refer to the ten European (former Roman Empire) nations that the Antichrist controls. "Blasphemy" refers to the Antichrist's claim of deity. Even in Roman times the emperors were worshiped as gods. The Emperor Domitian called himself "Dominus et Deus noster" ("Our Lord and God"). The description of the beast in verse 2 is similar to the description of the terrible fourth composite beast in Daniel 7:7. "Deadly" (v. 3) is the same word describing the slain lamb in Revelation 5:6. It can refer to the death of the Antichrist or a crushing military defeat from which he miraculously recovers. This *resurrection* would be at the midpoint of the tribulation period as he then is dominant for the next forty-two months (v. 5, cf. 11:2). "Who is able to make war with him?" is a rhetorical question but it will receive an answer in chapter 14, tribulation saints can!

The book of life (v. 8) is patterned after the typical citizen's lists of the ancient cities. All citizens were listed until they died, then their names were erased. Honored citizens were even inscribed in gold lettering. Verse 9 contains a sentence repeated seven times in Revelation 2-3, but now has one phrase missing, "…what the Spirit saith unto the churches." This strongly implies that the church is no longer on the planet and that these saints should be identified as *Tribulation saints*, not *church saints*.

 Life STEP   Even in the world's darkest hour it is clear that God is still in control and that His people will be remembered and protected.

Friday **16**

Revelation 13:11-18

What is the writer saying?

How can I apply this to my life?

pray *France – Outreach among the growing Muslim population. Islam is now the second religion of France.*

This section introduces a second beast, the *false prophet.* His job is to promote the Antichrist. He comes from the "earth." Since "the land" in Scripture often refers to "the land of Israel," this description may indicate that the false prophet comes from Israel. We now have three main characters in Revelation 13. The dragon is Satan, *the father.* The first beast is Antichrist, *the son.* The false prophet, *the unholy spirit,* completes Satan's counterfeit trinity. This *false prophet* also illustrates Satan's desire to imitate the messianic offices of prophet, priest, and king. The false prophet calls down fire from heaven like the two witnesses did in Revelation 11. Ezekiel 38 also predicts the use of fire to destroy an enemy of Israel during the tribulation period. Perhaps the false prophet is also claiming that the Antichrist defeated this enemy of Israel. Believers are warned in Deuteronomy 13:1-

3 to ignore miracles if they lead to the worship of other gods. The false prophet will oversee an image of the Antichrist which Matthew 24:15 and 2 Thessalonians 2:4 indicate will be placed in the temple in Jerusalem. Those who refuse to worship the image of the Antichrist by taking a distinguishing mark will not be able to buy food. They will also be liable for immediate execution.

The ancients used images to represent the power of a king, sometimes using tricks such as ventriloquism to manipulate the citizens. Even modern societies are fascinated with the image of a respected leader whether it is a painting, statue, or even the preserved body (cf. Lenin and Mao). Computer technology would certainly accomplish what is described here, but Satan could also use demons to control people.

Life stEP The infamous "mark of the beast" will certainly mean something to the believers who are on the planet at that time. For us, the best we can say is that *seven* is the number of perfection. *777* would then represent the trinity. Satan's unholy trinity is less: "666."

Revelation 14:1-7

What is the writer saying?

How can I apply this to my life?

In answer to the question, "Who *is* like unto the beast? Who is able to make war with him?" (13:4) Revelation 14 presents the 144,000. Instead of the mark of the beast (13:16) they have God's name on their forehead. The lamb with them would be the "Lamb as it had been slain" of Revelation 5:6. "Sion" refers to the temple mount specifically but Jerusalem in general. Powerful sounds emanate from heaven honoring their testimony. The four beasts (cherubim) and twenty four elders (representative Old Testament and New Testament saints) of Revelation 4 are there worshiping. The 144,000 are called "virgins" (v. 4). This could be physically true, although since Hebrews 13:4 says that the marriage bed is "undefiled," this might be a reference to spiritual purity. They did not defile themselves by association with Jezebel (cf. 2:20). They are "first fruits." This is a reference to the religious practice of giving some of the first grain to ripen to the Lord as thanks for the full harvest to follow. These 144,000 do not represent all the humans who are saved during the tribulation period, but rather the first group to be saved with many more to come. Deceit does not exist in their lives (as opposed to Satan). They are blameless (as opposed to the beast and false prophet).

The word "gospel" means *good news*. There are several *gospels* in the Bible. For salvation effectiveness they all rely on the cross work of Jesus Christ. However, they emphasize different aspects of God's good news for humanity. The gospel of the kingdom in Matthew is "Repent, for the kingdom of heaven is at hand." (Mt. 3:2) The Gospel of the Church Age is the death, burial, and resurrection of Jesus Christ (1 Corinthians 15:3-5). Here, the emphasis of the gospel of the tribulation period is *Repent; you have offended the Creator God*.

Life **stEP**   What a rude awakening when arrogant sinners are brought face to face with God their maker!

Sunday 17

Revelation 14:8-13

What is the writer saying?

How can I apply this to my life?

pray

Harry Bollback, Co-founder of Word of Life, as he and his wife Millie travel and minister.

Chapter 14 is actually a review of the entire tribulation period. In verses 1-7 we are re-introduced to the 144,000 Jewish evangelists, the message they preach, and the worship their lives will produce in heaven. In verses 8-13, we are reminded of the predicted defeat of all of God's enemies and the ultimate vindication of all the saints. This is the first of six references to "Babylon" in Revelation. Genesis 10:10 contains the first mention of Babylon (as "Babel"), where we are told that the city was founded by Nimrod. In Jewish legends, Nimrod was the inventor of polytheism. The Greek historian Herodotus (c. 450 B.C.) also claimed that Babylon was the source of polytheism. The next mention of Babel is in Genesis 11. After the flood, Noah's family was commanded to spread out across the face of the earth. Instead, some descendants decided to try to maintain their unity by building a tower on the flat plain of Babylon. Ever since Genesis 11, Babylon has been a symbol of man's government in rebellion against God. The early church referred to the Roman government as "Babylon" (cf. 1 Peter 5:13). Therefore, Babylon probably refers to the government of the Antichrist. In Revelation 17-18 this will have political, economic, and religious aspects as the Antichrist seeks to develop a unified world governmental system.

Ancient wine was cut 50-66% before being used as a daily beverage. The wrath of God against sinners will not be diluted (v. 10). There are some verses in the Bible that could be understood to teach that sinners are burnt up and go out of existence when they are cast into hell (theologically, this is called the "Annihilation Theory"). Here in 14:11 it is clear that not only is their status permanent, but their conscious punishment is also never ending.

Life STEP

God has the power to stop persecution. He clearly chooses not to for His own purposes. Notice, however, He has compassion and encouraging words for those who must endure a brief moment of affliction for His namesake.

Revelation 14:14-20

What is the writer saying?

How can I apply this to my life?

The tribulation review in chapter 14 concludes with the battle of Armageddon at the second coming of Jesus Christ. The "white cloud" and title "Son of Man" come from Daniel 7:13-14. "White" speaks of purity. "Clouds" are often associated with the glory of God. "Son of man" was Christ's favorite title for Himself. He used it twice as often as any other title (e.g., "Son of God"). "Son of" means *characterized by*. This is demonstrated in the response the Jews had to Christ's claim to be the "Son of God" (i.e., "characterized by deity"). They hated Him for making that claim and called it blasphemous. "Son of Man" identifies Jesus with us; he is a man like we are.

God the Father in the heavenly temple sends an angel to tell Jesus to start the final harvest. "Ripe" (v. 15) is the word for "over-ripe" such as sun-dried *golden waves of grain*. The "sickle" (v. 16) would be the large instrument used for harvesting grain. The next "sickle" (v. 17) would be a smaller instrument, designed for cutting grape stems. "Fully ripe" (v. 18) means *peak condition* and for grapes would mean *full of juice*. The juicy clusters of grapes represent sinful humanity with their life-preserving blood. In ancient times, grapes were thrown into large stone vats with a framework overhead from which straps hung. The unmarried men and women would remove their sandals, hike their robes, hang onto the straps, and crush the grapes as they joyously stamped to music. In this final judgment, the blood of Christ's enemies will flow the entire length of the land of Israel (about 200 miles). A horse's bridle stands about 4.5 feet from the ground. Assuming a literal river of blood about five feet wide, these dimensions would require about one billion people.

Life stEP While God is a loving God, He also is a just God. While gruesome, the judgment of sinners is legally and eternally just for they deserve the punishment that they receive.

Revelation 15:1-8

What is the writer saying?

How can I apply this to my life?

pray   *Columbia – For boldness and perseverance among missionaries who live with the threat of violence.*

Chapter 15 re-introduces the last series of judgments. In Revelation 10:6 and 7 we were told these judgments will come quickly, be intense, and climax the tribulation period. However, as a literary device, God keeps us in suspense through chapters 11, 12, 13, and 14. The sea of glass would magnify all the colors and lights in heaven. That "fire" is reflected from the sea of glass heightens the sense of impending doom and judgment. The martyrs sing the "song of Moses." Moses created two songs in his public ministry. Exodus 15 praises God for the safe and miraculous exodus from Egypt. Deuteronomy 32 covers all of Israel's history up to Moses' day. Here they not only praise God for His attributes, but as fitting to the context, they specifically praise Him for His intent to judge their enemies. John sees the temple in heaven open. The inside is described as the "tabernacle." This word means *tent* or *dwelling* place. It underscores the fact that in the tabernacle and later in the temple built by Solomon, God dwelt with His people. He was present in the Holy of Holies, residing above the ark of the covenant (testimony) between the two sculpted cherubim. The top of the ark was called the mercy seat because on the day of Atonement (Yom Kippur) the *covering* blood was sprinkled on the top and God was *satisfied* (*propitiated*) that the just price for sin had been paid. Here we see mercy and punishment emanating from the same location. The seven angels are dressed like priests indicating that their job of judging was a holy, priestly job. One of the four beasts (cherubim) passes out the seven bowls of wrath. The temple is filled with smoke, as it had been with God's glory cloud when Solomon dedicated his temple in his day (cf. 1 Kings 8:10-11). The temple is then closed until the job is complete.

Life stEP   God's payday is coming someday. We might be frustrated now with the arrogance of sinful man, but God's longsuffering will come to an end.

Revelation 16:1-12

What is the writer saying?

How can I apply this to my life?

pray *Czech Republic – For the young people to search for answers in the Word.*

The first four bowl judgments parallel the first four trumpet judgments. They are, however, more devastating. In the trumpet sequence, only one third of each category was damaged. In the bowl sequence there is total destruction in each category. The first bowl produces horrible skin eruptions on all the beast worshipers. The second bowl kills all life living in salt water by making the water coagulate like blood does. The third bowl kills all life living in fresh water by turning it into blood. The saints and angels in heaven find this particularly appropriate since the beast worshipers were so quick to shed the blood of God's saints. The fourth bowl intensifies the effects of the sun. This may just be increased heat or it could include the damage produced by unblocked ultraviolet light as well. Not only does ultraviolet light increase the incidence of skin cancer, but it also hastens cataract formation, inhibits crop growth, and damages plankton in the sea. Sinful humanity refuses to acknowledge God's hand in these events and repent. Perhaps they think these are natural disasters or the result of human (nuclear?) warfare. While perhaps not believing in God they still use His name in their curses!

The fifth bowl plunges the world into a tormented darkness. Perhaps the pain is psychological (fear and dread). Or maybe they stumble around hurting themselves even more. Or perhaps the darkness lets them sit still and concentrate on the pain of their existing wounds. The sixth bowl causes the great Euphrates River to dry up allowing troops from the east to easily march to Israel. For years now Turkey has had the power to shut off the flow of the Euphrates with a system of hydroelectric dams. This is also predicted in Isaiah 11:15.

Life stEP One of the necessary features of "free will" is that it is free to be totally irrational. Man's depravity produces the most illogical response, which leads to eternal loss.

Thursday 17

Revelation 16:13-21

What is the writer saying?

How can I apply this to my life?

pray *Pray that the leadership of your church might be able to take a time of rest with their families.*

Frogs are *unclean animals* (Leviticus 11:10). These demonic frogs perform *sign-miracles* to convince the kings of the earth to come to Israel. The phrase "I come as a thief" is never used in Scripture of the Rapture. It always is used of the judgments associated with the day of the Lord in general, or the second coming specifically ("great day of Almighty" and Battle of "Armageddon," vv. 14, 16).

The word "thief" refers to a *cat burglar*, not an armed robber (hence the popular phrase, *thief in the night*). Even after all these *signs of the times*, the unsaved at the end of the tribulation period will still be caught off-guard by the appearance of Christ, *the thief*. The surviving saints, however, will discern the times and welcome their Messiah.

"Armageddon" comes from two words, "Har" ("mountain") and "Megiddo" ("place of troops"). Megiddo was the name of a strategic city that controlled the roadway through the Carmel mountain range into the huge Jezreel (*God Sows*) Valley. It is in the shape of a triangle about 20 miles on a side. It also goes by the name *Plain of Esdraelon* (Greek form of Jezreel). It has always been a fertile valley. The earliest battle in human history with recorded details (on the walls of the Temple of Karnack in Thebes, Egypt) occurred there between the Canaanites and Thutmose III around 1450 B.C. During the time of the judges, Barak and Deborah fought the Canaanites there, who were led by Sisera, the man eventually killed by Jael as she drove a nail through his head while he slept. Gideon also defeated the Midianites in this valley. Unlike the seal judgments and the trumpet judgments, the seventh bowl judgment is a specific judgmental event. It caps all the judgments with the worst earthquake this old world has ever seen. In addition, 100-pound hailstones rain down on what remains of the earth.

The final conflict leads to eternal victory for the people of God and His Christ.

Revelation 17:1-8

What is the writer saying?

How can I apply this to my life?

In Revelation 13, the beast represents the Antichrist and his kingdom. Here a woman rides the beast, which is now described as a "scarlet" beast. Isaiah 1:18 compares the stain of sin to "scarlet" and "crimson." She is an immoral woman and has immoral connections with all the kings of the earth. She is symbolically named Babylon. In the Old Testament, God likened the pagan religions to strange lovers and accused Israel of spiritual adultery when she went after the other gods (cf. Ezekiel 23:37). The woman is dressed like royalty. Purple traditionally has been the color of kings because the color was so expensive to produce. It took 10,000 murex shellfish to produce one ounce of the colorfast purple dye. "Mystery" probably refers to the deceitfulness and treachery of false teaching. She is "the great" because of the size of her organization, activities, and the extent of her apostasy. 2 Thessalonians 2:3 indicates that the revelation of the Antichrist will be accompanied by "the falling away (apostasy)." She is the "mother" of harlots and abominations as the source and greatest offender. In addition to false teaching and immorality, she is guilty of murdering those who love the Lord. John is puzzled and the angel begins to explain the scene. He first describes the beast. Satan loves to counterfeit Christ's program in an attempt to replace it. Note the similarities between Revelation 17:8 (describing the antichrist) and Revelation 1:18 (describing Christ). Both have a *death*, *burial*, and *resurrection*. In the tribulation period, the Antichrist will start to organize his kingdom in the first half (v. 8, "was"). He will then be killed or suffer a devastating political setback ("and is not"). He will descend into Hades, be indwelt by Satan, and then arise to renew his goal of world domination ("and yet is").

Life Step Good people are not necessarily holy. Some of the greatest evils are done in the name of or hiding behind God.

Revelation 17:9-18

What is the writer saying?

How can I apply this to my life?

Revelation 17:3 says that the woman is sitting on the beast with seven heads. Verse 9 says she is sitting on seven mountains. Both "heads" and "mountains" are used symbolically of kings or governments elsewhere (cf. Isaiah 14:13; Ezekiel 35:2; Daniel 2:44-45, 7:6). They could be simultaneous and in fact the horns and crowns (12:3, 13:1) do seem to refer to contemporary associates of the Antichrist. They could also be sequential, and that seems to be the case here. "Five are fallen" (v. 10) in Israel's history would be Egypt, Assyria, Babylon, Persia, and Greece. "One is" in A.D. 95 would be Rome. "The other is not yet come" would be the revival of Rome under the Antichrist. "He must continue a short space" refers to the first half of the tribulation before the Antichrist is *killed*. Notice that there is a connection between the "seventh" and the "eighth." The Antichrist is also the "eighth" as the satanically indwelt *resurrected* wonder for the second half of the tribulation period.

The number ten is interesting. In Jewish thought, her enemies come in groups of ten (cf. Genesis 15:19-21; Psalm 83:6-8; Jeremiah 41:1). Revived Rome under the Antichrist will probably control the same territory as ancient Rome. Rome controlled all of Western Europe to the Rhine and Danube Rivers. She controlled northern Africa and the Middle East to Euphrates. The Mediterranean was the *Roman Lake*. The Antichrist and his associates use the woman until they have no more need for her and then they discard her. If she represents a false religious system, then her destruction would take place at the middle of the Tribulation when the Antichrist enters the temple for the world to worship him.

Life stEP There was a time when the Vatican was the most powerful city in Europe. For a short time, another religious center will have temporal power.

Revelation 18:1-8

What is the writer saying?

How can I apply this to my life?

pray Pray that your pastor will have God's wisdom and guidance in the area of counseling.

Chapter 17 seems to emphasize the religious aspect of "Babylon" as the Antichrist's ecumenical movement, the *One-World Church*. Even so, 17:18 still maintains the political connection, as does 18:2 where "Babylon" is viewed as a place where things live. It would seem that chapter 18 emphasizes the political and economic influence of this "city." It is not unusual for a literal city to also represent a philosophy, way of life, or entire government. Therefore, we can't say whether the passage is referring to the ancient geographic location of the city of Babylon (somewhat restored in modern Iraq), a religious center (The Vatican or Jerusalem), a region (the European Union), a commercial center (New York City), or the evil system in general. Just as God urged Lot to flee Sodom, believers are warned to vacate corrupt Babylon (v. 4). Babylon smugly says to herself that she will never be a widow or mourn, implying that her husband (the Antichrist? Satan?) will

always be a victorious soldier. It is fitting that on October 12, 539 B.C. the ancient city of Babylon fell "in one day" as Cyrus of the Persians diverted the river that ran under her walls and sent soldiers into the city by way of the riverbed. At the second coming of Christ, He will speak and the Antichrist and the false prophet will be thrown alive into Hell. The armies will be killed and in a brief period of time, "Babylon" will be punished with utter destruction. Nimrod ("he rebelled") founded Babylon. He is called a "mighty hunter before the Lord" (Genesis 10:9). The phrase can also mean *against the Lord*. Legends claim he was the first idol worshiper and that after his death his wife, Semiramis, miraculously conceived and bore Tammuz, his reincarnation. She was the original *mother goddess*. From Babylon spread this cultic idea, which was eventually absorbed into Roman Catholicism with the adoration of Mary and the Christ child.

Life **stEP** Satan's program changes shape over time but is still recognizable.

Revelation 18:9-19

What is the writer saying?

How can I apply this to my life?

pray Fiji – For ministries to the University of the Pacific in Fiji, which impacts students from each island.

The destruction of the kingdom of the Antichrist and the city that represents his achievements is greatly lamented by those who benefited from her financially. The items listed are typical of any great port city in the first century. John spent time at Ephesus and certainly would have firsthand knowledge of these pleasant, desirable, and decadent luxuries. Since this is a vision and is designed to convey truth through *signs* or symbols, we do not need to imagine each detail happening only as it is described here. The fulfillment will be even more involved than the details provided in this selective report. For instance, it says that the kings of the earth stand a way off from her and lament her destruction. This does not necessitate that every king be present. That others would eventually hear the news or view it on television and mourn would also be included. The implication is that the devastation is so great that whomever was present would react the way these kings and merchants react. This concept would also apply if "Babylon" were not just one city, but representative of the whole kingdom of the Antichrist. As the news gets out about the kingdom's destruction and the inability of the Antichrist to benefit the economies of the world, the whole world slips into depression and mourning. Notice that the destruction is sudden and completed in a short amount of time (v. 10). "Thyine wood" is a dark hardwood used by the ancients for fine furniture. Cinnamon is interesting because in the ancient world it was only grown and exported from Southeast Asia indicating the amazing trade network in John's day.

In addition to all the products, God curiously adds the "souls of men." Is this an elaboration on the horrors of slavery, or is it a frank admission that Babylon as the source of ancient polytheism and the seat of the Antichrist's false religion was a trafficker in the very souls of men?

Revelation 18:20-24

What is the writer saying?

How can I apply this to my life?

While sinners lament on earth, the halls of heaven ring with praise for the destruction of this icon of Satan's attempt to overthrow the kingdom of God. "Apostles" (*sent ones*) only appear in the New Testament. "Prophets" appear in both. Satan has motivated the death of both in history, but in the context it seems to be referring to people living during the tribulation period. The two prophets certainly would be avenged by this destruction. Perhaps the 144,000 would be considered "apostles" in the sense that they were *sent* on their mission and supernaturally protected as they performed their ministry. We must be careful how we express this because the *office of apostle* is defined as someone who had seen the resurrected Lord (Acts 1:22) and performed miraculous signs (2 Corinthians 12:12). This office was limited to the early church as we are built on the *foundation* of the apostles and prophets (Ephesians 2:20).

A heavy stone thrown violently into the sea represents the violent overthrow of Babylon. In addition to earthquakes and volcanoes, modern man is concerned about devastating tsunamis (tidal waves). A wall of water from a sudden shock (landslide, earthquake, or asteroid strike) sends a swell of water outward. In open water the wave does not look like much, but great volumes of water moving at hundreds of miles per hour grow to high walls of water in the shallow coastal areas and violently strike the shore. John is told that joyful sounds will be silenced in that doomed city. Even everyday work sounds, like the grinding of grain, will cease. Babylon will be erased from the earth and from the memory of man. "Sorceries" refers to the magical (demonic) arts, but is the translation of the Greek word "pharmakeia," the root for the English word "pharmaceuticals." Mind-altering drugs are part of Satan's arsenal.

Life **stEP**   Satan was a murderer from the beginning. His world system continued that character flaw but now, hallelujah, she is no more.

Revelation 19:1-8

What is the writer saying?

How can I apply this to my life?

Hallelujah ("alleluia") is such a popular word of praise that it is hard to believe that it only occurs in one chapter in all the New Testament: Revelation 19. There are four hallelujahs: one for salvation (v. 1), one for judgment (v. 3), one for worship (v. 4), and a final one for the sovereignty of God in all these judgments (v. 6). In these verses we have the answer to the question asked by the souls of the martyrs under the altar in Revelation 6:10, "And they cried with a loud voice, saying, How long, O Lord, holy and true, dost thou not judge and avenge our blood on them that dwell on the earth?" The twenty-four elders and four beasts of chapter 4 are still part of the story, here worshiping God in the courts of heaven. We can't tell who the owner of the voice is. It could be one of the four beasts or an unnamed angel. "Our God" almost implies a human, which would be one of the twenty-four elders, but Revelation 7:12 has the four beasts using the phrase "our God" in worship. "Omnipotence" (*all powerfulness*) requires demonstration, otherwise it can't be known by others. It is now an observable characteristic of human affairs. God is obviously on the throne and His will *will* be done on earth as it is in heaven. It is announced that the "marriage of the Lamb" is come. His bride is ready, not just willing but also spiritually qualified. She had been impure, but as a redeemed individual her past has been forgiven and forgotten. She is given white clothing to illustrate her purity. What does the fashion-conscious person wear in heaven? They wear white trimmed with white and are adorned with white accessories!

Nothing can match the beauty and excitement of a bride on her wedding day. What a day that will be when our Savior we will see and our Bridegroom He will be.

Revelation 19:9-16

What is the writer saying?

How can I apply this to my life?

The person talking is not identified beyond the statement that he is a fellow servant and not worthy of the worship due God. He is an angel. Angelic guides are a normal feature of Jewish prophetic literature (cf. Zechariah 1:19; 2:3; 4:1). The angel tells John that those called unto the "marriage supper of the Lamb" are blessed. This, in effect, is what the two witnesses and 144,000 will be doing for the entire seven years of the tribulation period. The "marriage of the Lamb" (v. 7) takes place at the Rapture of the church. In ancient Jewish weddings, for the first seven days after the wedding, the bride was kept in seclusion. At the end of that week, the groom would proudly bring her out of the bridal chamber and introduce her to the wedding guests. They would then enjoy another week of celebration with their guests.

At the second coming of Christ, the bride of Christ will return to the planet to reign with Him. Those who accept Christ as their Savior during the Tribulation will be *friends of the bridegroom*, a designation that John the Baptist used of himself (John 3:29). They will enter the messianic kingdom and rejoice, as the marriage supper of the Lamb will be the first order of business when the 1000-year reign begins. The "spirit" of prophecy refers to its ultimate purpose. The ultimate purpose of the "revelation" of Jesus Christ is the unveiling of His glorious person for all to admire and worship. Revelation 19:11-16 describes this wonderful person as He returns to take possession of His rightful property as per the title deed of chapter 5, namely, planet earth. *A secret name* (v. 12) implies that even in the next mode of existence there will be mysteries to explore and learn. Christ returns to the planet like a Roman general in a triumphal parade of *spoils* before his adoring countrymen. He has His title on His thigh, where a Roman soldier would wear his weapon, the sword.

Life stEP   What a day that will be when the rightful heir returns to His throne.

Revelation 19:17-21

What is the writer saying?

How can I apply this to my life?

The imagery in Revelation is calculated to inspire awe. Here the angel has the sun as his backdrop, implying the glory of God that cannot be directly viewed by mere mortals. Everything is done on a large scale. For the thirteenth time in the book, something is described as "loud." Another feature of inspired Scripture is the intricacies woven into the story line. In Revelation 19:9 we have an invitation to the marriage feast of the Lamb. Here in Revelation 19:17 there is an invitation to the marriage feast of the Antichrist! In this case, it is not humans but rather the carrion-eaters of the avian world that are invited. Humans are invited (16:14) but they are invited to be eaten, not eat. Every stratum of human society winds up on this gruesome banquet table. The Antichrist and false prophet escape becoming a meal only to find themselves cast alive into hell.

Revelation 19:14 pictures the armies of heaven following Christ back to the planet. This is a common Old Testament concept. Jehovah "Sabbaoth" means *Lord of Armies.* "Sabbaoth" is sometimes translated "hosts" or "almighty" which obscures the point that the angels in heaven also perform a military function. Despite all this fire power, which would include both the holy angels and the Church Age saints, notice that only Christ does any fighting, and that by the spoken word. This episode is the conclusion to Satan's complicated maneuverings during the last half of the tribulation period. He has "resurrected" the Antichrist, empowering him to kill the two witnesses, to claim worship from the world, to reject the ecumenical church, and to further his quest for world domination. Satan, knowing that Christ will attempt to return to the planet, wants all available fighters present. He entices the kings of the east to attack the Antichrist. As they prepare to fight each other at Armageddon, they see Christ return and join forces against Him.

All of Satan's efforts are thwarted with just the words of the Lamb.

Revelation 20:1-6

What is the writer saying?

How can I apply this to my life?

Satan, the mastermind, is treated with greater severity than the Antichrist. He is placed in the lowest part of hell. The chains and locked door depict maximum security. Revelation 20 is the first time in Scripture that the messianic reign is said to last for one thousand years. All statements to this point have been open-ended. This number is repeated six times in the chapter, leading some commentators to conclude that it is to be taken as a literal, not symbolic figure. Good and godly men have argued otherwise. A popular conclusion is that the entire Church Age, at least since the A.D. 70 destruction of the temple in Jerusalem is this one *thousand year reign of Christ*. They conclude that the binding of Satan is also figurative, implying a drastic restriction on his activities, but not total inability to function. This interpretation not only handles "a thousand" figuratively, but also many other statements in Scripture about the nature of the messianic reign. We then have the problem of limited men deciding that their multiple and subjective conclusions are better than a literal and objective conclusion, pointing to a specific future scenario. Since the number "a thousand" is used elsewhere (Psalm 90:4) to describe the difference between man's time and God's time there is reason to believe that the number is not arbitrary but purposely chosen. God's original perfect lifespan was one thousand years. Adam sinned and died in the "day" (less than 1,000 years) that he sinned. Now as Christ returns there is a restoration of Eden-like conditions including the lengthening of the human lifespan. This is reinforced by Isaiah's contention that a human struck dead by Christ for disobedience at one hundred years of age has died tragically as a "child" (Isaiah 65:20).

Life **stEP**   In Scripture there are only two options. Either we are saved and part of the "first resurrection" (Old Testament, New Testament, Tribulation and millennial saints) or we are unsaved and part of the "second death."

Revelation 20:7-15

What is the writer saying?

How can I apply this to my life?

pray *Korea – Complete renewing of the mind for South Koreans saved out of Buddhism and Confucianism.*

Elsewhere in Scripture the messianic era is described as a period of blessedness for all mankind (Jew and Gentile) under the benevolent dictatorship of Jesus Christ. He will not tolerate any open rebellion. The Spirit will be poured out on all flesh, and holiness will be the hallmark of that time. Humans will enjoy freedom from disease and natural disasters. There will be no war or crime. Every human need will be met.

Despite these great conditions, there will be humans born during this long period of history who will outwardly conform, but never truly acknowledge the Lordship of Christ over their personal life. At the end of this initial phase of the messianic kingdom, Satan will be released for a brief period, enabling him one final opportunity to spark a rebellion. While seemingly unbelievable, the father of lies will once again succeed in deluding men with their inherited sin nature into joining his cause. The rebels are called "Gog and Magog." These were actual Gentile peoples first mentioned in Genesis 10 and later in Ezekiel 38. In Ezekiel 38, they are involved in an attack on Israel during the tribulation period. The occurrence of the same names does not automatically mean it is the same event. It is not unusual in secular or biblical literature to use one catastrophic human event as an illustration of another. For instance, we say that someone has *met his Waterloo* to refer to a humiliating defeat. This is based on Napoleon's defeat at Waterloo. Likewise, this post-millennial event is presented as similar to the mid-tribulation event of Ezekiel 38. They both involve treachery by Gentiles and conclude with God's enemies in flames. In preparation for *eternity* (by definition, no more babies being born to continue human history) John views the final judgments that result in sinners of all ages receiving their fair trial and assigned degrees of punishment in hell.

Life stEP If you can't make fire fall from heaven and He can, obey Him.

Revelation 21:1-8

What is the writer saying?

How can I apply this to my life?

pray *Germany – For God to remove the blindness of humanism and hostility toward Christianity.*

Human history is complete. Sinners and saints have been evaluated, rewarded, and placed in their respective eternal homes. Several passages describe the renovation of the physical universe to purge it of all vestiges of sinful humanity (cf. 2 Peter 3:10-13). Why would God's heaven need purging? Job 1 pictures Satan and his demons coming to the halls of heaven, so even God's abode will be renovated. John views no sea in the new earth. The "sea" speaks of sinful nations in turmoil. It was also the *front door* by which evil Gentile armies entered Israel. Instead of the false religious system, the harlot of Revelation 17, we now have the New Jerusalem as a bride. Psalm 37:29 promises, "The righteous shall inherit the land." For all eternity, "heaven" will be on earth. In the book of Hosea, God says that Israel will be "lo ammi" because of their rebellion. The phrase means, *not My people*. Now (v. 3) redeemed humanity will be "ammi" (*My people*). The blessedness of heaven includes healed memories. Imagine the release a godly rape victim will experience when that horrible memory will no longer affect her. Some would argue that God has to wipe tears of regret from our eyes. Since this passage is 1007 years after the judgment seat of Christ, that would not be an appropriate conclusion. Even once safely entered into eternity, we are reminded that salvation is a free gift (v. 6). Being "fearful" (v. 8) does not seem like a gross sin worthy of eternal damnation. In context, it is referring to a lack of respect for God and the shame a sinner has in associating with Christ. This "fearful" unbelief condemns an individual to a Christ-less eternity. There are several words for after-life punishment. "Sheol" (Hebrew) and "Hades" (Greek) are the terms for the current place of punishment. Gehenna (Hebrew), hell, and the lake of fire refer to the eternal place of punishment.

Life stEP Heaven will be greater and hell worse than we could ever imagine.

Revelation 21:9-16

What is the writer saying?

How can I apply this to my life?

pray *El Salvador – For believers willing to commit to the discipleship of new converts.*

Earlier in Scripture, the church is called the bride of Christ. Here the eternal abode of the church (the New Jerusalem) is called the bride. It is a glorious sight. John chooses the prettiest gemstones of his day to describe the beauty that he sees. "Jasper" usually has some color (light green) but here it is clear like crystal (no impurities, the impurities impart the color). The city is well protected. It has a high wall, gates, and guardian angels. It is laid out in a square with three gates in each wall. On each gate is inscribed the name of one of the tribes of Israel. Each gate is made of a single pearl (v. 21). Must be amazing oysters to produce those pearls! The city has twelve foundations and on each is the name one of the twelve apostles. This very graphically indicates that while God has a separate program for Old Testament Israel and the New Testament church, both are treated equally as brothers and sisters in Christ for all eternity. The city is huge. The conversion from reeds to miles would give 1500 miles per side. The tabernacle Holy of Holies, where the Shekinah glory of God dwelt, was a cube. Perhaps the three equal dimensions are designed to remind us of God's holiness and His presence with His people. However, the text does not require a cube. It could also be describing a pyramid (which has a square base, v. 16, and in the center rises to the same height as the length and width). Either way, this is a tremendously large object to reside on the planet. The distance of 1500 miles would be from Maine to Florida and the Atlantic to beyond the Mississippi. There are satellites that orbit the earth at an altitude of ninety miles, which makes the height of the city seem amazingly high. Physically, it would be impossible for the current earth to rotate with that lopsided weight, but of course this would be on the new earth designed for such a city.

Life STEP Eye has not seen nor ear heard all that God has prepared for His saints.

Revelation 21:17-27

What is the writer saying?

How can I apply this to my life?

Italy – For perseverance among missionaries, as an average of only 10% return for a second term.

pray

Converting from cubits to feet, the wall would be 216 feet high. That is impressive until you imagine a building towering 1500 miles above it. Note the incidental information that angels (at least when they appear to men) are the same size as men. The wall is made of clear crystal. The city is made of gold, but it is also described as clear glass. Perhaps John is describing the purest, shiniest gold imaginable. It is from this chapter that the popular image of heaven emerges with pearly gates and streets of gold. John goes on to describe the twelve gemstones used for the foundation. The exact identities of these stones are debatable as the various types of gemstones had different names in various periods of human history. It is interesting to remember that the High Priest's breastplate also contained twelve gemstones representing the twelve tribes of Israel.

Several times in chapters 4 through 19 John saw the temple in heaven. In the new heaven, there is no need for a temple. First, everyone is saved so there is no need for the atonement represented by the temple. Second, Satan is no longer entering the courts of heaven so all of heaven itself can now be the temple without fear of any contamination.

In the new heaven there is no need for the sun or moon, for God will provide the light from His person. "Gates" (v. 25) represent both access and safety. However, the city is so safe that they are never closed. The passage talks as if there are people other than the citizens of heaven living on the new earth and coming into the New Jerusalem. It is better to say that among the citizens of the New Jerusalem are kings and representatives of the various nations (Gentiles).

The Old Testament Hebrew society was agricultural, so the Old Testament pictures "heaven" as an agricultural paradise (cf. Zechariah 3:10). The New Testament Greek society honored city life, so it pictures heaven as a city. Actually, heaven will be on the new earth.

Revelation 22:1-7

What is the writer saying?

How can I apply this to my life?

pray · *Bahamas – For committed Christians to stand up and do the Lord's work.*

This sinful world is contaminated with a depressing amount of moral and ecological sewage. In heaven, the moral and ecological climate will be perfect, as pictured by the crystal-clear water flowing from the throne of God. One of the strong arguments for the intelligent design of the universe is the fine-tuning necessary to produce the narrow range of parameters in which biological life can exist. One of those important ingredients is water. A little closer or further away from the sun and our earth would not have water. A large percentage of our body mass is *just* water. We can survive for weeks without food, but only a few days without water. In our eternal home, life-giving water is in abundant supply. Apparently, our glorified bodies will process food. There is no mention of beefsteak, but twelve kinds of fruit that sound refreshing. The tree reminds us of the Garden of Eden, where man's moral problems began. One of the stated reasons for expelling fallen Adam and Eve from the garden was to prevent them from eating of the tree of life and thereby sealing themselves in their fallen state for eternity. Now the saints have returned to Eden and can profitably eat of the tree of life. The leaves are for "healing." If heaven is perfect, why would there be a need for healing? "Healing" does not require a pre-existing sickness. It is a preventative or therapeutic health regimen.

God the Father and Jesus Christ the Lamb both have thrones and are a delight to the citizens of heaven. We will see God face to face. He will be our light. His name, instead of the mark of the beast, will be on our foreheads. The saints will reign. What will they reign over? That is one of the mysteries not revealed in Scripture. Verse 6 begins the conclusion to the whole book. The trustworthiness of the information is affirmed. Christ speaks stating that He will come "quickly" meaning that He can come at anytime, unannounced.

Life step · If these things are so, how then shall we live?

Revelation 22:8-15

What is the writer saying?

How can I apply this to my life?

pray *Pray that God will give your church a greater burden to reach the lost in your community.*

John solemnly reaffirms he indeed observed and heard the prophecies that he wrote. For a second time he tries to show respect for the angel who has guided him through his vision. For a second time the angel reminds him that he is only a fellow servant and that worship should be reserved for God and God alone (cf. 19:10). The angel tells him not to keep the information private, but to share it with all believers. This is different from the command given to Daniel in Daniel 12:4, "But thou, O Daniel, shut up the words, and seal the book, even to the time of the end." The Tribulation information revealed in Daniel was not imminent since so many other things had to happen first. John's prophecy was and still is imminent in that nothing has ever had to happen first before the timeline predicted in Revelation could start. That is why the angel can say, "The time is at hand" and Christ can say, "And, behold, I come quickly." These phrases do not require that Christ come *soon*, but rather that He can come at anytime, and when He comes, it will be abrupt, sudden and then all the events in the book will in succession quickly unfold. These statements of imminent divine intervention would also strengthen the warnings to the seven churches in chapters 2-3. The tribulation period might not start for 2,000 years, but Christ's chastisement upon the church at Laodicea might be fulfilled within a few years.

Verse 11 seems contradictory to God's normal challenge for sinners to repent. Perhaps it is phrased to warn that at any moment the world is liable to be swept into the final judgments and that if you want to be on the side of righteousness you need to be there today, tomorrow will be too late. Christ refers to Himself as "Alpha and Omega" (v. 13), a description that God the Father uses of Himself in Revelation 1:8.

Life stEP The company on the road to hell and outside the gates of heaven is not the sort of people that we would want to have as neighbors!

Revelation 22:16-21

What is the writer saying?

How can I apply this to my life?

It is interesting how the identity of the speaker to the reading audience changes without warning. John is writing it all down, so he is often the speaker (as in 22:8). Sometimes God the Father speaks (1:8). Sometimes Jesus speaks (16:15; 22:7, 12-13, 16, 18). The whole chain of Revelation starts with Jesus (v. 16), goes to an angel, then to John, next to the seven churches of Asia Minor, and finally, down through the centuries to us. In the Old Testament, "the branch" is a messianic title referring to the Messiah's connection with the "soil" of humanity in general and the family of David specifically (cf. Jeremiah 33:15). The "morning star" is the planet Venus because it is the brightest of the heavenly bodies after the moon and is often visible just before dawn. "Lucifer" is the Latin name for "morning star," applied to Satan in Isaiah 14:12 (in the sense that he has attempted to usurp the title). The Messiah is the "light" to the Gentiles (Isaiah 9:1-2). The "Spirit" (v. 17) is the Holy Spirit. The "bride" could be a personification of the New Jerusalem (as in 21:9), implying that the city calls out for more inhabitants. It could also refer to believers (as in 19:7) and would be a timeless representation of one believer calling another of the elect to salvation. This is illustrated by the next phrase, "And let him that heareth say, Come." Verse 18 pronounces a curse on those who tamper with the material. Some commentators have tried to use this as proof that the Book of Revelation is the final book of inspired information in human history. However, the word "book" is the Greek word for "booklet" and therefore refers only to the Book of Revelation, not the whole Bible. In fact, an identical statement occurs in Deuteronomy 4:2 and 12:32. It obviously means that nothing should be taken away from or added to the information in that book. Only an unsaved person would do so, hence the warning of eternal damnation.

Life **STEP**   "Maranatha" (1 Corinthians 16:22) is Aramaic for *Our Lord Comes!*

Disobedience...
Domination...
Deliverance

Disobedience...
Domination...
Deliverance

Disobedience...
Domination...
Deliverance

So goes the cyclical pattern of this historical narrative. The book contrasts God's faithfulness with Israel's disobedience and apostasy.

The book covers the period of Israel's history from the death of Joshua (after the Exodus, forty years of Wilderness Wanderings, and conquest of the Canaanite nations) to the first king of Israel, Saul. A chief feature is that the Twelve Tribes failed to drive out the Canaanite peoples like God had commanded and eventually intermarried with them as God feared leading to religious and spiritual compromise.

The Hebrew term for "Judges" means "deliverers." There are thirteen Judges including Samuel who is also a prophet. Some of the Judges ministered at the same time in different parts of the country. We often speak of the "400 years of the Judges with seven cycles of spiritual highs and lows" but the actual time covered in the book is closer to 330 years.

There is no way of knowing for sure who wrote Judges as the writer is never identified. Later Jewish tradition states that Samuel wrote the book. The key for us is that godly men and women in ancient history trusted the original author and his material and therefore the book has consistently been received as inspired scripture by Jews and Christians alike.

Each cycle takes the nation of Israel further and further from God. The book itself is thematic rather than chronological. The foremost theme is seen in God's power and deliverance of the people (by His covenant mercy) from the consequences of their sinful disobedience.

Key Verse: Judges 21:25 "In those days there was no king in Israel: every man did that which was right in his own eyes."

Outline of Judges
I. The Prologue -- The Disobedience of Israel (1)
II. The Judgment of Israel (2:1-3:6)
III. The Deliverers of Israel
   A. First Cycle (3:7-11)
   B. Second Cycle (3:12-31)
   C. Third Cycle (4, 5)
   D. Fourth Cycle (6:1-8:32)
   E. Fifth Cycle (8:33-10:5)
   F. Sixth Cycle (10:6-12:15)
   G. Seventh Cycle (13-16)
IV. The Epilogue -- The Disunity in Israel (17-21)

Sunday 20

Judges 2:1-12

What is the writer saying?

How can I apply this to my life?

pray — Finland – For more Finns to respond to the call to full – time Christian service and missions.

Today's passage jumps into the middle of the long introduction to the book of Judges (v. 1:1 to 3:8). Judges was written when David was king and after the 330-year time period of the Judges had ended.

As Joshua had earlier instructed (v. 1:1), the two southern tribes, Judah and Simeon, had began to drive out the "remaining" Canaanites (Joshua 13:1). At first they had victory albeit incomplete; they "could not drive out the inhabitants ... who had chariots of iron" (v. 1:20). Next, the other tribes of Israel also all failed to "drive out the inhabitants" that still dwelt in their portions of the new land.

We begin with the "Angel of the LORD" reminding all of Israel of their promise, made before Joshua died, to keep God's Covenant (see Joshua 24). However, Israel had already begun to break these commands:

▶ Yet, the Lord "will never break His covenant" with Israel. He had kept His part of the "contract" when he had made of this "slave people" a new nation. His past blessings now remind them of their duty!

▶ Israel was to make "no league" with the Canaanites (v. 2). Even so, they made the Canaanites (v. 30, 33) paid "tribute" (v. 28, i.e. "taxes"). Thus, when Israel "was strong" (v. 1:28), they choose to make a profit rather than to obey God.

▶ Israel was to "throw down the altars" (v 2) of the Canaanite gods. They did not, and soon they were "serving" the god, Baal, and goddess, Ashtoreth (vv. 11, 13), at these Canaanite altars!

▶ Israel recognized their sin and "lifted up their voices and wept" [the place was called "Bochim"; "place of weepers"].

▶ When Israel did not drive out the Canaanites completely, this enemy became the "leaven" that affects the entire "loaf of the bread" of Israel.

Life stEP — Oh, that all would consider the lesson here taught of the fearful consequences, not merely of commissions of sin, but of omissions of duty, such as prove so fatal to Israel! What have you allowed in your life that is a disregard to God? How can you make things right?

Judges 2:13-23

What is the writer saying?

How can I apply this to my life?

pray Germany – Pray for theologically sound Bible schools and staff to emerge for the training of workers.

Today's passage continues the long introduction to Judges. Now it presents Israel's second failure to "*keep the way of the LORD to walk therein*" (v. 22). Listen again to the final command of Joshua to the former generation, "Now therefore fear the LORD, and *serve* him in *sincerity* and in *truth*" (Joshua 24:14). 3 times over the next several verses the people declare, "We will serve the Lord (24:18, 21, 24). The section closes with an observation that "Israel served the LORD ... all the days of the elders that over lived Joshua" (24:31).

While the older generation was committed to a *way of life* where "We serve the LORD; for He is our God" (Joshua 24:18), this next generation "turned quickly out of the *way* which their fathers walked in, obeying the commandments of the LORD" (v. 17). These took a *different way* when they "forsook the LORD, and served Baal and Ashtaroth" (v. 13).

Our introductory passage reviews "Cycle of the Judges" that will be repeated seven times in this book. Judges defines the Cycles as follows:
(1)   The Cycle begins with *Sin*, identified by the repeating phrase, "Israel did evil in the sight of the LORD" (v. 11).
(2)   Secondly, as a result of their sin, the LORD "*delivered them* into the hands" (v. 14) of the enemies around Israel for a time of *Servitude*.
(3)   After a time of "*distress*" (v. 15), the people would "cry unto the LORD" (e.g., 3:9) bringing a prayer of *Supplication* to the LORD.
(4)   Then the LORD brings *Salvation* to His people as He "*raised up judges* to delivered them out of the hand of the spoilers" (v. 16).
(5)   Lastly, there is *Silence* during a period of *rest* for a specified number of years, e.g., 3:31, "and the land had *rest* for "X #" of years."

Life stEP There is a principle here for us Christians: Disobedience results in sad consequences and personal "distress." Notice also that the Lord will respond when we "cry unto the Lord" asking for forgiveness and help to deliver us from our troubles (e.g., see 1 John 1:9). For what sin-induced troubles do you need to ask God for forgiveness and deliverance?

Judges 6:1-10

What is the writer saying?

How can I apply this to my life?

Today we jump to the fourth "*Cycle of the Judges*" [We did not cover the "judgeships" of Othniel, Ehud, and Deborah [with Barak].

Again Israel "did evil in the sight of the LORD" (v. 1) so God punishes His people by "delivering" Israel to the Midianites, allowing the Midianites to "prevail" (v. 1,2) for seven years (likely 1169 to 1162 BC). The Midianites "oppressed" Israel by annually "sweeping" through central parts of Israel at the time of harvest to consume or destroy Israel's harvest (v. 3-4). The people of Israel were unable to resist, they fled to caves in the mountains and becoming "greatly impoverished" (v. 6).

When Israel "cried unto the LORD" (v. 6), God responded by sending an *unnamed* "*prophet*" (v. 8) and then by sending *Gideon* as a *Judge* (v. 11). Likely this unnamed "*prophet*" moved from one community to the next in the areas most affected by the Midianite "destruction" as the "prophet" repeatedly delivered his message from God.

We are given only a summary of the *prophet's* 2-part message: First, he reviews what God had done some 300 years earlier when:

1. God "delivered" Israel up out of their "bondage" in Egypt (v. 8-9).

2. Next, God "drove out from before" Israel the several peoples who resisted Israel as Israel approached their Promised Land.

3. And finally, God "drove out" all Canaanite nations who had been dwelling in the Land promised to Israel (v. 9).

Second, the *prophet* points out the source of Israel's troubles:

1. The people of Israel were "fearing the gods of the Amorites," which is to say Israel was breaking the *First Commandment*; "Thou shalt have *no other gods* before me" (Deuteronomy 5:7).

2. Thus Israel had not been "obeying the voice" of the LORD (v. 10).

Judges 6:11-24

What is the writer saying?

How can I apply this to my life?

Our passage deals with the LORD's quiet but persistent calling out of *Gideon* to do the His special service. The Lord used this unexpected approach to transform Gideon's lack of faith in God.

When the angel of the LORD [an Old Testament appearance of Jesus!] appeared to Gideon, he was threshing wheat in the wine press.

Gideon's actions point out the distress of the people of Israel as they were being *oppressed* by the Midianite "raiders"! Normally farmers would thresh wheat on hilltops "threshing floors." The grain was repeated tossed in the air to allow the chaff to blow away, leaving just grain behind. All of this produced lots of noise, dust, and unwanted attention!

So Gideon was working quietly in a secluded wine press [a walled, outdoor "factory" at the bottom of a hillside]. Since there would be little wind here, lots of chaff would be left in the finished grain.

But it was better to endure a little chaff so as to keep your grain and your life!

Notice the Lord's patient prodding of Gideon; He says, "The LORD is with thee, thou *mighty man of valor*" (v. 12). What irony! A "man of valor" hiding in the winepress! Yet the Lord also saw more in Gideon. It was the Lord's intent to instill into Gideon the valor he would need!

Again, the Lord repeats," I will be with thee" (v. 16) to enable you to "smite the Midianites" (v. 16). To which Gideon requests a sign to confirm the Lord's promise. He requested for his Visitor to wait while Gideon prepared a large banquet-like meal of goat-meat and bread (v. 19). When the meal was placed before the Angel, he raised His staff, which "consumed" the meal by fire. This provided Gideon the sign, which he had requested (v. 17; Lev. 9:24; 1 Kings 18:38).

Life stEP

Do you believe God can use you? How has God been *nudging* you along to make you into the mighty person of faith? While Gideon required a sign to confirm the Lord's strengthening, the Lord will work in quiet ways to demonstrate his faithfulness to you. How has the Lord shown Himself faithful to you?

Judges 6:25-40

What is the writer saying?

How can I apply this to my life?

pray   *Ghana – Development of harmonious relationships between national pastors and missionaries.*

On the same night that Gideon built an altar to the LORD (v. 6:24), God told him to destroy another one – the altar of *Baal* (v. 25). *Baal*-worship was the primary "evil" that Israel had done in the "sight of the LORD" (v. 1), which had brought on the present "Cycle of Oppression."

The worship of *Baal, the storm god*, the *"Bringer of Rains,"* centered on the growing of crops, multiplying herds, and having children.

When we compare the strange inconsistencies of Gideon's father, Joash, *before* (v. 25, 27) and *after* (v. 31) Gideon's "casting down" of the Baal altar, we see that Israel's problem was not their abandonment of *Jehovah* but rather their adding on of a worship of *Baal*, which was forbidden by the First Commandment (Deuteronomy 5:7). *Gideon's First Assignment* was to purify his father's household from idolatry while at the same time offering a burnt offering, which sanctified ["to set apart"] his own life as a Judge called by *Jehovah*. The best explanation for the *"second bullock of 7-years"* (v. 25) would seem to be that the Lord instructed Gideon to take the younger ["second in age"] of the father's 2 oxen, which was *7 years old*, and sacrifice it as a declaration that Jehovah intended to use Gideon as a Judge to save Israel from the *7-year oppression* of the Midianites (see v. 1).

For the first time, Gideon's father, Joash, now stands up with "believing courage" in *Jehovah* and defended his son (v. 31). We suspect that his son's courage fueled Joash's own renewal of faith in Jehovah as he also turns away from his trust in *Baal*, the "Bringing of Harvests"!

Thus a new name was given to Gideon, "Jerubbaal" which means "Let Baal Fight." Since *Baal* could not harm Gideon, this name became a title of honor for Gideon, who had fought against Baal.

How can you, like Joash, have a clear testimony in your world? Are things in your life that have caused you to have an *inconsistent walk* with the Lord Jesus? Is there someone you could call today, someone with a faith like Gideon's, who could help you regain your own "believing courage" and confidence in God's faithfulness?

Friday 20

Judges 7:1-14

What is the writer saying?

How can I apply this to my life?

In this chapter we have the account of a remarkable battle. The enemy troops numbered 135,000 (Judges 8:10). God's people totaled 32,000 (v. 3). The ratio of 4 to 1! Yet the Lord says to Gideon, "The people that are with thee are too many ..." (v. 2). The Lord intended to make it clear that God alone was to receive credit for the coming victory.

Incredibly the Lord *twice* orders a reduction in the size of the army of Israel. In the second reduction, Gideon was to observe how his men drank at a river; only those used their hands to lap up water like a dog [implying alert and ready to respond to an emergency] were retained.

Gideon was left with 300 men (v. 7). Now the ratio was 400 to 1! Clearly the victory was to be the Lord's, not men's (see Psalm 115:1f). Add to this the fact that his men had no conventional weapons; resulting in the most unusual confrontation. With a trumpet in one hand and a pitcher in the other, the troops went off to battle. Yet, Gideon's "faith" (see Hebrews 11:32) in the Lord's promise of victory remained steadfast.

God's point is clear; mere numbers themselves are no guarantee of success; it is the presence of the Lord that ensures victory and success (Leon Morris). Similarly, the Lord is making the point that He is able to do marvelous things with even just a handful of dedicated believers.

Consider the contrasting use of the word "saved" in v. 2 and in v. 7. The Hebrew word, "yaw-shah" is used over 200 times in the Bible. It is used in the literal sense here, meaning, "To delivers, rescue, save, or defend" [i.e., to cause to be safe and free from a danger]. It is also used in a spiritual sense: (1) negatively it means, "Being saved from God's judgment upon the sins." Also, (2) positively, it means, "changing the character of a person to reflect the character of God."

Life stEP — Have you ever wondered why God was working in seemingly odd ways in your life? Often God wants you to learn the same lesson of faith as seen here and God wants you to know that the results are His doing! So then, how has God been directing in your life? And how can you properly respond by faith to what He has directed you to do?

Judges 7:15-25

What is the writer saying?

How can I apply this to my life?

pray — Guatemala – For the rapid and accurate completion of the 17 Bible translation projects in progress.

Our story of Gideon continues with an assurance from the LORD. The Lord instructs Gideon (v. 9) to slip into the Midianite camp at night. Gideon, by divine arrangement, overhears the "telling of a dream" (v. 13-14) by one Midianite to another of the "armed men of the host" [v. 11, likely a reference to the disciplined elite corps of the Midianite army].

By this Gideon knew that the superstitious Midianites were fearful that their fates had been sealed. The "tumbling" round loaves of "barley bread" (v. 13) could only mean one thing; God was going to "deliver" the Midianites to army of Israel who would "roll over" them.

Gideon divides his little army into 3 companies. They were to take trumpets and lamps hidden inside pitchers as they approach the sleeping enemy. When the trumpets blow, the men were to shout, "the sword of the LORD, and of Gideon!", break their pitchers, and hold up their lamps.

The signal was given after the beginning of the 2nd watch [v. 19, thus at 10 PM.]. This would add to the confusion when returning troops were interpreted as infiltrators who had already penetrated the dark camp!

Each was to "stand in his place" (v. 21) like "pathfinders" who were marking the lanes that would use to "roll down" upon the Midianites.

Since the Midianite army was an "alliance of convenience" between the Midianites, the Amalekites, and the Arabians of the deserts (v. 12), when "every man's sword was against his fellow" (v. 22) likely some were suspicious that other had betrayed them and joined the Israelites.

After the battle, the Midianites fled southeast towards the Jordan River. The formerly fearful "men of Israel" from northern Israel gathered to "pursue" the Midianites (v. 23). Messengers were sent to "all Ephraim" [v. 24, a large Israelite tribe in central Israel] to join in the pursuit. Gideon wanted Ephraim's men to "take" [i.e., "block"] the routes that would be used by the retreating Midianites "before they" could arrive (v. 24).

Life Step — Are you facing fearful things in your life, as did Gideon and the army of Israel? Remember, in your fear and weakness, God desires to shine. God is looking for modern Gideons who will trust Him. How can you by faith allow the Lord to work in you and through you today?

Judges 8:22-35

What is the writer saying?

How can I apply this to my life?

pray *Hungary – For the Church to mature in its ability to evangelize and overcome feelings of inferiority that restrain boldness in its witness.*

Three events are given here as a summary of the lengthy remainder of Gideon's continuing "Judgeship."

First, we find the "men of Israel" (v. 22) offering Gideon to take the position as king. This attitude would continue in Israel; they wanted the continuity of a royal family and a monarchy. 100 years later the nation gathers to ask the last Judge, Samuel, for a king (1 Samuel 8:4-5). Gideon responded properly by declining; "the Lord shall rule over you" (v. 23)! Any desire to achieve personal glory was set aside as Gideon recognized his own duty and God's place of supreme honor.

Second, Gideon then does an odd thing; he asks for a portion of the spoils taken from the Midianites. Gideon was given 42 pounds of gold! With it he makes an "ephod" (v. 27a, an elaborate 2-side apron).

While King David later wears a similar "breast-plate" [also called an "ephod"], as commonly worn by civil magistrates (1 Chronicles 15:27), the root idea in Israel of an 'ephod" refers back to the "apron" which only the high priest was to wear (Exodus 28:6). So it would seem that Gideon, by wearing this politically powerful symbol, was competing for power and prestige with either the priests or princes of Israel!

Thirdly, the "ephod" became a source of sin for Israel as they went "whoring after it" (v. 27). This means they became unfaithful to God by "prostituting" themselves to it as a substitute to the true worship of God at the Tabernacles. Just as Gideon was not to be Israel's king, neither was he to be their high priest! Since Gideon and all Israel knew this, the "thing" became a snare (v. 27) unto him, his family, and Israel!

In spite of Gideon's incomplete faithfulness, the text closes with a *final observation.* God blessed Gideon and Israel with "quietness" during the next 40 years of his judgeship.

It is so easy to be like Gideon. Sometimes we avoid personal pride as we give true glory to God alone. Then we do "odd things" and seek personal advancement, power, and prestige. What is there in your life that is threatening to be a substitute for your true worship and honoring of God? How can you give God honor by your conduct?

Monday 21

Judges 13:1-14

What is the writer saying?

How can I apply this to my life?

pray — Italy – Pray for godly officials in a government believed to receive 23 billion annually from extortion.

Here we see the announcement of Samson's birth and that he was to be "set apart" for special task, he would *begin to deliver Israel"* (v. 5).

The story of Samson is given more space (chapters 13 to 16) than any other Judge. In several ways he was unique amongst the Judges:

• The 40 years of Philistine oppression was the longest (v. 13:1).

• Only Samson was called to his task before his birth (v. 5).

• Only Samson's "judgeship" did not include a time of "rest" for Samson did not deliver Israel from their oppressor, the Philistines. Rather, Samson was called to "begin to deliver" Israel (v. 5).

• Only Samson died in the hands of Israel's oppressor (16:20). Note that the prophecy his parents received indicated that the deliverance, which Samson was to "begin," was to be at a time in the future. It is also important to notice the character of parents of Samson in that it fell to them to faithfully bring up this deliverer of Israel:

• Samson's mother was, for his sake, required to practice the rigid abstinence of the Nazarite Law (Numbers 6:3). Also notice her great spiritual insight, easing the needless fears of her husband (v. 23).

• Samson's father, Manoah, responds with a time of intense prayer desiring that the LORD might "teach" them what they were to "do" (v. 8). Manoah's actions were prompted not by anxieties but by "his great desire to follow the instructions given" (Jamieson, Fausset, Brown).

• Manoah and his wife were just ordinary people of faith ("a certain man," v. 2) who took serious their responsibility to carry out the Lord's will. For almost 20 years their lives would be an example to us of a couple that illustrates the declaration of the Lord Jesus, "Blessed are they that have not seen and yet have believed" (John 20:29).

Life stEP — We too must consider what we must do to carry out the Lord's will for our lives. How can you follow Manoah's example of faith? What important issues in your life need your intense prayer as you seek clarity how the Lord would have you proceed in these matters?

Judges 13:15-14:4

What is the writer saying?

How can I apply this to my life?

pray | *Honduras – For God to provide the teaching staff and funding needed to keep Bible schools operating.*

The Story of Samson continues with a 2-verse summary of his early days and youth (13:24-25). The story tells us these few details:

▸ Like Gideon, Manoah is given an authenticating sign; in this case the Angel ascended in the midst of the flames of the "burnt offering" (v. 16). Thus Manoah came to know his visitor was "God" (v. 22) and he was confident that the Angel's message was true.

▸ A woman, who had been barren, "bore a son" (v. 24) as promised.

▸ As the child, Samson (v. 24), "grew," he was raised with *careful and vigilant instruction* in that he was to "begin to deliver Israel" (v. 13:5).

▸ Somehow as Samson grew, others saw that he was "blessed" of the Lord (v. 24). The Lord was preparing the child for the task ahead.

▸ Perhaps as a teen, the "Spirit" began to "move" Samson (v. 25; meaning "to impel" = "to be driven forward"). Thus the Spirit began to impart upon Samson his unique "tool" for ministry; his great strength.

Samson first used this Spirit-supplied strength at his marriage to a Philistine girl. The story tells us that he sees a woman from the Philistine town of Timnah and he tells his parents that he wants her for a wife. They rightly protest (v. 14:3; Deut. 7 3-4)! But Samson would not listen.

Note that the text makes it clear that this was *divinely arranged*, "of the LORD," for the wedding was to provide an "occasion against the Philistines" (v. 4). Thus Samson was doing something *great* and *good* by means that were *selfish* and *evil* [obviously not a pattern we are to follow!]. It was the Lord who worked it out to fulfill His *good* purposes.

Sadly Samson was held by his *fleshly desires*; a pattern we see throughout his life. He saw the woman and she "pleased him well" (v. 3). Samson was not thinking that she was wise and virtuous woman but rather he saw something in her appearance that caught his fancy.

How is the Lord Jesus *impelling* you to "*move forward*" in your life? An important key is to carefully listen to the wise counsel of the godly people around you! Who has the Lord put in your life as a source of counsel? And how can you better listen to their guidance or warnings?

Judges 14:5-20

What is the writer saying?

How can I apply this to my life?

Let's begin with a question: Since Samson demanded of his parents, "*get her for me*," why then did he "*go down*" to her town of Timnath for the marriage? It seems that Manoah had gone with Samson (v. 5) to arrange a marriage contract with the woman's family. Only after such an agreement would Samson have been allowed to "*talk*" to her (v. 7).

It also seems that the Philistine family did not wholly endorse this marriage. Thus an Arabic "sadiqa" marriage was arranged, i.e., the wife stayed with her family and the husband was allowed to visit her (15:1).

Notice also that the 30 "companions" [including his "best-man"! v. 20] were Philistine men and not, as customary, Samson's kinsmen and friends. Clearly, "*when they saw him*" (v. 11) to be a strong, mighty man, they brought these 30 "*companions*" as guards for the family's safety!

Let's ask a second question: Why did Samson, a Nazarite, wander away from his parents to be alone in a vineyard (v. 6)? Likely, he was purchasing the wine for the coming wedding "*feast*" [v. 10, literally, "a drinking"]! Since wine was expressly forbidden for a Nazarite, Samson seems to have wanted to do this disobedient act apart from his parents!

And yet, it is here amidst Samson's "*dubious detour*," that the "*Spirit of the LORD came mightily upon him*" (v. 6) allowing Samson, without a sword, to kill a powerful, young lion. Obviously, the LORD wanted Samson to know his strength so as not to fear the great dangers ahead!

The phrase "*after a time he returned*" (v. 8) implies *about a year*. A year's betrothal was also according to custom. Likewise, a year would be necessary for carrion animals to hollow out the carcass, bees to then make in their beehive, and stock it with honey from which Samson would take, eat, and to give to his parents. By this Samson blatantly violates a second Nazarite requirement; not to touch anything dead.

Twice here Samson blatantly ignored what he knew to be right and good as he chooses to do what is clearly against the principles that defined his life! How about you? Are you making choices that also ignore what you clearly know to be right and good? What choices are before you? How can you, with God's help, avoid "*dubious detours*"?

Thursday 21

Judges 15:1-20

What is the writer saying?

How can I apply this to my life?

Paraguay – For God to call laborers to the more than 400 interior villages that remain unreached.

"… in the time of wheat harvest" (v. 1), i.e., the end of May. The *"shocks"* [v. 5, stacked grain] were still in the fields. It was the dry season!

What were Samson's motives for his exploits here? Was it revenge? Was it pure anger? Or were these controlled actions intended by Samson to further his God-given mission? Consider the following:

▶ Previous, we saw Samson's anger "kindled" (v. 14:19). But not here!

▶ If he was uncontrollably "angry," he would have taken revenge upon the father-in-law and challenged the new husband to a "duel"!

▶ Yet he takes no immediate action. The story begins "a while after"; likely several months time. Samson had time to think, to plan.

▶ As a Judge, Samson was God's agent for the "delivering of Israel" (v. 13:5). So likely, on returning for his wife, he was seeking an occasion against the *Philistines people* and not just *the woman's family.*

▶ Also Samson, a judge of Israel, devised a plan where the Philistines would retaliate against *him* personally and not *his nation,* Israel.

After setting fire to their harvest, Samson retires to Etam, in Judah. When the Philistines pursue, the Judeans, fearful of them, bind Samson and give him to them. Notice that the Judeans were not held responsible for Samson's act of "personal" revenge. Samson submitted to the Judeans but, after he is given to the Philistines, "the Spirit of the LORD came mightily upon him" and he kills 1000 of them with a jawbone!

After the victory and in great thirst, Samson, first declares that God had provided this victory. Then he cries out to God for water. So God provides water by splitting the rocks. This making an important spiritual point that even the strongest man is still dependent upon God (v. 18)!

When offended, does your anger get "kindled"? Do you act rashly and foolishly? Then consider this question: How can you delay your response so that you may consider your responsibilities as an "agent" of the Lord Jesus? Since you are His ambassador in your world, how can you be an "agent" for what is right, good, and glorifying to Him?

189

Judges 16:1-17

What is the writer saying?

How can I apply this to my life?

Today we begin with an unusual incident of Samson carrying away the gates of a Philistine city (v. 1-3). We are *picking up* the story after Samson had *quietly* "judge Israel ... 20 years" (v. 15:20 &16:31).

Earlier events (ch 14 & 15) covered about 2 years and these later events cover up to 3 years. Leaving 5-years of Samson's *quiet judging* in Israel. Likely the Philistines were satisfied with this *quiet peace*.

Yet Samson again goes to the Philistines as he "sought an occasion against them" (v. 14:4). Apparently, their fear of Samson dimmed. God intended to use Samson's strength to again "deliver" Israel.

Observe 4 things concerning Samson's entering the Philistine city:

1. Some 16 years before they had tried to take him by force and he had killed a 1000 of them. Yet here they attempt the same thing!

2. In that Samson left the harlot at midnight instead of waiting until morning as the Philistines expected, Samson was likely spiritually troubled by his own spiritual weakness after his sin with the harlot.

3. We must conclude that Samson, with a repentant heart after submitting to sin, had returned to his life's purpose of furthering God's will to "begin to deliver Israel" (13:5) from the Philistines.

4. Thus we come to understand the purpose of Samson in tearing off the city's gates and carrying them back to the Judean provincial capital of Hebron: By this phenomenal feat of strength the nature of the true God of Heaven was being declared.

Leon Wood aptly notes, "It is sad, by true, that God often finds necessary the use of His servants, in spite of the fact that there is serious sin in their lives. ... Despite the fact that Samson had fallen into such an entrapment of Satan, God would ... accomplishing His goal. ... How shameful for Samson that this has to be the case!" (The Distressing Days of the Judges, p. 327)

Life **stEP** Christian friend, God, because of His greatness, will use you in spite of your own sin. Yet a much better path of life for you is to walk a holy life that faithfully seeks His purpose for you! Take some time now to talk to God, asking Him to forgive you and enable you to serve Him.

Judges 16:18-17:6

What is the writer saying?

How can I apply this to my life?

pray   *Germany – For youth ministries to develop creative and relevant means of sharing the Gospel.*

Samson has now fallen in love with a third Philistine woman, *Delilah* (v. 16:4). She however is a shrewd prostitute in the business of making money and only pretended to love Samson. Soon she accepts an offer by the Philistines to "entice him" to tell the secret of his strength (v. 5).

Samson knew he was in a risky game (v. 16). Repeatedly he gave dishonest answers to her incessant requests. But Delilah was also being dishonest when she declares, "The Philistines are upon you" (v. 9, 12, 14) for she was cautiously testing him, not giving a signal to the men in hiding.

We must conclude that Samson was aware of her deceit and of the men "lying in wait." Yet, we only see his pride, self-confidence, and careless attitude towards sin; "I can play and win this game."

Yet Delilah is persistent in her task, for Samson's "soul becomes vexed unto death" (v. 16). And so Samson reveals his source of strength. Delilah again has him sleep on her lap while the seven locks of his head are shaved off. He didn't even know he had lost his strength! Perhaps if Samson had not been so *blind* to his sin, he would have kept his *sight*!

And so Samson pays the price for being a fool; they put out his eyes (v. 21)! Yet he had trusted a woman that he knew was full of deceit. So Samson lost the risky game! He also lost his pride and self-confidence.

The Philistines brought him to Gaza (v. 21), bound with chains, and made him grind grain in his prison. They also made "sport" of him (v. 25).

But there is good news. Note that God quietly gave Samson a second chance, "the hair on his head began to grow again" (v. 22)!

During these days of shame Samson repented, "O Lord God … may I be avenged of the Philistines for my eyes" (v. 28). As he destroys their temple and dies with the Philistines (v. 30), he has his greatest victory.

Although we too fail and sin against our Lord, He is still quick to forgive us as well (1 John 1:9). Have you, like Samson, act foolishly as you played "risky games" with sin in your own life? Why not, like Samson, confess those sins to God so that God might forgive you too!

There are twelve *Minor Prophets*, so called, not because they are unimportant, but because they are smaller than the *Former Prophets* (Moses, Joshua, Judges, 1 & 2 Samuel and 1 & 2 Kings) and the *Major Prophets* (Isaiah, Jeremiah, Ezekiel, and Daniel). The Minor Prophets cover some of the same themes as the other prophets, but in addition, they emphasize social justice and true worship. Nine of the Minor Prophets were written before the destruction of the Temple in 586 B.C. while the last three were written after the return from the Babylonian Exile (the *Post-Exilic Prophets*—Haggai, Zechariah, and Malachi). One was written against the country of Edom (Obadiah). Two books were written about Nineveh (Jonah and Nahum). Two other books condemn the Northern Kingdom or Israel (Hosea and Amos). Seven are directed to the Southern Kingdom or Judah (Joel, Micah, Habakkuk, Zephaniah, Haggai, Zechariah, and Malachi).

Amos was a Judean farmer sent to preach against the apostasy in the Northern Kingdom of Israel. His home was in Tekoa, about ten miles south of Jerusalem. He calls himself a "herdman" and a "gatherer of sycamore fruit" (*figs*, 7:14). He also states that he was not a "prophet, neither was I a prophet's son" (7:14), but he nevertheless demonstrates a sharp wit, knowledge of international affairs, and a solid knowledge of the Word of God. He ministered during the reign of wicked King Jeroboam II (793-753 BC) who had a residence in Bethel. In Judah, the king was Uzziah (792-740 BC), who was somewhat godly, and apparently a hero to Isaiah (Isaiah 6:1). Both kings enjoyed long reigns and prosperous times. It may be that Jeroboam felt that Jehovah was blessing him as both Elisha and Jonah had predicted a time of physical blessing for the northern kingdom (cf. 2 Kings 13:14-19 and 14:25). Amos condemns Jeroboam's misuse of his success and wealth. Hosea was a resident of the Northern Kingdom who also condemned Jeroboam and Israel about this same time. Amos gives no indication of knowing Hosea or Isaiah (Isaiah was part of the aristocracy in Jerusalem). He does, however, include Jerusalem and Judah in his prophecies, but his primary focus is on the sins of the Northern Kingdom. After King Solomon, the nation was divided. The ten northern tribes never had a godly king. Their first king, Jeroboam I (931-910 BC) did not want his citizens going across the border to worship at the Temple in Jerusalem, so he erected a Temple to his god, the golden calf, in Bethel about twelve miles north of Jerusalem. Ironically, *Bethel* means House of God. It was the place where God gave Jacob the vision of the ladder ascending to heaven. Amos's name means, burden. Despite his lowly background as a farmer, God burdened him over the sins of his people. The theme of his book is *Repent or Perish*. The outline of the book is:

Judgment on the Nations	1-2
Judgment on Israel	3-6
Symbolic Visions	7-9:10
Final Blessing	9:11-15

Amos 1:1-2; 3:1-7

What is the writer saying?

How can I apply this to my life?

Amos was a unique person. His background as a herdsman and gatherer of fruit makes him a most interesting person. He was, in every sense of the word, a layman called by God to preach a most unpopular message. He was from Judah but prophesied to the Northern Kingdom during the reign of Jeroboam II. Conditions were the *best ever* as far as prosperity was concerned, but they were at a low ebb spiritually. When you read the book, you are impressed that he was humble, industrious, observant, honest, and very simple and clear in his message.

In chapter three Amos speaks of their guilt. He makes it clear that where there is privilege, there is also responsibility. The words "You only have I known" (v. 2) are important. Israel had a special place in the heart of God, but they had sinned. (See the word "therefore.") Both cause and effect follow in vivid descriptions. 1. The lion that roars (3:4) shows the effect of the cause; he has taken something. The lesson is: God will warn them when He is prepared to act in judgment. 2. The snare (cause) (3:5) is laid for a bird to fall into it (effect). The lesson: God will use various instruments against those who disobey. 3. The trumpet is blown (cause) (3:6) and the people are afraid (effect). 4. The evil (calamity) in the city (cause) (3:6b) means that the Lord has done it (effect). God was about to judge His people who had forgotten how to do right.

Life **stEP**

We are also *known to the Lord* (see John 10:27). We are special to Him. But with that relationship comes responsibility. "Whom the Lord loveth he chasteneth" (Hebrews 12:6). Let's stay sensitive to His will and His Word to avoid such calamity.

Amos 4:1-13

What is the writer saying?

How can I apply this to my life?

pray Uruguay – For God to reveal truth in a land where spiritists and cultists outnumber true believers.

Strong language — verses 1-3
One couldn't find stronger language to describe the luxury-living women in Amos's day. They are called, "...ye kine (cows) of Bashan..." (v. 1). The cows in this area were known for their well-fed condition. The women *were wanton women of Zion* (see Isaiah 3:16-26; 32:9-13).

Irony and judgment — verses 4-5
Amos uses irony to drive home his point. This isn't a real invitation to sin. The Lord was exposing hypocrisy. He was taunting them for being so careful in their ritual and yet so very sinful in their daily life.

Won't you ever learn? — verses 6-13
The word "yet" is the key to the paragraph. We find the Lord listing all His dealings with Israel – hunger (v. 6), drought (v. 7), mildew and blasting (v. 9), locusts (v. 10), and wars (v. 10b)..."yet have ye not returned unto me."(v. 9b). It was as if the Lord

was saying, *What is it going to take to get you to turn again to me and stop your evils ways?* The answer is found in the "therefore" of verse 12.

The bottom line is "prepare to meet thy God" (v. 12). The Lord was about to bring His hand hard and heavy on His people.

Life stEP
Anyone who does not know Christ as Savior *will* meet the Lord as Judge. This is applicable in our nation. We are affluent; we have privileges and knowledge in proportions unprecedented in world history. This should be a warning to those who do not know Him.

Amos 5:4-15

What is the writer saying?

How can I apply this to my life?

pray Jamaica – For Jamaican believers to have greater access to and interest in Christian resource materials.

In your reading you will note that we are instructed to *seek the LORD* four times in this chapter (vv. 4 , 6, 8, 4). After the lamentation (5:1-2) we have the explanation (vv. 3-17): Seek the Lord, He will not tolerate the sinful substitutes of idolatry (vv. 5-6). The reference to turning "judgment to wormwood" (v. 7) means that they did not respect God. Justice was a joke. To "leave off righteousness" (v. 7) means to throw it or cast it to the ground. Doesn't that sound familiar in today's society? The seven stars and Orion (v. 8) (Pleiades and Orion) were well known constellations. (See Job 9:9; 38:31.) God's sovereignty and omnipotence are seen in this passage. "Calleth for the waters of the sea..." (v. 8) probably referred to the Noah's flood. The thought seems to be that God would judge Israel's sin just as He judged sin that day. While the manner of judgment would be different, the *fact* of judgment was assured. We have the thought of hatred both in the beginning and at the end of this paragraph (vv. 10-15). Note the hate of the unrighteous for those who tell the truth. We hear people say, *Tell it like it is.* Yet when this is done it receives the same unwelcome reception that it received in the days of Amos. There is a price to be paid for telling the truth. To seek the good (v. 14) is to hate the evil (v. 15).

Life stEP

As Christians we are to love the Lord. When we do that, we hate evil. "Ye that love the Lord, hate evil" (Psalm 97:10). While we readily acknowledge that God is love, it should be remembered that He is also hate. He loves sinners, but He hates sin. We need to love as God loves and hate as God hates. Let's determine that whatever the price, we are going to seek the Lord.

Amos 5:16-27

What is the writer saying?

How can I apply this to my life?

pray Philippines – Funding for the staff and supplies needed to continue Bible correspondence courses.

Verse 16 expresses more sorrow. The farm worker and the skilled laborer will both lament. Their forefathers knew the meaning of the Passover as a time of deliverance from judgment. But this people would not turn from their sin. We are looking here beyond the day of Amos to the future Day of the Lord. The first "woe" (there are two) was to them "that desire the day of the LORD" (v. 18). The view here seems to be *All right, I've sinned! So what? Where is the Day of the Lord you have been talking about? Let it come!* It was blatant defiance. Another view of this passage makes the speakers pious pretenders, who were saying, *If only the Lord would come and deliver us* but it was just words, not coming from the heart. Are there people who sing and talk about prophecy and the Lord's return, yet give no outward evidence that they are ready? Many know all the Biblical details of future events but are not personally prepared to meet their God. Today the believer's hope is the Day of Christ – the Rapture. Here in the Old Testament, the Day of the Lord referred to the Tribulation. Christ is coming with His saints and will initiate the Millennium. The days are different and the hope different, but the application is similar.

Verse 19 assures us that Israel, however crafty, cannot escape God's judgment. We see a man fleeing a lion and meeting a bear, then escaping the bear and going to a house, only to lean on the wall and be bitten by a serpent. Judgment is inevitable. Their feast days no longer meant anything to God and the songs they sang were only "noise" (vv. 22-23).

 Life **stEP** The Lord's return is very precious to us. Let us be careful that it is not simply a known doctrine, but that it has an effect on the way we live. (See Titus 2:11-13; 1 John 3:1-3.)

Thursday 22

Amos 8:1-12

What is the writer saying?

How can I apply this to my life?

pray   *Hungary – For God to call witnesses to the hard – to – reach groups: Gypsies, Yugoslavians, and Jews.*

The imminence of judgment is seen in the basket of overripe fruit. Verse three describes what would happen. The literal translation of the last part of the verse is "He casts forth; hush!" They would be aware that God was punishing, and their silence would be a submission to the deserved dealings of God.

Treatment of the Poor (v. 4)

Verse 4 speaks of their forcing the people to labor without adequate compensation. They were exploiting the poor.

Shame in their Religious Attendance (v. 5)

While they felt some obligation to attend Temple services, they were anxious to *get it over with* in order to get back to the desire in their hearts – outdoing the other man.

Cheating (vv. 5b, 6b)

Amos doesn't simply tell of their evils; he lists how they were cheating. He names sin.

1. Making the ephah small (v. 5). This is a unit of dry measure (like our bushel basket). Perhaps they used false bottoms or smaller containers to cheat their customers.

2. Making the shekel weight heavier requiring the person buying to place more silver on the balance (v. 5).

3. Buying the poor for silver (v. 6). This was the sin of slavery, condemned by God. (Leviticus 25:39).

4. Selling the refuse of wheat (inferior grade of wheat) (v. 6b).

God also lists specific dealings with His backslidden people (vv. 8-14). Note and mark the "I wills" in verses 8-12.

Life stEP

God wants each of us to be circumspect in our day to day dealings with others. Honesty, integrity, and a clear awareness of God's high standard are so important. God's standard is high for each of us. Consistency in our day-to-day living is important.

Amos 9:8-15

What is the writer saying?

How can I apply this to my life?

pray — *Indonesia – For Muslim's (80% of India) hearts to be open to the truth of Jesus Christ.*

God's eyes were on the sinful people (v. 8). He promised to destroy them. He would "sift the house of Israel among all nations" (v. 9). This is one of the many times in Scripture that this prophecy is given. For almost three thousand years they have been scattered.

Victory for the People of God (vv. 11-15)

The events in this paragraph are yet to be fulfilled and will take place after the Rapture of the Church. The Tribulation will follow. Then Christ will come in great power and great glory *with His saints* and establish His Kingdom.

The Tabernacle of David (v. 11)

At this point it would be helpful to read Acts 15:14-17. The setting is important. The Jews were mystified that the Gospel was offered to the Gentiles. James made it clear that it is God's will to take out a people from among the Gentiles first and then return and do a work for Israel.

Note the order:
1. Israel judged and scattered (Amos 9:8)
2. A people is taken out for His name (Acts 15:14)
3. He rebuilds the Tabernacle of David. Other passages also make this promise: 2 Samuel 7:1-29; Psalm 89:1-52; Isaiah 9:6 & 7; Jeremiah 23:5. Amos insisted that the people would be punished for their sins and then restored again – a literal kingdom. Some of the Millennial conditions are described in the last three verses.

Life **stEP** — The prayer "thy Kingdom come" in the *Lord's Prayer* will be answered. God is good to His Word and will do what He promised. How comforting it is to know that we can depend on our God in every promise He has made to Israel and the Church.

There are twelve *Minor Prophets*, so called, not because they are unimportant, but because they are smaller than the *Former Prophets* (Moses, Joshua, Judges, 1 & 2 Samuel and 1&2 Kings) and the *Major Prophets* (Isaiah, Jeremiah, Ezekiel, and Daniel). The Minor Prophets cover some of the same themes as the other prophets, but in addition, they emphasize social justice and true worship. Nine of the Minor Prophets were written before the destruction of the Temple in 586 B.C. while the last three are written after the return from the Babylonian Exile (the *Post-Exilic Prophets*—Haggai, Zechariah, and Malachi). One was written against the country of Edom (Obadiah). Two books were written about Nineveh (Jonah and Nahum). Two condemn the Northern Kingdom or Israel (Hosea and Amos). Seven are directed to the Southern Kingdom or Judah (Joel, Micah, Habakkuk, Zephaniah, Haggai, Zechariah, and Malachi).

Obadiah means, *Servant of Jehovah*. There are twelve men with this name in scripture. We do not know anything personal about this man, not even his father's name or his city of residence. The material in this short book of only twenty-one verses is vague in historic references so we can't even date the book effectively. The theme of the book is the *Doom of Edom*. She is condemned for harming the children of Israel during a time of national crisis. Since the 586 BC destruction of Jerusalem by Nebuchadnezzer, and the subsequent deportation of the

bulk of the population was a huge crisis, we assume that Obadiah is writing about the sins of Edom at this time. Also, verses 1-9 are similar to Jeremiah 49:7-22 written during the period of the Babylonian attacks upon Judah. The outline of the twenty-one verses is:

Judgment Announced	1-9
Judgment Justified	10-14
The Day of the Lord	15-21

The Edomites lived south of Judah in the rugged and desolate area south of the Dead Sea. They were known for the defensibility of their mountain retreat, and the wisdom of their diplomats in trade and political negotiations. Obadiah predicts that God will confound both advantages. The Edomites descended from Esau, the twin brother of Jacob (whose name was changed to *Israel* and his sons became the heads of the Twelve Tribes of Israel.). The word *Edom* means *red* and is a reference to Esau (*hairy*) who had red hair and sold his birthright for a mess of red pottage. Esau and Jacob had a tense relationship due to Esau's lack of spiritual sensitivity and Jacob's deception. The Edomites were a constant source of frustration to the Israelites. The last known Edomites in ancient history were the Herods of the New Testament (by then known as *Idumeans*.). Petra, the famous *Rose City* of the Nabatean Arabs is in the territory of ancient Edom (modern Jordan). In Revelation 12 we are told that during the tribulation period

Jews will flee from the Antichrist and find refuge in the mountains of Edom. During the Messianic Era (Millennium) God says that Edom will be left desolate as a warning to those who contemplate rebelling against Him (Isaiah 34).

Obadiah 15-21

What is the writer saying?

How can I apply this to my life?

The Day of the Lord is highlighted here (v. 15). God is pleased to carry us to that distant day when all nations will be judged. The Day of the Lord is mentioned more in the Minor Prophets than any other section of Scripture. Remember, the day begins after the Church is raptured and includes the Tribulation, Christ's Second Coming in glory, and His millennial reign. Often, as in this passage, it refers to Christ's coming to judge the nations just prior to His reign.

In many ways the conflict that existed between Edom and Israel reminds us of the conflict that exists between the believer's old and new natures.

1. There was conflict and struggle between Edom and Israel. Compare this with "For the flesh lusteth against the Spirit, and the Spirit against the flesh …"(Galatians 5:17).

2. There is a continued self-importance promoted by the flesh. It loves to exalt and flaunt itself.

3. The flesh is strong, and there is only one way to deal with it. We are to "… make not provision for the flesh…" (Romans 13:14). This *Edom nature* of ours will bring us to failure every time we depend on it (Romans 7:18). Fully recognizing that *Edom* is still alive, we should be conscious that God has broken the flesh's power over us, and the law of the indwelling Spirit makes us free (Romans. 8:2).

4. The Spirit does the work of the Lord "in us" and we "walk not after the flesh [Edom] but after the Spirit" (Romans 8:4).

To *walk in the Spirit* is to allow the Lord to control our lives. It is a walk of faith and dependence on Him. While in the "flesh" there is "no good thing," our dependence on the indwelling Spirit is the secret for a life of victory.

The beloved Apostle John penned the fourth Gospel around A.D. 90. Early tradition holds that he wrote his Gospel from the city of Ephesus. One might wonder why God commissioned four biographies of His Son's earthly life, but certainly, each account gives us a new appreciation and perspective of our Savior. Matthew writes to Jews, presenting Jesus of Nazareth as their prophesied Messiah. He quotes many Old Testament passages in the process. As such, Matthew presents Jesus as the Lion of the Tribe of Judah, taking his genealogy back to Father Abraham. Mark writes to a Gentile Roman audience that knows so little about the Jews that he has to inform them that the Jordan is a river. The Romans care little for Jewish customs but know a lot about slavery, servanthood, and obedience. As such, Mark presents Jesus as the perfect servant. No one cares about the background of a servant so Mark provides no genealogy. Jesus is pictured as a busy man, *immediately* springing into action as He bustles around doing the will of His Father in heaven. Luke writes for a Greek audience. They admired the human intellect (Plato, etc.) and the physical body (the Olympics). As such, Luke presents Jesus as the greatest man who has ever lived. He takes Jesus's genealogy all the way back to Adam. Finally, John presents Jesus of Nazareth in His full-blown deity. Since God always existed, there is no need for a genealogy of Jesus in John. John differs in comparison with the other Gospels in that it contains twenty seven personal interviews, and the mention of six Jewish holidays. Jesus Christ is presented as greater than the law, temple, shekinah, and holidays. John records seven great "I AM" claims.

- The Bread of Life (6:48)
- The Light of the World (8:12)
- The Door (10:7)
- The Good Shepherd (10:11)
- The Resurrection and the Life (11:25)
- The Way, the Truth and the Life (14:6)
- The True Vine (15:1)

The purpose for the fourth Gospel is clearly stated by John in 20:31 "But these are written, that ye might believe that Jesus is the Christ, the Son of God; and that believing ye might have life through his name."

The miracles recorded in this book are signs of Jesus's deity that should lead people to believe unto eternal life. In fact, *sign* is the only word that John uses to describe a *miracle*. In this book, John presents seven signs, each highlighting an aspect of the salvation that only Jesus Christ could provide.

Sign   =   Salvation
1. Water into wine = the outpouring of God's grace
2. Cleansing the temple = the future perfect sacrifice
2. Nobleman's son = the necessity of faith
3. Lame man   = the sovereignty of God
4. Feeding of the 5000   = the sufficiency of Christ's sacrifice
6. Blind man   = the cleansing of forgiveness
7. Raising of Lazarus = the resurrection unto eternal life

Belief is the response that John seeks. The word *believe* occurs ninety eight times as compared to only eight times in Matthew, thirteen times in Mark and nine times in Luke.

Dr. Merrill Tenney, whose commentary on John is highly recommended, provides the following outline. It is based on the reaction of the Jewish authorities to the person of Jesus Christ.

1. Consideration   chapters 1-4
2. Controversy   chapters 5-6
3. Conflict   chapters 7-11
4. Crisis   chapter 12
5. Conference   chapters 13-17
6. Consummation   chapters 18-20
7. Commission   chapter 21

John 1:1-14

What is the writer saying?

How can I apply this to my life?

John starts his account of the person of Christ in a style reminiscent of the book of Genesis, "in the beginning." Here, *beginning* does not imply a time when God did not exist, but rather just the opposite. John is saying that at the origin of human history, God was already there.

The terms *Word* (Greek, *"Logos"*), *life* (Greek, *"Zoa"*) and *Light* (Greek, *"Phos"*) here applied to Jesus Christ, speak of His being the revelation of God to mankind (see John 14:8-9), and the source of eternal life to those who believe.

Verse three plainly states that Jesus Christ is the Creator. What a blessing to read the account in Genesis 1 knowing it is an infallible account of the creative work of the Son of God. In verse five, we see the *Light* was met with opposition—*darkness*. The darkness is said to not comprehend the Light. The idea is not that the *darkness* did not understand the *Light*, but rather that it could not overpower it.

This section also introduces us to one sent to testify about the Light, John the Baptist. John is the prophesied forerunner (Isaiah 40:3; Malachi 3:1, 4:5, 6). Those who should have been the best prepared to receive the Light, the Jews ("His own," v. 11), rejected Him. To those who received the true Light, He gave the power (right) to be called children of God. Verse 13 states that this new birth came about by the will of God and not by any agency of man.

Jesus Christ became flesh and blood that He might take upon Himself the sins of mankind. God became one of us so that He could be our substitutionary sacrifice… What sacrifice are you willing to make in return?

John 1:15-28

What is the writer saying?

How can I apply this to my life?

In this section, John again turns his attention to John the Baptist. Here we see two aspects of John's life: his ministry and his message.

John the Baptist's ministry had created no small stir, evident in the fact that the Pharisees sent a delegation to investigate who he was and what he was doing (vv. 19, 24). John gave clear testimony to the nature of his ministry in verses 20-23. He told his investigators clearly he was not the Messiah; neither did he claim to be Elijah (Malachi 4:5), or the prophet (Deuteronomy 18:15). John simply referred to himself as "the voice" (see Isaiah 40:3).

Not only do we learn of John's ministry in this passage, but more importantly his message. John's ministry was to prepare the nation of Israel to receive Jesus. He proclaimed His eternality. Even though Jesus was born after John, and began his ministry after John, He was *before*. This is a clear declaration of Christ's pre-existence. He was from eternity past. John also describes the nature of Christ's ministry. Two Old Testament character qualities define His ministry: grace (loving kindness) and truth. He provides one gracious gift after another (1:16). Moses gave the law, not without grace and truth, but Christ would usher in a new dispensation that would fully unveil the grace of God in truth. Jesus Christ is the One who declares or explains the Father to us. The Greek root form of the word being translated *declared* is the source of our word *exegete* (to explain or unfold divine mysteries). Jesus explained the truth of the Father to man (1:18).

The ministry and message of John the Baptist points us clearly to Jesus Christ as the promised Messiah of Israel. John teaches us that Jesus is the eternal Son of God and the ultimate demonstration of the grace of God. Have you received God's gracious gift of salvation?

John 1:29-42

What is the writer saying?

How can I apply this to my life?

pray *Japan – Praise the Lord for the new openness caused by economic, social, and natural disasters.*

It is clear from his calling Jesus the *Lamb of God*, that John knew Jesus was the promised Messiah (Isaiah 53:5-11). In the Jewish sacrificial system, an unblemished lamb was sacrificed during the celebration of Passover for each household. The blood of the sacrifice was a covering for sin, but could never take their sin away (Hebrews 10:4). John recognized that Jesus was the Promised One who would become the substitutionary sacrifice that would take away the sins of those who placed their faith in Him. Jesus's sacrifice was sufficient to atone for all of mankind (1 John 2:2).

The Jews were looking for their Messiah, but they were looking for one who would come and deliver them from their national political problems. What a tragedy that most were not alert to the time of their visitation (Luke 19:44)! John gives us insight into how he knew Jesus. God revealed to him that the One upon whom the Holy Spirit descended and remained was the Christ.

The first four chapters of John describe a period of consideration when seven different people or groups of people consider the claims of Christ. First, John the Baptist recognizes Him as the sacrificial lamb. The second consideration involved the calling of His first disciples, Andrew and John. Andrew later brought his brother Peter as the third disciple. Andrew is most prominently seen introducing others to Jesus (see John 6:8-9; 12:22). Andrew tells Peter they have found the Messiah, and John adds a translation note that Messiah means Christ. When Jesus meets Peter He gives him the name *Cephas*, which is Aramaic for *rock*.

Life stEP Meeting Jesus is life changing. John and Andrew were never the same. John the Baptist pointed them to the Lamb of God, and they followed. Whom are you pointing to Christ? Whom are you following?

Wednesday 23

John 1:43-51

What is the writer saying?

How can I apply this to my life?

pray *Pray that the Lord will give you the strength to overcome temptation (Matthew 26:41).*

In John 1:43-51 Jesus adds Philip and Nathanael as disciples. Philip is from Bethsaida, as are Andrew and Peter. Bethsaida will later be one of the cities Jesus pronounces a woe upon (Matthew 11:21) for their lack of repentance, even in the face of some of Christ's greatest miracles.

Philip, like Andrew, found someone else to introduce to Christ, Nathanael. Nathanael, however, is not impressed with the news that Jesus is from Nazareth. Nazareth was small, had poor soil with no well, and housed a Roman garrison. This later became the basis for accusation of Jesus's illegitimate birth.

The fig tree (v. 48) was a place of meditation and study. *Guile* is *supplanter*, the name for Jacob in Genesis 28. Perhaps Nathanael's meditation on that passage and Christ's knowledge of his thoughts convinced him of Jesus's Messiahship and thus his declaration *Son of God, King of Israel.* Jesus is amazed that Nathanael so quickly turns from skepticism to belief. Greater evidences lay ahead for Nathanael as He would soon see Christ do the first of many miracles that demonstrated His deity. The reference to angels *ascending and descending* is another connection to Jacob (Jacob's Ladder).

Son of Man was a favorite title the Lord used of Himself. This is the first of eleven times the title occurs in the book of John and carries the idea of Christ's union with mankind through the incarnation. At His birth, He became fully man so that He might be able to offer Himself a sacrifice for mankind. Jesus willingly laid aside the glories of heaven to become the ultimate servant and all-sufficient sacrifice (Mark 10:45).

 Life stEP

When introduced to Christ, people react in different ways. Some, like Philip, are immediately sold-out. Others, like Nathanael, are skeptical and cautious. What a great example we see in Andrew and Philip, men who did not need the spotlight but quietly brought others to Christ.

John 2:1-12

What is the writer saying?

How can I apply this to my life?

pray   *Jamaica – For effective gospel outreach within schools and an increase in children's Bible clubs.*

The wedding at Cana of Galilee provided the third opportunity for considering the person of Christ. We are told that the wedding was on the third day, which would be Tuesday. This seems strange to us, but actually, this was a popular day for Jewish weddings. Perhaps the reason Mary felt compelled to do something about the wine shortage was because so many extra people had gone to the wedding with her (Jesus and His disciples). This also points to the fact that Jesus was not seeking notoriety, for the occasion of His first sign was a small, family type of gathering. Christ's response to Mary's request was not impolite. *Woman* was a proper title similar to saying *lady*. Jesus protests that His hour (to reveal Himself as Messiah) had not yet come. The six large pots held water for washing hands. If only the guests knew where the wine came from! His creative act, bypassing both the growth stage of the grape and the proper aging of the wine, underscores God's ability to create with the appearance of age just as He did when He created Adam and Eve. Jesus came to bring the new wine of God's grace in a measure that exceeded man's need just as surely as the six large pots of wine surpassed the need of this small wedding party. This is the first sign of seven signs that John records. Remember, John's goal is to bring the reader to a place of *belief* in the deity of Jesus Christ. Surely, His power over natural processes was very convincing to those who knew and understood what had taken place.

Life STEP

So far we have seen Jesus as the Word, God, Creator, Light, only begotten Son, Lamb of God, Son of God, Messiah, King of Israel, and Son of Man. Which title best speaks to you in your relationship with the One who even concerns Himself with trivial happiness and avoiding social blunders at a wedding?

John 2:13-25

What is the writer saying?

How can I apply this to my life?

pray   *New Zealand – The need for focused Youth Pastors and leaders.*

During the Passover, many people of the scattered Jewish nation made a pilgrimage to Jerusalem. They wanted to take part in the celebration and remembrance of God's grace, mercy, and deliverance from their bondage in Egypt. Because many had traveled in from distant lands, merchants had developed a thriving business providing the animals for sacrifice and the necessary currency exchange so those traveling would be able to pay their temple tax. Jesus charged these merchants with making God's house a place of *merchandise*. The word being translated for merchandise is the word from which we derive our word emporium. Jesus's zeal was for purity in the house of God! (See Psalm 69:9.) Jesus demonstrated the power to overturn the hypocritical spiritual state that was so prevalent and restore purity in the worship of the Almighty God. The Jews questioned His authority to challenge this accepted compromise. They demanded a sign as a sort of credential. The sign He offered went right over their heads as He spoke of His bodily resurrection. Here, as in other places in this book, John gives us a glimpse of the effect these events had on the disciples. His disciples, remembering this event later, were strengthened in their faith (John 12:16).

During these days in Jerusalem Jesus obviously did other signs (2:23) that were causing people to believe He was a great man, *believing in His name*. That their belief was surface curiosity, and not saving faith in Him as the Christ, is evident from the statements in John 2:24-25. Jesus knew their hearts, and knew the quality of their belief and was not willing to *believe* in them.

Life **STEP**   God is not interested in the show of religion, but in purity of heart. He demands this not only from those who would worship, but especially from those who take part in the leading.

John 3:1-12

What is the writer saying?

How can I apply this to my life?

pray — Hungary – For churches to mature in their giving and support of nationals involved in Christian work.

Christ's fourth encounter in chapter two was no low-key event. On His first trip to Jerusalem, He marches into the temple and runs out the moneychangers, instantly gaining the attention of the rulers of the Jews. The temple was to be a place of worship, not merchandise. In chapter three, we meet one of these rulers as Jesus has His next encounter with a ruler named Nicodemus. Nicodemus was a Jew and he came to Christ with intellectual needs. In the religious circles Nicodemus traveled in, he was a recognized authority (v. 10), yet he was spiritually blind. He was a Pharisee, a teacher (3:10), and part of the Sanhedrin. Jesus introduced Nicodemus to his need for rebirth. He initially understood this to be a physical rebirth, which would be impossible. Jesus helped him to understand that He spoke of a second birth into spiritual life (v. 6).

Jesus uses the wind (v. 8) to illustrate the ministry of God's Spirit to Nicodemus. Just like the wind, God's Spirit moves according to His sovereign will and His effect is unmistakable upon the hearts of mankind.

Nicodemus is only mentioned in the Gospel of John and only three times. In the three passages, it seems that John focuses on the progression of his spiritual life. Nicodemus appears first in chapter three, but leaves with no apparent change. Then in John 7:50-51 we find him defending Jesus against charges made by the Sanhedrin. Last, we find him at the Crucifixion (John 19:38-39), with Joseph, boldly and publicly standing as a disciple of Christ.

Life step

Many who are brilliant and highly intellectual have a hard time grasping the simple truths of God's Word. Have you been born twice? To be alive is to have experienced physical birth. To be born again is to receive eternal life through placing your faith in Jesus Christ. You must be born again!

John 3:13-24

What is the writer saying?

How can I apply this to my life?

Nicodemus was not a novice. However, when Jesus taught using a simple earthly comparison between physical birth and spiritual birth, this great teacher could not grasp the simple truth. How would he ever understand heavenly things, which no one had seen (3:12-13)?

Jesus was trying to relate to Nicodemus in terms he could grasp. He uses the account from Numbers 21, which tells of a time in the history of Israel when they complained against Moses and God sent serpents among the people. Many were dying, and God instructed Moses to make a bronze likeness of a serpent and raise it on a pole. Those who were bitten were to look upon the serpent and they would not die. This required them to believe and look in faith. In the same way, at the cross, Jesus Christ would be raised up, and those who place their faith in God's substitutionary sacrifice would be saved. Nicodemus eventually appeared to understand (John 19:39).

Verse 16 shows the breadth (*world*); length (*gave*); depth (*not perish*) and height (*everlasting life*) of God's love. Christ has paid the price for the sin of all men of all time: past, present, and future (1 John 2:2). That means that the only issue left is whether men will believe and receive what has already been provided for them. This means that men go to hell, not because of their sins (plural), but because of the sin (singular) of unbelief. Once in hell, they then pay for their own sins (plural), having rejected Christ's gift of eternal life.

Again, John picks up the theme of light and darkness. Jesus came to bring light to those in darkness. Those who desire to know God are attracted to the light. Those whose deeds are evil reject the light and flee from it, not wanting to be exposed by it.

Life
st**E**P   Are you attracted to the things of God or do you avoid them? Those who are of the light, love the light and want to be near it.

John 3:25-36

What is the writer saying?

How can I apply this to my life?

Pray for your church to have wisdom and integrity in dealing with the finances entrusted to it.

Jesus was from heaven, and as such, His ministry was superior to that of John the Baptist. John was among the greatest of men, but did not compare to the Son of God. Jesus came with a message from heaven, but many were not receiving the message. Those who did receive Him had gone on record to the fact that God is true. However, those who rejected Christ were rejecting God and calling Him a liar, for they rejected His messenger and therefore His message. (See Luke 20:9-18.)

Believers in Jesus Christ have the Holy Spirit living within them (1 John 4:13; Ephesians 1:13-14). At salvation, we have all of the Holy Spirit there is to receive. Verse 34 does not teach that Jesus had the full measure of the Holy Spirit, while we only get small allotments; but rather, this is in contrast to the Old Testament prophet who was only temporarily empowered by the Holy Spirit for a specific task. Jesus had the Holy Spirit permanently, as do those who place their faith in Him.

Verse 36 ends chapter three with a clear statement of what it means to be saved. The one who is saved is one who believes and by faith receives His Son, who alone gives everlasting life. In the same way, those in Numbers 21 had to believe Moses and look upon the serpent to escape death. The one who does not obey reveals a heart of unbelief, and will not see everlasting life, but will remain under God's wrath. God's abiding wrath is not a new condition, but rather a continuation of the condition they were already in due to their unbelief.

Life stEP

The Holy Spirit is not given to believers in installments. The question is not how much of the Holy Spirit do you have, but how much of you does the Holy Spirit have? Obedience is not a requirement of salvation, but rather a demonstration of it.

John 4:1-15

What is the writer saying?

How can I apply this to my life?

Thailand – For God to raise up honest leadership to establish a framework for a just government.

The woman at the well, a Samaritan woman with deep spiritual needs, will prove to be everything that Nicodemus was not! The rulers, in this case the conservative Pharisees, were concerned about Jesus's growing success and, unlike John the Baptist, they were not happy. Unwilling to escalate the confrontation at this time, Jesus leaves the area of their concentration (Judea) and heads for safer, neutral ground in Galilee. Galilee was safer because ever since 930 B.C. non-religious Jews, and then even Gentiles starting in 722 B.C., had inhabited the area. In verse 4 *must* is a moral necessity, not physical, as they could have done what religious Jews did when traveling north. They could have bypassed the Samaritan area by crossing the Jordan River and traveling up the east bank. The sixth hour was high noon, normally too hot for the work of carrying water, but apparently this woman avoided the other women of the city out of shame for her lifestyle. Jesus does the unexpected and asks the woman for a drink. Note that John finds it necessary to explain that socially Jews would normally not stoop to speak to a Samaritan, much less a woman. Jesus crosses both boundaries to reach this woman. Jesus uses a known item, *water*, to introduce this woman to the unknown, spiritual life. The gift of God that He offers is salvation. Those who have been born again become life-giving streams to those with whom they share the good news of the Gospel.

To catch fish you have to go where the fish are! Christ takes the road less traveled and is busy doing His Father's business. Jesus used things people knew and understood to unfold spiritual truth.

John 4:16-30

What is the writer saying?

How can I apply this to my life?

pray Slovakia – For the church planting to be successful in bringing the Good News to many unbelievers.

Up until this point, the Samaritan woman has been proud and argumentative. Jesus responds to her graciously, obviously impressing her since Jewish people of the day disdained the Samaritans as *half-breeds* and theological competitors. Racially, they were the product of the Assyrian foreign policy of population transfer to quell rebellion. The Israelites were moved out and Gentiles brought in.

Verse 18 indicates that marriage is more than sexual relations. Christ's request to return with her husband would cause her to walk a mile in the noonday sun. Embarrassed and confused, the woman resorts to the tactic of changing the subject and launches into a *theological discussion*. She tries to bog the conversation down by introducing a point of contention between Jews and Samaritans: where they should worship. The word worship comes from *worthship*, recognizing and appreciating the worth of God. The central issue was not where one was when worshipping God, but rather the heart with which they approached God. God desires a pure and true heart from those who would worship Him (Psalm 24:4). Jesus intercepts her and brings her back to the central issue, a vital heart relationship with the Creator.

The disciples return, oblivious to the ministry that has been taking place, and are amazed that Jesus has crossed this cultural line. The Samaritan woman leaves her water pot and rushes to the city to tell her fellow-citizens, "Come, see a man, is not this the Christ?"

Life stEP

Jesus was more concerned for the spiritual needs of this woman than what people would think about Him talking to her. Are you allowing culture to decide whom you will tell about Christ? The woman's first response was to try to avoid conviction with a debate. Are you seeking truth or holding to tradition?

John 4:31-42

What is the writer saying?

How can I apply this to my life?

Upon returning, the disciples try to get Jesus to eat. He refers to the spiritual food He was already enjoying and confuses them in the shift from the physical to the spiritual realm. As the Samaritans were making their way down the road from the village to the well, Christ explained to His disciples that the harvest was not four months away, but that the fields were *white* unto harvest. Heads of grain would look white, but Jesus is probably referring to the white robes of the Samaritans coming toward Him! At a time like this, food should be the last thing on their minds. During the harvest, the reapers often are focused on the task of getting in the harvest to the neglect of meals. This is the case here. This is no time for eating; it is time to bring in the crop. Jesus also shares an important ministry principle. Not everyone gets to do the harvesting. Some plant, some water, some cultivate, and others often bring in the harvest. In the case of the disciples, they now had an opportunity to reap that which others had sown.

The final verses of this event (vv. 39-42) show us that the Samaritans first believed because of the woman's testimony. However, to the people of this culture, the testimony of a *woman* was inadequate. They would have to hear and see for themselves! Jesus did not share this condescending attitude toward women as was evident from His dealings with her.

Life
stEP   Are you willing to set aside your comfort for the sake of the ministry God gives you to accomplish? Are you looking to the needs of others or are you too preoccupied with your own needs to see others? What part are you playing in the harvest of God?

John 4:43-54

What is the writer saying?

How can I apply this to my life?

pray · Canada – Pray for churches to hold fast to biblical truth, ethical integrity, and evangelical zeal.

Unlike the argumentative initial response of the Samaritan woman, in this section we see the humble plea of a father for his child. This sign was again to demonstrate who Jesus was in order that the people might believe and be saved. Cana, where Jesus met this nobleman, was over twenty miles from Capernaum where the boy lay sick. Jesus, being God, is omniscient, and therefore just as capable of healing this child at a distance as if standing at his bedside. Jesus's first response to the nobleman seems rather harsh but is probably intended for the broader audience who may have heard. The Jews were always seeking a sign and were often reluctant to receive Christ at face value. The nobleman was more than likely a Jew, possibly an important member of Herod's court. The nobleman did not appeal to his position, nor did he defend himself in light of Jesus's charge, but rather in earnest faith again appealed to Him to save his dying son. The man asked Jesus to come to Capernaum, but Jesus sent him away with the simple statement, "...your son lives." The nobleman did not question, but returned the twenty miles home. When he learned of the hour of his son's healing, the nobleman believed, and in turn led his family to belief in Jesus.

Life stEP Are you willing to take God at His word? How often have we seen God deliver only to then question it or explain it away? The miracles of Jesus demonstrated who He was, so that men might believe, not to draw attention or attract a crowd.

John 5:1-14

What is the writer saying?

How can I apply this to my life?

Unlike the nobleman in the previous section who sought Jesus out to heal his sick son, the man in this passage had been sick for thirty eight years! He was not even aware it was Jesus who healed him! The description of the angel stirring the water and subsequent healing of the first to enter the water (vv. 3b-4) is not found in the earliest manuscripts prior to A.D. 400. The fact that this may have been only a local legend adds to the sadness of the situation. How many today cling to false hope built upon the traditions of men rather than the Word of God? This type of healing is unique in Scripture. Jesus has compassion on this individual knowing the number of years he has suffered. His direction to the man is simple, "Rise, take up thy bed, and walk." The Jews give the man a hard time about carrying his pallet, seeing this as a violation of the Sabbath rest. This once again is an example of man's tradition being exalted to the same level as God's Word. Jesus obviously did not stay around to be mobbed by the others at the pool. By sovereign choice, He had shown grace to this man who did not even know Who He was. Later Jesus found him in the temple and warned him. His condition may have been the result of his sin. A similar situation is found in Matthew 9:2, where a man's sins are forgiven resulting in his healing.

Life stEP

In the world many cling to false hope and false religion based upon myth and superstitions. We who know the truth are to be a light in the darkness for those who are lost. Many of life's great tragedies are directly traceable to lifestyle choices!

John 5:15-27

What is the writer saying?

How can I apply this to my life?

pray *Pray that the married couples of your church will nurture and protect their relationships by a dependence upon God's Word.*

The first four chapters of John were characterized by consideration but we now move to a new section of John, chapters 5-7: The Period of Controversy. The controversy begins as Jesus heals a man, who had been lame for thirty eight years, on the Sabbath. He meets the man at the Pool of Bethesda (*beth* is *house* and *hesed* is *loving kindness*, one of the Old Testament words for *grace*). Verse 16 demonstrates the Pharisees' irritation over Sabbath desecration. Verse 18 voices another complaint, that He claimed equality with God by calling Him *His Father* (Greek *idion* as in idiosyncrasy). Jesus will say, *My Father* or *Your Father*, but not *Our Father* in His discussions with the Pharisees! In today's passage, Christ builds on His claims to a special relationship with God, which the Pharisees correctly interpret as claims of equality with God. Throughout this passage, Jesus declares His commitment to doing the Father's will. He had come to fulfill all that the Father had given Him to do. His statement in verse 17 and following made it clear that this was only the beginning, and He would continue His work as the Father directed. Verse 24 makes it clear that one cannot have a valid faith in God the Father apart from a faith in the Son of God.

Many today live their Christian lives under a cloud of dos and don'ts. The Pharisees missed Jesus because He did not fit their mold. God wants us to follow Him from the heart, not by a system of man-made religious regulations. The key is a relationship, not regulations.

John 5:28-38

What is the writer saying?

How can I apply this to my life?

pray   *Korea – For seminary graduates to humbly commit themselves to less prominent, rural pastorates.*

Jesus concludes His response to the challenge that came from the Jews by stating that the resurrection and subsequent judgment will verify His authority. Someday, all those who have died will hear His voice and arise (see Daniel 12:2). Two distinct outcomes await those who will arise. The open arms of their Savior will greet some, while others will meet their final Judge (Revelation 20:11-15). *Good* and *evil* in verse 29 are not conditions of salvation, but the evident fruit of their lives.

The Pharisees argue that a man cannot be his own character witness. Jesus, in 5:31, picks up this thought and states that if He alone bore witness of Himself, His witness would not be true. This statement is true here, in the sense of admission into a legal defense. Therefore, in verses 30-47, Christ brings five testifiers to the witness stand: 1) 5:30-31 – Himself.

The point here is not that He never bore witness of Himself. He did, but that He was not alone in His witness. 2) 5:32-35 – John the Baptist, whose life and ministry prepared the way for the coming of Christ. 3) 5:36 – His works. When John the Baptist doubted in prison, Jesus let His works speak for Him to assure John that He truly was the Messiah (Matthew 11:2-6). 4) 5:37-38 – His Father (three times: baptism, transfiguration, and after the triumphal entry). 5) 5:39-47 – Scripture.

The unbelieving heart is often oblivious to the evidence that is clearly seen by those who are open to hear God's voice. Hard hearts are often only softened by a consistent loving demonstration of the life of God lived out by those who truly know Him.

John 5:39-47

What is the writer saying?

How can I apply this to my life?

pray

Japan – Continued success of youth ministries working among the 3,000,000 university students.

The religious leaders of the day thought themselves to be experts in the Scripture. They equated their strict observance of the Law given by Moses with their salvation. Yet, Jesus turned this against them when He stated that Moses wrote of Him (v. 46). If they would not believe Moses whom they held in the highest esteem, how could they believe Him whom they despised? Even in the face of overwhelming evidence, the unbelieving heart often is not softened, but grows even harder. Jesus did not fit the mold they had cast for their Messiah. As a result, they were unwilling to hear Him, much less humbly confess their need before Him. Their pecking order was well established, yet He needed none of their recognition (v. 41). Their glory did not come from God, but rather was self-imposed as they compared themselves to one another.

Moses was the human author of the first five books of the Old Testament: Genesis, Exodus, Leviticus, Numbers, and Deuteronomy. One does not need to look far to find Moses's prophetic words relating to Jesus. Genesis 3:15 points directly to the cross work of Jesus Christ where He dealt Satan the defeating blow that sealed his doom. This is only the beginning of many such prophecies in Moses's writings.

Life stEP

Self-righteousness is the worst sort of blindness to plague mankind. The writings of Moses should have brought the Jews to a place where they were humbly seeking a Savior. Yet they twisted his words and missed his highest thoughts. How do you view yourself in light of God's Word?

John 6:1-14

What is the writer saying?

How can I apply this to my life?

The feeding of the multitude was the fourth sign done by Jesus. Each sign was a demonstration of Who He was, God the Son. John chose each one carefully to underscore an aspect of saving faith. John gives a tremendous picture of God's abundant supply for man's greatest need. Here bread was broken to meet man's physical need. In only a few verses Jesus will show that He is the true bread come down from heaven, and that His sacrifice is more than sufficient to meet the needs of all humanity (1 John 2:2). In this Gospel we learn of some interesting details the other synoptic Gospels do not give: the nearness of the Passover feast, the testing of Philip (vv. 5-6), and the type of bread used (barley was a coarse, cheap bread). Once again, Andrew is seen bringing someone to Jesus. Some would like to cheapen this event by saying that each person only received a small fragment, a token taste. However, verses 11 and 12 quickly dispel that notion. Each man ate all he wanted, and the fragments that were gathered amounted to twelve baskets full. Interestingly, Jesus's insistence that "nothing be lost" (v. 12) was nearly identical to His words in John 3:16; 6:39; 10:28; and 18:9 where He states that none of those who trusted Him for salvation would be lost.

Life stEP   Just as Jesus was not limited by physical circumstances, in the same way His sacrifice is sufficient to meet every spiritual hunger of mankind. Because He is God, His sacrifice is infinite and His gift of salvation is secure. Have you partaken of the Bread of Life?

Thursday 25

John 6:15-27

What is the writer saying?

How can I apply this to my life?

pray *Germany – Churches to return to a dependence upon the teaching of the Word of God to change lives.*

The response offered by those who had been miraculously fed was not what Jesus had intended. He wanted the people to see Him as their Messiah, but they wanted to make Him their king. His rebuke (v. 26) exposes their wrong motives. The miracles were proof of His true deity, yet the people were only thinking of the physical. Jesus instructs them to labor for *the meat that remains* (consider the water that satisfies in John 4:14). The food is Christ Himself.

As He often did, Jesus came apart from the crowd to be alone on the mountain. The place was on the western bank of the Sea of Galilee near the city of Bethsaida (Luke 9:10). Jesus had sent the disciples on ahead and had possibly agreed to meet them near Bethsaida (Mark 6:45) on their way to Capernaum. He had remained to see the crowd off and then had gone up into the mountain to pray (Mark 6:46).

The disciples had not expected to see Jesus coming to them walking on the sea. This fifth sign demonstrated His power over creation, and the ability to transcend the physical limitations that bind mankind. "With God all things are possible" (Mark 10:27). The crowds, upon discovering Jesus's departure, quickly follow to Capernaum. Jesus confronts them, exposing their motive in seeking only a free meal. *Sealed* in verse 27 is similar to our idea of something that is *certified*. The Father placed His certification upon the ministry of His Son.

 Many today seek after the miraculous and the spectacular. God's desire for man has not changed. It's that we might look to the Son, and upon seeing, believe. What is your motivation in following God?

John 6:28-40

What is the writer saying?

How can I apply this to my life?

John 6:35 is the first of the seven great "I Am" statements in John. Most of these statements have a predicate nominative (in this case, *bread*). Nevertheless, all reflect the naked "I Am" of Exodus 3, the covenantal name of Jehovah (Yahweh), by which God wished to make Himself known to His chosen people. Based on the Hebrew verb *to be*, it conveys both His eternality (past, present, and future or the eternal present) and His self-sufficiency. The backdrop to "I am the bread of life" is the miracle of the feeding of the five thousand (John 6:1-21). When confronted with the need for food to feed the fainting masses, Philip (the accountant) calculates that it would take 66% of a man's annual salary to feed the crowd. Andrew (the visionary) finds a boy's lunch and talks him out of it! This is the only miracle recorded in all four Gospels. Only John mentions that the people of Galilee were ready to force Jesus to be their king. The people are rather brazen in their request for more food and further signs of Christ's Messiahship. The implication of verse 31 is *Feed 2.5 million people for forty years like Moses did and then we'll consider your claims!* Jesus quickly corrects them stating that it was God who supplied the bread in the wilderness, and now the true bread from heaven was come down to them.

Life stEp   "Whose God is their belly" (Philippians 3:19). It is not a pretty picture when human existence is reduced to *gimme, gimme.* Let us not overlook true spiritual food in our lust for physical things.

John 6:41-58

What is the writer saying?

How can I apply this to my life?

pray — **Guatemala – Pray for missionaries to develop successful discipleship programs to train rural believers.**

Jesus has an extended conversation with the people of Galilee. They want Him to throw off the yoke of Rome and meet their physical needs. However, it is clear that they are not interested in His spiritual program. Verse 44 makes it abundantly clear that apart from the working of God, no one would come to Christ. Jesus states that the bread, which He was offering, was different from the manna, which their fathers had eaten in the wilderness (v. 49). Those who ate that bread were dead. He was offering Himself as the true Bread of Life, which brings eternal life. Elsewhere, Christ told His disciples that He spoke in parables to discourage the unbelievers (Matthew 13:13). In this passage, He uses a similar tactic, making His teaching sufficiently difficult to weed out the marginal disciples. They don't follow the analogy of eating His body (appropriating His sacrificial death) for (spiritual) nourishment. In light of the emphasis on salvation by believing, and the many analogies that Christ uses in John, it is clear that He is not referring to taking Communion as the basis of salvation, and *eating* the body and blood of Christ. The entire passage speaks of a spiritual consuming and internalization of Him, the logos of God, via belief.

Life **stEP** — Those who have partaken of the Bread of Heaven will never hunger again. It is only through the broken fellowship of unconfessed sin that the pangs of spiritual want return. Is your soul satisfied today?

John 6:59-71

What is the writer saying?

How can I apply this to my life?

pray *Jamaica – Leadership within the government and churches to be untainted by corruption or compromise.*

Apart from the work of the Holy Spirit, genuine belief would not be possible (v. 63). The statement that Jesus knew from the *beginning* uses the same Greek word as found in John 1:1 where we read that the Word was with God in the *beginning*. This is a clear statement of His foreknowledge, an attribute applicable only to God. As He stated earlier (John 6:37), He again declares the need for God's intervention to bring man to saving faith. Left alone no one would come to the light. Verse 66 makes it clear that even being a follower does not guarantee that a person is a true believer. As some drift away, Jesus challenges the disciples. Spokesman Peter eloquently professes their trust in Him. He uses a perfect tense of the verb (a present condition based on a previous act) saying, *We have been and are currently believing that You are the Holy One of God* (v. 69). It is interesting that elsewhere a demon makes the same identification (Mark 1:24). Jesus responds (v. 70) by saying, " ...one of you is a devil ." Again, John switches roles from that of the narrator of the story to interpreter, as he explains to the reader that Jesus's words in verse 70 are directed toward Judas. Judas, although chosen to be one of the twelve, was simply going through the motions of belief, but did not posses genuine faith.

Life stEP Profession and possession are not the same. True faith is not a matter of mere words. A living faith will be active and visible in the fruit of the life. Those who only profess faith will not endure over the long haul (1 John 2:19).

John 7:1-13

What is the writer saying?

How can I apply this to my life?

During this time in Jesus's ministry, it was getting dangerous for Him to travel openly in Judah for the Jews sought His life. However, during the Feast of Booths (Tabernacles), He again teaches in the temple in Jerusalem. The Feast of Booths was a time when the Jews were reminded of God's provision during their wandering in the wilderness. They were to make booths and stay in them for seven of the eight total days of the feast (see Leviticus 23:42). Each day offerings of the fruit of the harvest were being made. The eighth day all were to gather for corporate worship and offering.

Some think that to have been alive when Christ walked among men would have been a great advantage to believing. In the last chapter, John has shown that many of Jesus's followers did not believe in Him (6:66) and that even one of the twelve was not a true disciple. Now here, in this passage, we learn that His own brothers did not believe in Him (v. 5). Their tone appears to be taunting (vv. 3-4). Jesus is not prepared at the time to go up to Jerusalem, but chooses to wait and depart sometime after His brothers have already gone up. The climate in Jerusalem is volatile (vv. 11-13), but He begins to openly teach in the temple in spite of the danger.

Life stEP   The deceitfulness of the human heart can blind even those of great opportunity to observe the work of God. Be careful never to get so accustomed to seeing God work that you treat His grace and mercy as a common thing.

John 7:14-24

What is the writer saying?

How can I apply this to my life?

When Jesus began to teach, the people marveled. They could not understand how one who had no formal training could teach with such power. Yet, the wisdom of the teaching of Christ was from above. The things He taught were from above, from the Father.

The requirement of God for man is to believe, to take God at His word by faith. Verse 17 is such an appeal, *Take me at my word and see the truth of what I am teaching.* Too often men look to one another instead of looking to God for truth.

The *one deed* (work), referred to in verse 21, is a reference to the healing of the lame man at the pool near the Sheep Gate (John 5:1-15). Because this healing had taken place on the Sabbath, the Jews had labeled Him a sinner, violating the Law. Jesus picks up on their discontent and reveals the hypocrisy of it. If it was not a violation of the Law of Moses to circumcise on the Sabbath, how could making the man whole be a violation? Judging by appearance (v. 24) was looking only at the letter of the Law and not the Spirit behind it. The Jews had reduced their worship of God to a legal code that must be followed to the letter. God was looking for heart obedience based in a relationship with Him.

 Life stEP

What is the basis of your faith? Is it ritual or relationship? Those who heard the Son of God speak were often too stuck in their ritualistic mindset to hear what He was really saying.

Wednesday 26

John 7:25-39

What is the writer saying?

How can I apply this to my life?

pray United Kingdom – Alcoholism is higher in the UK than in any other Western European country. Pray that the young people will not be drawn into this vice.

Many of those who had made the pilgrimage to Jerusalem were obviously not familiar with Jesus, but were able to connect Him to the whispering they had heard among the crowds. The Jews held a common conception that the Messiah would burst on the scene seemingly out of nowhere, but with Jesus, they knew where He came from. Jesus responded that while they may have known Him and where He came from, they do not know the Father who had sent Him. Many who heard His words were convinced that He was their Messiah and believed, yet the Jewish leaders only increased in the hardness of their hearts and their rejection. As Jesus began speaking of the time of His return to the Father in heaven, His words went right over their heads.

"Tabernacles" is the *harvest home* festival, much like our Thanksgiving. In honor of the forty years of protection in the wilderness, families would take their joyful meals outdoors in gaily-decorated shelters. Everyday the High Priest would lead a procession from the Pool of Siloam with water in a gold pitcher to pour out at the temple. With this as a backdrop, Jesus stands on the eighth day and calls out to the spiritually thirsty crowds (v. 37).

It was in this setting that Jesus proclaimed that He was the source of true satisfaction and that those who find this satisfaction would become a source of refreshment to all. John (v. 39) interprets His comments as pertaining to the Holy Spirit, whom those who believe would receive upon their salvation.

Life stEP Those who responded in faith to the ministry of the Savior found eternal life. There is a great difference between hearing God's Word and receiving it.

John 7:40-53

What is the writer saying?

How can I apply this to my life?

The opening verses of this section show the range of opinions about Jesus that swirled around the Jerusalem streets. Some said He was *the Prophet* (see Deuteronomy 18:15-18), while others (v. 42) said He was the Christ (Messiah), and yet others were sure that He could not be the Messiah, because He was to come from Bethlehem and they thought that Jesus was from Galilee. Their statements show both their lack of knowledge concerning Jesus and their impulsiveness, for in verse 44 they are ready to seize Him. Their inability to lay hold of Him shows that everything was moving forward on God's timetable; not man's.

In typical pharisaical fashion, they upbraided the people for being *taken in* by Jesus's words. Their statement says little about their knowledge, but much about the hardness of their hearts. The claim that none of the Pharisees believed in Jesus (v. 48) begins to lose its weight as Nicodemus speaks. The first time John introduced Nicodemus was in chapter 3. There, he came in the darkness to interview Jesus having seen the miracles He did. Now, he defends Jesus's right to a fair hearing. The response of the Pharisees (v. 52) "Art thou also of Galilee?" was an insult and an erroneous one at that, seeing that the prophet Jonah was from Galilee (see 2 Kings 14:25).

Our words always reveal the attitudes of our hearts. James said it best when he asked if the same fountain could bring forth both fresh and bitter water. What are your words telling about the condition of your heart?

John 8:1-11

What is the writer saying?

How can I apply this to my life?

The episode in chapter 8 is designed to entrap Jesus and discredit him. The scene begins on the Mount of Olives where He is already ministering to a constant stream of people (v. 2: "came unto him" indicates *constantly*). The Pharisees show up with a woman taken in the very act of adultery. (Where was the man?) The tense of the verb *say* (v. 4) indicates that they were *repeatedly saying*. Their statement about the Mosaic Law was accurate, although God in His grace did not always insist on capital punishment, such as in the case of King David. They were hoping to either accuse Him of contradicting Moses or of contradicting Roman law, which did not allow the Jews to inflict capital punishment. It seems that Jesus was embarrassed by the crassness of their treatment of the woman (v. 6). He brilliantly avoids the trap by putting it back on them to fulfill the Law, if they are worthy.

Christ succeeded in turning another challenge back on His interrogators when questioned about the tribute money ("Render therefore unto Caesar the things which are Caesar's; and unto God the things that are God's." Matthew 22:21). In neither case did He really answer their question, but rather He exposed their ulterior motives for asking the question. Out of gratitude for His gracious treatment, the woman awaited His direction. It is established that not one of the men stayed to pursue the matter. Jesus does not condone the woman's sin, but releases her with the admonition to cease her life of immorality.

Life stEP

We are to hate the sin, but love the sinner. Jesus associated with the dregs of society. They were the ones who needed the *doctor*. He did not water down His demands, however. Sinners were forgiven, but expected to repent and forsake their sin.

John 8:12-24

What is the writer saying?

How can I apply this to my life?

pray   *Peru – Apathy, doctrinal error, and cults are crippling churches. Pray for more trained Bible teachers.*

Jesus is still in Jerusalem at the Feast of Tabernacles. John again picks up the theme of light and darkness. This is the second of the seven great "I am" statements of Jesus that John records. The priests in the temple would light the Court of Women for dancing and singing, making large lamps and using worn out priestly linen garments as wicks. In the light of these festive hanging bonfires, Jesus made the analogy to His spiritual illumination. The Shekinah Glory had lighted the way of redemption for the children of Israel from Egyptian bondage and through the forty years of wilderness wanderings. That same light is now available for daily guidance in righteousness. Soon, at the Feast of Pentecost, it would descend from heaven and enter individual believers in the form of the indwelling Holy Spirit. Jesus's testimony was valid because He knew the answers to the big questions of life: Who Am I? Where did I come from? Where am I going? The Pharisees could not answer those questions. Christ's second witness of validity (satisfying the demands of the Law for two witnesses in a court of law) was the testimony of His own Father, who not only empowered Him for His miraculous works but also spoke from heaven on three different occasions stating His approval of His Son (baptism, transfiguration, and after the triumphal entry).

Life stEP

It is stunning to see the hardness of the human heart. The Pharisees were intelligent men. Though they argued vehemently with the Lord, they must have felt the power of His words. They never denied the reality of His miracles, yet in the face of such obvious power, they persisted in their opposition.

John 8:25-36

What is the writer saying?

How can I apply this to my life?

pray   *Hungary – Pray that many Bible school students here from central Europe will become leaders at home.*

This is the second time that Jesus mentioned that He was going away and that where He was going they could not go (because they weren't righteous and wouldn't be welcomed into heaven). The first time they wondered if He was planning to leave the country to live among the Jews in the area outside of Palestine (John 7:35). Now they wonder if He is planning to commit suicide (John 8:22). In 8:24, Jesus literally says, "...if ye believe not that *I Am he*, ye shall die in your sins." This again is an allusion to the name *Jehovah* in Exodus 3 (although they and many translators assumed He meant, *I am he*). Jesus is exasperated with their insolence, and rightly so, since He clearly claimed to be the Messiah sent from heaven with the signs to verify the claim. *Lifted up* normally means *glorified*, but here, as in chapter 3, it refers to His crucifixion.

Christ predicts His own death and specifies death by crucifixion so that when it happens, the people can remember His prediction and know that He was telling the truth.

True believers will automatically demonstrate their genuineness by their continuation in the faith. It is the unsaved pretenders who do not have the inner energy to persevere. Verse 32 mentions three highly prized commodities: knowledge, truth, and freedom. His Jewish audience bristles in their pride of being *Abraham's Seed*. Their claim of never being enslaved is strange in light of four hundred years in Egypt and their current domination by Rome (v. 33)!

The prophecies in the Old Testament about the coming of Messiah and the teachings of Jesus seem so clear to us living after the fact. How many teachings of our duties during the Church Age will seem equally clear *after* the return of Christ? We need to be diligent students of the Word so we are not embarrassed.

John 8:37-47

What is the writer saying?

How can I apply this to my life?

pray   *Indonesia – For Indonesian pilots to be trained so the missionary work can continue.*

The discussion gets heated as Jesus points out that their father is really Satan as demonstrated by their murderous intent (vv. 38, 44). When they attempt to claim Abraham as their father, Jesus exhorts them to act like it! Verse 41 comes out of the blue and might be a jab at the rumors surrounding Christ's virgin conception and birth (cf. v. 48). In 6:66 we noted that even *discipleship* does not guarantee that a person is a true believer. We see this as some drift away from Christ. In today's passage, Jesus shows that true discipleship depends on having the right Father. Jesus refers to *your father* three times (vv. 38, 41, and 44). The Jews claimed to be the sons of Abraham in verse 39, but Jesus shows this to be false. They were of Abraham's physical seed. This is true. However, Abraham is not their spiritual father. The Jews also claimed to be sons of God in verse 41. Again, Jesus shows this to be false by showing that if you love the parent, you will not hate the son, which they were doing. Last, Jesus says they are sons of the devil (v. 44), the father of lies, for they were knowingly doing his works as is seen in verses 38, 41, and 44.

Jesus substantiates His claim to be speaking the truth on the premise that no one could charge Him with sin. His enemies often debated whether Jesus was a sinner (John 9:24; 18:38; 19:4, 6). Christ answers His own question of why the Jews would not believe Him. They have rejected Him because of their relationship to the devil. Indeed, they were not of God!

There are many who claim to be disciples of Christ, but this does not mean that they are! The only way for a person to be a true disciple is to first have the right lineage. To whom do you trace your lineage? If it is to anyone but God the Father, then you are not a disciple of Christ.

John 8:48-59

What is the writer saying?

How can I apply this to my life?

pray · Bolivia – For caring youth ministry in a land where 80% of children are living in extreme poverty.

To call Jesus a Samaritan was the equivalent of calling Him a religious fraud. The Jews begin hurling all kinds of abuse at Him, even to the point of saying He was demon possessed! In verse 55, Jesus says that these *Sons of Abraham* had not come to *know* the heavenly Father (this word for *know* means *to come to know by experience*) while He *knew* the Father (a different word for *know* which means *to know inherently*). Jesus' words in verse 51 do not miss their target, as the Jews clearly understand the implication of *shall never see death*. They fume over the fact that these statements would clearly make Him superior to Abraham and the prophets! *Who do you think you are?* would be how we would say it today (v. 53). We can almost feel the indignation coming from the crowd! Jesus understands their frame of mind, but makes it clear He is not attempting to exalt (glorify) Himself, but simply carry out the will of His Father.

Your father Abraham (v. 56) is stated in the ancestral sense. He *rejoiced to see* the promise of future salvation coming through his seed. How much Abraham understood is not known. The Jews again are stuck in the present because they do not recognize the deity and therefore, the eternality of Christ. That Jesus would have first-hand knowledge of Abraham is beyond their comprehension. The discussion comes to an explosive climax with Christ's clearest "I Am" (Jehovah) claim in verse 58!

Life STEP

How do you respond when those who do not agree, challenge the basis of your claim to have a relationship to God? We can imagine in this event in Christ's life that His accusers were livid, while He remained calm and confident (see Philippians 1:28).

John 9:1-12

What is the writer saying?

How can I apply this to my life?

pray *Italy – Maturity in believers, as more churches have resulted from bitter splits than church growth.*

John 9 is the fascinating story of the Sabbath healing of the man born blind (the second Sabbath healing in John that infuriated the religious establishment). This is the only recorded miracle of one defective from birth. A number of Christ's miracles involved the healing of the blind in fulfillment of Messianic passages such as Isaiah 35:5. The event begins with a philosophical discussion among the disciples as to why the man was born blind. In verse 34, the Pharisees will voice one popular opinion. As far back as the book of Job, we find that those who suffered were considered to be under God's judgment for their sins. Christ however, states that it was for this very moment that he had been born blind, that the Father might be glorified. Christ makes clay, anoints the man's eyes, and tells him to wash in the pool of Siloam (*sent*). The clay encouraged the man to display faith.

Throughout his Gospel, John has highlighted specific miracles (signs) to show that Jesus is God and to bring his readers to the point of believing in Him. Jesus had previously stated before the crowd in the temple that He is the *light of the world* (cf. John 8:12; 9:5). Now He clearly illustrates this truth by bringing one born in both physical and spiritual darkness into the light. Just as this man had to wash the clay from his eyes, so our sins must be washed in the blood of Christ.

Life stEP We are all born blind. It is to the glory of God that some sense the *clay* of God's Word and respond in faith receiving their spiritual sight and a new way of life!

John 9:13-25

What is the writer saying?

How can I apply this to my life?

pray   *South Africa – For believers within the government to apply biblical principles in solving problems.*

This portion of John's Gospel shows the tragedy of following man's tradition rather than walking with God. Clearly there were no sustained doubts from anyone present that a miracle had occurred, but it was against the Pharisaic Code to knead clay on the Sabbath (vv. 13-15). Therefore they labeled Jesus a sinner (v. 16). Previously, when Jesus had healed the lame man at the Pool of Bethesda, the Jews had taken issue with the man because he had taken up his bed and walked, just as Jesus had told him (5:10). The religious Jews were so blind that they could look right past a great miracle and only see a technical violation of their tradition. Here in this passage the very same thing is again taking place.

The exchange between the Pharisees and the blind man is amazing! The blind man's opinion of the identity of Jesus goes from *the man* (v. 11), to *prophet* (v. 17), to *Lord I believe* (v. 38)! The response of the man's parents is sad. How could they not be overjoyed at the healing of their son? Yet their fear of the Jews caused them to shrink back from a great opportunity to embrace Jesus as the Christ. This is a great illustration of the truth taught in Proverbs 29:25, "The fear of man bringeth a snare."

Life stEP   The Jews' greatest deterrents to seeing Jesus as the Christ was their spiritual blindness and zeal for their traditions. What best describes your spiritual walk? Is it defined by religion or relationship?

John 9:26-41

What is the writer saying?

How can I apply this to my life?

pray **Korea** – *For godly Chinese businessmen to use their easy access to North Korea to share the Gospel.*

This passage shows a profound truth. Often the simple must instruct those who claim to be learned. The blind man holds to a simple faith, "...I was blind, now I see." He knows that God's power had been demonstrated through his infirmity and cannot do anything but believe in the One who made him whole. The Jews call Jesus a *sinner* because they placed their Sabbath regulations above the spirit of the Law. When one was born blind, the common belief was that the family was being judged for their sin. The disciples certainly thought this way (John 9:2). When the man refused to call Jesus a sinner (John 9:25), they turned on him and claimed he had been in sin since his birth (v. 34). "*Cast him out*" means they kicked him out of the synagogue, the local assembly of the Jews, similar to our churches.

Jesus, hearing the man was cast out of the synagogue, finds him and affirms His deity to him. How gracious of the Son of God, to care so much for this man that He sought him out. Obviously, the Pharisees are still hovering about this man (v. 40) and feel the weight of Jesus's statement about the blind receiving sight and the seeing being blind. Because they were not willing to admit their sin (blindness) and need for healing (salvation), they would remain in their blind state!

Life **stEP** What great darkness surrounds those who are religious, yet apart from Christ! Only by coming to the Savior will they ever truly see the Light of Life.

John 10:1-13

What is the writer saying?

How can I apply this to my life?

This section is a continuation of the exchange that took place between Jesus and the Pharisees at the end of chapter 9. Here He makes the third and fourth of the seven "I am" statements in the Gospel of John (vv. 7, 11).

Christ is the *door* to the sheepfold. The shepherd literally served as the door when he lay down in the doorway of the stone enclosure. Sometimes these enclosures were topped with brambles that acted as *barbed wire* to protect the sheep during the night. The enclosure had only one entrance. To get to the sheep one had to go through the shepherd first. Today many would like us to believe that there are many roads that lead to God. The message of the cross is very exclusive. There is one door (v. 7), one way (John 14:6), one God and mediator (1 Timothy 2:5).

The Pharisees were spiritual thieves, robbers, or at best, hirelings (vv. 8, 12). Perhaps Jesus had in mind the words of the prophet Zechariah as He made these statements (Zechariah 11:4-9, 17). Christ is the *Good Shepherd* because He gives His life for the sheep (v. 11, Psalm 22). For us, that is His *past* ministry. He is the *Great Shepherd* because He presently guides the sheep all the way to glory (Hebrews 13:20; Psalm 23). He is also the *Chief Shepherd* of the sheep and in the future will return to reward all the *under shepherds* or pastors (1 Peter 5:4 cf. Psalm 24).

Life **stEP** Christ is the only door into the security of the sheepfold. There is no other way of salvation than through the sacrifice of Jesus Christ. One of our great comforts as believers is the knowledge that the Great Shepherd has placed us in the fold.

John 10:14-30

What is the writer saying?

How can I apply this to my life?

The Good Shepherd has a special relationship to His sheep. This is seen by the nature of the relationship. The shepherd is not a hired hand, but rather the owner of the sheep (my sheep); and the relationship is reciprocal (know and known). The Father loves the Son because of His willing obedience. *Other sheep* (10:16) refers to Gentiles who would believe and be joined with the Jewish believers (this fold) into one body (see Ephesians 2:13-16). Verses 17 and 18 teach clearly that Jesus was in total sovereign control throughout the events leading to His crucifixion. No one took His life from Him but rather, He willingly offered Himself as our substitutionary sacrifice. A worthy shepherd would sacrifice himself to save his sheep. Jesus proved He was our Good Shepherd at Calvary.

John indicates (v. 22) that this confrontation takes place during the time of the Feast of Dedication, which took place in the winter. This feast is present day Hanukkah. It was a celebration of the rededication of the temple by Judas Maccabeus in 165 B.C. after its desecration in 168 B.C. by Antiochus Epiphanes.

Even though it had been weeks since Jesus' last confrontation with the Jews much hostility toward Him remained. The Jewish leadership continues in their unbelief, which shows they were not a part of God's fold (v. 26). This section concludes with a powerful declaration of the security of our salvation (vv. 27-30).

Life stEP

Believers are in a spiritual war zone. The battle has already been decided, yet it still rages. To bring men to Himself, Jesus endured much suffering and abuse. How willing are you to stand for Him?

John 10:31-42

What is the writer saying?

How can I apply this to my life?

If anyone ever doubted whether Jesus claimed to be God, He put the question to rest as He plainly says, "I and my Father are one!" (v. 30). The Jews understood perfectly that by making such a statement Jesus claimed to be God. In response, they lashed out stating that His claim was blasphemy! Yet Jesus used the Scripture to silence their complaint. In the passage He quoted (Psalm 82:6), the psalmist used the common Hebrew word for God, *Elohim*, to identify key men who spoke for God. How much more should the incarnate Son Himself be free to speak of His oneness in nature with the Father!

Once again, Jesus was willing to let His works speak for Him (vv. 37-38). If they could not believe His words, they only needed to examine His works to see that He did all that the Prophets had said that Messiah would do when He came (cf. Isaiah 35:4-6).

As so many times before, the Jews wanted to grab Him, but He eluded their grasp. Each time we are reminded that Jesus was in complete control of every situation (v. 39).

Withdrawing to the Jordan, His ministry now comes full circle to where it all began (John 1:28 ff.). Though most of the religious leadership had rejected Him, many sought Him and believed upon Him there.

Life Step The security of our salvation stems from the trustworthy nature of the one who provided it. He endured the painful sacrifice required to purchase our redemption and has an active involvement in keeping those who have believed unto salvation.

John 11:1-15

What is the writer saying?

How can I apply this to my life?

pray — *Japan – For an end to cult growth, which far exceeds the growth of Christianity.*

Chapter 11 contains the last and greatest of Jesus' sign miracles prior to His own resurrection. Bethany (*house of dates*) was a small village on the backside of the Mount of Olives about two miles from Jerusalem.

Lazarus (*Whom God aids!*) is not as well known as his two sisters, Mary and Martha. On hearing the news of his friend's sickness, Christ explains that this episode is predestined to glorify the Son. He means not just in the miracle, but also in the aftermath for this miracle was to cause the final confrontation leading to His crucifixion. Verse 9 poetically relates that as long as you are walking in the center of God's will, no harm can befall you. Verse 14 is also a miracle because He knew what took place over twenty miles away. Verse 6 tells us He waited two days and verse 17 tells us that Lazarus had been dead four days. (The Jews believed that the soul did not leave for heaven until three days had passed.) Christ purposely waits until the fourth day to increase the drama and impact of this, His crowning sign miracle before His death.

Throughout his Gospel, John has highlighted many miracles done by Jesus, but draws particular attention to seven that he identifies as signs, each underscoring some aspect of what it means to believe. This final sign points to the newness of life that awaits those who have trusted Christ as Savior.

Life stEP — Christ taught the masses but focused on individuals. He poured His life into individuals who then turned the world upside down when He was gone.

John 11:16-29

What is the writer saying?

How can I apply this to my life?

pray   *Jamaica – That key individuals among the Rastafarian group would be saved and become witnesses.*

Didymus means *twin* (as does Thomas), perhaps the twin brother of Matthew because they are frequently mentioned together. Thomas gives us a glimpse into what is going through the minds of the disciples. They were greatly concerned about the mounting hostility against Jesus.

The contrast in the personalities of Mary and Martha makes an interesting study (John 12 and Luke 10). Luke 10 is the famous *Martha/Mary Syndrome* where Martha is busy preparing a meal for the Lord and rebukes Him for allowing Mary to sit and listen to Him while she did all the work. Martha is told that Mary has chosen the better part, sitting at the feet of Jesus! Here in John, Martha is active, running out to meet Jesus while Mary passively mourns in the house. Martha aggressively announces her hurt in losing *my brother* (Greek emphasis), whereas Mary tenderly mourns *my brother* (v. 32). Martha is vocal and Mary is tearful. Christ and Martha have a rational discussion about the resurrection, whereas Mary just falls at Christ's feet and worships. That Martha called Jesus the *Teacher* (*Master*) is interesting because the Pharisees would not teach women, but Jesus did (v. 28). Their friends, who have come to comfort, are staying close to Mary, while Martha must have appeared to be holding her own.

Life **stEP**   God always deals with us as individuals. Martha needed instruction while Mary needed to be comforted. Ask God to help you meet people where they are. What a blessing it is to know that those who believe in Jesus will live even if they die!

John 11:30-44

What is the writer saying?

How can I apply this to my life?

pray *Mexico – For discipleship programs that would effectively teach how the Bible impacts family life.*

Jesus' response in verse 33 is a display of anger at Satan for the heartache he has brought to mankind. *Groaned* is used as the snorting of a warhorse. Death, to Christ, was not an impassable barrier, but a call to battle! The *wept* of verse 35 was a quiet, dignified weeping.

This passage is filled with emotion. Martha goes to fetch Mary having had a few moments with Christ outside the village. She calls her sister unobtrusively. The Jews, who had been consoling Mary instead of going out with Martha when she went to meet Jesus, followed Mary as she rises to leave. They thought she was going to the tomb to weep, and they wished to share in this activity. Mary's words were almost identical to Martha's and as such were a firm conviction that Christ's power could have saved Lazarus from death. No one was expecting a resurrection! But then, Jesus exceeds all that we ask or think, doesn't He?

At the tomb, Christ orders the stone removed and reminds Martha of His previous statement to her. He offers a thanksgiving prayer before the miracle. Lazarus, upon hearing the voice of the Omnipotent, responds and comes forth! Christ had to specify, "Lazarus, come forth," lest the whole cemetery empty out!

Life stEP Many Christians are like Lazarus as he comes out of the tomb... alive in Christ, but still bound by the grave clothes of the world. They cannot work for their hands are bound, nor witness because their mouths are bound. Christ wants us to be free! Oh, that we would proclaim Christ's words to those dead in sin, "Whosoever will may come!"

John 11:45-57

What is the writer saying?

How can I apply this to my life?

pray *Netherlands Antilles – Openness to the Gospel in a land where religious freedom has yielded little fruit.*

When Jesus gives the command to loose Lazarus, it would appear that the miracle is finished. There is more though! In verse 45, we see that because of Jesus' power, many believed! Sadly though, some merely went to report the incident, their hearts hardened to the truth. The religious authorities were not happy campers! The *place* they were afraid of losing was the temple. Caiaphas offers what he believes is the expedient thing to do, sacrifice one man for the good of the whole nation. Caiaphas, being the High Priest, is speaking prophetically (v. 51), yet he himself does not have God's will in mind but rather the removal of a nuisance for the good of the whole. Earlier, Jesus had told them they were of the devil and would do his works ("a murderer from the beginning," John 8:44). Here we see them plotting that very thing. Verse 52 speaks of the scope of Christ's sacrifice, sufficient not only for the nation of Israel but for the Gentiles also. This day marked the beginning of the Jews' open plans to kill Jesus. Verse 55 is an amazing backdrop. The Passover was at hand! Jesus was soon to be the ultimate Passover lamb. The blood He would shed would be a once-for-all sacrifice that would serve not as a covering for sin but as the satisfaction of God's righteous demands (1 John 2:2) and the basis of cleansing from their sin, to those who believe (Hebrews 10:10-14).

Life STEP The substitutionary sacrifice of Jesus Christ on the Cross is the basis for our forgiveness. This forgiveness is made available to every man yet is only known by those who believe and place their faith in Christ. What a tragedy to know of God's grace and yet not receive it.

John 12:1-11

What is the writer saying?

How can I apply this to my life?

We are now six days before the crucifixion. It has been no more than three months since Lazarus was raised (from the Hanukkah of John 10 to Passover is about one hundred days). Martha is still active, and Mary is worshipping! This was apparently a special meal as the Greek text says that they reclined at the table. Only the wealthy regularly ate this way. The poor would only do so at special meals like Passover. In the reclining position, it was easy for Mary to reach the Lord's feet. Normally a servant would wash the feet. It was also unusual for a woman to let her hair down in public. These acts of humility are impressive. The value of the perfume is overwhelming. Three hundred pence (denarii) represents about a year's wages for a common laborer. The spikenard (nard) was expensive because the closest that it was grown and processed was northern India.

The mean-spiritedness of Judas is shocking. It is hard to imagine whom he thought he was to interfere. The Lord graciously protects Mary and turns Judas' complaint back on him. If he was so interested in the poor, he could make that his personal ministry for the rest of his life! John interjects the commentary that Judas was insincere, although no one suspected him at the time. In verse 10, we see that sinful intent is multiplying. The religious leaders started with plans to kill one man *for the sake of the nation*. They have now added a second. Having crossed the line, they now can rationalize almost anything to preserve their place.

Life stEP Martha, Lazarus, and Mary are wonderful examples of service, fellowship, and worship. All are necessary, but worship is the starting point.

John 12:12-22

What is the writer saying?

How can I apply this to my life?

This section, often referred to as the Triumphal Entry, is common to all four Gospels. Here, many in the crowd of people coming to Jerusalem to celebrate the Passover began to continually call out (the verb is in an imperfect tense) to Jesus as He enters the city.

The palm branch, a symbol of happiness, is used to this day in the Feast of Tabernacles celebration. *Hosanna* is a transliteration of the Hebrew or Aramaic meaning, *please save*. Both this phrase and *he who comes* are found in Psalm 118:25, 26. The crowd obviously has these messianic ideas in mind as they greet Jesus. His entry, riding on a donkey's colt, is a direct fulfillment of Zechariah 9:9.

Unlike the pomp and circumstance usually associated with the coming of a king, Jesus' entrance is humble. Nonetheless, the Pharisees are greatly agitated and are stirring one another up as a result of their perceived ineffectiveness at squashing His popularity with the people.

John editorializes the event (v. 16), showing the disciples' lack of understanding about what was happening as the events unfold. Later, after the Lord's Resurrection, they were able to put the events together.

Throughout the book it is clear that John is writing both to a Jewish and Gentile audience. The mention of the Greeks (vv. 20-22) is important in that Jesus' death was for the sins of all of mankind, not just the Jews.

Life **stEP**   The fulfillment of Scripture is a common theme among the Gospels. God's Word will not fail. The things written concerning Jesus will all be completely fulfilled. Are you ready for His promised return?

John 12:23-36

What is the writer saying?

How can I apply this to my life?

The Greeks (previous section) were *God-fearers*; Gentiles who were impressed with Judaism but didn't want to be circumcised. Possibly, they came to Philip since he had a Greek name (*Lover of Horses*) and was from a Greek area. It is touching to see the way Philip goes to Andrew for advice. You will notice that no more mention is made of this request, but Jesus uses it as an opportunity to predict His imminent death, (*the hour*) towards which the entire story has been moving. It is significant that Gentiles trigger this announcement because through His death we are elevated to equality with Jews in the family of God!

Verse 24 applies *the law of the harvest* to the spiritual realm. Verse 25 is a paradox. Those who wish to save their life, living for their own selfish ends, will destroy (present tense) that to which they desperately cling. Those who hate their lives (by comparison), gain (future tense) that which is true life indeed.

The Father thunders His approval from heaven (v. 28). *Lifted up* (v. 32) normally means *exalted*. The cross is a triumph, not a defeat! It was here that the serpent received its head wound (Genesis 3) and the prince of this world system was cast out (v. 31)! John returns to familiar themes of light versus darkness and that which leads to belief. Jesus' warning is to respond (in faith) to the light at hand, lest the opportunity for belief is snatched away due to their procrastination (vv. 35-36). See also (Matthew 13:4, 19).

We fear death because it makes no sense to us that out of death and decay can come another life. Nature encourages us, whether it is the *dead* grain of wheat or the stunning metamorphosis of the lowly caterpillar into a mass of jellied protein, and then the stunning butterfly!

John 12:37-50

What is the writer saying?

How can I apply this to my life?

pray — Italy – For the northeastern Veneto region of 4,437,000 people of which approximately 2,000 are believers.

Verse 36 announces Christ's withdrawal from the public. In chapters 13-17, He limits His ministry just to the disciples. Verse 37 announces the reason for going private. Verse 38 quotes Isaiah 53:1, and verse 40 is part of Isaiah's call to the ministry (Isaiah 6:10). In Isaiah's day (700 B.C.) he was told that he would have a ministry of hardening and so did Jesus. Those who reject the deity of Christ did so with the claim that in Scripture Jesus is not referred to by the name *Jehovah* (the Greek *Kurios* for *Lord* can also mean *sir*). John 12:41 is the one place in Scripture where there is a direct connection between Jesus and the name Jehovah. In Isaiah 6:1, it is Jehovah *high* and *lifted up* that Isaiah views, but John tells us that the prophet was beholding the glory of Jesus! Like Nicodemus, some of the Jewish religious leaders were coming to faith in Christ (v. 42). However, they kept this to themselves fearing the reproach of their peers. Though they are generally the exception, not all of the priests would remain hostile to the Gospel (see Acts 6:7). John, looking back upon this event, notes that it was the fear of men that motivated their silence. They sought the approval of men more than the approval of God.

Those who reject Jesus Christ will only have themselves to blame ultimately. Jesus makes it clear that those who hear and reject the Gospel will be judged by the very Word of God from which they have turned away (vv. 47-50).

Life stEP His contemporaries missed the predictions of Messiah's death (Psalms 16, 22; Isaiah 53). We are tempted to give them the benefit of the doubt, but Christ expected them to know these *hard* passages.

John 13:1-11

What is the writer saying?

How can I apply this to my life?

pray *Nigeria – For committed Christian leaders that will follow through with real preparation of Bible lessons and true discipleship.*

Chapters 13-17 contain seven lectures designed to prepare the disciples to carry on Christ's work in His absence. Seven times in these chapters He says, "*These things have I spoken unto you.*" In four of these, we are given the purpose for His teachings:
1) For their joy (15:11)
2) For their confidence (16:1)
3) For their memory (16:4)
4) And for their peace (16:33)
Chapter 13 contains the account of the Last Supper. Verse 1 states that Christ loved His disciples *to the uttermost* (fullness of His love). He leaves them with an example of humility to follow. Prior to chapter 12 Jesus had four times stated that His hour had not yet come. Now however, it had come. *Hour* is a reference to the whole series of events leading up to and including His death, burial, and resurrection.

In the exchange between Peter and Jesus (vv. 6-11), much more than dirty feet are being discussed. Peter's initial refusal quickly becomes an overreaction as he requests a complete cleansing. The reply of Jesus (v. 10) is a reference to salvation. *He that is washed,* (saved) needs only to wash his feet (confession of daily sins for unbroken fellowship). The statement that they are *not all clean* is a reference to the unbelief of Judas.

Life **STEP** Peter always tries to control the situation. In his befuddlement, (probably because he was seated where the assigned foot washer would sit) he first rejects the washing then requests a whole bath. Consistent with 1 John 1:9, Christ strikes the balance. Believers are bathed in the blood of Christ for salvation and kept in fellowship by the confession of daily sin.

John 13:12-20

What is the writer saying?

How can I apply this to my life?

pray   South Korea – For seminary graduates to humbly commit themselves to less prominent, rural pastorates.

Jesus has just washed the disciples' feet. This was a task performed by the servant of a household. In the absence of any subordinate, no one was jumping to be the one to carry out this task. Jesus takes on the role of servant to the group and performs this menial task.

Returning to His place at the table, He now explains the importance of this act to His disciples. His pre-eminence among them was never an issue (v. 13). The terms they addressed Him by were terms of respect and honor. If their teacher, the Lord, was not too good to serve them by washing their feet, they too were not too good to serve one another. The example (v. 15) He left them was not of washing feet but rather of service. Blessing (v. 17) is found not in the knowledge of what pleases God, but in doing those things that please Him. Verse 18 is a fulfillment of verse 19. Jesus was going to tell His disciples plainly of His betrayal before it occurred, so when it happened, their faith would not be shaken but rather strengthened. The Cross was not a mistake but part of God's plan. The betrayal was a necessary element on the road to Calvary.

Verse 20 shows the connection between the Lord and His servants. Those who minister unto the servants of God are ministering to the Lord. A great example of this is found in the Olivet Discourse (Matthew 25:34-40). The heartbeat of God is that of service. If our Lord was not too good to wash the feet of His disciples, then who are we to consider ourselves above any aspect of ministry unto our brethren?

Service is not glamorous, but it is Christ-like. Jesus was not pretending to be a servant, but using this opportunity to demonstrate vividly that to humble one's self to serve others was not below Him, and should not be too much to ask of us!

John 13:21-38

What is the writer saying?

How can I apply this to my life?

In the next section (13:31-14:31), Christ tells His disciples, *Brace yourselves, I'm leaving!* He affectionately calls them *little children* and certainly they would behave so in the next seventy two hours!

Peter persuades John (the disciple whom Jesus loved, v. 23) to ask Jesus who His betrayer would be. Jesus plainly identifies Judas, however many of the disciples are still oblivious to his treachery (v. 29).

Peter ignores the Lord's challenge to love the brethren and goes back to His statement in verse 33, "Whither I go, ye cannot come." When Christ said that to the religious authorities (7:34; 8:21), He implied *never* (since they refused to repent and believe). In verse 36, He softens the statement for the disciples indicating that their separation would be temporary, not permanent. Peter gets the drift and protests his intent to lay down his life

as well. Christ calls his bluff and states the reality that at the time of crisis, no one will stand with Him. He will go through the valley of the shadow of death alone. Peter's denial is recorded in all four Gospels.

In this first private discussion after Judas' departure, Christ is asked four questions by the puzzled and increasingly alarmed disciples. Peter: Where are you going? (v. 36) Answer: Somewhere you can't.

Thomas: How can we get there? (14:5) Answer: Through Me!

Philip: Can we take a peek? (14:8) Answer: Look at Me!

Judas (not Iscariot): Why the change in the program? (14:22) Answer: Belief required.

Despite being truly repentant of their sins and desirous of obeying God and His Christ, the disciples had the same disease that afflicted the Pharisees. They wanted physical manifestations of the kingdom of God in this world. Where have you set your affections?

John 14:1-14

What is the writer saying?

How can I apply this to my life?

pray — *Jamaica – For Jamaican churches to have a hunger for God's Word and a passion for missions.*

Christ does not want His disciples to be in turmoil. Belief is the key. *Mansions* is from the Greek root *meno*, meaning *to abide*. It is not referring to palatial country estates but rather, *dwelling places* (rooms in a father's house for the children). The only other time this word occurs in scripture is in 14:23 where it refers to our heart as Christ's home!

Christ promises to return for the disciples. Theologically, this is a unique proposition since up to this point in their understanding of the Bible; the coming of Christ was for the sake of establishing a kingdom on the earth, not taking saints back to heaven. As such, verse 3 becomes a major witness for the Pre-tribulation Rapture of the church! Believers will spend the seven years of the tribulation period in seclusion with the Bridegroom in the heavenly bridal chambers before returning to help establish Christ's Kingdom in the same arena where He was originally rejected.

Verse 6 contains the sixth of Christ's great "I am" statements. Jesus, being one with the Father, was of the same essence as the Father. To know Him was equal to knowing the Father. Those who know Jesus know the way home.

In response to Philip's request (v. 8), Christ offers His own life as an open book about the Father. The astounding statement that the disciples would do *greater works* should be understood as works greater in scope. Christ was localized and could only minister to so many people per day. However, when He leaves and sends the Holy Spirit, the Holy Spirit will work through all believers.

What work could be greater than seeing the dead being raised? Today we have the privilege of seeing lives changed through the power of the Gospel. To know Christ is to pass from spiritual death to spiritual life.

John 14:15-24

What is the writer saying?

How can I apply this to my life?

Italy – Pray for the more than 30,000 communities without an established gospel witness.

Christ will ask the Father to send another Comforter. There are two words for *another* in Greek. *Heteros* is *another of a different kind* such as the false gospel that was no gospel at all in Galatians 1 or our word *heterosexual*. The other word is *allos*, which means *another of the same kind*. Both Jesus and the Holy Spirit are *comforters*.

In 1 John 2:1, the term being translated *comforter*, is used of Christ and translated advocate. When we slip into sin, Jesus Christ is our *advocate* with the Father. The Greek term is *paraklete*, a compound word composed of *para* (alongside; parallel) + *kaleo* (to call): *one called alongside to help in time of need*. It was used as a legal term: aide, counsel, or intercessor. Even our English word *comfort* helps us appreciate the Holy Spirit's ministry. It too is a compound word, *com* (with) and *fort* (strength). He doesn't just comfort us when we get hurt but strengthens us before we go out into battle!

Verses 15 and 24 are like the bookends of this section. The life of the true believer is characterized by obedience to the commandments of God. Jesus had set the ultimate example of love and obedience and now expects His followers will walk according to that pattern. The one who says he loves God and yet lives a life of habitual disobedience to the Word of God is deceiving himself but not God (1 John 2:4). This being said, maturity does not happen instantaneously when one is saved. We must leave room for the immature Christian to grow into maturity and obedience as their knowledge of God increases.

Life stEP

The function of the Spirit is to make the reality of God convincing to all men in the same way that Jesus did to His disciples. How are people being impacted by your life and testimony?

John 14:25-31

What is the writer saying?

How can I apply this to my life?

pray   *Guatemala – For medical ministries to reach the 55,000 war orphans and 5,000 street children.*

One of the ministries of the Holy Spirit was temporary and limited to the disciples. This resulted in the book we hold in our hands almost 2,000 years later, the Bible. He would cause the disciples to remember all that Christ said, even though they didn't understand much of it at the time it was spoken.

He emphatically states that, "My (kind of) peace I give unto you (not the world's peace)" (v. 27). Christ wants the disciples to be happy for His imminent reunion with the Father. He also implies that He has to go away for this special gift of the Holy Spirit to come. It is clear that the ministry of the Holy Spirit is different after the cross than before. The event that makes the difference is the Cross work of Christ. The actual payment for the sin of mankind gave the Spirit of God greater influence in the lives of men than what was normally experienced by the Old Testament saints. This could be one of the reasons why we see so many of the Old Testament saints falling into gross sin (cf. David and Solomon) while most heroes of the New Testament stayed faithful to the Lord.

Christ knew that the disciples were in a state of shock, but He informs them of these things now so when they happen, the disciples will have further proof that He was right and indeed is the Messiah.

The *prince of this world* (v. 30) is a reference to Satan, who soon would throw everything he had at the Son of God. In unwavering obedience and submission to the will of the heavenly Father, Jesus Christ walked full face into the adversary's fury.

Life Step

It is sometimes tempting to say, "God is not doing anything special in my life. I want to see some power!" But in the sweep of human history, the impact the Bible has had on culture is a demonstration of incredible power!

John 15:1-11
What is the writer saying?

How can I apply this to my life?

Uruguay – For God to save and call witnesses among the upper middle–class, which is estimated to be the largest group not evangelized.

pray

Chapter 15 is lecture number two, a lecture on relationships. At the end of chapter 14, Christ said to the disciples, *let us go* (from the site of the Last Supper). As they make their way out of the city to the Garden of Gethsemane (*Olive Oil Press*), He uses an agricultural analogy to describe the relationship of the believer to Himself (vv. 1-11). The grapevine was a powerful symbol in Israel, like our *bald eagle.*

The progression given (v. 2) is that of increasing fruitfulness. The vinedresser works with the branches of the vine to maximize their fruit bearing. Jesus told His disciples that they were already *clean* or *pruned* because of the word He had spoken to them. They were ready to bear fruit, but the key for them would be their abiding in Him, the vine (v. 4). On their own they could produce nothing (v. 5) but in Him they would bear much fruit.

The branches that are burned (v. 6) can picture the following things: 1) unproductive Christians who are taken home prematurely because of their disobedience 2) branches containing dead wood that is cut away during the pruning process. Here the *branch* is only the dead wood that is thrown into the fire, and not the whole person. 3) Those, like Judas, who professed to be followers of Jesus Christ but did not continue in faith, demonstrating that they were not genuine (1 John 2:19). Verse 7 is not a blank check but rather a promise that as His disciples walked in obedience they could rely on Christ to meet their needs. The relationship that Christ was unfolding for His disciples was based upon love (v. 9) and obedience (v. 10) just as His relationship with His Father. Their walk of love and obedience would result in glory to the Father and fullness of joy for them.

Notice the progression of what Christ expects from His vines (15:2, 5): *fruit; more fruit; and much fruit!* How do you measure up?

John 15:12-27

What is the writer saying?

How can I apply this to my life?

pray *Ukraine – For God to give youth a passion to live for Him and reach their land.*

Christ's second lecture to His disciples involves relationships. First, He discusses their relationship to Him as the vine and the branches (vv. 1-11). Second is their relationship to each other in brotherly love (vv. 13-17). Finally, He discusses their relationship to the world (vv. 18-27).

In the new set of circumstances, no longer will believers be the servants of God or just the children of God but rather adult sons in God's family (the theological definition of the New Testament word *adoption*). This gives us great authority, privilege, and responsibility. It is significant that the Church Age began at Pentecost, the anniversary of the giving of the Law. The great transition from the Age of Law to the Age of Grace begins on the same anniversary in the calendar. On that day, the disciples went from being children under the tutelage of the Law (Galatians 4) to adult sons! In their day, students chose the rabbi they wanted to study under. Christ says that He reversed the process by choosing them (v. 16). He chose them to be fruit bearers. The authority they have in prayer is to fulfill that commission.

Jesus gives them fair warning that the world is not going to treat them kindly. There is a chain of *guilt by association*. The world hates the Father; therefore, it also hates the One sent from the Father (the Son). Since it hates the Son, it also hates those associated with the Son. It also resents that the Son has chosen them out of the world (v. 19). Verse 26 returns to the coming of the Comforter who will energize the disciples in their relationship to the world (as that of light, witness, and testifier). He is called the Spirit of Truth. Notice that His job is to magnify Christ, not Himself.

 We are free... free to choose to show our gratitude to our Savior by working for Him and His glory! Christ wants us to bear fruit, fruit that remains and thus glorify the Father.

John 16:1-11

What is the writer saying?

How can I apply this to my life?

The fourth relationship that Christ discusses is that of believers to the Holy Spirit. The parents of the blind man in chapter 9 were afraid of being excommunicated from the synagogue. In chapter 12 we find out that some of the Pharisees did believe in Jesus, but they were afraid to lose their position of prominence in society. Being put out of the synagogue was a serious event for a Jewish person. The Pharisees controlled the synagogue system (whereas the Sadducees controlled the temple). The synagogue controlled all birth certificates, marriage certificates, bills of divorce, and burial rights. All of Jewish life and society centered on the synagogue. Jesus warns them of their own excommunication so they are not caught off guard when it happens. By warning them ahead of time, He wants to keep them from despair, which can lead to apostasy.

The Apostle Paul is a good example of verse 2. Christ says it will be *profitable* to them for Him to leave (v. 7). This is the same word used by Caiaphas when he said that it was *expedient* for one man to die to save their position! The Old Testament does not say much about the Holy Spirit's ministry of conviction. Now we are informed of three areas of conviction in verse 8 which are explained in verses 9-11: *sin* (of unbelief, v. 9); *righteousness* (now that my example is no longer in front of their eyes, v. 10) and *judgment* (since it is coming soon, v. 11). The following are the several different special relationships and ministries of the Holy Spirit. The Spirit convicts the world (v. 8), it guides the disciples (v. 13), and the Spirit glorifies Christ (v. 14.).

Life stEP The fear of man is a snare. Let us not be concerned about our appearance in man's eyes, but rather, let us serve Christ in obedience. Satan is a defeated foe! He still roars and is dangerous in his death throes, but we can claim the victory in the power of the Spirit.

John 16:12-22

What is the writer saying?

How can I apply this to my life?

Having spoken of the Holy Spirit's convicting ministry, the Son of God now turns to His teaching ministry. By His use of the Old Testament Scriptures, quoted in various places in the Gospels and Acts, Jesus put God's stamp of authority on those writings. Beginning in John 14:26, Jesus pre-authenticates all of the New Testament writings. "Bring all things to your remembrance" (John 14:26) speaks of the Gospels. "Guide you into all truth" (v. 13) would occur as the Epistles were penned under divine inspiration. These letters would give the early church the direction and instruction it so desperately needed. "Shew you things to come" (v. 13) was the promise of the blessing of the completed canon, as the book of Revelation would foretell the final chapter of human history and the glorious future of those who enter into God's rest.

Today, we have the Scripture in totality. There is no need for new revelation. However, the Spirit of God still guides believers in understanding God's revealed Word found only in the Bible. "He shall glorify me" (v. 14); the ministry of the Holy Spirit is never to bring attention (glory) to Himself, but to bring glory to Christ.

We saw in verse 16 how puzzled the disciples were since they had not comprehended the death, burial, and resurrection of Christ. Within twenty four hours, He would be gone, but within another forty eight hours He would be with them again in His resurrected body! He does not spell it out to them, but further illustrates the significance of their mood swings over the next seventy two hours. They will be plummeted into the depths of despair. Their despair will be bitter as they hear the religious authorities mocking and rejoicing at His demise. Verse 22 speaks of the fullness and permanence of their joy at the other end of these events.

Life
st**EP**

Anything said to be of the Spirit should match exactly the pattern laid in Scripture. One should ask, "Who is being glorified and what is the purpose?"

John 16:23-33

What is the writer saying?

How can I apply this to my life?

pray — Indonesia – For the unity and continued growth of churches in the midst of intense persecution.

The phrase, *in that day* (v. 23), is a reference to the time after Jesus's resurrection. Up to this point, prayers were not offered in the name of Jesus. Christ explains the pattern of prayer that is followed during the Church Age. We are to make our requests to the Father in the name (authority) of the Son. This does not mean that it is out of the question to pray to Jesus or the Holy Spirit but that the normal pattern is to pray to the Father in the authority of the Son and empowered by the Spirit. The direct access to the Father that Jesus reveals to them would be a tremendous source of encouragement. The disciples say, *Yes, now we understand*. One would think they would have been filled with questions. They clearly overstate their grasp of that which Jesus is saying to them as seen by His reply.

Jesus is clearly skeptical (v. 31) knowing that in a few hours the sheep would scatter (Zechariah 13:7). Even with that depressing acknowledgment, Christ leaves an example for us to follow in our lonely times as He rightly observes that the Father will be with Him. (This sets the stage for the horror of the three-hour period when even this was not true as He bore the sin of the entire world on His back and was temporarily abandoned by His own Father.)

Jesus states the reason that He has spoken these things to them is that they might have peace in the midst of the turmoil that was to come upon them. *Overcome* in verse 33 is the same as *conquerors* in "we are more than conquerors" (Romans 8:37). Three different Greek prepositions describe Christ's relationship to the Father in this section: v. 27, "out from" (*para* indicates authority or commission); v. 28, "out of" (*ek*, source); v. 30, "from" (*apo*, separation from the Father).

Life stEp — It is hard to think that anything could be better than having Jesus living with you in the flesh. In the plan of God, the indwelling Holy Spirit and His written Word gives us a richer relationship with the Godhead!

Sunday 31

John 17:1-13
What is the writer saying?

How can I apply this to my life?

pray Kenya – For believers to forsake previous ethnic religious practices and be unified by biblical truth.

John 17 is the real *Lord's Prayer*; His *High-Priestly Prayer of Intercession*. (Matthew 6 is better called *The Disciples' Prayer*). The structure of John 17 is very interesting. The *bull's eye* is *eternal life*, with the following three sections forming three concentric circles. Each of these sections is broader in scope than the former.

1) Verses 1-5 have two commands: *glorify thy Son* (that is, His authority as the Son to give eternal life due to His work on earth) and *glorify thou me* (that is, return my person to its pre-incarnate glory with the Father).

2) Verses 6-19 contain two more commands: *Keep them* (that is, protect my disciples from evil) and *sanctify them* (that is, set them apart for the continuation of my work on earth).

3) Verses 20-26 contain two requests: *I ask* (v. 20) is a request for unity among all believers. *I desire* (v. 24) is a request to unite all believers with their Savior in glory.

Eternal Life (v. 3) is defined, not as endless existence (although it is that!) but as a living contact with God. *Know* is the present tense, which means that even in heaven the contact and growth is ongoing throughout all eternity! (*Know* means more than just imparted knowledge.) The *life* now enjoyed by the disciples is revealed in this prayer as enlightenment (v. 8) and preservation (except Judas whose betrayal was predicted, Psalm 41:9, 11).

Life STEP Eternal life is not luxurious idleness, but purposeful labor for the Creator, both now and for eternity!

John 17:14-26

What is the writer saying?

How can I apply this to my life?

Bahrain – For the American Mission Hospital, which is well regarded, to see fruit from the tactful witness of believers employed there.

pray

Continuing from yesterday, the *life* (v. 3) now enjoyed by the disciples is revealed in this prayer as joy (v. 13), sanctification (to set apart for *God's use*, v. 19), and employment (v. 18, *So send I you!*). It is revealed in the prayer as unity of common belief, worship, service (v. 23), and fellowship (v. 24) now and for eternity!

The disciples are not of the world, as demonstrated back in verse 8 by the fact that they: 1) accepted His words, 2) recognized that Jesus came from the Father, and 3) believed Him. That sets the disciples apart from the Pharisees. In verse 17, note the close association between sanctification and revealed truth. Verse 18 likens our mission to Christ's. We take up where He left off. Christ says that He set Himself apart that the disciples might also be set apart. Of course, His sanctification was His self-sacrifice on the cross (v. 19)!

With these eleven disciples, there begins a long chain that reaches down the corridors of time to the 21st century, which has resulted in our salvation! There is much work to be done, but Christ looks forward to that grand day when labor is over and we can all meet in the Father's house. Jesus is anxious to introduce us to His Father! His Father is a very prominent theme in John, occurring over 120 times. *Holy Father* only occurs once in the Bible in 17:11.

The unity of the disciples was important for the evangelistic outreach of the early church. Verse 23 says that their unity will be a signal to the world that Jesus was the Messiah. The united testimony of the transformed disciples was the validation to the world that the Father truly sent the Son.

What can a watching world conclude by the relationship of believers in your town? Are you a promoter of unity or are you weakening the local Christian witness by sowing discord?

John 18:1-14

What is the writer saying?

How can I apply this to my life?

pray *Panama – Increased educational opportunities for those in or considering full-time ministry.*

We now enter the fifth major outline section of John, the Period of Consummation (chapters 18-20). Jesus and His disciples are just arriving at the Garden of Gethsemane. Apparently, chapters 15-17 were spoken en route, or they stopped at another private location for these lectures. The other Gospel accounts speak of Jesus praying in the garden although, here in John, He has already prayed an extensive prayer. It could be that the prayer of John 17 was spoken in the hearing of the disciples for their benefit; whereas the other Gospels mention the private agonizing that He did in the garden with only a few of the details known by the disciples (because they were asleep!).

The Kidron was a steep valley between Jerusalem (The Temple Mount) and the Mount of Olives. A stream runs through it all the way down to the Dead Sea seventeen miles to the east. Today it provides a strip of green lushness in an otherwise bleak wilderness.

The band (cohort) of men that Judas brought would number 300-600 soldiers. Christ responds with the name of Jehovah, "I Am (he)." This display of raw power is a reminder that Jesus did not have His life taken from Him but that He laid it down willingly. The prediction that verse 9 fulfills was only minutes old, having been prayed in 17:12! Peter tries to take charge of the situation, however he does not realize that what is happening is a part of God's plan. Jesus stops him from any further embarrassment and announces His intentions to go with the men. He is taken to Annas, the real power behind the current High Priest Caiaphas (who had been deposed by the Romans earlier for political reasons).

Life STEP Only the hardness of the human heart, blindness of sin, and trickery of Satan could have produced this type of foolishness! How faithful are you to study God's Word that you might know truth from error?

John 18:15-27

What is the writer saying?

How can I apply this to my life?

Another disciple was John. He doesn't mention his name out of humility, but is the best candidate. John apparently came from a wealthy family who could move in such circles. Only two of the twelve have stayed with Jesus; nine have scattered already.

The dignity of Jesus is in stark contrast to the seething anger of these men. The high priest's questions were directed in two areas: Jesus' disciples and His teaching. The religious leaders have often been concerned about the number of people who were following Him (compare 12:19). Not only is His first response logically accurate, but His rebuke to the one who struck Him is also eminently reasonable. It further includes a legal term, *bear witness* which contains an implied request for a fair trial. As Isaiah 53 predicts, the suffering servant will be the victim of a judicial murder. Annas then sends Jesus bound to Caiaphas. Although each of the Gospels mentions progressions in the arrest and examination of Jesus, John's Gospel is the only one to tell us that this initial examination occurred before Annas. The office of High Priest was for life and although he had been deposed, Annas still wielded much influence among the Jewish leadership.

Interwoven with Jesus' questioning is the drama of Peter's denials in the courtyard. Comparing the other Gospels, some have complained that there is a discrepancy on the identity of his questioners. We need to realize that *selective reporting* is not the equivalent of *error* or *deception*. Many people around the fire could have questioned Peter. Each author reports the questioner that caught his attention in the retelling of the events of that fateful night.

Life stEP   When the heat was on, most of the disciples scattered. How will you fare if persecution comes to you? Jesus remained calm under the pressure of examination. His strength is available to us as we stand for Him!

John 18:28-40

What is the writer saying?

How can I apply this to my life?

pray   *Netherlands – For those crossing social and cultural barriers trying to spread the Gospel to the lesser reached people.*

The Praetorium (v. 28) is a reference to the governor's official residence (see Acts 23:35). In order to remain ceremonially clean the Jews would not enter into a Gentile home. John notes that they did not want to be defiled so that they might observe the Passover. How strange, in light of the fact that they were in the process of carrying out a murder!

As Pilate examines Jesus, we see another example to avoid. Pilate was not convinced that Jesus had committed any crime worthy of death. His decision was politically motivated and devoid of justice. The Passover was at hand, and Jesus, like the Passover lamb, was the innocent being offered for the guilty. Both Jew and Gentile had a part in His death. The Jews needed the participation of the Romans since the Jews were not allowed to execute anyone (v. 31). This seems strange in light of the fact that they had often taken up stones to stone Him! John interjects that their situation served to fulfill what had been prophesied concerning His death (v. 32).

As Pilate again interviews Jesus, he tries to verify the accusations the Jews apparently made that He is a political rival (19:12). Jesus tells Pilate clearly that He is a king but that His kingdom is not of this world. It is amazing that Pilate does not probe this profound answer, but simply concludes that He is indeed claiming to be a king.

Much has been written concerning what is meant by Pilate's question, "What is truth?" However, what he does next seems to indicate that it was a pessimistic dismissal of Jesus' words. Pilate appears to neither believe in Him nor find Him to be a threat and looks for a basis for setting Jesus free.

Let us be quick to desire justice and not what is expedient.

John 19:1-11

What is the writer saying?

How can I apply this to my life?

pray Korea – For the unblocking of Christian radio broadcasts that reach into North Korea with the gospel.

Pilate was the Roman governor of Judea from A.D. 26-36. He had a history of stormy relationships with the Jews that displeased his Roman superiors. He was anxious to avoid having another bad report sent back to Rome.

The crucifixion of Christ is variously dated from A.D. 29 to 33. In any case, Pilate would have already been in Judea for a number of years and would have several years thereafter to re-consider the error of condemning an innocent man. Despite his care here, Rome eventually recalls him for misadministration in another matter. Pilate was not willing to execute an innocent man, and flogged Jesus to satisfy inherent blood lust. Perhaps he hoped to arouse pity to let Jesus go. He also allowed his soldiers to take out their frustrations on the Jews by mocking their *king*. The Romans played a game called *the game of the kings* to while away time. The climax involved mocking an innocent bystander, which might be the cultural background to their mockery of Jesus.

The original charge brought against Jesus before Pilate was that of treason (18:33) since the Sanhedrin thought that would be easier than explaining the real charge of *blasphemy*, which now slips out in their anger (v. 7), further confusing the issue. Jesus maintains a dignified silence (v. 9) fulfilling Isaiah 53:7. Jesus minimizes Pilate's role in His execution, placing the burden on the theocratic representative of the chosen people, Caiaphas (v. 11). Pilate skillfully baits his enemies into professing a heresy of their own: "We have no king but Caesar" (v. 15).

Life stEP Pilate was in over his head, both in Judea and in this trial. You may lose (in this life) if you live according to your principles, but you will always lose if you don't.

John 19:12-22

What is the writer saying?

How can I apply this to my life?

The point of Roman crucifixion was two-fold. First was the agony of the event, designed to discourage rebellion. The other was the total humiliation and the cruelty of carrying your own instrument of death (like digging your own grave). There was also the shame of public nakedness, and the prying, scornful eyes of those who passed by and read the published charges. Paul, in Colossians 2:14 wrote that it was really our charges that were nailed there.

Jesus' death was the substitutionary sacrifice for the penalty of man's sin. His death is sufficient for every man but is only made effective to those who place their faith in Him. Pilate further insulted the Jewish authorities by having *The King of the Jews* placarded between two common thieves! Golgotha *(skull)* has been identified as a rocky outcropping just north of the current (Turkish) walls of Jerusalem, called *Gordon's Calvary*. It is a nice visualization of what the site might have looked like, but probably the real site was at The Church of the Holy Sepulcher, which is inside the Turkish walls today. In Christ's day it was just outside to the northwest.

John does not detail the horrors of the crucifixion. Archaeologists have discovered victims with the spikes going through the heel bones as though the feet had been nailed to the side of the cross. Death came through a combination of blood loss, shock, and suffocation.

Life **stEP**

We are physical beings. It is natural to concentrate on the physical horrors of crucifixion. Don't forget the spiritual ramifications of the humiliation, selfless love, sin bearing, and the spiritual death that were also involved.

John 19:23-30

What is the writer saying?

How can I apply this to my life?

Psalm 22:18 and 69:21 are being fulfilled. You would have to stay up many nights inventing *fulfillments* of such passages in a fictitious story. God's sovereignty is evident, even down to the attitudes of soldiers present at His crucifixion, and their casting lots for His tunic (v. 24).

Also present are His mother, her sister (while the passage could be read to understand her name was Mary also, this would seem highly unlikely), two other devoted women, and John. While John does not record Jesus' prayer for His executioners (Luke 23:34) or His pardon of the repentant thief (Luke 23:43), he does record His words to His mother and the *disciple He loved*. His concern for His mother is touching. *Woman* was not a disrespectful way to address one's mother in that culture (John 2:4). "Behold thy son" was instructive to Mary as He commends her to the care of John, *whom He loved*. The care of a widow was the responsibility of the oldest son. Jesus entrusts his mother to the care of John, rather than His unbelieving brothers (7:5).

Notice that He controlled His life to the very end and at the proper time He dismissed His spirit from His body (see John 10:18) after the victorious statement, "It (the provision for the salvation of mankind) is finished!"

Life st**EP** Jesus' love and concern for others was evident to the end. Even on the cross, His thoughts were for the needs of those with Him. Lord, help us to see with your eyes!

John 19:31-42

What is the writer saying?

How can I apply this to my life?

pray · Paraguay – For Bible school students to earnestly seek God's guidance for future areas of ministry.

Despite suggestions for a Wednesday or Thursday crucifixion, Friday still is probable. All the biblical data can be explained to fit with a Friday crucifixion and it has the respectability of tradition behind it. (Lest we be too skeptical of *tradition*, let's remember that we also worship on Sunday for the same reason. Sunday worship can be illustrated, but not commanded from Scripture!)

This particular Sabbath was a *high day* because it occurred during Passover (either the first full day of Passover or the first day of the seven-day Feast of Unleavened Bread). It is possible that Christ celebrated the Passover with his disciples Thursday night according to one religious calendar (Essene). He was then crucified the very afternoon that Jewish fathers were butchering their lambs for the Passover meal Friday night. This would be true according to the other calendar (Pharisaic).

John injects strong emotion in verses 34-37, identifying himself as an eyewitness (*the disciple* of v. 26) of the proof of Christ's death (*water* is the plasma that separates from the red blood cells once the heart stops) and His fulfillment of yet more specific Old Testament prophecies (Exodus 12:46; Zechariah 12:10). Two influential men procure the body, allowing it to suffer no more indignities. Nicodemus supplies a large amount of spices, such as would be used in a royal burial (2 Chronicles 16:14).

Life stEP · Not many mighty, not many noble are called into the family of God. Queen Victoria once praised the Lord for the letter "m" as it saved her from *not any*!

John 20:1-10

What is the writer saying?

How can I apply this to my life?

pray   *Nigeria – Protection for those working among the Fulani people and other Muslim groups.*

Another argument for a Friday crucifixion is that the women were coming on Sunday to further adorn the body for burial, something that should be done as soon as possible. In this case the Sabbath day intervened.

It is interesting that John records Mary Magdalene as the first eyewitness of the empty tomb (although she doesn't realize that Christ is alive until verse 16). She was a devoted follower of Jesus ever since He cast seven demons out of her (Luke 8). Actually, if John was making this story up he probably would have chosen a more respectable first witness since in that day, women were not allowed to testify in a court of law.

John was younger and faster than Peter but not as bold, and it was Peter who entered the tomb first to inspect the proof of Jesus' resurrection, the empty tomb, and the abandoned grave clothes. That point in human history is the launch pad of the church, the event that turned cowards into dynamic, fearless testifiers of the risen Lord!

The *ironic tragedy* of the life of Christ, which is resolved in the resurrection, is this: "Although virtuous, He suffered all possible indignities; majestic, He died in disgrace; powerful, He expired in weakness. He claimed to possess the water of Life but died thirsty; to be The Light of the World, but died in darkness; to be The Good Shepherd, but died in the fangs of wolves; to be the Truth, but was executed as an imposter; to be Life itself, but He died quicker than the average crucifixion victim. The greatest example of righteousness the world had ever seen became a helpless victim of evil!" (Merrill Tenney, *John*, p. 52.)

Life **stEP**   The resurrection of Jesus Christ was a powerful demonstration of victory won over sin and death. Those who know Christ as Savior will experience this newness of life.

John 20:11-18

What is the writer saying?

How can I apply this to my life?

John explained in verse 9 that no one expected Christ to rise immediately from the dead. It wasn't until after the resurrection that they began to understand it from Scripture (such as Psalm 16:10, "For thou wilt not ...suffer thine Holy One to see corruption.").

Mary missed Peter and John on the way back to the tomb and didn't receive any encouragement from their newfound conviction. She was sobbing broken heartedly (literally, *wailing* as in 11:33) when she decides to look inside. She sees the angels and talks with them, but nothing is registering. She must have thought it perfectly natural for two men to be sitting in a tomb! As she turns, she notices another man and launches into a fresh attempt to locate the body of her Lord. The inability of Mary and others (like the two disciples on the road to Emmaus) to recognize the Lord at first, argues strongly against the theory that the resurrection is a myth of wishful thinking. Finally, through the blur of her tears, noting the urgency in the familiar voice, she finally realizes that she is talking to her Lord! Two natural acts followed: first, use of the familiar name, *Master* (Rabboni, *My Teacher*, normally used in prayer to God Himself) and then a grip that hinted she would never let go. Jesus did not want Mary to cling to Him because she needed to make the transition from reliance on Him to reliance on the Holy Spirit.

Life stEP   Those forgiven much, love much. Jesus of Nazareth meant the world to Mary Magdalene, physically, spiritually, and emotionally. The day He died; her lights went out. Now, after forty eight hours of weeping, her nightmare is over! What an explosion of joy.

John 20:19-31

What is the writer saying?

How can I apply this to my life?

New Zealand – For Bible schools and churches to convey a mission emphasis among their people.

The word of Christ's resurrection must have spread like wildfire through both the ranks of the disciples and the Sanhedrin. Matthew records the attempts of the religious authorities to silence the *rumor* of the resurrection with hush money.

John does not tell us how many people were gathered with the disciples. They were afraid of the Jewish authorities, but imagine how they must have been dissecting every little detail that Mary, Peter, and John could provide. Suddenly without a door opening, Christ is standing there in their midst! (Item #1: Glorified bodies can pass through solids!) He could have said a million different things but He settles on a routine *Hello* (*shalom aleichim*). The routine greeting of peace also allayed their fears, both of the sudden appearance and concern about the cowardly behavior less than seventy two hours earlier. His next comment concerned their commission, which requires empowerment (v. 22). It is symbolized by His breath (creative power), and actualized at Pentecost.

Since only God can forgive sin, verse 23 is talking about the results of the disciples' preaching ministry. Some will respond, be saved and as a result, have their sins forgiven by God. Thomas (*the Twin*) was not there and will forever be known as *Doubting Thomas* by his comments. Before we are too hard on poor old Thomas, let's remember that the very proof that he requested had already been provided for those who were there that night (v. 20). Those who believe having not seen the resurrected Lord (like us) are commended for their belief (v. 29). Thomas's testimony is the fitting conclusion to John's thesis, and John says so in verses 30 and 31.

Life stEP

We would like Jesus to be physically here, but the power of the Word and the internal confirmation of the Spirit are sufficient for us today.

John 21:1-14

What is the writer saying?

How can I apply this to my life?

pray — *Nicaragua – Salvation among the Sandinista and Contra soldiers left disillusioned from the war where they saw many atrocities.*

John 21 is the final section of our outline: the commission. Having established the believability of the life and message of Jesus Christ, John now tells us how this message was spread throughout the world.

Seven of the eleven disciples gather together in their home territory of Galilee. That Christ would appear to them on their familiar home ground negated any lingering sense they might have had that perhaps what they experienced in Jerusalem was a product of their confusion and fear in a hostile environment. Once again, Christ appears unto people who should have recognized Him, but they do not. His question implies that He knows they didn't catch any fish. Now that it was daylight, the fish would be able to see and avoid the nets. They nevertheless obey the voice of the stranger on the shore with startling results. Christ had called them to the ministry with a similar miracle three years earlier (Luke 5).

Propriety (not necessarily modesty) called for Peter to be properly dressed to greet his Lord, despite the fact that it would be harder to swim thus attired. The Lord had already procured some fish (small sardines), which are cooking on the breakfast fire, a considerate gesture for men who had worked all night. We can only imagine the rush of memories, as Christ broke the bread and fish and fed them once again from His own hands. It left an indelible mark on Peter as he refers to it in Acts 10. This meal is a not-so-subtle reminder that He can provide for all of their needs. Just as a miraculous draught of fish initially convinced them to leave all and follow Him (Luke 5), they are to do so once again.

Life step — Hard work is therapeutic. It is proper to be busy as long as we are sensitive to the Lord's direction in our life when higher business calls.

John 21:15-25

What is the writer saying?

How can I apply this to my life?

pray *Philippines – That Christians currently working within the government will use their influence wisely.*

Peter had publicly denied the Lord three times after protesting greater love than the rest. Now, Christ gives Peter three chances to publicly affirm his chastened love for the Lord in front of the other disciples. Peter is not confident enough to tell the Lord that he *agapes* Him (self-sacrificing love, love given with no thought of a return) but *phileo* is strong enough (brotherly love as in Philadelphia). Christ probes the deepest in the third question by using *phileo* saying, *Okay, you can't say 'agape,' but do you really 'phileo' me?*

Both *lambs* and *sheep* are mentioned, representing all kinds of believers in different stages of development. The master shepherd mentions two aspects of shepherding: feeding the flock and caring for all their needs. Christ predicts Peter's death by martyrdom. The last command to Peter was "Follow me." He still is a little slow and turns around to see what everyone else is doing. He spies John, still nameless but identifiable by the descriptive phrases John uses. Peter blurts out, *What about John?* Jesus, no doubt with exasperation in His voice, says, *Mind your own business, and do what I told you to do! Follow me!* A rumor developed from Jesus' actual words, a rumor that John wanted to quell. However, he probably wasn't very convincing since, by the time this is written, all the others had met martyrs' deaths, and he was still going strong! He nevertheless asserts that his life is an eyewitness account of the greatest story ever told. His years of service, communion, and reflection have made him quite the wordsmith as well. He closes his Gospel with a precious tribute to the grandeur of the greatest man who has ever lived!

Life **stEP** God is so gracious. Not only does He forgive our sins, He also uses us in His work giving us reward for what He plans, energizes, and executes through our lives!

Proverbs

In the Bible, the word "proverb" denotes a concise saying of practical wisdom and often conveys moral direction. A proverb is a kind of truth that is most commonly true but is not what is certainly true. A proverb was designed to be a teaching tool in which a pointed, compact saying would give an insight into the governing of one's conduct in life.

Proverbs, as used in several ancient cultures, were designed for oral transmission [While they did have books, most people could not afford their own copy. Rather they would memorize large portions of Scripture!]. They were artfully structured in several ways to impact the hearer so he could *see* the teaching and also for ease of memory.

1. Frequently a *contrasting couplet* was used: "a fool *uttereth all* his mind; but a wise man *keepeth it in* till afterwards" (Proverbs 29:11).
2. "Commit thy works unto the LORD, and thy thoughts shall be established" (16:3) is an example of a *completive couplet*.
3. Whereas, "Better is a *little* with righteousness than *great revenues* without right" (16:8) is a *comparative couplet*.

Proverbs 1:1, 10:1, 25:1 and Ecclesiastes 12:9 tell us that King Solomon both *authored* proverbs and *collected* and *edited* other wise sayings already in existence. The exceptions are the last two chapters where Proverbs tells us that Agur and Lemuel authored those portions.

According to 1 Kings 4:32, Solomon "spoke three thousand proverbs" [thus, our book of Proverbs holds only some of his proverbs]. 1 Kings 4:31 says "he was wiser than all men." That statement, of course, was no longer true when Christ became a man, for in Him "are hidden all the treasures of wisdom and knowledge" (Colossians 2:3). The story of how Solomon acquired such wisdom is found in 1 Kings 3:5-13.

Some of the virtues commended in Proverbs are the pursuit of wisdom, respect for parents, liberality, marital fidelity, honesty, humility and piety. Vices condemned include lust, drunkenness, lying, cheating, laziness, strife, greed, pride, folly, gluttony and vengeance.

The principle theme of the book is *wisdom.* Thus words *wise* and *wisdom* occur more than one hundred times in the text. Similarly, Solomon's use of contrasting words, fool, foolish, etc., are also used over one hundred times! The intent was for this book to be a source of instruction for Solomon's *own son*, Rehoboam (1:8; 2:1; etc.). But Solomon also intended for these proverbs to guide all *youth* (4:1) and ultimately for *all men* (8:1-5).

Just a word about why we are starting and ending in the middle of Proverbs: We note that most subjects in Proverbs are presented a "*little at*

Proverbs

a time" but "*again and again.*" This was an ancient teaching style that reinforced the teachings on a subject over time. For this reason the Quiet Time Diary also presents a portion of Proverbs each year throughout its 6-year cycle. This year you get chapters 16 through 20!

Proverbs 16:1-11

What is the writer saying?

How can I apply this to my life?

Today's passage is an excellent place to begin the habit of using colored pencils to mark important, repeating words. As nowhere else in Proverbs, nine times in these eleven verses the word "*LORD*" is used. This is to focus in on the contrasts being made between how our own hearts tend to lead us and how the *LORD* wants to direct us! A common *color-code* is to lightly *box in* with a purple pencil all words related to God the Father.

Of course, the word "*LORD*" is the common way English Bibles translate the Hebrew word "Jehovah" [or, it may be pronounced "Yahweh"], which means *He is* and implies *He truly exists.* With this as a start, let's note what contrasts with the *LORD*'s ways; our "*heart*" (v. 1), our "*own eyes*" (v. 2), a "*proud in heart*" (v. 5), our "*iniquity*" and "*evil*" (v. 6), our "*ways*" (v. 7), our desire for "*great revenues*" (v. 8), our heart-directed "*way*" (v. 9), and, by implication, *unjust weights* (v. 11, i.e., implying *basic*

business practices). Perhaps you could *box in* these with an orange pencil for *rusting* or *corrupting.*

Let's take a closer look at one of these verses, v. 9. The verse begins with the observation that people are reasonable, logical, purposeful creatures that plan to achieve desired outcomes. The words "deviseth" (v. 9) and "preparations," in verse 1, both picture the actions of a commander of an army who places things in order and arranges his troops in preparation for a coming battle. Similarly, in our *hearts* (v. 9), we *calculate* our best plan of advance (see Proverbs 19:21); with *cunning* we weigh our various options, goals, and methods. The truth is also presented that only God is sovereign and only He [and not men] "directs" what will actually take place. The Hebrew word for *direct* is most often translated *establish* or *prepare,* all of which mean that only God can *fix* His plans so that they will take place.

 Are you *devising* a plan for your life that is pleasing to God? Only then can you be confident that God will *fix* things to bless your plans! Otherwise, your *devisings* will be thwarted by His *directings.*

Proverbs 16:12-22

What is the writer saying?

How can I apply this to my life?

The prevalent form of government during Solomon's reign (970-930 BC) was monarchy. He was the predominant king of his time (1 Kings 3:13, 4:34). Since he was known for his wisdom, he wrote a number of his proverbs to advise other kings how to conduct themselves (v. 10-13). He also advised people how to act in the presence of kings (v. 14-15).

Next to be considered are the errors of powerful people, like kings. Their personal achievements, possessions and power result in great "folly" (v. 22). "Pride" (v. 18) is that self-sufficient attitude which gives oneself the credit that is rightly due to God. Haughtiness is a *high opinion of oneself*, often manifested by showing *contempt for others*.

Solomon then moves on to advise powerful people in their *handling of matters* (v. 20). First, we note that, although knowledge is extolled elsewhere in Proverbs (20:15), *wisdom* (v. 20-21) and "understanding" (v. 22) are given more prominence and value throughout Proverbs (3:13-15, 4:7). *Knowledge* usually has to do with *input*. It is the orderly assimilation of information by the intellect. In order to be useful, it must first be *thought through* before it can be properly utilized.

Wisdom is the *judicious use of knowledge*. Thus the "wise in heart" (v. 21) are those who use *well-thought-out judgments guided by godly principles* before acting upon what they know! *Wisdom* has to do with *output* (vv. 20-22). Our world often exalts knowledge with little regard for its wise utilization. Unfortunately this often leads to the *non-judicious* use of knowledge. This leads to the failure of "fools" in their "folly" (v. 22).

Life stEP

The little phrase "understanding is a wellspring of life" (v. 22) is good advice. Just as one has to dig a well before finding a refreshing source of water, so we must dig for the thought-out judgments guided by godly principles to guide our response to what is known. Is there a "matter" that you know you need to act upon? How might you wisely pray and meditate upon the actions you will take?

Proverbs 16:23-33

What is the writer saying?

How can I apply this to my life?

pray — Peru – Funding for more scholarships that will make Bible training accessible to the poor.

The subject of many proverbs is the *good* or *evil* wrought upon others by our spoken words. Verse 23 teaches that the effects of words are largely dependent upon the "*heart*" purpose of the speaker. *A heart of love* and concern can bring joy, hope, and comfort to the hearer. Words spoken by a *heart filled with evil intent* can bring strife and destruction, by using the various tools of the *mischief-maker* (vv. 27-30):

▶ The *digger of evil* v. 27a; such a person first spends a great deal of effort to find a *golden nugget* of innuendo or suspicion which can then be manipulated into an evil story of gossip or slander.

▶ The *speaker of fire*, v. 27b (James 3:5-6); once a *nugget of suspicion* is prepared, the evil heart will use it to *smoke*, *scorch*, or to *completely burn* his neighbor's reputation!

▶ The *planter of strife*, v. 28a; a "*froward*" person finds a *perverted pleasure* in *overturning* others by planting gossip-seeds.

▶ The *whisperer of divisions*, v. 28b; a powerful tool is a half-true tale shared secretly. A clandestine slander is a most effective divider of friends by means of doubt, mistrust and anger.

▶ The *influencer of violence*, v. 29; while he will use *violence* to achieve his evil desires, he will often *entice* others with *deceit* and *persuasion* into the way of evil which he has planned.

▶ The *deviser of evil things*, v. 30; such a person becomes so evil that he shuts his eyes to better meditate upon and see how his plans will come to pass.

How can you begin to *rule your spirit* (v. 32) and teach your mouth (v. 23) not to be an evil digger, speaker, planter, whisperer, influencer, or deviser? Wow, what a task! Perhaps you know a *hoary headed* [white-haired] old person, who is a *righteous* friend (v. 31) who has learned to *rule his spirit* (v. 32). He could be a great help to you! Take a minute and write him a note asking for his advice and prayers!

Proverbs 17:1-9

What is the writer saying?

How can I apply this to my life?

pray   *Poland – For God to protect missionaries and ministry equipment from criminal activity.*

While each of these proverbs has a distinct message, they are also related to the general topics here of either *"strife"* (v. 1, *fighting with words*) or *harmony* ["quietness," peace] in our personal relationships. Let's look at Solomon's wise advice about choosing a *"better"* way of life:

▶ *"Better"* (v. 1) is *stale bread* and *harmony* than a *house full of feasting* and *fighting with words*.

▶ *Better* is a "wise servant" (v. 2, *one who heeds instruction*) than a disgraceful son who causes "shame" [i.e., *failing to be trustworthy*].

▶ A *"wicked doer"* [v. 4, he deliberately causes injury to others] and a *"liar"* [he speaks falsely] will readily listen to "naughty" stories, i.e., information from gossip that will bring ruin and disaster upon others.

▶ These *evildoers* will ridicule the poor (v. 5a) and are amused when others are ruined (v. 5b).

▶ *Better* are the people suffering from poverty or calamities (v. 5) since they are highly regarded by their Creator [He watches after them!], who will punish anyone who makes light of their plight.

▶ *Better* to speak *valuable, superior* words like a noble *prince* than the *"lying"* words of a *fool* [a rare word here for "fool"; one, who like a *withered corpse*, is now *senseless* to the needs of others].

▶ A *better* way to live is to be motivated by *"love"* [e.g., he chooses not to be *senseless* to others]. Rather he will *cover* [v. 9, Lit: To *cover with a cloth*; thus *conceal the matter*] someone's sin rather than repeat the story as he gossips with friends.

Life STEP

Solomon would insist that it is "better" if you make it your habit to consider your words before you speak like a "fool." How about writing on a card, which you can carry throughout the day, these four questions that summarize Solomon's advice:
Proverbs 17:1-9 asks me to consider my words: (1) Are they true? (2) Are they kind? (3) Are they loving? (4) Should I keep them to myself?

Proverbs 17:10-19

What is the writer saying?

How can I apply this to my life?

pray   *Argentina – Funding for students with a desire to study God's word at camps and Bible schools.*

Here we have various topics relating to the general subject of *strife* and peace. Nine verses refer to some form of *evil* or *foolish* conduct.

"*Reproof*" [v. 10, also translated "*rebuke*"] sets the tone for this collection. *Reproof* expresses *strong censure* or *disapproval*. An honestly delivered *reproof* is intended to be a *check* that causes us to stop and examine our course of action or our attitudes. Properly given, a *reproof* should, first, express what is wrong and, <u>second</u>; guide a person to a right course of conduct.

A deserved *reproof* will "entereth more" [i.e., *cut more deeply*] into a humble man's character than will one hundred lashes cut deeply into the back of a fool. Since the Law restricted punishment to forty lashes (Deut. 25:2-3), this exaggeration is intended to express the *severest punishment.*

The point is that it is difficult for us to accept a *reproof*. So let's consider some things we must remember [lest we react like a "fool"!]:

▶ That the person giving an honest reproof is a courageous friend (27:6)!

▶ That God, our Friend, gave us Scripture to *reprove* (2 Tim. 3:16).

▶ That the Holy Spirit of God is often our *Reprover* (John 16:8).

▶ That it is difficult to admit that our actions or attitudes can be wrong!

▶ To allow reproof's *check* requires a humble admitting of a flaw!

▶ To allow the *check*, assumes that we are willing to adjust our ways!

▶ Just as a one hundred-lash punishment will take time to heal, so we must endure the *healing time* needed for God to repair our character.

▶ The truth is that a *reproof* is a mild substitute for the harder treatment [the one hundred-lash picture!] that God will bring upon the fool!

Note that our *response* to a *reproof* is one of those things for which it is best if we have decided upon an intended reaction before it is received!

Life **STEP**   So, how can you ask the Lord to help you wisely respond to an *honest reproof* given by a *true friend*? Take a minute and write out your intended response; "I am going to pause, think, and then …"

Proverbs 17:20-28

What is the writer saying?

How can I apply this to my life?

pray   *Portugal – For the churches to raise up full–time workers of the Gospel.*

Again, in today's passage, we have various topics relating to the general subject of *strife* and peace. Once more the word *"fool"* is prominent. Be sure to note that it is contrasted here with *the man of understanding* (vv. 24, 27, 28). While many proverbs form contrasts, in verse 20 the second clause advances on the subject of the first clause. Thus the *lying tongue* gives evidence to that which is in the *crooked heart*. The observation is that *thoughts* carry over to both *words* and *deeds* (see also Mark 7:21-23).

Consider the phrase *"a perverse tongue"* (v. 20). While the English word *"perverse"* means the same thing as the Hebrew word here; we do not understand the root idea of our own word! *"Perverse"* has a root meaning of *to turn about*; thus *"a perverse tongue"* describes someone who *turns words about with his tongue.*

"Perverse" implies *turning words* in three different ways:

(1) To *twist* or *wind* words so as to brashly falsify the truth.

(2) To say one thing at one time and something quite *contrary* at another [this idea is picked up by the Greek Septuagint which reads, *"Easily changed* in tongue,"* [i.e., to change what has been said already].

(3) To say one thing to give a certain impression which *twists* the facts to conceal the true attitude of a person's heart [this idea is picked up by some modern translations that use, "a deceitful tongue"].

One reason why a "man of understanding" speaks only sparingly (v. 27) is that he is not *turning* and *twisting* his words to <u>pervert</u> the truth! This subject is picked up by both our Lord Jesus (Matthew 5:37) and by James (James 5:12) when they say *let your yea be yea; and your nay be nay ... for whatsoever is more than these cometh of evil.*

Once again we are faced with one of those areas where it is best if we have decided upon intended conduct before we act! So then, write the Lord a note and ask for His help to enable you to honestly and truthfully speak with a *straight tongue* and not a *twisted tongue*.

Proverbs 18:1-12

What is the writer saying?

How can I apply this to my life?

Hungary – Effective outreach and godly teachers in public schools where Christianity is welcome.

In typical fashion, each of the several proverbs here is the next in the ongoing *string* of scattered lessons related to its topic.

An interesting *pair* of proverbs here is verses 10 and 11, which are intended to be a contrast in *sources of security*.

First we are given the source of *true security*, "The name of the LORD *is* a strong tower" (v. 10). In the ancient world, a person's name was intended to describe his character. This proverb is saying because God is loving, good, all-powerful, all-knowing, everywhere-present, and the Keeper of His promises, we can be *safe*. We can spiritually "run" to Him when things in life are threatening to us!

The phrase, "a strong tower" brings to mind a picture of a pleasant valley with farmers tending to their fields who are then troubled by an invading army. These farmers flee to the hill in the center of the valley. On the hill sits a *massive fortified castle* that is ready to defy the threats of the invaders. The LORD (the English for Jehovah!) is that Fortress for us. Our security is in His strength. He is always there, with open gates, at the center of our life's *valley*. He is ready to protect!

The second verse in this pair presents a *deceptive security*. When trouble threatens the "rich man," he believes he can run to the safety of his "wealth." Obviously, this proverb was placed second to show us how to evaluate its message. We must conclude that wealth is not like the Lord; it is not always holy, loving, good, powerful, knowing, present, or able to deliver. So this rich man is *deceived* as he anticipates his wealth to be an *unconquerable defense* that will keep him safe. In his "*conceit*" he believes he is safe but that is only what he *pictures* in his own mind!

Life stEP

To what *fortified castle* do you run when your life gets hard? Since the Lord is the only genuine protection, is He in the center of the *valley of your life*? What danger in your life is threatening your *valley*? What can you tell the Lord about your situation so that He can be your *unconquerable defense*?

Sunday 34

Proverbs 18:13-24

What is the writer saying?

How can I apply this to my life?

pray *Canada – That Canada's churches will keep evangelism a priority.*

Today we again have a series of independent proverbs. Several of these proverbs are aimed at guiding our use of our words:

▶ *Talking too soon!* (vv. 13, 17) Many are the dangers of speaking out on an issue when only one side of the issue has been heard! Withhold an opinion until every facet is known. Similarly, ask the advice of a "neighbor" (v. 17) or co-worker before you promote a cause that will benefit you! Their perspective can be of great value!

▶ *Talking too much!* (vv. 15, 16) Learn to be "*prudent*"; that is , *wisdom applied to practice, thus, cautious, discreet, and considerate.* Use your "heart" and "ear" *more* and your mouth *less!* Work to gain "the knowledge of His will in all wisdom" (Colossians 1:9). Similarly, consider how God has *gifted* you (Romans 12:3-11) with natural talents and spiritual gifts. Then, let your consistent work and faithful service become your best *words* of promotion (v. 16)!

▶ *Talking too offensively!* (vv. 19, 21) Be ever mindful of the power of words and the consequences of all that you say! Your words can be either *deadly* (v. 21) or a source of "life" for others! So, think before you put your mouth into action; remember, once your words have offended a brother, it will be really hard to "win" him back.

▶ *Talking too harshly!* (vv. 20, 23) Learn to talk wisely so as to avoid conflict and you will continue to earn your daily food (i.e., you will keep your job!). Remember an old saying, a dog with a wagging tail is fed but a barking dog is driven away! Similarly, practice talking in a "friendly" manner (v. 24)—don't be the angry, barking dog! You "show yourself friendly" by having a *kind stance*, [consider a dog with its tail wagging!], an *amicable tone* that expresses a willingness to get along, and *helpful intent* that seeks to serve.

 Life stEP Which of the above needs your attention most? Consider the coming day, who will you be meeting? Ask the Lord to help you now as you prepare the stance, *tone* and *intent* of a coming conversation.

Proverbs 19:1-9

What is the writer saying?

How can I apply this to my life?

There are many external distracters that seek to draw a person away from his walk on the *path of integrity* [*a focus upon moral goodness*]. It is this path that is pleasing to God. Let's link together this set of proverbs with this observation.

▶ *Hunger* is a great distracter! When we are hungry and poor it is easy for us to justify stepping off the path of right (vv. 1, 4, 7). God often uses this situation of poverty to teach a person the lesson of upright character. Low circumstances can be used by God to teach a high standard of honest, moral conduct!

▶ Let us be careful to distinguish between the *fair-weather-friends* of today's verses (4, 6 & 7) and the *true friend* that "loveth at all times" (17:17) and "sticketh closer than a brother" (18:24). May we not seek some economic advantage by our friendships!

▶ One of the subtle lessons presented in these same verses is that the *person of integrity* will seek to be a *neighbor* or a *brother* to the man who is poor! After all, God Himself delights in being known as the friend of the fatherless and the widows (Psalm 68:5)! Mimic God in this!

▶ A disadvantage of wealth is that it makes the discernment of *true friendship* difficult. It can often be feigned for personal benefit. When a wealthy person gives to someone in need, he must then determine whether a thankful response is genuine or a ploy for more gifts (v. 6)!

▶ Notice the repeating subject of *perverse words* in our passage (vv. 1, 3, 5, 9). We will often have the opportunity to *twist* or *distort* an event or statement to gain some monetary, legal, or social advantage. Yet, such *twisting* of the truth is another dangerous distracter from one's *path to integrity*. We are also reminded that the Lord, who sees all, will not allow such *distortions* to go "unpunished" (vv. 5, 9)

Life
STEP   How can you strengthen you own *path of integrity*? Let's start with a basic question: What in your life is *off the right path*? What do you need to do today to step back onto the *right path*?

Proverbs 19:10-19

What is the writer saying?

How can I apply this to my life?

pray Kenya – For the believers to live an exemplary life and speak out against what is wrong.

Typical of Proverbs, today's verses present recurring themes found elsewhere in the book. We have several proverbs relating to *family relations* [wives and sons], several relating to *riches* and *the poor*, and others, which we will look at here, relating to *anger* and *wrath*.

▸ *Anger deferred* (v. 11, compare with v. 19): The man who controls his anger by *lengthening* or *drawing out* the time allowed before responding has *good sense* ["discretion" is a component of wisdom]. Similarly his "glory" [this word means *a garland given to honor the one who wears it*] will be overlooking offenses, knowing that to respond will only lead to more trouble.

▸ *Anger combined with power* (v. 12): Solomon is warning leaders to be careful in how they respond, for their reactions have great influence in the ability to *frighten* (the roar of a lion) or to *encourage* (the welcome sound of rain in a dry place). Notice that Solomon is saying that both anger and favor are proper tools to be used in governing if they are used with a careful and wise hand.

▸ *The penalty of a hot temper*: The root for "great wrath" (v. 19) is translated elsewhere as *to be hot*. Thus our word means *hot rage* or *fiery emotions*. A man's failure to control his *hot rage* will repeatedly get him into trouble. It is also hard to overcome!

This warning comes after a verse (v. 18) on the *chastening of a son*. Two implications apply here:

1) *A father with a hot temper* must control his own "wrath" to deal with a son that needs *chastening*, that is, *punishment that teaches*.

2) A father with a *hot tempered son* must "chasten" his son so that the son learns self-control. Only then will the son be *delivered* from greater *punishments* which life will deliver him!

Life stEP

How can you win over your own *hot temper*? First of all, you can only win one day at a time. Ask yourself, "When insults come against me today, how can I respond with *discretion* and *control* so that at the end of the day I will have earned the *garland of good sense*?

Proverbs 19:20-29

What is the writer saying?

How can I apply this to my life?

In today's collection we have several contrasts between the "*wise*" (v. 20) and the "*fool*" (v. 29), as they are influenced by either *God's counsel* (vv. 20, 21, 23) or *false counsel* (vv. 22, 27, 28).

Let's consider the "*wise*" person:

▶ He listens to "*counsel*" (vv. 20, 21) means *advice and plans to guide choices*.

▶ He listens to "*instruction*" (v. 20) means *training that corrects conduct*.

▶ While he should make plans for his future (see 16:1, 9), a wise man will recognize that God may *overrule* and *redirect* these plans (v. 22).

▶ He *fears* the LORD (v. 23). This means his knowledge of God's holiness causes him to watchfully obey God's commandments, that is, "thou shalt not ...," for he knows God will discipline His own children!

▶ As a "*simple*" man (v. 25), that is , one who is untaught but *open-minded* and *willing to learn*, will learn by seeing the penalties delivered upon others who *scorn* the right way to live and speak (vv. 25a, 28).

▶ He *truly listens* when he is *reproved* (v. 25b) means *a careful pointing out, in love, of the causes of a wrongdoing* (see Leviticus 19:17-18). Properly given, a *reproof* not only seeks to *expose someone's sin* but also seeks to *call the person to repentance*. Thus a wise man will truly value receiving a *reproof* because a friend is seeking to help!

▶ He is *cautious* about some "instruction" that is *bad advice* (v. 27); it causes a "son" to "err" [*to be drawn towards an evil way*, see 28:10]. Thus all advice must be compared to *known godly words* (v. 27b).

When advice is contrary to the Word of God, the wise will "*cease*" listening. "Cease" here carries the idea of *leaving* the bad advisor or *refraining* from listening to him any further.

Proverbs 20:1-10

What is the writer saying?

How can I apply this to my life?

An interesting contrast is presented in this grouping of proverbs! While we are given several *ingredients* that make up the *cake mix* of a good character, we are also reminded twice (vv. 6, 9) that a real example of a person who lives out this life of personal "*integrity*" (v. 7) is hard to find! As a result, be sure to notice the warning here; we are wisely advised to look "*deep*" into a person's "*heart*" (v. 5) before we believe a person's *proclamations* of "his own goodness" (v. 6) or his claim to have a *clean heart* and a life *pure from sin*.

Since the larger topic looks at our *walk in personal integrity* (v. 7), let's consider the opening proverb, which gives a contrast to a godly and wise walk. "*Wine*" [fermented grape juice] and "*strong drink*" [fermented drinks made from barley (beer), dates, or pomegranates] are such powerful influences in a person's life that these are here *personified*, that is, given the abilities of *people*! Watch out, these powerful and influential *people* are *mockers*, *brawlers* and *deceivers* (v. 1a). It is "not wise" (v. 1b) to *listen* to their conversations.

▶ "*Mocker*": Also translated "scorner," means, *to talk big with no respect for others*. It expresses *complete contempt* as it *boasts of itself* or painfully *ridicules others*.

▶ *Brawlers* [KJV = "Raging"]: Literally *to growl or howl* and is likely best illustrated in Isaiah 59:11, "we roar all like bears … ." It is used to describe us when our *actions are intentionally loud* so as to cause uproar, turmoil and distress.

Life *stEP*   The only way to be men and women of integrity is to be clothed with the righteousness of Christ "by the washing of regeneration" (Titus 3:5).

Proverbs 20:11-20

What is the writer saying?

How can I apply this to my life?

pray   *Spain – For an end to the government's selective restriction and closure of Christian radio stations.*

Every person, even a child, possesses a conscience that lets him know some things are wrong. The problem is that one's sin nature is stronger than one's conscience. There are two forces that act to keep one from violating the conscience. One is fear of consequences. The other is love. A child can fear the one in authority or love that one sufficiently to behave properly. When we receive Christ as our Savior, He imparts His love to us. We yield to the power of that love and therefore desire to please Him by abiding in His Word (1 John. 2:14). Thus we overcome the temptations of the world, the flesh and the devil.

Our hearing and seeing are from the LORD. Unfortunately, our sin nature leads us to use these gifts for self-gratification. By reading the Word, God can teach us how to use these gifts to glorify the giver. The Holy Spirit will then empower us to obey the Word as we yield ourselves to Him.

Interspersed through the book are proverbs admonishing about laziness (v. 13), trade ethics (vv. 10, 14) and obligations to parents (v. 20). Others exhort us unto knowledge (v. 15) and practical wisdom (vv. 16-18).

The word translated "flattereth" in verse 19 is not the usual word for flatter. More often it is rendered "entice," as in Proverbs 1:10 and 16:29. This is one of the many verses that counsel concerning the use of speech. We are not to consort with those who disregard God's rules concerning use and misuse of the gift of speech.

Life stEP

The Book of Proverbs, when studied in the light of New Testament truth, guides us in practical Christianity. Satan, his world system, and our sin nature lead us from God's purposes for our lives. The righteous use of ears, eyes, minds, mouths, feet and hands is necessary in God's program on earth.

Proverbs 20:21-30

What is the writer saying?

How can I apply this to my life?

pray   *Taiwan – For godly national Bible teachers and evangelists who understand this people's unique mindset.*

One who is intent upon building an estate in this life will surely lose an eternal perspective. He will glory in that which he has amassed and lose sight of spiritual values for himself and his progeny.

David is a good Bible example of one who practiced the principle of verse 22. He was wickedly pursued by Saul for years and had a number of opportunities to avenge himself. Instead he waited, trusting the Lord to recompense evil.

Let the one who cheats another be aware that the Lord keeps accurate records.

"In all thy ways acknowledge Him, and He shall direct thy paths" (Proverbs 3:6). It is not for us to fully comprehend how the Lord directs our steps. It is for us to trust Him for direction step by step (Proverbs 3:5).

"Better is it that thou shouldest not vow, than that thou shouldest vow and not pay" (Ecclesiastes 5:5).

Upholding mercy and truth, it is government's responsibility to thresh and winnow the evil out of society for the benefit of the whole (vv. 26, 28).

Neither spiritual nor physical darkness can hide evil intents from the Lord. He has a lamp that sheds light upon the innermost recesses of the heart.

Corporal punishment can cause bruises but it can bring discipline that cleanses evil.

Life stEP   We speak of a *generation gap* between youth and age. However, each stage of life has its values for the individual and for society. Strength and vitality are gradually replaced by wisdom and composure. The aspirations of youth can develop into the accomplishments of age. Let each be appreciated.

Zechariah

At least twenty-eight men in the Bible are named "Zechariah." The name means *Jehovah Remembers.* This may refer to the prayers of his parents or more likely, his mission of reminding Israel that God does remember them in their plight.

The man who gave us the book of Zechariah was from a family of priests. He returned from the Babylonian Exile with about 50,000 others under the leadership of Zerubbabel in 538 B.C. (Nehemiah 12:4, 16). His father was unimportant, or died young, since he is not mentioned in Nehemiah. His grandfather, Iddo, was a contemporary of Zerubbabel, Governor of Judah, and by tradition, a member of the *Great Synagogue* (the governing body of the Jews that preceded the Sanhedrin of the New Testament Period).

Solomon's Temple stood for almost four hundred years. In 586 B.C., the Babylonians destroyed it. God explained this as a punishment on His people for their spiritual idolatry and disobedience. When the people returned to Jerusalem, their first task was to rebuild the temple, which was the center of Jewish national life. Local opposition, fearful of being dominated by the Jews, opposed the reconstruction. Rather than call upon God for help, the people gave up and did not finish the temple. After sixteen years of apathy and inactivity, God stirred up the people to obedience.

Zechariah and his contemporary prophet Haggai ministered together, encouraging the people to finish the temple construction. They were preachers of hope for a disheartened people, God's men for the hour. They succeeded in that the temple was finished four years after they began their ministry.

Time Line

605 B.C.	Start of the Babylonian captivity
586 B.C.	Solomon's Temple destroyed
538 B.C.	Zerubbabel starts back to Jerusalem with 50,000 Jews
536 B.C.	Foundation of Temple laid
534 B.C.	Work on the Temple is stopped (Ezra 3:1 4)
520 B.C.	Sixth Month: Haggai's first sermon (Haggai 1:3 11)
520 B.C.	Sixth Month, 24th Day: The people respond (Haggai 1:12 15)
520 B.C.	Eighth Month: Zechariah's first sermon (Zech. 1:1 6)
520 B.C.	Eleventh Month, 24th Day: Zechariah's eight visions (Zech. 1 6)
520 B.C.	Eleventh Month, 25th Day: Symbolic crowning of Joshua prefiguring Messiah as the *King-Priest* (Zech. 3:8)
516 B.C.	Twelfth Month, third Day: Completion and dedication of the Temple 70 years after destruction of the First Temple

480 B.C. Esther
458 B.C. Ezra returns to Israel
445 B.C. Nehemiah returns to Israel
433 B.C. Malachi's ministry

There is reason to believe that Haggai was an old man and Zechariah was rather young. The emphasis is slightly different for each prophet. Haggai was concerned with the immediate task of getting the Temple up. Therefore his message is immediate, local and external. Zechariah's message places more emphasis on heart realities and therefore is futuristic, universal, and inward. His vision gazes all the way into the Messianic reign on a renewed planet Earth.

Zechariah has the most information about Christ in the Old Testament after Isaiah, giving details of both His First Coming (3:8; 9:9; 11:11-13; 13:1, 6, 7) and Second Coming (6:12; 12:10; 14:1-21). The most interesting prophecies are the predictions of the donkey ride on Palm Sunday and the betrayal for thirty pieces of silver.

Other prophetic events mentioned include the last siege of Jerusalem, the initial victory of the enemies of Israel, the dividing of the Mount of Olives in half, the Lord's return to save Israel, judgment on the evil nations, topographical changes in the land of Israel, the Feast of Tabernacles in the Millennium, the ultimate holiness of Jerusalem, and the false shepherd (the Antichrist).

Zechariah's favorite title for God is "Lord of Hosts (Armies)" which occurs over fifty times. This military title indicates that He has adequate resources to establish His kingdom.

Theme: Jehovah Remembers
Outline:
I.   Call to Repentance (1:1-6)
II. Eight Symbolic Visions (1:7-6:8)
   A. The Horsemen among the Myrtle Trees (Jehovah Still Caring for Israel) (1:8-17)
   B. Four Horns and Four Smiths (Jehovah Fighting For Israel) (1:18-21)
   C. The Man with the Measuring Line (Jehovah Rebuilding Jerusalem) (Ch. 2)
   D. Joshua the High Priest in Filthy Garments (Jehovah Redeeming Israel) (Ch. 3)
   E. The Candlestick Fed by the Olive Trees (Jehovah Making Israel a Witness) (Ch. 4)
   F. The Flying Roll (Jehovah Refining the World) (5:1-4)
   G. The Woman Flying in a Basket (Jehovah Eliminating Sin) (5:5-11)
   H. Four War Chariots (Jehovah Eliminating Sinners) (6:1-8)
III. The Coronation Scene (6:9-15)
IV. True Worship (Ch. 7 & 8)
V.   Two Burdens of Messianic Prophecy (Ch. 9-14)
   A. Emphasis on the First Coming of Christ (Ch. 9-11)
   B. Emphasis on the Second Coming of Christ (Ch. 12-14)

Zechariah 1:1-6

What is the writer saying?

How can I apply this to my life?

Darius I (Hystaspes) reigned over the Persian Empire from 522 to 486 B.C. Jewish legends considered him to be a pleasant Gentile king and most (about 2.5 million Jews) elected to stay in Persia under his rule while the 50,000 returnees struggled in Jerusalem. The date corresponds to November of 520 B.C. Dating the event by the reign of a Gentile king underscores the fact that Israel is under Gentile domination in the *Times of the Gentiles*. Archaeologists have found an inscription from the time of Darius called the Rock of Behistun. It is famous since it was written in three languages (Persian, Babylonian, and Assyrian), which was the key to unlocking the ancient cuneiform script.

"Sore displeased" (v. 2) in the Hebrew text is a graphic phrase, *angry with anger* (i.e., *very angry*). Note the repetition of the special military title for Jehovah—"Lord of hosts (armies)." The implication is *I know that you feel small and powerless, but I am the One who owns the cattle on a thousand hills, as well as the wealth in every mine, and control the angelic armies of heaven. Is there anything too hard for Me?* "Turn" (v. 3) is the root concept of *repent*. The New Testament equivalent speaks of *a change of mind, a turning from one way of thinking to another.* The "former prophets" (v. 4) would include Moses through Jeremiah. These noble men spoke faithfully to their fellow countrymen, but very few repented, and as a result, they were swept away by the *long arm of the law* in the Assyrian and Babylonian captivities (722 and 586 B.C.). While both sinful men and saintly prophets have a limited shelf life, God's Word is eternal and infallible. Verse 6 concludes this brief but potent call to repentance, with the people of Zechariah's day agreeing with God's assessment of their fathers' behavior, and repenting themselves.

Life Step Zechariah's public ministry started with an emphasis on a right relationship with God through repentance. Once the heart is right then the blessings can follow.

Zechariah 1:7-17

What is the writer saying?

How can I apply this to my life?

Pray that you will not be discouraged by delayed answers to prayer (Luke 18:1).

About 114 days after the brief message on repentance and the positive reaction from the Jewish people in Jerusalem, Zechariah receives eight visions in one night of visioning. The night of visioning came on the twenty-fourth day of the month. In the Jewish calendar there is nothing significant about that particular day of the month. However, in Haggai 1:15, it was on the twenty-fourth day of the month (the sixth month) that the people repented at Haggai's message to have faith and get busy rebuilding the temple. God uses positive reinforcement by giving additional encouraging messages on that day of other months (cf. Haggai 2:10, 20).

"Behold" (v. 8) introduces each of the eight visions and also occurs several other times in the book. It is a Hebrew term of exclamation, implying excitement and awe: *Look at that!* The "bottom" (*ditch*) is the Kidron Valley outside the eastern walls of Jerusalem where there would be water to nourish the myrtle bushes. "Myrtle" (Hadassah) is the Hebrew name for Esther. It is a beautiful, small tree growing 8-30 feet tall with broad evergreen leaves, white flowers, and edible berries. It is used as a decoration in Jewish festivals. This tree symbolizes Israel. While pleasant, it is not a mighty oak (the Gentile nations in comparison to Israel).

The horsemen are God's angels patrolling the earth. They report back that everything is peaceful. This enforced peace with the Gentiles dominating Israel is not good. Like the *Pax Romana* (*Peace of Rome*) it is a peace that benefits the overlord, not the subjects. The "angel of the Lord" down in the ditch indicates God's concern for Israel's condition. The 70 years would be the period of time the temple was in ruins (586-516 B.C.). God concludes that He used the Gentile nations as a tool to chastise Israel, but they went too far and now stand condemned.

Life stEP
God chastises His erring children but He also heals. God is down in the ditch with us as we go through the trials of life.

Zechariah 1:18-21

What is the writer saying?

How can I apply this to my life?

The second vision is very brief. Zechariah is again startled by what he sees ("behold"). The horns he sees are animal horns. Sometimes in language, a part stands for the whole. Here we should not think of bodiless horns, but rather the business end of a powerful ram charging at us. Notice that God gives an interpreting angel to help Zechariah understand what he is seeing. This is normal in visionary prophetic literature such as what also occurs in the Book of Revelation. "Scattered" is an interesting choice of words since in the book we will meet Zerubbabel, the Jewish governor of the province of Judea under the Persian government. His name comes from the same Hebrew root and means *Seed of Babylon* (he was born in Babylon during the Babylonian Captivity). Notice also the unusual way to refer to Israel by mentioning Jerusalem (the capital and seat of both David's throne and God's throne in the temple), Judah (the Southern Kingdom), and Israel (the Northern Kingdom). Even though Israel was divided around 900 B.C. and the Northern Kingdom put out of existence by the Assyrians in 722 B.C., this prophecy envisions them being reunited. The four horns that scattered Israel are probably Babylon, Persia, Greece, and Rome. Egypt and Assyria would be two other candidates. After the four horns, Zechariah sees four carpenters. These are men with strong tools that can carve wood, stone, and metal. They can use their sharp tools to whittle the four horns down to size, and in fact, out of existence. As it turns out in history, the horns and the craftsmen are the same nations. God used Persia to defeat Babylon. Greece defeated Persia. Greece is defeated by Rome. The final carpenter is not a horn but rather the ultimate craftsman, namely the Messiah who will defeat revived Rome (the kingdom of the Antichrist).

Life stEP When our strength all but fails, the Master comes and uses His skills to reduce our obstacles to a manageable size.

Zechariah 2:1-13

What is the writer saying?

How can I apply this to my life?

It is the second member of the Trinity who appears in many of these visions to offer help to Israel. In the first vision, He is the rider of the red horse in the ditch among the myrtle trees. In the second vision, He is the fourth carpenter coming to whittle down the enemies of Israel. In this passage He is the man with the measuring line, coming to rebuild Jerusalem. "Measuring" speaks of ownership. Even though the temple in Christ's day was corrupted, Jesus nevertheless called it "My Father's house." Note that Zechariah is called a "young man." "Fire" occurs over five hundred times in Scripture. It speaks of purity, purification, power, holiness, glory, and punishment. The "four winds" speak of the four points of the compass. See Jeremiah 49:36 and Ezekiel 37:9 for other statements about the scattering of Israel and her ultimate restoration. In context, the "land of the north" (v. 6) has to refer to Babylon (cf. v. 7). Two years after the warning there was civil unrest in Babylon. Many Jews probably lost their lives in the 518 B.C. turmoil because they did not heed this warning to "deliver" themselves. Jesus gave a similar warning for believers to flee Jerusalem when it was surrounded (Luke 21, fulfilled in A.D. 70). Likewise in Revelation 17 and 18 people are warned to flee Babylon. There is no part of the body more sensitive to a poke than the eye. Woe to the person or nation that pokes God in His eye. The "me" of verse 11 must be another member of the Godhead. "Judah" is the territory around Jerusalem, the area geographically that the Jews of Zechariah's day controlled. "All flesh," not just Israel, is affected by this promise. "Raised up" signifies that God is making preparations for judgment. Ultimately this will be fulfilled in the Tribulation period.

Life stEP · Mark 4:39 is a great example of *hush*. Christ stilled the storm on the Sea of Galilee, using a phrase that meant *to muzzle an animal*. In effect, He said to the winds, *Shut your mouth, back to the kennel!*

Zechariah 3:1-10

What is the writer saying?

How can I apply this to my life?

pray *Nigeria – Pray for the infrastructure of Nigeria to improve. There is not constant electricity and good drinking water in most regions.*

The "angel of the Lord" is the preincarnate Christ. Joshua was the High Priest in Zechariah's day. "Satan" and "resist" are from the same Hebrew root, therefore it could read: *the Resister standing to resist him or the Opposer standing to oppose him.* The repetition in verse 2 is for the sake of emphasis. Joshua (and the 50,000 he represents) had just been snatched from the fires of the Babylonian Captivity. The word for "filthy" is the crudest term for objectionable material in the Hebrew language. It refers to animal refuse from slaughtering, such as manure, blood, and guts. Salvation involves both cleansing (forgiveness) and clothing in Christ's righteousness (justification). The High Priestly garments were very ornate with the following colors: gold, blue, purple, scarlet, and white. They were decorated with embroidery, gemstones, and golden bells. Zechariah realizes that he is viewing the Day of Atonement in which the High Priest wore *work garments* to do the sacrifices, but then changed into his beautiful garments (v. 5). The "fair mitre" (headdress) had *Holy to the Lord* written on it. "Branch" (v. 8, as in plant life) refers to *origination* and therefore emphasizes Christ's humanity as the second Adam from above. "Eyes" (v. 9) can refer to the facets of a gemstone. God engraves Christ, the gemstone, in His hands at Calvary to reveal the flashing splendor of His internal greatness and love. Christ is referred to as a *stone* in many passages with a variety of emphases. He is the stone: smitten by God, rejected by Israel, stumbling to the lost, corner to the church, tested by Satan, and shattering to the nations. Ancient people lived in an agrarian culture. Their *heaven* was an agricultural paradise.

Life stEP The fourth vision is a picture of the cleansing and justification of Joshua the High Priest, and by extension, Israel and all men who come to God in faith believing.

Zechariah 4:1-14

What is the writer saying?

How can I apply this to my life?

Zechariah views olive trees with an abundance of olives. The oil is running out by itself, flowing by gravity to the lamp stand. This visual speaks of the abundance of power God Himself supplies to make His people a light to the watching world. Here there is one lamp stand with seven lamps indicating the national testimony of Israel. By contrast, in Revelation 2:1, the church's testimony is represented by seven individual lamp stands underscoring our international character. One day, apostasy will extinguish the Church's light and Israel will be re-ignited (Romans 11:21-29). Zerubbabel the governor and Joshua the high priest are the two olive trees.

Revelation 11 applies this vision to the two witnesses. The point of verse 6 is: "Not by (human) might nor by (human) power, but by my Spirit, saith the Lord." In the New Testament, the Holy Spirit is called our "Comforter" (Greek *paraclete: One called alongside to help*). *Comfort* means *with (com) strength*

(fort). In Romans 8:37 we're said to be "more than conquerors." In Greek this is *hupernikon* (*hyper conquerors!*). In Latin it is *supervincemus* (*super conquerors*: super men and super women for God!). "Shoutings" (v. 7) is the Hebrew word *Shoah* which means *great tumult* and is also the word Jewish people use for the *Holocaust*. "Grace to it" means *may God bless it or how elegant it is.* "Despised" (v. 10) is the Hebrew word *buz*, reproducing the angry sound of a scornful crowd. "To and fro" is a military term for *patrol* as seen in 1:10. "Branches" (v. 12) is the word for *ears* of grain, which indicates the abundance of olives. "Golden" is the color of olive oil and speaks of deity, especially picturing God's purity, beauty, and value. Many Scriptures indicate God's original intent of making Israel a missionary force to the Gentile world (cf. Exodus 19:6; Isaiah 12:4; Deuteronomy 32:8; and Ezekiel 5:5).

Life stEP   Once saved, Israel was to be a bright testimony to the watching world. Likewise, we are saved to shed forth glimmerings of God's grace.

Zechariah 5:1-11

What is the writer saying?

How can I apply this to my life?

pray *South Africa – For loving outreach by those in youth ministry to a very vulnerable generation.*

Today we cover two visions. The first pictures the rooting out and punishment of sinners. The second vision pictures the removal of sin from Israel with an attempt by Satan to protect sin. To convert from cubits to feet, calculate eighteen inches for one cubit. The largest Biblical scrolls (such as would contain the book of Genesis or Isaiah) are thirty feet long but only fifteen inches high. The holy place in the tabernacle was exactly thirty by fifteen feet. The dimensions of the scroll therefore represent the holiness of God. In the stone copy of the Ten Commandments, there were five commandments on each tablet. *Swearing falsely by God's name* (perjury) is the third commandment and *theft* is the eighth commandment (both are the *middle commandment* on their side). This symmetry is a figure of speech, which uses a *part* to represent the *whole*. Therefore, the entire law is meant, not just these two *central* commandments. An "ephah" is like a bushel basket. A "talent" is round and would be heavy (about 76 pounds). Some have suggested that since both the ephah and the talent were used in commerce, part of the emphasis is on the sin of greed (*commercial idolatry*), which was a problem after the Babylonian Captivity (cf. Nehemiah 5; Malachi 3; James 5; and Revelation 18).

There is nothing viler than an evil woman. In the Old Testament men are considered *childish* in their evil and regarded as *naughty*. Women, however, are the well-spring and foundation of the next generation. When the women of a society are evil, there is no hope left—the foundation is gone. The stork is an unclean animal; therefore, these women represent demons that are trying to save "wickedness" by taking her to her ancestral home, Babylon, located on the plain of Shinar. Once there, Satan will seek to establish a power base for the final conflict. All throughout Scripture, Babylon symbolizes man's rebellion against God.

Life **stEP** Sin always destroys. Holiness always blesses. The choice is ours.

Zechariah 6:1-8

What is the writer saying?

How can I apply this to my life?

The "two mountains" refer to the Mount of Olives and the Temple Mount (Mt. Zion) with the Kidron Valley in between. This is also called the Valley of Jehoshaphat (*Jehovah Judges*). By Jewish, Muslim, and Christian tradition, it is the place of final judgment. Brass (or bronze) is symbolic of judgment (cf. the bronze altar, bronze serpent, bronze feet of Jesus in Revelation 1). The four horses are very similar to the four horsemen of the apocalypse (Revelation 6:1-8). "White" speaks of victory; "red" of bloodshed; "black" of famine and disease; "grisled" of death in general. In Revelation 6 grisled is a pale green color such as in the figure of speech, *a little green around the gills*. The concept of apocalyptic terrors to judge sinners is first mentioned in Deuteronomy 28 and then specified in Ezekiel 14:21 as "sword," "famine," "noisome (wild) beasts," and "pestilence."

It is difficult to tell from the Hebrew text exactly where the different horses traveled. The only thing that is clear is that a country to the "north" received special attention in this judgment. "North" is the direction from which Israel was usually attacked since the desert to the east made attack from that direction difficult. Therefore, although Babylon is due east of Israel, she is referred to as an enemy from the north. Since only the waters of the Mediterranean are to the west of Israel, this vision obviously is designed to encompass the entire earth. "To and fro" is the military term for *patrol*. While ultimately the judgment is on all Gentile nations, it is interesting that two years later (518 B.C.) and six years later (514 B.C.) the Persians punished the citizens of Babylon for attempted revolts.

Life stEP God climaxes human history with the destruction of the Gentile world powers and the installation of His Son as the King in Jerusalem. This glorious truth should motivate believers to purity of life and zeal in witnessing.

Zechariah 6:9-15

What is the writer saying?

How can I apply this to my life?

pray *Netherlands Antilles – For doctrinally sound literature to be printed in the Papiamento language.*

These men from Babylon, though Jews, foreshadow the Gentile Magi who would come from Babylon to worship the Christ-child. Why would Babylonians even care about the birth of the Jewish Messiah? Maybe because they were the spiritual descendants of godly Daniel! Perhaps the gold represents the deity of the Messiah and silver represents His humanity. The crown was set on Joshua's head for two reasons. First, if it was placed on Governor Zerubbabel's head (who was the grandson of the last legitimate Davidic king) the Persians would have considered this a treasonous act. More importantly, the ceremony was designed to show that the Messiah would be both a king and a priest. "Grow up out" comes from the same Hebrew root as "branch" and could be translated *branch out* as a play on words. The Hebrew word for "memorial" is *zikkaron*, which comes

from the same root as "Zechariah" (*God Remembers*). According to Jewish tradition, this crown was placed in the window of the temple in the front gable where everyone coming to the temple could look up and see it. Theoretically, Christ could have seen it hanging there as He rode the donkey into Jerusalem on Palm Sunday. Notice that one man has a nickname (v. 10 cf. v. 14; "Hen" means *grace*).

When Christ offered the kingdom on Palm Sunday, it was a bona fide offer of the kingdom. The establishment of the kingdom was contingent on the obedience of the people (v. 15). Of course, the crucifixion was necessary both as the established means of salvation and also as a predicted event. If the Jewish leaders of Christ's day had obeyed Him, then His crucifixion could have come another way, such as by the Romans on the charge of insurrection.

Life stEP The horrors of the tribulation period will ensure that the majority of the Jews are believers and therefore worthy of receiving the kingdom when Christ returns.

Zechariah 7:1-14

What is the writer saying?

How can I apply this to my life?

Two years have elapsed since the eight visions of Zechariah 1-6. In two more years the temple will be finished and sacrificial worship restarted. In chapters 7-8, Zechariah receives four messages from God warning against the dangers of vain, ritualistic, ceremonial, heartless worship. In this passage, men come from Bethel, about twelve miles north of Jerusalem. Bethel has a rich religious history, including visits from Abraham and Jacob. Here Jacob had his *ladder* dream and later returned to build an altar. It would have taken almost a whole day to travel that far. The men's determination to do right is commendable. "Sherezer" means *protect the king* and "Regemmelech" means *friend of the king*. The fast on the Day of Atonement was the only fast required by the Law. These other fasts mentioned in Zechariah 7-8 were man-made (cf. Amos 8:10). To this day, Jews observe the fast of the *Ninth Day of the Fifth Month*

(Tisha B'Av). They believe a variety of evil events occurred on this same day in the calendar year, including the destruction of both temples (586 B.C. and A.D. 70). Verse 1 tells us it was the ninth month. The very next fast in the annual cycle of religious holidays would be the fast of the tenth month (cf. 8:19), which remembered the start of the Babylonian siege in 588 B.C., exactly 69 years and 11 months earlier.

God lists the Old Testament fruits of the Spirit in verses 9-10 (cf. Galatians 5:22-23). In comparison to the population of Zechariah's day, the land of the "former prophets" was heavily populated, even in the marginal wilderness region to the south. The rebellion of their fathers led to the current sparse population. "Adamant" was a very hard stone. "Scattered" (v. 14) means *blew away*, like wind driving away the chaff when winnowing grain.

Life stEP The people of Zechariah's day were excited because they were close to finishing the temple. God did not want their worship to become stale and routine. How can we keep the right heart attitude in our worship?

Zechariah 8:1-13

What is the writer saying?

How can I apply this to my life?

pray United Kingdom – For God to raise up a new generation of vibrant, doctrinally sound Bible teachers.

"Jealousy" in the Hebrew text is literally, *redness of face*. Jehovah looks forward to the completion of the temple that Zerubbabel, Joshua, Zechariah, Haggai, and the people are building. He will dwell in the Holy of Holies in Jerusalem once again. The word "Jerusalem" means *City of Peace*. God says that it will also be called *Jeruemet*—"city of truth." "Holy mountain" is *Har Kadosh*. It refers to the temple mount specifically, but all of Jerusalem in general. (Technically, the mountain that the temple was built on was Mount Moriah. Another mountain nearby was called Mount Zion or Sion but that name eventually was given to all Jerusalem as well.). "Old men and old women dwell in the streets," indicates that there has been a long time of peace and prosperity for there to be old people. "Boys and girls playing in the streets" indicates that the streets are safe. "Remnant" (v. 6) refers to a small number of people. However, it is often used of the small group of the faithful.

While the remnant of Zechariah's day may have their faith stretched to imagine such prosperity, their lack of vision does not affect God's ability to perform. "East" and "west" as points on the compass implies *universality*. (Jews will come from everywhere in the world to live in Jerusalem.) Ezekiel 48:35 and Revelation 21:3 also anticipate the greatness of the day when God will dwell with His people.

The "prophets" of verse 9 are Haggai and Zechariah. In the book of Haggai and again here in Zechariah, God reminds the people that when they disobeyed Him, He would curse their crops, but when they obeyed Him He would bless their farming efforts. He concludes that while the Jews had been proverbial for a cursed people over the previous seventy years, now they would be proverbial for a blessed people. Everyone will want to be their friends.

Life **STEP** Do unsaved people look up to us as good-luck charms or accidents waiting to happen?

Zechariah 8:14-23

What is the writer saying?

How can I apply this to my life?

pray   *Ghana – For evangelistic outreach in the northern region, which has had less exposure to the Gospel.*

God continues with an emphasis on the character qualities that He respects and expects from His people. Jewish courts met in the gates of the Israelite cities (cf. Ruth 4:1). God not only expects truthfulness in everyday activity but also in the courtrooms of the City of Jerusalem.

Biblical buzzwords from this section: Truth and Peace ("Emet" and "Shalom" in Hebrew). "These six things doth the LORD hate: yea, seven are an abomination unto him: A proud look, a lying tongue ..." (Proverbs 6:16,17).

In verse 19 we have all four fasts listed. The fast of the tenth month remembered the start of the siege of Jerusalem in 588 B.C. The fast of the fourth month remembered the breaching of the walls in 586 B.C. The fast of the fifth month remembered the destruction of Solomon's temple (*the First Temple*) in 586 B.C. The fast of the seventh month remembered the murder of the Jewish governor Gedaliah in 585 B.C. Interestingly enough, even though the two men of 7:2 asked if they had to continue to observe these fasts, God never answered their question. Their logic was, *Now that we are rebuilding the temple and God is blessing our crops, do we need to keep fasting for these sad events?* God's logic was, *Did you ever observe these fasts because you were repentant and loved me or were you just having a pity party?* God does give the encouraging word of *one day your fasts will be turned into feasts.* (This play on words is in English, not in the Hebrew text unfortunately.) God envisions the day when the most exciting, the most popular activity on the planet will be to take a trip to Jerusalem to worship the Lord. In that day, Gentile teachers will retire and Jewish teachers will be the experts people seek to further their knowledge of the Lord. The Day of Pentecost was a foreshadowing of this day (Acts 2).

If the rejection of the Jew leads to Gentile blessing and salvation, how much greater will be the benefit to the Gentile when the Jew is accepted!

Zechariah 9:1-9

What is the writer saying?

How can I apply this to my life?

Alexander the Great defeated Darius III of Persia at the Battle of Issus (in southeast Asia Minor) in October of 333 B.C. Strategically, this left all of Syria and Israel open to the Greeks. The Phoenicians became fabulously wealthy as sea merchants and colonizers of the Mediterranean world. At one point, their colony at Carthage, in Northern Africa, challenged Rome under Hannibal (notice "Baal" in his name!). "Dust" (dry) and "mire" (wet) are the two *normal* conditions of ancient streets. The city of Tyre had an island fortress a half-mile out in the Mediterranean with 150-foot high walls. What the Assyrians could not accomplish in five years, and Nebuchadnezzar could not crack in thirteen years, Alexander did in just seven months. He defeated the island fortress by scraping the mainland city into the sea. This formed a land bridge (mole) two hundred feet wide out to the island. He executed two thousand citizens and enslaved thirty thousand more. Today, you can visit Tyre in Lebanon and see the bedrock where fishermen spread their nets to dry (cf. Ezekiel 26:14!).

There were five cities of the Philistines on the coastal plain of Israel (vv. 5 & 6). Ekron was furthest north and would be attacked first. Gaza was the largest and most strategic city, located right on the coastal highway that ran from Damascus to Egypt. Gath, the fifth and unmentioned Philistine city, is missing probably because by this time it had already been absorbed into Judah. The Jebusites were Canaanites that eventually converted to Judaism. Ekron became a Jewish city around 160 B.C. "Oppressor" (v. 8) is the term used of the Egyptians who enslaved the Israelites. By Jewish tradition, God used a dream to warn Alexander not to harm Jerusalem. Abruptly, the passage turns from Alexander on his white war stallion to Jesus on His donkey.

Life stEP Predictive prophecy is a great demonstration of the supernatural character of Scripture. History is *His Story*. Both Alexander and Jesus died at 33. There the comparison ends!

Zechariah 9:10-17

What is the writer saying?

How can I apply this to my life?

"Ephraim" was the largest of the ten northern tribes, and therefore represents the entire Northern Kingdom of Israel, with the capital at Samaria. God envisions a day when all Israel, Judah, and the capital of Jerusalem will be peaceful, prosperous, and free from Gentile domination. "Sea to sea" (v. 10) would be from the Mediterranean in the west to the Dead Sea in the east. "Blood of thy covenant" (v. 11) refers to the animal sacrifices that ratified the various covenants God made with His people, such as the Abrahamic and Davidic Covenants. Because of God's unconditional promises, He will take the cursed Jews who perish for lack of water (like Joseph thrown in the dry well by his jealous brothers) and restore them to Jerusalem in blessing. "Double" (v. 12) is the inheritance of the firstborn son. For instance, if there were five children in a family, the father would divide his inheritance in six parts. Each child would get one part except the oldest son who received two portions.

The height of the clash between the Jews and Greeks occurred between 175 and 164 B.C. as Antiochus Epiphanes, a Greek ruling in Syria, and a foreshadowing of the Antichrist, afflicted the Jews. He desecrated their temple by offering a pig on the altar and erecting an idol. This sparked a revolt led by the Maccabbean family. The subsequent Jewish victory and rededication of the temple created the Jewish holiday of Hanukkah (called the "feast of the dedication" in John 10:22). Storms from the south are especially oppressive since they bring blast-furnace heat out of the Arabian Desert. The Arabic word for these hot winds is "sirocco" (the name given to one of the models of the Volkswagen cars). It will be a holy war (v. 15). The restored land and people will be a great, sparkling testimony to the watching world.

Life STEP   God has torn. Can He also heal? Can He restore the years the locusts have stolen?

Zechariah 10:1-12

What is the writer saying?

How can I apply this to my life?

In chapter 10, the Good Shepherd offers blessings. But, in chapter 11, the willful sheep reject the Good Shepherd and follow the evil shepherd. Israel has two rainy seasons, one in the fall (*former rains*) and the second in the spring (*latter rains*). The fall rains are needed to get the winter wheat started and the spring rains promote the growth and ripening of all the crops. "Shepherds" represent kings and "goats" speak of exceptionally evil men. "Judah" refers to both the *kingly tribe* (Genesis 49:10) and also the *Southern Kingdom* (which at the split in 930 B.C. contained two tribes, Judah and Benjamin). The "nail" or "tent peg" (v. 4) was important, not only for holding the tent up, but also for displaying prized possessions within the tent. All four of the items in verse 4 illustrate the Messiah that would come from Judah ("oppressor" is better translated as *ruler*). "Joseph" represents the *Northern Kingdom* (which at the split in 930 B.C. had 10 tribes, two of the more prominent being the sons of Joseph: Ephraim and Manasseh). Therefore Judah + Joseph = United Israel. The "hiss" of verse 8 is a shepherd's whistle.

Ever since 722 B.C. (the Assyrian Captivity) there have been more Jews living outside the land of Israel than inside. Today world Jewry numbers about 15 million with about 5.5 million living in Israel. Over seventy different languages are spoken in Israel representing the different cultures from which Israelis have returned to Israel. Gilead would be part of Jordan today; Lebanon is still called Lebanon (although currently occupied by Syria). The analogy is to the Exodus from Egypt when God dried up the Red Sea and later the Jordan for miraculous crossings. Likewise in Revelation 16:12, the Euphrates river dries up. Here the "pride" of Assyria (the Tigris River) dries up.

There is a way that seemeth right unto man, but it might be the path of the evil shepherd. We must discern and follow the Good Shepherd.

Zechariah 11:1-11

What is the writer saying?

How can I apply this to my life?

"Lebanon" means *White Mountains* (snow-capped). They soar to fourteen thousand feet. The cedars of Lebanon were famous for their beauty. The wood was highly prized because of the rosy grain and strong sap that made the wood impervious to insect attack and rot. The fir tree (cypress) was not as beautiful or valuable as the cedar, hence the mourning for the destruction of the cedar. "Bashan" is the rich grazing area of the Golan Heights to the east of the Sea of Galilee. The "pride" of Jordan is the thick vegetation along the Jordan River. It was normally thick enough for lions to live there. All of the areas and vegetation mentioned here were known for their lushness.

The evil shepherds (kings) who abuse the flock are Jewish since they exclaim, "Blessed be the Lord" when they sell the sheep (v. 5). "Beauty" (v. 7) can also mean *favor*. "Bands" is the idea of *unity*. The breaking of the staff in verse 10 would indicate that God is removing His *favor* from Israel. The "three shepherds" (v. 8) might be leaders of Zechariah's day who despised him for his rebukes, or more likely refers to the three governmental offices (*Prophet, Priest, and King*), which were stripped from Israel in A.D. 70 by the Romans. Zechariah is acting out the part of the shepherd as the Messiah of Israel. The three shepherds loathed the Messiah. This is reminiscent of the Jewish leaders that called for Christ's crucifixion. Siege conditions sometimes led to cannibalism (cf. 2 Kings 6:28). Josephus records that this was also true in the A.D. 70 destruction of Jerusalem. The "poor of the flock" would refer to true believers who understood the predictions that Zechariah was making and were watching in stunned silence.

Zechariah 11:12-17

What is the writer saying?

How can I apply this to my life?

pray *Thailand – For pastors to accept their responsibility to lovingly confront believers engaging in sin.*

Knowing that God often had his prophets act out some of their prophecies (cf. Ezekiel 4), most likely Zechariah was actually doing this *shepherding* in front of people on the streets of Jerusalem. He would have dressed like a shepherd (with a heavier robe than city dwellers to use as a sleeping blanket at night). He would have the tools of a shepherd, including the two staves already mentioned. Perhaps he even tried to get some of the people (*sheep*) to follow him around. He then announces to the puzzled crowd that he is ready to be paid for his shepherding efforts. At that point, perhaps a wise guy in the crowd throws thirty pieces of silver at his feet. This would be a cheap wage. In Exodus 21:32 it is the price to buy a slave. Since the wage is cheap, the Lord's response in verse 13 is dripping with sarcasm ("a goodly price"). This pictures Israel's opinion of Jesus. The New Testament notes the fulfillment.

Judas betrayed Jesus to the Sanhedrin for thirty pieces of silver (Matthew 27:3). When he was consumed with guilt for causing the death of Jesus, he returned the silver. The Sanhedrin could not use the money in the temple since it was *blood money* so they used it to buy an exhausted potter's field (clay) to use as a pauper's graveyard (Matthew 27:7). The field was no good because all the clay was gone and it couldn't be farmed but the holes were already there in which to bury the poor.

The Shepherd's crook was a composite made of pieces of wood held together by leather straps. Verse 14 envisions the breaking of the bands of the shepherd's staff. The evil shepherd is so greedy he even tears apart the sheep's hooves apart looking for meat. The "right eye" was the eye used to aim the arrow (v. 17).

Just as Saul, *The People's Choice*, was followed by David, *God's Choice*; likewise, one day *The People's Choice* (the Antichrist) will be followed by *God's Choice* (Messiah Jesus)!

Zechariah 12:1-14

What is the writer saying?

How can I apply this to my life?

pray   *Paraguay – For pastors to actively model the disciplines of prayer, Bible study, and witnessing.*

God narrows the discussion down from the broadest category (the heavens) to the narrowest (each individual person). God's judgment reduces the nations to a drunken stupor. "In that day" is similar to the Old Testament phrase, "the Day of the Lord" and is repeated sixteen times in chapters 12-14. Jerome, an early church father, lived in Israel and reported watching the local teenagers *pump iron* with rocks. Despite the best efforts of the weight lifters, Jerusalem will remain firmly in her place. Tents (v. 7) do not afford much protection against marauding armies, so Jehovah will *hover protectively over* Israel. Israel has never experienced the destruction of all her enemies as described in verse 9. According to verse 10, apparently some unsaved Jews will accept Christ even as He returns in the air at the Second Coming; abruptly, like Saul on the road to Damascus! Grace is "unmerited favor." They will ask for even more grace ("supplications"). They will "look" (and "live" – Numbers 21:8) in belief.

"Me" is Jehovah, but as the "Me" turns to "Him" we obviously have two members of the Godhead in view. "Pierced" cannot be weakened to just *emotionally hurt*, as it normally means *physical puncturing*, and there is a parallel drawn to the death of godly King Josiah. This verse is also applied to Christ in John 19:37. Hadadrimmon was a city near Megiddo, the place where Josiah died as all levels of society mourned: king, prophet, priest, and commoner. The amazing thing is that we even know what the mourners will say—just as clearly as if we had read it in the newspaper the next day. "Who hath believed our report? And to whom is the arm of the Lord revealed?" (Isaiah 53:1). Thus is fulfilled Romans 9-11, "And so all Israel shall be saved..." (Romans 11:26)

Life **stEP**   Israel's National Day of Atonement is a picture of the salvation that is available to us right now. Future blessings motivate to present responsibilities.

Zechariah 13:1-9

What is the writer saying?

How can I apply this to my life?

pray   *Honduras – Pray for salvation decisions to result from radio broadcasts.*

"In that day" is the day in which God invades space – time – history and takes overt control of human history. For the remnant that remains and believes, salvation and cleansing is provided. This fountain is based on the cross of Christ but accessed at the Second Coming. It is "opened" never to be shut again for the Jews. It is for the cleansing of "sin" (*to miss the mark*) and "uncleanness" (*ritual impurity*, Numbers 8:7). Revelation chapter 9 indicates that *end time* religion will be demonically inspired. Not only will the idols, prophets, and unclean spirit be removed from millennial earth, but also the very *names* of the false gods will be forgotten! "Thrust him through" (v. 3) is the same word as "pierced" in 12:10. The rough garment associated with the *Holy Man* was also the type of clothing a farmer/herder might wear, so this will become a convenient alibi for the exposed false prophet. If verse 6 is still referring to the false prophet, then the cuts were part of their pagan rituals (a vain attempt to produce sympathy in the aloof god, cf. 1 Kings 18:28). If referring to the Good Shepherd, then it is a very appropriate description of the betrayal and crucifixion of Christ. The word "man" is actually "strongman" in Hebrew. "My fellow" means *my close relative*. The two together become a good, strong statement of the humanity and deity of the Messiah. The early church father Tertullian commented: "The death of the Son of God [at the hands of His own Father] is by all means to be believed *because* it is absurd." (It is too preposterous to have been invented by man!) In the horrors of the tribulation period, 66% of the Jewish population of Israel will be destroyed. Among the 33% remaining would be the 144,000 sealed Jews (cf. Revelation 7:3). Israel's "Lo-ammi" period of Hosea ("Not My People") will turn into "Ammi" ("My People").

Life stEP   Where God's grace is spurned, His just judgment is sure to follow. But, even in His judgment, He still is gracious and a remnant is saved.

Zechariah 14:1-11

What is the writer saying?

How can I apply this to my life?

"Nations" occurs thirteen times and "Jerusalem" twenty three times in chapters 12-14. The Jewish people are a resilient group. Even in the horrors of the Holocaust, they had great hope. Writings found in a cellar in Cologne after WWII: "I believe in the sun when it is not shining. I believe in love when I feel it not. I believe in God when He is silent." Normally, "people" stand, not just "feet" (v. 4). The unusual phraseology is calculated to emphasize that this is a literal return to the Mount of Olives (His *feet* will touch that sod again!). Acts 3:21 tells us that He will be in Heaven *until* the time of restoration comes. Then He will return to the planet! Revelation 12:6,14 show Israel fleeing from the Antichrist into the wilderness around the Dead Sea.

Daniel 11:41 states that Ammon, Moab and Edom (modern Jordan) will not fall into the hands of the Antichrist. Likewise, at Christ's return, the valley caused by the division of the Mount of Olives will provide an avenue of escape for trapped Jerusalemites. The earthquake will produce tremendous topographical changes in Israel. One of these will involve a new river running from Jerusalem down to both the Mediterranean Sea and to the Dead Sea with the result that these areas, which are frequently dry a good part of the year (especially the Dead Sea region) would now have abundant water for crops (Ezekiel 47:8). The earthquake of Uzziah's day (v. 5) occurred over two hundred years earlier, yet God treats the Jews as a unit. Daylight was affected when Joshua fought in the Valley of Aijalon (vv. 6, 7). In preparation for the Millennial capital and the masses of people who will come to worship the King (cf. Ezekiel 40-48), this whole area – roughly forty miles north/south – will be leveled, leaving the temple exalted in the middle, near ancient Shiloh, the first city to host the tabernacle.

 Life stEP

We may be the *terminal generation*. We may be witnessing the *birth pangs* of a new age. Are we ready?

Zechariah 14:12-21

What is the writer saying?

How can I apply this to my life?

Christ will control physics to melt his enemies. He will control psychology to confuse His enemies. Great spoil will be left behind for Israel. The feasts of Israel are symbolic of the ministry of Christ (He is our Passover Lamb; He was the Firstfruits from the dead, etc.). The only feast not fulfilled by the end of the tribulation period is the Feast of Tabernacles, which speaks of the blessings of the millennial reign of Messiah. It is the *harvest home festival* much like our Thanksgiving. Jewish people take their meals outdoors in festively decorated tents and then go *home* the eighth day. Likewise we will celebrate the millennium for *seven days* and then go home (to Heaven!) on the eighth. The Egyptians (v. 18) may be singled out because they were the first Gentile nation to harass the Israelites. It may also be that with the mighty Nile River, they need special warning not to treat the required feast observance lightly, as the plague will surely spread to them if they disobey. So great will be the holiness of that blessed kingdom that even common everyday items like the bells on the horse's bridles will be "HOLINESS TO THE LORD" (also on the turban of the High Priest).

A Legend: Two knights on horseback were traveling strange territory at night. As they crossed a dry riverbed, a voice cried out of the darkness: "Halt!" They instinctively obeyed. The voice continued: "Dismount and fill your pockets with stones." This task accomplished, the men remounted and continued into the night with one remaining statement ringing in their ears: "Tomorrow you will be both glad and sorry." At first light the men eagerly dug into their pockets to fathom the meaning of the mysterious statement. To their amazement, in their hands shone gorgeous gemstones—rubies, diamonds, and emeralds! And then they understood the statement. They were both glad and sorry. Glad they took some, but sorry they did not take more. Moral: Take all of the Word of God that you possibly can!

Hebrews

Erdman says, "The Epistle to the Hebrews differs in form from all other epistles in the NT. It begins as an essay or treatise; it progresses as a sermon or lecture; and it ends like a letter." The book is of high literary order in that it presents and develops a definite theme, and its arguments are carefully composed and arranged.

Hebrews develops the theme of Jesus Christ in His present office as our Great High Priest. Nowhere else in the NT is an analysis of the character and ministry of Jesus Christ so long sustained. A thorough knowledge of Jesus is intended to provide all readers, both Jewish and Gentile Christians, with a *goal for life*; 6:1, "... let us go on to perfection."

The *purpose* of the letter is three-fold:

1. *To present* needed, detailed information about our Great High Priest to its first readers, Jewish Christians. They possessed a good knowledge of the Old Testament, but still had *spiritual ear troubles* since they were "dull of hearing," (5:11).

2. *To encourage* the Jewish Christians. They were coming under religious pressure to once again conform to the Mosaic Law. This epistle seeks to have these believers consider the claims of Christ and then make a total commitment to Christ. Thus, the writer says thirteen times, "let us ....," as he exhorts the Jews to whole-heartedly follow the Lord.

3. *To warn* the readers about apostatizing from the truth. Hebrews warns that the cost to Jewish believers (and Gentile believers as secondary readers) of not being a totally committed Christian is much higher than other costs.

The *key word* in Hebrews is *"better"*: used thirteen times. It literally means *higher in rank; thus, more prominent*. It came to mean: *more useful, more excellent*. "Better" is used in the Book of Hebrews to build a series of comparisons:

a. Christ is a *better* messenger than prophets or angels (1:1-2:18).

b. Christ is a *better* apostle than Moses (3:1-6).

c. Christ gives a *better* rest than Joshua (4:1-10).

d. Christ is a *better* priest than Aaron (4:14-7:28).

e. The New Covenant is *better* than the Old Covenant (8:1-9:28).

f. Christ is a *better* sacrifice than the OT sacrifices (10:1-18).

g. The Christian life of "faith" is a *better* way to live (10:32-12:29).

Sunday 38

Hebrews 1:1-7

What is the writer saying?

How can I apply this to my life?

Our text literally bursts forth with a majestic declaration; in the past God used prophets, but this time God has used His Son to speak to us!

The first 4 verses form a single sentence. Note that this prologue is fulfilling its purpose; introducing the central themes to follow:

▶ The Son was appointed "*heir* of all things" (v. 2). Note God in eternity past assigned to the Son a kingdom, all of creation (Psalm 2:6).

▶ This is as it should be since the Son is also the *Maker* of the universe ["worlds," v. 2b]. This is an indication that the Son is Eternal.

▶ The book of Genesis tells us that God spoke the worlds into existence. Here we hear that the Son now holds all together (v. 3b)!

▶ The Son, in relation to God, is declared to be "the brightness of His (the Father's) glory" and "the express image of His (the Father's) person" (v. 3a).

▶ First, the Son is the "brightness" or *a flashing forth of a flood of light* that reveals the splendor of God.

▶ Also the Son is the "express image" of God, meaning *to engrave* a coin. Thus, the Son is the exact representation of God's being. Jesus, by becoming a man, made God's *person* known to us.

▶ The Son has "purged our sins" (v. 3c). We now move to His high-priestly work of providing sinful people with purification of sin.

▶ The Son, having finished His great work of redemption, then "sat down at the right hand of the Majesty on high" (Psalm 110:1; Romans 8:34).

▶ The angels are wondrous beings with amazing attributes (2 Samuel 14:20; Psalm 103:20). However, they have not been appointed *heir of all things* and are not seated *on the right hand of the Majesty on high*.

In verses 5-7, the writer quotes from four Old Testament passages to show that our Great High Priest is superior to angels He has also been given – *a more excellent name* – the name *Jesus* means *Savior*.

Life stEP Since God the Father sent Jesus into the world to declare the Father's message, how closely are you listening to His instructions? Consider the person and character of Jesus, what about His life has impressed upon you the *spiritual appearance* of God the Father?

Hebrews 1:8-14

What is the writer saying?

How can I apply this to my life?

Our passage continues the exaltation of the "Son" (vv. 2, 5). It uses OT quotations to present the eternal kingdom of the Son.

Verses 8 and 9 are quoting from Psalm 45:6-7. That Psalm is one of several *royal Psalms* that describe the Messiah as the King.

▶ First we must note that God here declares the Son to be *true deity*. We hear *one person* of the Godhead, the Father, calling *another person* of the Godhead, His Son, God!

▶ Second, God the Father declares the greatness of the Son who has a *throne*, a *kingdom*, and a *scepter* of a kingdom.

▶ Thirdly, God the Father declares the eternal character of the Son's kingdom; it will continue through all the *ages of time*!

▶ Fourthly, God declares the character of the Son's kingdom. It will be a *righteous* kingdom.

Next, verses 10-12, from Psalm 102:25-27, declare the Son's final victory.

▶ While the angels are always presented as powerful beings, Jesus Christ is declared to be the *Omnipotent One* [all-powerful], which is demonstrated in His works of creation. This would include the angels, who are the inhabitants of Heaven!

▶ The Son made the world; therefore he had the original right to govern it!

▶ Note that the Son is unchangeable while the earth and the heavens "shall perish." The phrase implies a violent end. Verse 13 quotes Psalm 110:1. This verse emphasizes the victory of the Son, who awaits God's conquests of the Son's enemies.

Verse 14 points out that this was the Son's victory, not the angels'. The angels will serve those who inherit the Son's salvation.

Life
stEP   Hebrews 1:14 indicates that God appointed angelic protectors for each of us (Psalm 34:7; 91:10-12; Matthew 18:10). The holy angels become an example to us by their desire to serve God whom they love. How can you follow this example and be of service to God's people?

Hebrews 2:1-9

What is the writer saying?

How can I apply this to my life?

pray Romania – For the lifting of government restrictions, which are hindering effective ministry growth.

The second chapter begins with *"Therefore."* This word draws the proclamations of the first chapter together with the application that is now before us. Neglecting the salvation, which these Jewish Christians had received, presented a danger of drifting away (cf., 5:11-12). The first readers of this letter were characterized by being spiritually *hard of hearing*.

Notice the five we's: *"we have heard,"* "lest *we* let slip," etc. This warning was to *believers* who, through "neglect" (v. 3), were allowing a spiritual deterioration to take place.

The Greek word here for *"neglect"* (v. 3) is the *negative* [by adding an "a" to the front of a word; like our *uncaring*] of *to think about*. It means *not responding appropriately to*, or *not pay attention to*, or *not caring about*. The point is that this new salvation in Christ should be that to which we give *particularly close concern*!

• This same word, without the negative, is found in 1 Peter 5:7, "…He *cares* for you!"; thus, Jesus pays *close attention* to us!

• A form of this word is found in 1 Timothy 4:15, *"Meditate upon* these things; give thyself wholly to them; …" here we are to *ponder how to carefully put certain principles into action*.

Now, let's notice God's *careful attention* to give us so great a salvation (vv. 3, 4, & 9):

• The Lord Jesus Himself has *spoken of this salvation* (v. 3b).

• The Lord then sent out His disciples to be *witnesses* (v. 3c)

• At the same time God empowered "those who heard Him" (v. 3c) to exhibit the powers of *this new life in Christ* (Hebrews 6:5) by means of *signs, wonders, miracles,* and the *gifts of the Holy Spirit* (v. 4).

 Christian friend, since the phrase, *to neglect*, is the negative of *to look after*, which of these have characterized your walk before God? What <u>neglected aspect</u> of your walk as a Christian needs some *careful pondering* of how to put it into action? Then consider: In what areas of your life do you need God's *attentive help* to accomplish some remolding? Pray and ask God for His divine help in these areas.

Hebrews 2:10-18

What is the writer saying?

How can I apply this to my life?

Yesterday we looked at the *"glory"* (vv. 7, 9) of Jesus who became a man so that He could "taste death for every man" (v. 9). Today's passage proclaims the result; Jesus brings "many sons unto glory" (v. 10).

Jesus is declared "the *captain of their salvation"*; that is, He was the *originator who caused salvation to happen*. Thus in verse 10, we see that Jesus *established a way for us to come to salvation*!

"Glory" (v. 10) is continuing from the earlier quote of Psalms 8:4. The *glory* upon which Jesus is crowned has also become the *glory* of "many sons," that is, those people who have believed on the great work of God.

"Glory" means *being given a high status or exalted condition*; which is to say Christ's *tasting death* (v. 9) changes everything for *those who believe*. Believers have become a *shining brightness* since:

▸ They have received God's *"salvation,"* v. 10, meaning *having been made safe from a difficult situation* which was (1) sin's power over a person and (2) God's pending judgment upon sin.

▸ They have been *"sanctified"* by God (v. 11). This is the verb form of the common word, *holy*, [*thus being made holy*]. It means to be (1) *separated from* our former life in sin and (2) *dedicated to* God and to the special service which He assigns us. It also carries the idea of *to cause to have the qualities of holiness"* (1 Thessalonians 5:23).

▸ They have become his *"brethren"* (vv. 11, 12, 17) and are *"children"* (vv. 13-14) who take part in God's family. The writer illustrates this truth with 3 quotes. In verse 12, Psalms 22:22 is quoted. In verse 13, Psalm 18:2 is quoted, followed by Isaiah 8:18. When the *brothers* of Jesus, *children of God*, gather together, they are to praise, glorify, and fear Him!

How long has it been since your own *"salvation?"* When considering your own salvation, what can you praise and glorify God about? Your *"salvation"* set in motion the on-going work of God's *sanctifying* in your life. What aspects of your life still need God *to cause to have the qualities of holiness* about them?

Hebrews 3:1-6

What is the writer saying?

How can I apply this to my life?

The *holy brethren* of 3:1 are the *brethren* of 2:11, 12 and 17. These brethren have been given high privileges as "partakers" in God's "heavenly calling." These privileges include:

▶ Jesus, their "*captain*," calls them to be His family (2:11-12)!

▶ Jesus became their "*high priest*," (2:17) in that He made "reconciliation" to God for their sins.

▶ Jesus has "*sanctified*" them [2:11, *to make holy*].

▶ Jesus is now "*bringing many sons unto glory*" (2:10) by inviting them to *partake* in a "*heavenly calling*" (3:1). This is an invitation to take part in God's heavenly kingdom and in the work of the *hope of our calling.*

The Greek word for "*partakers*" (3:1) is also used in 1:9, 3:14, 6:4, and 12:8. The word translates "fellows" or "companions." We see the literal use of the term in Luke 5:7, "And they beckoned unto *their partners*, …in the other ship … come and help them. And they … filled both the ships …" It means *those who have together* thus like modern *shareholders.*

Our passage asks us to "*consider*" [to observe in your thoughts] this Jesus who is the "*Apostle and High Priest of our profession*" (v. 1):

▶ He is an *Apostle* and was *one sent forth with a mission to complete.* Thus Jesus was sent to be God's greatest "spokesman (1:1-2) and revealer of God's "express image" (1:3). The NT teaches that God "sent the Son" (I John 4:14) who in turn has now *sent us* (John 20:21).

▶ As *High Priest*, Jesus completed the job of the *chief officer* of the Old Testament sacrificial system as revealed by God to Moses. The High Priest's chief responsibility was to "*make reconciliation* for the sins of the people" (2:17). So Jesus has made a way for us to come to God! He now continues his work of *interceding* for us by offering up prayers to the Father on our behalf (7:25), which allows us to draw near to God (4:15-16).

Life stEP   A member of the family of God cannot be *unborn* out of God's family! Membership in His household carries with it both privileges and responsibilities. What are some of your responsibilities as a *shareholder* in the business of His household?

Hebrews 3:7-13

What is the writer saying?

How can I apply this to my life?

Today's passage begins with a long quotation (vv. 7-11) from Psalm 95:7-11. Verses 12 and 13 then apply the psalm's warning to us. The psalmist points out that Israel's ancestors missed God's blessings because they had "hardened" their hearts against God.

Let's look at the warnings of the quotation that are to apply to us:

▶ *"Harden* not your hearts" (v. 8): *"Harden"* means *to dry up; to become stiff* as did Israel's faith in God during their *"provocation"* and *"temptation"* against God in the wilderness (Exodus 17:1-7).

▶ "When your fathers *tempted* me, *proved* me" (v. 9): This phrase means they did not trust God during their wanderings in the wilderness. They were *trying out God* [*"tempted"*] before they would *approve or truly accept* [*"proved"*] Him as their God.

▶ *Always they err with the heart* (v. 10): The heart was seen as the center of a person's being: will, feelings, and personality. God was "grieved" because their *hearts* were always *wandering away from the right path*, which is picturing a planet that appears to wander through the stars of a constellation.

Let's now look at the application to Christians:

▶ *"Take heed*, brethren" (v. 12): He gives a caution, *You who claim to be Christians, look about you, be on your guard!*

▶ "An *evil heart* of unbelief" (v. 12): Like Israel in the wilderness, do we refuse to fully believe and trust in God? Are some of us *trying out* God to see if we want to *truly accept* Him later?

▶ Sadly, some will *depart from the living God* (v. 12b) as they are either *drawn away from* or *withdraw from* God.

▶ *"Exhort* one another daily" (v. 13): This is a key principle in our defense against being *drawn away* or *withdrawing from God*. We "exhort" one another as we *come alongside one another to comfort, encourage, strengthen, instruct, and support.*

Life **stEP** What can you do today to keep from *wandering away* from your walk with God? How can you be *on your guard*? Also, what can you do *"today"* (vv. 7, 13) to be an exhorter of others?

Hebrews 3:14-19

What is the writer saying?

How can I apply this to my life?

Today's passage illustrates *God's rest* (vv. 11, 18; the illustration will continue in 4:1,3,5,8,9,11!). This *"rest"* refers back to the days of Moses when God wanted to provide His people, Israel, an abundant life in the land He had promised them (see Joshua 1:13; 21:43-45).

The record of Israel's *"unbelief"* (vv. 18-19) is in Numbers 14:1-4. The writer of Hebrews points out that, at the *"beginning"* (v. 14) of Israel's story, Israel did exercise their faith in God to bring them out of slavery. Thus they *believed* God was going to free them from their slavery when they applied the blood of the Passover Lamb (Exodus 12:1-28). *Believing, they* passed through the Red Sea, escaping the power of Pharaoh and their slavery in Egypt. They also *believed* that God was going to "bring them up ... unto a good land ... flowing with milk and honey ..." (Exodus 3:8).

Today's passage refers to two years later when Israel did not continue *"stedfast"* (v. 14) in their *belief* that God was going to deliver His *Promised Land* into their hands. They refused to believe they were going to *"enter into His rest"* (v. 18). Then for thirty eight years they continued to *grieve* God with many other acts of "unbelief" (e.g., Exodus 17:2-7).

Notice that those who, in Moses's day, refused to believe God's promise to give them this *"rest"* were then denied *entry* (v. 19) into God's Promised Land because of this sin (v. 17) of "unbelief" (v. 19). Joshua and Caleb believed God and later entered in because they *wholly followed the* LORD (Numbers 32:10-13).

Now as a warning to us (vv. 12, 14), the writer of Hebrews says that as a result not continuing "stedfast" in their belief in God, God removed some of His blessings from them and so they died in the wilderness (v. 17). Likewise we must *today, hear His voice, and harden not our hearts* (quoting from Psalm 95:7-8).

Life stEP

If we fail to hear God's exhortations and heed His warnings, we too will suffer loss. Are you spending your Christian life following your own agenda, while your Great High Priest, Jesus Christ, desires to work in you that which is pleasing in His sight (Hebrews 13:21)?

Hebrews 4:1-11

What is the writer saying?

How can I apply this to my life?

pray   *Japan – For the Holy Spirit to help believers overcome ancestral influences by the study of God's Word.*

Today's passage continues to warn Christians using the tragic example of *unbelieving* Israel. The first generation, freed from slavery in Egypt, failed to "enter into God's rest" (3:11). The Lord had intended *three stages of rest* for the nation of Israel:

1. The *redemption rest* from slavery in Egypt (3:11; Exodus 6:5-7).
2. The *possession rest* in the Promised Land (Deuteronomy 12:9, 10).
3. The *kingdom rest* when Messiah reigns on earth (Isaiah 11:10-16).

These 3 *rests* parallel *three stages of rest* God intends for believers:

1. The *rest of salvation* provided by Jesus as a gift at the time of a Christian's salvation (4:3; Matthew 11:28).
2. The *rest of a life in Christ* attained by being a productive part of the Lord Jesus's present earthly program (4:5-6; Matthew 11:29).
3. The *eternal rest* received when this life is over and we are with Christ (4:9-11; Daniel 12:13). This rest is still a future hope to us.

The warning of Hebrews 4 is that saved people today can miss the *second stage* of their rest as did Israel.

▶ Notice that God, after His work of Creation, entered into a *day of rest* (4:4; Genesis 2:2). "We who have believed" (4:3) are to enter into enjoying our inheritance as new members of the family of God!

▶ Yet, many Christians *come short* of the deep sense of satisfaction which is intended to be part of a Christian's experience each day. Notice the "today" of 3:7, as each of us walk in our *life in Christ*.

▶ The *unbelief* of Hebrews 3:12, 18, 19 and 4:6, 11 is the failure to trust God for all those additional victories needed in all of our *today's* (v. 7)! We too must face the hard things of life, which are like figurative *walled cities* and *giants* in our daily lives. We must daily *walk by faith* as an extension of our having been *redeemed by faith*.

The key to finding our rest needed for "today" is learning more about God. You must learn to trust in Him to give you victory over your *walled cities* of sin and *giants* of daily troubles. What giants will you face today that tempt you to *harden your heart against God* in unbelief?

Hebrews 4:12-16

What is the writer saying?

How can I apply this to my life?

Today's passage brings to a close the warning and exhortations of 3:12 to 4:11. The writer concludes with an admonition to his readers to diligently appropriate the "rest," (v. 11) which God has offered. His objective is to keep us from *falling* (v. 11) into unbelief, as did Israel.

3 resources are given to aid in *holding fast* (v. 14) to our faith in Christ:

1. *The Word of God*: The writer points out that the Old Testament is filled with historical examples to us that are applicable to our lives now! As we consider the actions, choices, and character of the people in the Bible, we allow the Bible to penetrate our hearts as it spotlights our hidden errors of thought and deed. It also displays what is *spiritual* in our life and what is just fleshly or natural (v. 12).

2. *The Son of God*: When the Word points out our fleshly errors, our *unbelieving* misdirection, and our sin, we are reminded to "hold fast our profession" (v. 14). Our "profession" gives us access to the care of our Great High Priest who is able to "sympathize" (v. 15) with us. He continually prays and intercedes for us before God the Father.

3. *The Grace of God*: As a result, we, in spite of our sin, may "come boldly" before God's "throne of grace" because Jesus continues to provide us with a means to "obtain mercy" (v. 16).

Don't miss the *turn of expression* given here in the words "*throne of grace.*" In the ancient world, when a person had wronged his king, he was brought before the king's throne of judgment to hear what judgment was to be pronounced. Yet we are reminded that, even though our sin is known to God ("open to the eyes of Him," v. 13), when we come in repentance before His throne, we are not given our deserved *judgment* but instead are given His *mercy* and *grace!*

Life stEP

"Let us therefore come boldly unto the throne of grace, that we may obtain mercy, and find grace to help in time of *need*" (v. 16). What spiritual *need* is there in your life? What sin have you gotten into that (a) needs God's *mercy*, instead of the judgment you deserve, and (b) needs God *grace* to "help" you out of the mess you have made?

Hebrews 5:1-8

What is the writer saying?

How can I apply this to my life?

pray   *Ukraine – For the teachers, textbooks, buildings and scholarships essential for leadership training.*

Our passage continues to build upon the theme of Jesus, our "great high priest," who is carrying on His ministry from "heaven" (vv. 4:14-16).

We are given a description of an Old Testament "high priest":

1. A priest must be selected from "*among men*" (v. 1) so he might officiate on behalf of men. Note Jesus was *a man* (Hebrews 2:14, 16).

2. A high priest was "*ordained for men*" [v. 1, i.e. *appointed*] since he was to be their representative who was able to approach God in hope.

3. He was to "*offer both gifts and sacrifices for sin*" (v. 1; "*offer*" means *to carry forward*). God had stipulated that a person who brings a sacrifice had to rely upon a priest who carried sacrifices to the altar.

4. A priest must be "*called of God*" to his office (v. 4). Even Jesus did not elevate Himself to this position, (v. 5) but rather was called to it by His Father. The writer (vv. 5-6) proves this by quoting from

Psalm 110:4; showing that the Messiah was to be the royal king. The story is from Genesis 14:18, where *Melchizedek* was both a king and priest.

5. The High Priest was to be a man of "*compassion*" (v. 2). He *deals gently* with men who bring offerings to him. Some offerings were brought to deal with sins of *ignorance* (v. 2a; Numbers 15:22-31, sins done by those *not knowing* God's Word). Still other offerings were provided to cover sins done by those who have been <u>*lead away*</u> into sin, literally, *caused to wander* from known truth (v. 2b).

Our passage points out that every priest understood that he was "*compassed with infirmity*" [v. 2b]. This is to say that each was aware that he was *completely encircled* by his own wickedness, moral weakness, and sin.

In this aspect Christ was different than the OT priests. He was "*without sin*" and thus He did not need to first "*offer up sacrifice*" for His own sins (see Hebrews 4:15; 7:27).

Have you fallen into sin because of *ignorance* of God's ways or because you have been *lead away* into sin? If so, call unto Jesus, your faithful High Priest who desires to *deal gently* with you and your sin if you will confess your sin and turn to Him (1 John 1:9).

Hebrews 5:9-14

What is the writer saying?

How can I apply this to my life?

The writer has barely begun to explain that Christ was a "high priest after the order of Melchizedek" (v. 10), when he felt obligated to stop [he picks up on this theme again at 6:20]. He then reprimands many of his readers because they had stagnated in their Christian lives and had not matured spiritually. He makes four accusations:

1. *You are dull* of hearing (v. 11b). "Dull" was a common Greek word used only rarely in the Bible. It could refer to someone who was sluggish, lazy, careless, or, as used here, slow to learn.

2. *You are* in need of being taught again the "first principles" (v. 12a). This phrase, "first principles," was used of school children who were just beginning to learn their ABC's. Many believers needed to go back and review their spiritual ABC's!

3. Spiritually, *you are babies* when you should be of *full age*! You ought to be adults able to digest meat (v. 12b). What a picture… perhaps a 25 year-old who still has no teeth to chew his food, so he sits on his mother's lap and is fed milk from a bottle!

4. *You are unskillful* in the words of God about righteousness (v. 13). Unskillful referred to a person who was not trusted; *not yet tested*. Such *inexperienced* persons lacked the skill needed to distinguish between good moral choices and evil.

One more thing needs to be pointed out; these four *you are's* are to be understood as *you have become*. The implication is that these believers had *at one time* been learning and growing but then had *become* dull and stagnant.

Life stEp

Don't miss an insight given by the writer! He is pointing out how to become a *full aged* believer who can "discern both good and evil" (v. 14): (1) How can you exercise your spiritual muscles today? (2) What can you read to help you get beyond your spiritual ABC's? (3) How can you make the Bible a part of a daily *dietary plan* (1 Peter 2:2)? (4) If you are an *untested* and *inexperienced* Christian, who can be your *tested* and true spiritual coach, teacher, trainer, and example?

Hebrews 6:1-8

What is the writer saying?

How can I apply this to my life?

Our writer insists on our moving beyond the *beginning "principles* of the doctrine of Christ"* (v. 1). They include *"repentance from dead works"* [literally, *acts that lead to death*, which includes repetitive religious ritual, 9:14] and *"faith* towards God"* [which refers to a firm belief in the nature, attributes, and deeds of God, including His bringing us salvation].

He points out that our *going on to perfection* (v. 1) is something *we will do with God's help* [*God permitting*, v. 3]. This reminds us that God alone assists us in reaching the goal of *"perfection."* It is *bringing to completion* our spiritual maturity in Christ, which began at our salvation.

He then gives a solemn warning (vv. 4-6) about the tragic alternative to spiritual growth. Apparently there was the grim possibility of his readers retreating from the spiritual progress which they had made. He warns these Christians of the danger of moving from a position of true faith to the extent that they become disqualified for further service (1 Corinthians 9:27, *lest I become a "castaway,"* i.e., disqualified from further use; used of impure silver that was *unworthy* to be used in making coins) (The Bible Knowledge Commentary, 2:794). Consider the following:

• *"Once enlightened"* (v. 4, *having clearly understood*) describes the Christian's conversion experience (10:32; 2 Corinthians 4:3-6)

• *"Have tasted of the Heavenly Gift"* (v. 4) is an understanding of the first concepts of salvation (John 4:10; Romans 6:23; James 1:17-18).

• *Having shared in the Holy Spirit* (v. 4; 3:1, 14) is a reference to having received the gift of the Holy Spirit and then giving evidence of His work of transforming their lives (e.g., "fruit of the Spirit").

• *Having tasted the power of the Word of God* (v. 5) refers to being instructed by Scripture and seeing it transform their character.

Life stEP — Sadly a Christian's persistent rejection of the Spirit's call to repentance will make him an unusable castaway to God; disallowed in the race. Has the Spirit of God been prompting you to turn away from some sin? How can you allow the Spirit to transform that area of your Christian walk making you *worthy* of service to God?

Hebrews 6:9-15

What is the writer saying?

How can I apply this to my life?

In verses 9 and 10, the writer assures his "*beloved*" readers that he anticipated *better things* of them than the *thorn-bearing, in-danger-of-being-cursed, doomed-to-burning* backslider described in verse 8!

He has become "*persuaded*" (v. 9, a *settled conviction*) concerning them, that is, he has overcome doubts by his observations. The convincing evidence had been their *ministering to the saints* (v. 10). This was clear evidence that the Holy Spirit had produced His fruit in their lives (v. 4)!

Their *ministry to the saints* had also been a "*work and labor of love*" toward God. He intended to encourage them to keep at their service to fellow Christians, knowing that God would not fail to notice and assist.

He then exhorts these Hebrew Christians to continue in a manner of life, which *diligently* (v. 11) serves others *with faith and patience* (v. 12).

1. "*Diligence*" means *to continually exert oneself or to make every effort*. It pictures a runner who is *leaning into his stance* as he eagerly awaits the starting signal.

2. "*Slothful*" (v. 12) is a contrast to *diligence*. It is a *lack of exertion*, thus *slowness, laziness*, and *idleness*. Such a manner of life leads to the rejection of service for others.

3. "*Faith*" for us who are already Christians is *a firm conviction of a truth* [i.e., Jesus truly lives and directs the steps of our lives]. Such a "*faith*" becomes the basis for our daily choices. It is guided by our confident "*hope*" (v. 11b).

4. "*Patience*," a companion quality to "*faith*," means *long-angered*, the opposite of *hasty anger* or being *short tempered*. It is *putting up with circumstances for a long time*. Notice that this is a quality of the Lord Himself! He is "*longsuffering* toward us" (2 Peter 3:9).

Life stEP

Do you have a "*diligence*" or *eagerness to get at* the service of your fellow Christians? Or do you exhibit a *slowness* in your service to others [after all, if you delay maybe someone else will help]?
How will your "*faith*" guide you in the choices you must make today?
How can you let "*patience*" be a companion to your "faith" today?

Hebrews 6:16-20

What is the writer saying?

How can I apply this to my life?

Our passage examines an "*oath*" by God. *Oaths* were used in legal matters to give reliability to promises. A part of an oath was the naming of one who would insure that the promise was carried out. Verse 13 said that God had made a "*promise*" to Abraham and He confirmed it by *swearing* [a solemn pledge] an *oath* (Genesis 22:16-18). Since God intended to keep His promise to the "*heirs of promise*" (v. 17), He is declared to be its co-signer! Galatians 3:6-29 explains how we Christians have become *heirs of Abraham* (v. 7, 9, 16, 29).

The point is also made concerning God's "*immutable*" promise to us Christians! "*Immutable*," indicates both *an unchangeable determination to do a thing* and *the power to bring it about*. It is applied to:
1. The "*immutability of His counsel*" (v. 17). "*Counsel*" speaks of *intentions* or *purposes* based upon God's deliberate reflection and decrees. "Counsel" is enforced by His "immutability" which is

to say what *God resolves to do* He also has the *power* to bring it about!
2. The *surety* of His *confirming oath*, which is to say He, as His own co-signer, will make sure the promises are brought to pass!

These two immutable things become our "*strong consolation*" (v. 18), our "*hope*," and the "*anchor of the soul*" (v. 19).
1. "*Consolation*": an *encouragement or admonition* that strengthens a believer in his faith (12:5; Romans 15:4; Philippians 2:1).
2. "*Hope*": Not our everyday conversation "hope," but *a certainty concerning the future that influences present actions* (Titus 2:13).
3. "*Anchor of the soul*": Ship anchors were iron hooks used to grapple onto rocks (Acts 27:29; I Timothy 1:19). An anchor was *sure and steadfast* when it had grabbed onto the rocks below and would not slip. Such is the picture of our *hope* in God's promises to us!

The Bible describes someone with *hope* as restful, glad, strengthened, happy, rejoicing, abounding, righteous, consoled, good, steadfast, and purified. How has God kept His promises to you? And how has His *immutable counsel* brought you hope?

Hebrews 7:1-10

What is the writer saying?

How can I apply this to my life?

pray Panama – For believing fathers committed to biblical principles in a land where 72% of births are illegitimate and domestic violence is on the rise.

Today's passage thoroughly describes *Melchizedek* (5:6, 10). Verses 1-3 examine 6:20, a quote of Psalms 110:4. Melchizedek was a contemporary of Abraham, and the following is known about him (Genesis 14:18-24):

1. "*King of Salem*": An early name for Jerusalem (Psalm 76:2) when it was a Gentile or Canaanite city.

2. "*Priest of the most high God*": A name for God used by Jews (Psalm 91:1), and Gentiles (Numbers 24:16; Daniel 4:2) to identify God as the <u>Supreme One of Heaven</u> who is above all other men and gods.

3. After the battle when Abraham rescued Lot, he gave a tithe of his victory spoils to Melchizedek who was the priest of God. Abraham did this because he desired to honor God. By this he acknowledged that his victory belonged to God. Thus, Melchizedek was the *recipient of worship* to God.

4. At the same time, Melchizedek, as God's representative, *extends God's blessing* upon Abraham (Genesis 14:19-20).

5. Melchizedek's name means both *king of righteousness* and *king of peace*. These are pictures of the attributes of Jesus Christ.

6. "*Without father, without mother, without descent* (*genealogy*, in contrast to the sons of Levi) … abideth a priest continually" (v. 3). All of these are intended to present Melchizedek as a *type* or picture of Christ. Of interest to us is that Melchizedek belonged to an order of God's priests of which Christ was its high priest.

After considering Melchizedek's credentials, the second half of the passage (v. 4-10) begins with "*now consider*" (v. 4, *to weigh with careful thought*). We are to consider "*how great*" or *superior* was Melchizedek's priesthood in comparison to the priesthood of the "sons of Levi" (v. 5). It was they who were represented "in Abraham" when he recognized the exalted role of Melchizedek's priesthood. This was accomplished by paying the tithe to God through Melchizedek!

Life stEP Like Abraham, do you desire *to honor* and *give back* to God? He has in so many ways given you victory in the battles of your life! As a part of your own personal thank-you to God, perhaps you could take a minute and write out a twenty-five word declaration to honor God.

Hebrews 7:11-17

What is the writer saying?

How can I apply this to my life?

pray *Ukraine – For believers willing to begin a work within each of the 20,000 villages without a single believer.*

Why did there need to be a change of *Levitical priesthood*? The *Levitical priesthood* could not *make perfect* [or *accomplish the goal of salvation*] those who sought a right relationship with God (v. 11a; 10:1). The Levitical priesthood could only direct people to the "*better hope*" which it was "*bringing in*" (v. 19). The word "priesthood" refers to *ministry in service* to God by the *Levitical priests*.

Verse 12 of the passage declares "*the priesthood being changed*". This means *to transpose to a different form*, i.e., God has *switched* his priesthood from the Levitical priests, the "order of Aaron," to the "order of Melchizedec."

Next the passage reminds us that the *Law of Moses* (v. 12b; i.e., *The whole religious system of Israel started by God's instructions to Moses*) was bound to the *Levitical priesthood*. Thus the *Law* could not function without the Levitical priesthood (v. 11b) of Aaron.

The Lord's decree is repeated (v. 17 Psalm 110:4) to show God's intent for "another priest" to *arise* (v. 15) after the *order of Melchizedek of the tribe of Judah* (v. 14). This was not possible under the *Law of Moses*.

Therefore, the *Law*, along with its *Levitical priesthood*, must be *annulled* v. 18, *cancelled*). This means *to repeal a law by right of an authority*. By this act God made way for "*another priest*" (v. 15), who is Christ Jesus of the tribe of Judah (v. 14), to begin His office as an "endless" Priest of God (v. 16; the "for ever" of Psalm 110:4).

The incarnation, death, and resurrection of Jesus Christ opened the way for Jesus to become our great high priest with the *power of an endless life*. That power comes from His being impervious to death or any other destructive power. Because He became a man, He knows our human needs. Because he is God, He has the power to meet our needs.

Life stEP

Jesus has completed His great work providing us with redemption and salvation. He has also entered into another great service as our "endless" High Priest by presenting our needs to God!
So then, how can Jesus help you with your needs and accomplish God's goal of drawing you closer to God the Father?

Hebrews 7:18-22

What is the writer saying?

How can I apply this to my life?

pray *Pray that the leaders of our country would be sensitive and obedient to the leading of the Holy Spirit.*

Two contrasts are presented between the *new covenant* of Jesus and the *old covenant* of the Old Testament Law (v. 19):

1. First, the old covenant "*made nothing perfect*" (v. 19). Rather, it pointed the way to the Lamb of God, Jesus, who would be God's *perfect sacrifice* by allowing us to "draw nigh unto God."

2. Second, the Old Testament priests performed their duties without offering an "oath" as a promise. But God made an "oath" to guarantee (v. 20) that Jesus, as a member of an order of everlasting priests (v. 21), would serve a better covenant (v. 22)!

Thus we have a "*better hope*" (v. 19) than did the Old Testament believers because we were brought to God by a "*better covenant*" (v. 22).

The word *surety* (v. 22) is often translated *guarantee*. It is a special type of guarantee. Webster's dictionary defines a *surety* as "one who assumes the obligation on default or failure in duty of another." Suppose a merchant needs funds. The bank will say, "We have the money to lend, but we aren't confident that you will sell enough goods to repay the loan." The merchant must find a *surety* whom the bank knows can and will make up his shortage if he fails. The bank will enter into an agreement with him, but the one who is the *surety* must sign also.

In his distress, Job cried out for a surety (Job 17:3). The psalmist expressed need for one (Psalm 119:122). An Old Testament priest could not be a *spiritual surety* to those he served. But we praise God in that Jesus was made our "surety of a better testament" (v. 22). The great declaration of today's passage is that Jesus has signed with His blood as our *surety* who guarantees we will receive God's promises.

Many Christians live from day to day with a sense of insecurity, guilt, or frustration. This passage declares that God's promise concerning our salvation is as *sure* as *money in the bank*. Since the work of Jesus Christ makes you "perfect" before God, how can you live in spiritual victory this week?

Hebrews 7:23-28

What is the writer saying?

How can I apply this to my life?

pray   *Jamaica – For churches to model compassion to the poor, who receive minimal exposure to the gospel.*

Today's passage continues the theme of the superiority of Christ's priesthood over that which was available under the Law of Moses.

First is presented the *permanent priesthood* of Jesus (v. 23-24). The Old Testament Priesthood changed when a high priest died, whereas the priesthood of Jesus will never change. Therefore our Great High Priest, uninterrupted in ministry, is able to *"save them to the uttermost"* (v. 25).

The word *"uttermost"* is a Greek compound word, *"all + to-the-end"*, and means *unto the completion of all*. Thus, Jesus serves us as priest until He has brought about our complete salvation. He ensures we will receive all the promises of eternal life! He will also continue transforming us until we are *totally and eternally* made into the image of Christ!

Next, the nature and station of our High Priest is presented (v. 26).

• He is *holy* and therefore can bring us to a state of holiness.

• He is *harmless,* that is, He is *free from evil* and has no motive except for *our ultimate good.*

• He is *undefiled.* While on earth, Christ proved His sinlessness in that he was not stained by sin while in a world full of sinners!

• He is now *separated from sinners,* that is, he has now been exalted to his heavenly state as our High Priest.

• He is now *higher than the heavens.* There is no position in Heaven or on Earth more exalted than His (1:4; 4:14)! Verse 27 shows us that once upon the Cross, Jesus provided an *all-sufficient sacrifice for sin.* Under the old system, the high priests offered sacrifices every day. The high priest also offered sacrifices, consecration offerings, for his own sins. Our Great High Priest was consecrated forever by an oath of one who cannot lie (6:17-18).

Life stEP   Christ is going to *continue serving until the completion* of your transformation into a Christ-like Christian. What can you ask Him to help you change in your life today? He is making intercession for you right now. What help do you need to be successful in holy living?

Hebrews 8:1-6

What is the writer saying?

How can I apply this to my life?

Perhaps the best way to understand this passage is to review the Old Testament *tabernacle* which our passage refers to. After the LORD gave Moses the Law (Exodus 20-23), God gave him details for the construction of a *sanctuary* called the *tabernacle in the wilderness* (Exodus 25-27). The structure was 45' long, 15' wide, and 15' high. It was divided into two rooms separated by a heavy curtain. This tent-building was inside an enclosed courtyard made of a framework covered by a linen curtain. Inside the courtyard's entrance was a large brazen altar where sacrifices were made (see Exodus 35-38).

Today's passage says that this *tabernacle* was an "*example*" (v. 5, *a copy imitating an original*, see 9:23-24) and a "*shadow*" (v. 5, used metaphorically here; *an image that 'foreshadows' a future object*, see 10:1) of a building in Heaven called the *true tabernacle* (v. 2).

Verse 5 quotes from Exodus 25:40 (also Numbers 8:4), which made clear that the *earthly tabernacle* and its furnishings were to be made according to God's *specific pattern*. This *earthly tabernacle* was an *imprint* or *impression* of the *true tabernacle* in Heaven.

We learn that the Lord Himself "pitched" this *true tabernacle*. He is now involved there in a ministry that is "more excellent" than that of angels, prophets, Moses, Aaron, or the Old Testament priests.

He has become the *mediator of a better covenant* (v. 6; 9:15; 12:24, 1 Timothy 2:5). This word "*mediator*" referred to a *middle man* or *arbitrator* between two arguing parties. This word describes the work of the Lord Jesus coming between God and us to *establish* (v. 6b, *to carry into effect*) God's better covenant.

Life STEP — We know that our sin separated us from our holy God. Now we must rejoice and praise the Lord Jesus who has *mediated* a new and "better" covenant relationship between God and us! Do you have an old hymn book somewhere nearby? If so, look up an old hymn about Christ as our Savior, perhaps "I Will Sing of My Redeemer," and then sing through the hymn as a prayer of thanksgiving to our Lord!

Hebrews 8:7-13

What is the writer saying?

How can I apply this to my life?

pray   *Italy – For missionaries working in a culture that is spiritually ritualistic, apathetic, and cynical.*

Our terms *Old Testament* and *New Testament* come from the *covenant* God made with Israel at Mount Sinai (Exodus 19:5-8) and the *new covenant* prophesied by Jeremiah (31:31-34). It is quoted here in verses 8-11. The words *testament* and *covenant* are the same.

The *"first covenant"* served as God's "schoolmaster" and "tutor" (Galatians 3:24; 4:2) to guard God's children, Israel. It was not a *"faultless"* (v. 7; *perfect in all its parts*) agreement between them. Some *parts* were faultless, like its revelation of God's holiness and its picturing the coming Lamb of God. The *"first covenant"* did have *faults*. One example of this is that it could not keep Israel *continuing* (v. 9b) in its covenant responsibilities. Instead, they acted ungratefully to God (v. 9a).

The articles [the terms of a contract] of the *new covenant* are presented here and we are amazed at their extraordinary character:

• God's laws will be put into their *minds* and written on their *hearts* (v. 10b). This is to say a Christian will be *conscious* of God's ways and will *love* God's ways. This results in the *courage* to act upon them.

• God will be *their God* (v. 10c), in that He will be near to His people to continually sanctify them. As a result, His people will truly be *His people* who love, honor, and obey Him in all things.

• All His people shall *know God* (v. 11). There will no longer be a need for priests or prophets to teach God's Word. God's Spirit will teach Christians all things (see John 14:26; 16:13). The Scriptures declare that we will be *taught of God* (Isaiah 54:13; John 6:45).

• God will pardon their "sins" and will not "remember" them (v. 12). Under the first covenant, sins were brought to mind every year due to the repetition of the sacrifices. Under the new covenant, sins have been forgotten and washed away by the blood of Christ!

Life stEP   Since this new covenant binds you to God, Christian, are you listening to your *conscience*? The Holy Spirit of God will talk to your spirit by means of your *conscience*! Are you allowing the Holy Spirit to teach you and guide you onto paths of holy living that please God?

Hebrews 9:1-10

What is the writer saying?

How can I apply this to my life?

Today's passage begins a contrast between the *old tabernacle* and the "greater and more perfect" *Heavenly tabernacle* (v. 11). This is where Christ ministers as our eternal High Priest (v. 24).

Notice the writer's respect as he describes the *old tabernacle*. He first describes the two halves of the Tabernacle [called here the "first" and "second" tabernacles] including its furniture (vv. 1-5). Second, he describes the "ordained" service of the priests (vv. 6-7); that is, once per year, not without blood, and by first offering for his own sin. Next, he explains that this design and service is to *signify* certain lessons (vv. 8-10) as follows:

a) The first lesson was that the "*way into the holiest of all*" [*the Holy of Holies*, the *back room* in the tabernacle] was not yet made known. This *inner tabernacle* was the dwelling place of God. The "veil" (v. 3) that separated the two rooms of the tabernacle stood as a symbol that the *path of free approach* was blocked.

b) We are also taught that the tabernacle was a "*figure*" [*a parable; a story teaching a lesson*] for that time period (v. 9). The tabernacle was an object lesson. It prefigured the "good things to come" when Christ served at the "greater ...tabernacle" (v. 11).

c) Next, the offerings made did not make the petitioner "*perfect*" [*to bring to completion*] in his "conscience" or *inner person*. The external ceremonies and sacrifices of the worshipper could not reach to the worshipper's *inner person*. Therefore, they could not bring about a sense of spiritual accord with God. Only the work of the Holy Spirit *purging* our inner spirit can *perfect* fellowship with God be obtained (v. 14)!

Life stEP

We have a great gift! First, we have a direct and continuous "*way*" to God. We now worship in the Heavenly tabernacle made available by the service of Jesus, our High Priest. We also rejoice knowing that the Holy Spirit is *perfecting* our *inner persons*. What area of your life does the Holy Spirit need to *bring to completion*? Since a "*way*" has been made open for you to approach God, how might you pray to God concerning this need?

Hebrews 9:11-15

What is the writer saying?

How can I apply this to my life?

pray — *Cuba – Fruitfulness and a greater area of outreach for the Christian radio feeds out of Latin America.*

Today's passage brings us to a climax. During the fourteen centuries under the first covenant, a new covenant was promised (Jeremiah 31:31-34). It would be "established upon better promises" (8:6-8).

This new covenant [or new testament] has now been established by the work of Christ. Note what He has accomplished:

• Christ, as our *High Priest* (v. 11a), has entered into the "more perfect" (v. 11b) Heavenly tabernacle and has "obtained *eternal redemption* for us" (v. 12). "Redemption" means *to loose something that was bound*. Redemption was used of captives released from their bondage when a ransom was paid (1 Peter 1:18).

• Christ, as our *Perfect Sacrifice*, needed only *once* to offer *Himself without spot to God* (v. 14). By this He *purged* [*to cleanse so as free from contaminants*] us from sin, therefore making us *perfectly* pure in our "conscience" [v. 14b, used here to refer to entire *inner person*].

• Christ, as our *Mediator*, served as the *contract negotiator* ensuring to both God and people, the ratification of the New Covenant (8:6; 12:24; Job 9:33, *daysman*; 1 Timothy 2:5).

Let's look at what was accomplished by this great *redemptive work*:

▶ We have received the *"eternal redemption"* that Christ "obtained ... for us." Since the value of His *one-time-for-all-times*" sacrifice (v. 12) was immeasurably great, so then our redemption was a *one-time-for-eternity* event. I only need to *get saved* once!

▶ We have a new life in Christ that begins with a *cleansed inner person* [*purged conscience*].

▶ We have a new purpose in life. No longer do we serve "dead works" (v. 14). Instead, Christ has made us fit to *serve* the Living God.

▶ We have also been "called" [an official summons into God's kingdom] to "receive" a "promise of eternal inheritance" (v. 15).

Life stEP — We have eternal redemption by His own blood (v. 12) through the ministry of the eternal Spirit (v. 14). Now we glory in our new life of service and the promise of an eternal inheritance (v. 15).

Hebrews 9:16-22

What is the writer saying?

How can I apply this to my life?

Since the words *"testament"* and *"testator"* are use six times here, we begin by looking at these words. The word literally means *to place between two* and refers to a contract between two parties. Often, in the Bible, it means a treaty or pledge between God and men. A *"testament"* could also, as it does here, refer to a *last will and testament* of someone who was about to die, that is, the *"testator."* Since ancient times, such a legal device was used to arrange for the disposal and distribution of the *testator's* property upon his *death* (v. 16b).

Here we see that Jesus Christ is a *"testator"* who has declared His desire to distribute His *"eternal inheritance"* (v. 15) to every believer. It is only *necessary* for the beneficiaries to accept the terms of His will!

We also see that this new covenant of Jesus is like the old covenant between God and Israel, which was put into *"force"* (v. 17) by means of the ceremony carried out by Moses (v. 19-20). This ceremony ratified their covenant with God (see Exodus 24:1-8) by the sprinkling of blood.

Our passage ends by pointing out that the *"shedding of blood"* (v. 22) was central to the Old Testament sacrifices (Leviticus 17:11) which provided a *"remission"* of sins or an *atonement for sin. Remission of sins* literally means *to cause one to stand away from their sin.* Hence, it speaks of our receiving *a deliverance from the penalty of our sin.* Often we simply say we have been *forgiven of our sin.*

We cannot leave this idea without pointing out that the central mission of the Lord's coming was to *shed his blood* so that He might provide us with *"remission of sins"* (Matthew 26:28). Jesus also, in His Great Commission, commands us Christians to be proclaiming this *"remission of sins"* to all nations (Luke 24:47).

Life stEP Some of our most cherished hymns honor the Lord Jesus and extol His shed blood which provided us with "eternal redemption" (v. 12). Perhaps you could likewise honor our Lord by looking up one of these old hymns [e.g., *Are You Washed in the Blood*], and singing it through to yourself as a way of personally thanking the Lord Jesus!

Hebrews 9:23-28

What is the writer saying?

How can I apply this to my life?

pray *Italy – For youth ministries to have an effective outreach among the 1,600,000 university students.*

Our passage picks up on the subject of *Christ, our High Priest* (vv. 11-12), who entered into the *heavenly tabernacle*. We are told that the tabernacle of Moses was only a *pattern* (v. 23) and a *figure* (v 24, *a copy*).

The writer is showing the incompleteness of the Levitical sacrifices. Christ our High Priest (vv. 23-24) offered a better sacrifice *to put away sin;* He only "*once*" had to offer "*the sacrifice of himself*" (v. 26)! Notice the contrast between the word "*often*" [used of the Old Testament priests, (vv. 25, 26) and the word "*once*" [used of Christ, vv. 26, 28).

Let us turn to another truth in our passage. It uses three *appearings* of our Lord to declare three great truths about His ministry:

• One is in the *past tense*. "He *has* appeared to put away sin by the sacrifice of Himself" (v. 26). This is to say that Christ died as a sacrifice for our sin!

• One is in the *present tense*. "*Now to appear* in the presence of God for us," (v. 24) says that Christ has ascended into Heaven as our High Priest who makes intercession for us (7:25).

• The third is in the *future tense*. "… unto them that look for Him *shall he appear* the second time without sin unto salvation" (v. 28). He will come to Earth again to complete His work of salvation in us.

In His past earthly ministry He saved us from the *penalty* of sin by what He did *for us*. In His present priestly ministry He is saving us from the *power* of sin by what He does *in us*. In His future ministry He will save us from the very *presence* of sin by what He will do *with us*.

Life STEP

Did you notice the two little words added after the statement, *Christ has entered … into Heaven itself and to appear now in the presence of God* (v. 24)? Yes, two little words, "*for us*!"

Would you act upon this great truth by asking your Heavenly High Priest, Jesus Christ, to intercede for you before God Himself? Pray that you might become all that God would want you to be!

Wednesday 41

Hebrews 10:1-10

What is the writer saying?

How can I apply this to my life?

pray United Kingdom – For God to create a thirst for and a commitment to God's word in the hearts of youth.

Today we begin the last argument (chapters 7-10) concerning the superiority of Christ and the new covenant which He put into effect.

Once again the writer presents the limitations of the Old Testament's *Law* (v. 8) and its *sacrifices* (v. 1) as a means of approaching God (v. 1-4). He points out that the priests of the old covenant had to *repeatedly* offer the same sacrifices "year by year" for the sins of "those who approach" (v. 1). The repeated sacrifices could not make those who drew near to God "*perfect*" (v. 1)! Those sacrifices *could not purge* (v. 2) their *consciences* because the sacrifices could not *take away* sins.

This *imperfect* sacrificial system lead by imperfect priests, is contrasted with Jesus Christ's "*once* for all" (v. 10) sacrifice. He offered his own body as a perfect sacrifice by which He "*sanctified*" (v. 10) and "*perfected*" (v. 14) those who place their faith in Him.

Let's look at what Jesus Christ has accomplished for us:

• He has "*purged*" our sins. This word means *to provide an inner cleansing from guilt and shame for sins* (v. 2). It draws upon the Old Testament idea of *atonement for sin* [i.e., *those who are guilty of sin must satisfy God's wrath upon sin*].

• He has "*sanctified*" us. *Sanctify* means *to make pure and holy* by the purifying influences of the Holy Spirit on our hearts! It carries an Old Testament picture of a thing set aside for special service to God.

• He is *perfecting* us. This literally means *to bring to a full end*. It implies a plan, a process or course, a work to do, and an intended final product. It is used here to express God's spiritual intention of *bringing us to a state of completion according to His plan for us*.

Life stEP

As a Christian, have you considered Christ's intent to complete His work of perfecting your life so that you might become God's intended finished product? What sin does He want to cleanse from your life? What special service does He specifically intend for you to do for God? What area of your character does He still desire to *bring to a full transformation* in your life?

Hebrews 10:11-18

What is the writer saying?

How can I apply this to my life?

pray *Uganda – For God to call witnesses to the Sudanese, Congolese, and Rwandan refugees.*

Today's passage continues a study of the *Superiority of Christ's Priesthood.* First notice (vv. 11-12) that the Old Testament priests offered sacrifices while they *stood* (v. 11). This signified that their work was never finished. The priests always offered the *"same sacrifices."* Some of these sacrifices were offered daily, some weekly, some annually, but *always again!* There was also no provision for the priests to be *seated.* By *daily standing,* they were pointing out that their offerings were never complete. The offerings were unfinished work, because they could *"never take away sins"* (v. 11). They could never *perfect* (v. 14, *bring to completion*) the Old Testament believer. With the completion of His one offering for sins, Jesus then *sat down* (v. 12)! Our Lord Jesus completed His one offering for sins and is now seated at the right hand of God waiting for the fulfillment of *"til his enemies be made his footstool"* (v. 13; a phrase from Psalm 110:1).

Verses 16-17 (re-stating 8:10-12) present a summation of the promised "new covenant" prophesied by Jeremiah (see Jer. 31:33-34):
1. The laws of God will be written in the hearts of His people;
2. God will erase the sins of His people from His memory;
3. There will be no more sacrificial offerings because forgiveness will be complete and believers would be *made holy* (v. 14).

Our section concludes with a warning to Jewish Christians. They had received God's prophesied "one sacrifice" for the *"remission"* of sins but they were considering returning to the *old ways* of sacrifices at the Temple. Our writer is pointing out that "there is no more offering for sin" (v. 18); that is, there was no going back! The temporary and anticipatory sacrificial system of the Old Testament had completed its purpose!

Life **STEP**   As noted, this passage was written to give early Jewish Christians confidence that they had correctly moved on to a new way of worshipping God. God had planned this for them! This passage should also give you the confidence that Jesus has finished His work of *taking away* your sins! Ask yourself this question, do I have a *confident faith* that Jesus has saved me from my sins?

Hebrews 10:19-25

What is the writer saying?

How can I apply this to my life?

Today we leave the doctrinal section of Hebrews (ch. 7-10). This is where the foundation was established for our *confidence* (v. 3:6; 10:35) in Christ's work of redeeming, sanctifying, and perfecting us!

Today's passage begins the writer's *application* related to the *privileges* that Christ has provided us. First, we are *privileged* to have *free access to God*. Previously, He had restricted access by separating Himself from Israel behind the "veil" (v. 20) of the tabernacle's inner room, the Holy of Holies. Now, because of Christ's new covenant, we may *boldly enter into this holy place* (v. 19) as we personally fellowship with God. We are also *privileged* to have *Jesus continuing to serve* us as our "high priest" (v. 21); presiding over this new "house of God." Today's passage picks up from where it had left off in the first section of the letter (ch. 1-6). In 4:14, the Hebrew Christians were urged to, "*let us* hold fast our profession" in "Jesus the Son of God." Note the little phrase "*Let us* ..." which was used five times earlier in this letter to make *application* to believers (4:1, 11, 14, 16; 6:1). This phrase is also used again three times in today's passage (v. 22, 23, 24) as it returns to application. The three "*Let us* ..." verses here relate the *duties* required of us:

• The first "*Let us* ..." deals with *our hearts* having the right kind of *"faith."* This faith must be true, full of assurance, cleansed from evil *inner desires* ("conscience"), and pure in outer actions ("bodies").

• The second "*Let us* ..." deals with *our words* ("the confession"). It declares "*our faith*," or better yet "*our hope*" in Jesus being faithful in the completion of His promises to us.

• The third "*Let us* ..." deals with *our conduct* as we put to practice our new life in Christ. We need to "*consider*" how we can "*love*" and do "*good works*" to one another.

Let us put these three *"let us"* statements into practice! What step of *faith* can you take to cleanse your *inner desires* and walk in a *pure manner*? How can you declare your *"hope"* in Jesus today? What *good* deed can you do today to express your *"love"* for another Christian?

Hebrews 10:26-31

What is the writer saying?

How can I apply this to my life?

Our passage now moves beyond the *strong urgings* for faithful Christians looking for the "day" of the Lord's return (vv. 22-25), to a *solemn warning* to wavering Jewish Christians. These were Christians who were about to *forsake* Christianity and return to their Old Testament ways. The writer returns to his earlier warning, "*How shall we escape if we neglect so great salvation*" (2:3).

Our passage begins with, "if we sin willfully" (v. 26). The context tells us that more than *a yielding to some temptation* is being looked at. Four descriptors concerning their sin of *defection from faith in Christ* are given:

• "*Forsaking the assembling ...together*," v. 25, stressing the importance of Christian fellowship in a church environment. These Jews could not leave Christ and His Church by going back to their Jewish rituals.

• "*Trampled the Son of God*," v. 29a, pictures *an insulting and contemptuous public rejection* of Christ as their Redeemer (9:12), Purger of their sins (9: 14), and Perfecter of their lives (v. 10:14)!

• "*Counted the blood ... wherewith he was sanctified an unholy thing*," v. 29b. The blood of Christ was used to *wash* away their sins (v. 22) and to allow them to share in His new covenant (9:15). Now they were calling this "most holy" thing "unholy" (Exodus 30:10).

• "*Insulted the Spirit of grace*" (v. 29c). The "eternal Spirit" of God (v. 9:14) was the one making application of God's redemption in their lives, therefore enabling them to serve God. Now, they were *shamefully rejecting* the Holy Spirit's work as a part of their rebellion against God Himself!

The end of this somber passage (v. 31) reminds us of the *second purpose* of the "*day*" of the Lord's return (v. 25). The first is to faithfully complete His promises to us (v. 23). The second purpose is to bring judgment upon those who reject the "Spirit of grace" and face the fearful "vengeance" of the Lord's "recompense" [a *repaying* of people for their sins, v. 30].

Life **stEP**
There is a lesson for us here; there is no going back to some other way of finding God. What then helps you to "hold fast" to your "profession" in Christ (v. 23)? How can you fellowship with other believers (v. 25a)? How can you "exhort" others in their hope in Christ (v. 25b)?

Sunday 42

Hebrews 10:32-39

What is the writer saying?

How can I apply this to my life?

Our past two passages looked at a *message of exhortation* (vv. 19-25) and then at a *message of warning* (vv. 26-31). Now the writer moves on to a *message of encouragement* (v. 32-39). The writer reminds his first readers of their past *endurance* (v. 32, literally they *stood their ground*, often translated *persevered*), not long after they were "*illuminated*" [i.e., *saw the light of the Gospel and got saved!*]. Their past endurances included three evidences of their genuine Christianity:

• *Faith* during "*afflictions*" (v. 33): At times they had been put on public display and then both insulted and beaten, likely during the early persecutions by the Roman government.

• *Love* for persecuted Christians, like the writer of the epistle (v. 34a): Their assistance of these persecuted brothers apparently had resulted in their own "goods" being confiscated by the government.

• *Hope* in God's *promised, heavenly reward* (vv. 34b, 36b): They had suffered the loss of their "goods" with *joy* knowing that they possessed a heavenly wealth that could not be touched!

Having laid this encouraging foundation concerning their past testimony, the writer now gives his challenge of encouragement for their present situation. *Cast not away ...your confidence ... be patient ... do the will of God ... continue to live by faith ...don't draw back ... for in a* "little while" He [Jesus Christ] "will come" (v. 35-39)!

• "*Confidence*" = *boldness in openly speaking and living for God in front of the watching world.* Note that this word is translated "*boldness*," v. 10:19 (also 3:6, 4:16), concerning our coming into God's presence!

This provides a picture of our *daily life of faith*; we *confidently* come into God's presence for fellowship and we can *confidently* walk each day knowing that we are *doing the will of God* (v. 36)!

Life Step

So then Christian, how is your walk when your life gets to be a "*fight of afflictions*" (v. 32)? How can you apply lessons of *faith, love,* and *hope* to today's troubles? How can you *stand your ground* while *confidently* placing your faith in God's directing you to do *His will*?

Hebrews 11:1-6

What is the writer saying?

How can I apply this to my life?

pray   *Portugal – To see lasting changes in the hearts and lives of those attending Christian camps.*

Today we look at the *Faith Chapter* which uses the word *"faith"* twenty three times. Since the word is used many times in the Bible, it is not surprising that the subject of faith is much larger than what is covered here. This chapter deals with the *enduring faith of a Christian* who places his confidence in the Lord's help. Notice how *enduring faith* has just been introduced: 10:32, "ye *endured* ... afflictions"; 10:35, "Cast not away ... your *confidence*"; 10:36, "Ye have need of *patience*" 10:39, "But we ... *believe* to the saving of the soul!"

This Faith Chapter begins with an introduction, v. 1-3, which gives us *three characteristics of enduring faith* in a Christian:

1. "*Faith* is the *substance* of things hoped for," v. 1a. "Substance" is the *underlying support that enables us to stand*, or the *ground of confidence* for our hope. Faith is *being sure* about God's promises.

2. *Faith* is "the *evidence* of things not seen," v. 1b. "Evidence" here further explains "substance." "*Evidence*" is used here as in a legal proceeding; it is the substantiation of a *conviction* by the *events seen* and the *facts presented* which prove a truth. Thus, *faith,* after seeing the evidence, is a firm conviction that God's promises are true.

3. *Faith* is an *understanding* that our *universe* was not made from "visible" raw materials (v. 3, see 1:2)! "*Understand*" means "*to perceive by reflective intelligence*" (Wuest, Romans 1:20). The glories of the *visible world* can only point to an *invisible Creator* as its source.

Do not miss the writer's intent here! The existence of the very world in which we live is itself the first and greatest *evidence of faith*! The world came into existence by God's word of revelation. We walk today by faith in this same word of revelation concerning our *enduring faith*. It is this that gives us hope!

Hebrews 11:7-12

What is the writer saying?

How can I apply this to my life?

pray Slovakia – For salvation decisions resulting from the witness of Christians working in public schools.

Abel exhibited his faith in his *worship* (v. 4). Enoch exhibited his faith by his *walk* (v. 5). Noah demonstrated his faith through his *work* (v. 7). A right spiritual relationship with God is reflected through a proper walk which produces good works.

Neither Noah nor his family gained eternal salvation by building the ark, rather they "*became heir(s) of the righteousness which is by faith*" (v. 7). "But Noah found grace in the eyes of the LORD" (Genesis 6:8) because he believed God. God chose (Genesis 6:8) and called (Genesis 7:1) Noah and his household. They responded to His call (Genesis 7:7) and God shut them in (Genesis 7:16). They were safe from God's judgment because they were sealed in by God's grace.

"By faith Abraham ... *went out*" (v. 8): After Abraham "*went out*," he "*went forth* ...into the land*" (Genesis 12:4, 5). Some of us launch out for the Lord but never really go forth into the place of restful service. When Abraham was tested, he "*went down* into Egypt" (Genesis 12:10). When we are tested, we also are prone to go back *into Egypt* after being saved out of bondage. Although Abraham found riches in Egypt, he never built an altar there because he was out of the place of fellowship. So he "*went up* out of Egypt" (Genesis 13:1) and then "*went on*" (Genesis 13:3) "unto the place of the altar..." at Bethel (Genesis 13:3-4, north of Jerusalem).

"He [Abraham] looked for a city ... whose Maker is God" (v. 10), this is referring to the heavenly "New Jerusalem" (11:16; 12:22; Revelation 21:2, 9-27). The word "looked" carries a progressive idea of *patiently and eagerly expecting* or *watching steadily for what is to be received* (as in Romans 8:19). This illustrates the character of Abraham's faith, that is, Abraham continually set his *gaze* on his real home in Heaven; all else was just a temporary pilgrimage (the idea of *sojourn*, v. 9a).

Life **stEP** As servants of God, we need wisdom from the Holy Spirit in discerning the difference between a *walk of faith* and an *out-of-place* life style that distracts us from a *patient looking to our heavenly home*. What can keep you steadily focused upon God's goal for you?

Hebrews 11:13-19

What is the writer saying?

How can I apply this to my life?

pray — *Peru – For local Christian television programs, which are able to reach the inaccessible upper classes.*

Notice the elements of Abraham's *walk of faith*: Abraham didn't know *where* God was leading him (vv. 8-10). He didn't know *how* God would fulfill His promises (vv. 11-12). He didn't know *when* he would receive the promises (vv. 13-16). He didn't know *why* God asked him to sacrifice Isaac (vv. 17-19).

In order that we may have the opportunity to *walk by faith*; God often doesn't let us know *where, how, when,* or *why*. Faith extends our *spiritual sight* beyond the limits of *vision* of our *eyes* or *earthly plans*. It does this in order to permit us to also *see afar off* (v. 13). Only faith lets us see a better, heavenly country before we get there! Only by faith may we in this life see the city God has prepared for us (vv. 14-16).

Verses 17-19 give us the solution to the enigma of the story of Abraham *offering up Isaac* in Genesis 22:1-14. God had given to Abraham the promise, "In Isaac shall thy seed be called" (v. 18, from Genesis 21:12). God had promised Abraham that only through Isaac would his descendants be as many as the *stars of the sky* and *the sand of the seashore*. Then surprisingly God told him offer up Isaac as a sacrifice! How could Abraham's slaying his son possibly permit God to fulfill His earlier promises? Yet he says, "I and the lad will go yonder and worship, and *come again to you*" (Genesis 22:5). What we see is Abraham exercising an *expectant faith* in God as he ascends the mountain knowing that somehow he was going to witness God's answer to this dilemma! Abraham was trusting God to fulfill His promise even after Abraham had put his son to death; even if that meant that God would somehow resurrect Isaac from the dead! What a beautiful figure of why God the Father was able to permit the sacrifice of His beloved Son!

Life step — "For we walk by faith, not by sight" (2 Corinthians 5:7). When we desire signs, fleeces, and other such manifestations, we hinder our own progress in an *expectant faith*. "Without faith it is impossible to please him" (Hebrews 11:6). What are you *walking towards* in your life that needs your *expectant faith* in God's dependable care for you?

Hebrews 11:20-29

What is the writer saying?

How can I apply this to my life?

pray — Honduras – Pray for the establishment of Bible – believing churches among the Amerindian people.

Today we have three instances of *faith* "concerning *things to come*" (v. 20; *future developments that will happen at God's appointed time*).

The Genesis account tells of many failings on the part of *Isaac* (v. 20) and *Jacob* (v. 21). However, Hebrews 11 is not concerned with failings, but with *faith that triumphs over failings*. For instance, after many years of struggling against God's future plan for his sons (see Genesis 25:23), *Isaac*, "trembled" and (Gen. 27:33), submitted his *faith* to God's plan. Remember, Isaac never doubted God's covenant promises to Abraham. Rather, Isaac desired to *adjust* God's blessing so it would go to Isaac's favorite son, Esau. The lesson Isaac and Rebekah learned was their inability to alter the will of God who is immutable [unchangeable]!

Similarly, Jacob, near death, acted on *faith* as he gave his blessing to the two sons of Joseph (v. 21, Genesis 48). While in Egypt, Jacob was confident in God's promise (Gen. 47:27-31) that their descendents would return to their Promised Land. Notice that Jacob, while giving this blessing, "leaning upon the top of his staff" (v. 21) indicating his conviction concerning God's faithfulness to His future fulfillment of His promises to Israel. The last recorded words of Joseph (v. 22, Genesis 50:24, 25) prove his *faith*. Even in dying, he had faith God would fulfill his promises and bring Israel, in the future, to the land He had promised to them.

The acts of the *parents of Moses* (v. 23) prove that God will honor faith that stands against opposition and hostility. Their faith in God made His infinite resources available to them.

Refused (v. 24), choosing (v. 25), esteeming (v. 26), respected (v. 26), forsaking (v. 27), endured (v. 27), kept (v. 28), passed through (v. 29); *faith* brought all of these *verb-resources* to Moses! By *faith*, he chose to "suffer affliction. *By faith, Moses saw him who is invisible* (v. 27b)."

Life Step — Consider what would have happened if Moses had chosen the *pleasures* of Egypt; he would have drowned with Pharaoh's army! Christian, you too must choose; will you *bow* to God's plan for your life? Will you *move forward* as a faithful steward of God's plan? Or are you wrongly trying to *adjust* God's plan to better serve your desires?

Hebrews 11:30-35

What is the writer saying?

How can I apply this to my life?

The conquest of Jericho, described in Joshua 6:1-16, depended entirely upon believing and acting upon instructions from God which at times made no logical sense [e.g., how does marching around Jericho help defeat the city? Wouldn't it be better to make battering rams?!].

Rahab aided that conquest because she believed, "…The LORD your God, *he is God* in heaven above, and in earth beneath" (Joshua 2:8-11). She proved her faith by her deeds (James 2:25) and therefore did not perish with Jericho. Note that this Gentile prostitute is someone we might consider to be an *unlikely person* to become an example of faith! Yet, her faith is clearly evidenced and greatly rewarded by God!

Two generations after Joshua's conquest, Israel forsook the Lord God and served idols. As a result, for nearly three hundred years, their history consisted of recurring cycles of rebellion, judgment, repentance, and restoration. God raised up a succession of leaders called Judges [four are mentioned here; Gideon, Barak, Israel's commander, was assisted by Deborah, Jephthah, and Samson]. God empowered them to miraculously deliver Israel from its oppressors. David, the foremost of Israel's kings, and Samuel, the last Judge and first Prophet (Acts 3:24) are mentioned next.

The exploits summarized in verses 33 and 34 were far beyond the capabilities of the humans involved. They were supernaturally accomplished in response to faith on the part of those chosen by God to perform His purposes. In the Old Testament, there are two accounts of women who received their dead raised to life again (1 Kings 17:17-24; 2 Kings 4:32-37). In each case, the one raised from the dead was an only son, pointing to the resurrection of God's only begotten Son.

Life stEP "And greater works than these shall he do" (John 14:12). When Jesus went to the Father, He sent the indwelling, enabling Holy Spirit to us. He did this so that each one of us might have daily involvement in His miraculous work; the transforming of hell-bound sinners into heaven-bound saints! How has faith been evidenced in your life? How have you stood by your faith in God when it has been challenged by the world?

Hebrews 11:36-40

What is the writer saying?

How can I apply this to my life?

We have already been given in this chapter a parade of examples of *what faith can do* when people act upon their *expectant faith* in God. Today's passage takes us in a different direction; today we look at *what faith can endure* when people choose by faith to trust in God's future blessing rather than yield to present persecution.

We are reminded that many who chose to accomplish the tasks God set before them had to have an *enduring faith* accompanied by a brave and patient heart! Note also that the world did not look kindly upon those who did not choose its easy path. Their choice to faithfully follow the Lord resulted in the world inflicting upon them cruel sufferings, afflictions, temptations, and loss of home and nation. Yet, their *faithful endurance* led to a "*good report*" (v. 39) concerning their conduct and the blessing of a "*better resurrection*" (v. 35b). Note that the Apostle Paul suffered all of the experiences of verse 36 (2 Corinthians 11:23-27). Zechariah (2 Chronicles 24:20-21), Stephen (Acts 7:57-60), and Paul (Acts 14:19-20) were among God's spokesmen who were stoned for their preaching.

The question arises, why does God permit such persecution upon His loved ones? One reason is to demonstrate to the world the power of *enduring faith*. Another reason is to *perfect* (v. 40, also 10:14; 12:23) the persecuted so that they "might obtain a better resurrection" (v. 35). For these, their afflictions will produce praise, honor, and glory at the appearing of Jesus Christ (1 Peter 1:6-7; 2 Corinthians 4:17).

Since Abraham "looked for a city" (11:10), we conclude (see vv. 13, 39) that he, and these great heroes of faith, have not yet "received" God's *promised* (v. 39) blessings! Note that it is *better for us* (v. 40) that their reward has been delayed so that we, who display this same *enduring faith*, might also be "*made perfect*" and become companions with them as the Lord Jesus leads us all into His promised future.

Life Step — After reviewing all these heroes of faith, we are amazed that God had us in mind when He permitted them to be subject to such trials! Through them, the Lord wants you to consider: *What can I do by faith and what can I endure by faith* so that I might receive His "good report?"

Hebrews 12:1-8

What is the writer saying?

How can I apply this to my life?

pray *Pray for your pastor and his family to grow in God's grace and maturity and to pursue righteousness.*

Chapter 1 of Hebrews presented the deity of our Great High Priest. After warning against neglecting our salvation, chapter 2 set before us His humanity. Chapters 3 and 4 exhorted and warned those who had no heart desire to progress into a walk of faith. Chapters 5 and 6 exhorted and warned those who manifested a willingness to serve, but never brought forth fruit because they didn't let the Word exercise them "to discern both good and evil" (Hebrews 5:14). In chapters 7, 8, 9 and the first half of 10, God supplied us with detailed information about our Great High Priest needful for understanding His program and purposes on earth. Chapter 10 then exhorted and warned concerning willfully sinning after becoming a knowledgeable servant. Chapter 11 presented a roster of those who victoriously lived by faith in carrying out God's program on earth.

Now we hold the baton in God's great relay race. Those who have gone before us have a great interest in our performance (11:39-12:1). We must give heed to the seven exhortations presented in 12:1-8:

(1) Let us rid ourselves of any encumbrance that would hinder our pace.

(2) Let us be aware of sin (especially unbelief) that can draw us aside.

(3) Let us run with patient endurance.

(4) Let us keep watching Jesus who originated and will perfect our faith.

(5) Let us consider what He endured as He completed His *race*.

(6) Let us not scorn or take lightly the Lord's chastening.

(7) Let us remember that fatherly rebuke indicates love in the family relationship and is not a cause for fainting along the way.

Life stEP

The lesson for Christians is that our lives are like a long-distance running race on a *marked out* ("set before us," v. 1b) track. You are to be like a spiritual Olympic runner. As such, how is your race going?

- Are you carrying the *right gear* [lose the *ankle weights!*)?
- Are you committed to the *right training* and the *right diet*?
- Are you setting the *right pace* for the long race ahead?
- Are you keeping the *right focus* so you will win your race?

Hebrews 12:9-15

What is the writer saying?

How can I apply this to my life?

Our passage begins with "furthermore" to introduce another aspect of our relationship to our spiritual Father [the "Father of spirits," v. 9c]. God is like to our own *earthly human fathers* ["fathers of our flesh," v. 9a]. God, as our spiritual Father, chastens and disciplines us. We need to respond to Him as we did our earthly fathers, with respect (v. 9b), with a child's *admiration* for his father's status, and with *fear* of his discipline.

Verse 10 notes that our earthly fathers were limited and prone to mistakes. Our earthly fathers only disciplined us for a "few" years of our childhood. They also acted according to "their own pleasure." This is to say *according to what, in the father's opinion, was an appropriate discipline.* Our spiritual Father is not so limited in His discipline. His correction is never in error. It never fails to accomplish its goal of growth in our character. Also, it continues not for a "few" years, but until we are in Heaven as eternal "partakers" of His holiness! Finally, our spiritual Father's discipline is always for "our profit" [i.e., *our benefit or good*]; He never acts out of anger but rather always out of love for us.

What then are God's intentions as He chastens or disciplines us?

• God desires "that we might be partakers of his holiness" (v. 10).

• God wants us to pay Him back with a yield [*a tree's return to a farmer*] of the fruit of "righteousness" (v. 11).

• God wants us to walk in "straight paths" (v. 13; i.e., on His clearly *marked highway*).

• He wants for us to "follow peace... and holiness" (v. 14). We are to pursue *harmony* with others as well as *holiness*. This is the principle character of our relationship to our spiritual Father.

It is our job, as God's children, to look "diligently" (v. 15) to God's goal for our lives. So then, are you staying on His *clearly marked highways* of "peace" and "holiness?" Or, are you tripping over rocks and stepping in mud as you walk away from His pathways? Are you producing "fruit of righteousness," or are you failing to produce good fruit?

Hebrews 12:16-24

What is the writer saying?

How can I apply this to my life?

pray *Fiji – For pastors to confront believers influenced by alcohol and the worship of ancestral spirits.*

Today's passage follows the serious warnings of v. 15, "looking diligently lest any man fail of [*fails to receive*] the grace of God," with a sad example of Esau's *turning away* from the things of God. Esau's error was two-fold. First, he chose the temporal at the expense of the eternal. Secondly, he forfeited his spiritual privileges for a simple meal! Thus he was spiritually "profane" (v. 16; *the opposite of holy; an absence of interest in things holy to God*) because he esteemed bodily gratification over seeking a holy walk that pleases God. His repentance only came after he had already lost his birthright (Genesis 27). Next we have a contrast between the Old Testament believers (v. 18-21) and New Testament Christians (v. 22-24). Moses and Israel, with *fear and trembling* (v. 21), could only come close to God at Mt. Sinai. They were warned that *they may not come* on it (v. 18; it was a holy place; God was there on it, see Exodus 19:9-23). In contrast, New Testament Christians are allowed to "come to Mount Zion" (v. 22). This phrase is a symbolized picture of our great entitlement to *come to God* in fellowship. This was only made possible by the work of Christ on the Cross.

The city (v. 22b) is a heavenly city prepared by God (11:16) for which Abraham looked (11:10) and for which the Old Testament saints are still waiting (11:39). It is the city for which we should be seeking (13:14). It is the place Jesus has gone to "prepare" for us (John 14:2)!

"God the Judge of all" (v. 23) and "Jesus the mediator of the new covenant" (v. 24) are at this heavenly city. God's created beings will also inhabit it. These beings include: the *innumerable angels* (v. 22), the "church of the firstborn" (v. 23), referring to all Christians saved by Jesus Christ, and the "spirits of just men made perfect (complete)" (v. 23). This includes the Old Testament people of "faith" referred to in chapter 11.

Life stEP What a great declaration! We, as believers in Jesus Christ, are on our way to God's heavenly "Jerusalem!" We are those who have "better" (v. 24) entitlements than did Israel of old! Take advantage right now of your privilege to walk spiritually by prayer into God's presence!

Hebrews 12:25-29

What is the writer saying?

How can I apply this to my life?

pray Portugal – Pray that saved teens will be encouraged to reach their unsaved friends through evangelistic outreach programs.

We have seen that Hebrews is a book of instructions, exhortations and warnings. Now we face the *final warning* of the book. The warning begins with the simple word *"see,"* meaning *see to it!* This warning is in response to the several *"better things"* available to us because of the *"new covenant"* which Christ has *mediated for us* (v. 18-24).

This is a warning about *refusing* (v. 25a-25b; *declining to receive* a gift). It is a warning about *turning away* (v. 25c, *abandoning* or *forsaking* God's words) after we have considered all the blessings described in Hebrews. We are now fully aware of what God has said when He *spoke to us by His Son* (see again 1:1-2)! We must not lightly regard these words from God by refusing to both receive and live by them. We are also reminded that God is still a "consuming fire" (v. 29). God has not changed since the days of Moses. We are to *"see"* that just as in the days of Moses. They [the people of Israel] did not escape God's judgment upon their hard-hearted sin. We must *"see"* that if we <u>turn away</u> from His grace we too will come under His judgment!

When God gave the law to Moses, the voice from Heaven shook the mountain and the people trembled (Exodus 19:16-19). Haggai 2:6-7 prophesied of a time when both heaven and earth will be shaken (See 2 Peter 3:10-12). God will replace the things that are "shaken" (v. 27a) with that which "cannot be shaken" (v. 27b). Our God, who is a consuming fire, has extended His grace to those who have heeded His voice and found refuge in a kingdom that will remain.

How fearsome is the future for those who refuse Him! How important it is for us who have taken refuge in His words to warn those who have not! "Let us have grace" (v. 28). To what purpose do we need His grace? "Serve God acceptably with ...godly fear" (v. 28).

Life Step Have you been *seeing* how God intends for you to respond to all these marvelous words? Have you *seen to it* that you have *received* His gift of salvation? How will you demonstrate today that you have not *turned away* from God's message to you?

Hebrews 13:1-8

What is the writer saying?

How can I apply this to my life?

This last chapter of Hebrews is a kind of appendix and summation to the main discourse of the letter, which was completed with yesterday's closing paragraph (12:25-29). It is appendix-like for it lists various subjects. It is like a summary in that it serves as a closing reminder for some of the directions in the letter's main body. The first paragraph of this summation is a list of "stand-alone" rules of Christian social conduct:

• *Brothers*: (v. 1) *brotherly love* (John 11:36; 13:35). Christians are to keep on developing their *kinship-love* with other Christians.

• *Strangers*: (v. 2) *Give hospitality* to Christian travelers (Romans 12:13). Literally, it says, *show brotherly love to those not known to you*. This is especially true if they are *messengers* on assignment from God!

• *Prisoners*: (v. 3) There are Christians ill-treated and imprisoned for His name's sake! We are to *keep remembering* them as if we were their *fellow-prisoners* (e.g., Onesiphorus, 2 Timothy 1:16-18).

• *Marriage*: (v. 4) Read this like the earlier commands here: *Keep marriage honorable!* It is highly esteemed by God and God will judge those who defile it with pornography or sexual unfaithfulness.

• *Coveting*: (vv. 5-6) literally, live *without money-loving*! The opposite here is *to be content* where *content* is related to *arithmetic*. It means, not seeking to '*add*' *more* or we could say, *being satisfied that we have enough. Contentment* is linked with living by faith in God's promise to *never forsake us*, meaning He will always care for us (v. 6) by *adding* those things that we *need* to what we already *have*!

• *Rulers*: (v. 7) This is in the past-tense thus, *spiritual leaders which have had the rule over you in the past*. We are to *consider* (v. 7b) their past conduct so that we might imitate their character! You should remember (v. 7), obey (v. 17), and salute them (v. 24).

Life stEP   The words "I will never leave you, nor forsake you" (v. 5b) is such a comforting truth! However, let us be careful about *not coveting* and about *being content* so that we can personally apply it! What choices can you make today that will cause you to live satisfied and contented? What can you ask the Lord to *add on* to your needs?

Hebrews 13:9-14

What is the writer saying?

How can I apply this to my life?

Today we look at a list of the Christian's *religious duties*. In particular, the passage is answering an assumed question from its original Jewish [or Hebrew] Christian readers (Those of us who are Gentile Christians will find some of these hard to understand.) For example, "Since we Jewish Christians agree that we must leave behind our "Old-Covenant" religious ways, what will guide us as we seek to live by this "New Covenant" in Christ?" The answers to this question include:

• Beware of teachings that are *widely different* and *unknown* in your Christian community (v. 9a).

• Especially beware of teaching about dietary restrictions; these are of no *profit* to Christians (v. 9b). Notice that at the center of our own rituals in Judaism were the priests at the altar who were not allowed to eat of the meat of those beasts sacrificed on the altar (v. 10)!

The priests were not allowed to eat this meat because it was considered *weighed down with sin*. When the animals were sacrificed, the priests symbolically transferred the people's sins to the sinless animal. Its blood was shed and burned on the Altar or applied to the Mercy Seat. Then the *sin-loaded body* of the animal was taken out of the city and burned.

• Let us consider the example of Jesus; He was the promised Lamb of God who came so that He might *sanctify our Jewish people with His own blood* (v. 12). He had to, however, make His sacrifice outside the *gate,* and thus outside of Judaism and all its rituals! The symbolism of the sacrificed animals was fulfilled when Christ was taken outside the gates of Jerusalem to bear His reproach as He carried away our sin!

• "Let us" (v. 13) do the same! We Jewish Christians must also "go forth" outside of Judaism and away from its rituals if we, Jews by faith, are going to seek God's "Heavenly Jerusalem" (12:22) and the "better things" (12:24) of the "new covenant" that He has made with us!

Life stEP — The point here is that we are sanctified (separated) unto Him when we go outside of the scope of religious procedures and place our trust solely in that which He suffered outside the city for us. Faith trusts what God says. "Let us" go to Jesus who is outside religious ritual!

Hebrews 13:15-25

What is the writer saying?

How can I apply this to my life?

"I will praise the name of God with a song, and will magnify him with thanksgiving. This also shall please the LORD better than an ox or bullock…" (Psalm 69:30, 31). Because the Lord Jesus Christ has offered for us the required blood sacrifice (9:22), we are privileged to offer that which now pleases God best; our "*sacrifice of praise*" (v. 15) to Him! Another pleasing sacrifice is sharing our material goods (Philippians 4:18).

Notice that the benediction to this letter begins by referring to Jesus as "that *great shepherd* of the sheep" (v. 20). In John 10:11, Jesus designated Himself as the *Good Shepherd* who gave His life for the sheep. In Hebrews 13:20, He is the *Great Shepherd* who, as our Great High Priest, works in us and through us. In 1 Peter 5:4, He is the *Chief Shepherd* who will come for us.

The Good Shepherd *in the past* did something *for* us that we might be free from the *penalty* of sin. The Great Shepherd *in the present* is doing something *in* us and *through* us that we might be free from the *power* of sin while being perfected unto *every good work to do His will*. These two aspects of our Shepherd are brought together in 1 Peter 2:24, 25. He "bare our sins in his own body on the tree" that we who "were as sheep going astray" might now be shepherded by the overseer of our souls. Next, Peter speaks of the Chief Shepherd who will *in the future* come *for us*, that we might be forever freed from the very *presence* of sin!

In verse 22, we are given the final exhortation of the book. It is a beseeching plea that we *listen to, respond to and patiently put to practice* [the intent of "suffer"] "the word of exhortation" [some thirty eight exhortations are found in Hebrews!] presented throughout the letter.

Life stEP

It is true that this letter to the Hebrews was originally fashioned by the Holy Spirit to meet the needs of a particular people at a particular place and time; that is, the Jewish Christians of the First Century. Yet, the Holy Spirit had your spiritual progress in mind as He worded the message of this epistle so that you too should *listen to, respond to, and patiently put to practice* these exhortations from God!

1 Corinthians

The book of 1 Corinthians is a prominent New Testament epistle. It has the great love chapter, the chapters that deal with spiritual gifts, the resurrection chapter, the marriage chapter, and the passage so often read at the Lord's Supper. We know so many of the components of this book that we don't always see how they fit together.

The apostle Paul wrote the book from the city of Ephesus on his third missionary journey. Paul describes this letter in 2 Corinthians as a *sorrowful letter*. He wrote it with a heavy heart because a disaster was taking place in the Corinthian church: it was falling apart at the seams.

Founded on Paul's second missionary journey, the church at Corinth was located in the most immoral city of the Roman Empire. Corinth was filled with shrines and temples of idol worship, and visitors had easy access to temple prostitutes. In the world of that day, to call someone a *Corinthian* was to question their morality. Corinth was located on the narrow section of land joining Achaia with the mainland, making it a heavily traveled land route. There was also a set of tracks used to transport ships from the Aegean to the Adriatic Sea. Thus, it was a bustling seaport as well. This location made it an ideal location for prostitution, debauchery and corruption.

In the church, a number of problems had developed. In fact, the church was breaking down into cliques. Each group had their favorite leader. Things got so bad that a delegation was sent to Ephesus with a letter to meet with the apostle Paul. 1 Corinthians is the response to that letter.

The theme of the book is *dealing with divisions within the church*. A simple outline of the book would be:

I. *Introduction* – vv. 1:1-9
II. *The Root of Dissension* – vv. 1:10 - 6:20

   Paul gives his perspective on problems known to be present at the church at Corinth.

   A. Man's Wisdom Versus God's Wisdom, vv. 1:10-2:16
   B. Man's Wisdom Produces Rationalism, vv. 3:1-23
   C. Man's Wisdom Produces Mysticism, vv. 4:1-21
   D. Man's Wisdom Produces License, vv. 5:1-13
   E. Man's Wisdom Produces Legalism, vv. 6:1-20

III. *The Symptoms of Dissension* –
vv. 7:1-15:58
Paul answers questions brought
to him by the delegation from
Corinth.

A. Sexuality; including
marriage, divorce and
celibacy – vv. 7:1-40.

B. Food Offered to Idols and
Pagan Festivals – vv. 8:1-11:1

C. Worship; including veiling of
women, the Lord's Supper,
and spiritual gifts – vv. 11:2-
14:40

D. The Resurrection of Jesus
Christ – vv. 15:1-58

IV. *Conclusion*; including the matter
of the collection for the saints at
Jerusalem – vv. 16:1-24

1 Corinthians 1:1-9

What is the writer saying?

How can I apply this to my life?

Paul begins by first identifying them as *saints* (v. 2). The word *saint* means "one who has been set apart." All Christians have been set apart *from sin* and *unto God*. Even if we are not living as we should, God is still in the process of making us holy.

Paul then thanks God for the church at Corinth. The church had many problems, but it still had many good qualities for which Paul could thank God. He thanks God for the grace He had shown them, and that they were secure in their relationship with Christ. It's interesting to note that although they were immature, they all had spiritual gifts (v. 7). Spiritual gifts are given at salvation and have nothing to do with whether or not we are spiritual. The use of spiritual gifts depends on one's walk with the Lord, but all who are saved have spiritual gifts. God will complete His work of *sanctification* (the on-going work of God to set believers apart unto God) in the lives of all believers (v. 8). This was a great hope for Paul, based on the faithfulness and sovereignty of God (v. 9).

What strikes us as we read this introduction is the positive nature of Paul's salutation. Here is a church torn by division and problems, yet Paul can find something in them for which to thank God!

God desires that we who are His people continually praise Him. What are you thanking God for in your life? Who can you encourage with the truth that God is working in their lives? Write a Christian friend a short note to tell them two things: (1) Express how you are thanking God for the encouragement you receive as you see God working in their life. (2) Encourage them by pointing out how you were reading that God desires to "enrich" (v. 5) His children.

Monday 44

1 Corinthians 1:10-17

What is the writer saying?

How can I apply this to my life?

pray — *Poland – Summer camp ministries safety, salvation decisions, and consecration commitments.*

In many of Paul's letters, he starts out with a theological section and then makes application to a certain problem the church is facing. In this epistle, Paul gets to the application part quickly, for there are so many issues to deal with.

The first problem he addresses is division in the church, both inward and outward. The word *contention* (v. 11) means "strife caused by rivalry." Paul's desire is that they would be *perfectly joined together* (v. 10). This phrase was used of setting broken bones. They needed to get back together, yet they were divided into four camps:

(1) Most likely, those following *Peter* were Jews who wanted to hold on to some of their Jewish traditions.

(2) Those following *Apollos* were Greeks who were impressed by his eloquence.

(3) Those who followed *Paul* included people he had led to the Lord and baptized (vv. 14-16).

(4) The fourth group thought they were the most spiritual because they were *of Christ* (v. 12). That sounds good at face value, but they probably had a proud attitude, thinking they didn't need a teacher.

Paul rebuked them all and said they should be united for the cause of Christ. Otherwise, divisions have the potential to bring the Gospel of Christ to "none effect" (v. 17).

Life stEP

We need to be sure that we are followers first and foremost of Jesus. Do you find yourself picking one teacher or pastor over another? Are you a person who works to promote unity in your church? What positive thing can you do this week to encourage the effectiveness of the Gospel message and a sense of unity at your church?

1 Corinthians 1:18-31

What is the writer saying?

How can I apply this to my life?

The "preaching of the Cross" (v. 18) would be *foolishness* (v. 23) to the Greeks because, while they believed that their gods died and came back, they would never conceive of one of their gods dying on a cross. The Jews saw death on a cross as shameful (Deuteronomy 21:23). The Gentiles wanted *wisdom* (v. 22) or *human reasoning*, while the Jews wanted miraculous signs (v. 22). Neither understood the Cross (v. 23) thinking it to be "foolishness."

Be sure to notice how God has turned the "wisdom of this world" into foolishness (v. 20) while at the same time He takes things considered "foolish" by the world – such as preaching "Christ crucified" (v. 23) – and makes of them the "wisdom of God" (v. 24)!

However, to believers, the Cross is what we glory in! Christians are saved by the preaching of the Cross and it is the power of God to salvation (Romans 1:16-17). It has become our "wisdom, and righteousness [right standing with God], and sanctification [a new standing with God] and redemption [our source of release from bondage to sin]" (v. 30).

Those who are called by God are not called because of their abilities or riches. God's call is always by unmerited grace. Grace has nothing to do with us; it has everything to do with God! God has chosen the insignificant and weak in order that He might get all of the glory. The believer has nothing to glory in, for the salvation they enjoy is totally given to them by the grace of God. Many mysteries in the sovereign grace of God are hard to understand, but one can understand how God deserves our praise for He has made us righteous.

Life stEP

Why does God call the weak and the lowly? Why is the Gospel a stumbling block to the Jews and foolishness to the Gentiles? Do you glorify God daily for your salvation? Go to the Lord now and thank Him for saving you by His grace and commit to give all glory and honor to Him.

1 Corinthians 2:1-8

What is the writer saying?

How can I apply this to my life?

Paul reminds the Corinthians that they were saved as a result of Paul preaching the Gospel. Paul had the ability to speak in a philosophical way that would impress his hearers (v. 4). While this was a highly respected skill among the Greeks, Paul did not succumb to that. Instead, he decided to stick to the Gospel, for God promises to bless His Word (Isaiah 55:10-11). The word translated *determined* means *to resolve beforehand*. Paul had determined to share the central truth of the Gospel, which is that Jesus died for our sins on the cross.

The fear and trembling that Paul mentions here (v. 3) can be seen in Acts 18:1-11. It is hard for one to imagine the great apostle being afraid, but he was. He had gone to Corinth alone, and fear in his heart had affected his ministry. The Lord appeared to him in a dream to encourage him and as a result, he had a fruitful ministry in Corinth.

The fruit of the ministry was a result of the power of the Gospel, not Paul's rhetorical skills. He wanted people to have their faith firmly placed in God and not on his personal abilities. He then assures them that there is wisdom in the Gospel of God, but it is not the wisdom of the world (v. 6): it is far beyond that; it's the wisdom of God which had been "hidden" (v. 7) but which was now being proclaimed by Paul and others (v. 1)!

Life stEP

Are you determined to declare to your world that Christ was crucified to bring "righteousness, and sanctification, and redemption" (1 Corinthians 1:30) to the people? Does your life give evidence of the transforming "power" of the Holy Spirit (v. 4)? How can you today be a "demonstration" of the Holy Spirit's life-changing "power"? Also, how can you "declare" a "testimony" that God has brought a saving message into the world?

1 Corinthians 2:9-16

What is the writer saying?

How can I apply this to my life?

pray   *Chile – For the Chilean church to overcome its spiritual isolation and develop a missionary zeal.*

In verse 9, Paul quotes from Isaiah 64:4. At first glance, we might think that the emphasis is on our future blessings when we get to Heaven; however, the context in Isaiah has to do primarily with the blessings God "has prepared" for us while we are here on earth! While Heaven is a glorious place awaiting us, God has great things prepared on this side of glory for those who love Him.

By the ministry of the Holy Spirit, God "has *revealed*" to us what He has "prepared" for believers (v. 10). Seeing that every believer has the Spirit living in him (v. 12), every believer can discern the will of God. Paul says that Christians have been given the Spirit of God so that they might know all the wonderful things God has blessed them with.

The *natural man* (v. 14) is the unsaved man. He is a *living creature* with a *soul* but he does not have a spirit (vv. 14 & 15) which is alive unto God.

The natural man is also a *foolish* man (v. 14) because he does not have a spirit that can interact with the Spirit of God. Thus he not only does not understand the things of God, he CANNOT know them. The reason the unsaved man cannot understand the things of the Spirit is because he is spiritually dead (Ephesians 2:1-3). However, when the Spirit of God draws a person to believe in Jesus Christ, the person is given two gifts: (1) God's *Holy Spirit* (v. 10) and (2) an *inner spirit* ("New Man") that is *alive* unto God and able to "know" the "things of God" (v. 11). Then the Holy Spirit becomes our teacher who guides our spirits into truth – usually by speaking to our spirits through our *consciences* (1 Timothy 1:5, 19). As a result, we can discern all things; that is, we can understand the Scriptures and apply them to our lives. That is what it means to have the "*mind* of Christ" (v. 16).

Life stEP

Are you listening to the Holy Spirit so you can understand God's direction in your life? Often, He will prompt your conscience as He "guides" you into God's truth. Take a minute and write God a note expressing your spiritual response to the Spirit's promptings in your life.

1 Corinthians 3:1-8

What is the writer saying?

How can I apply this to my life?

pray — *Brazil – Pray that Christians in high profile positions would keep a moral and ethical testimony.*

The apostle's desire was to talk to them as if they were spiritual, but he realized by their behavior that they were "carnal" (vv. 1, 4). The word *carnal* means "fleshly." Living in the *flesh* is when we are living with unconfessed sin in our lives, controlled by our own *fleshly* desires instead of being controlled by the *Spirit*. As a result of living in the flesh, the Corinthians had not grown in the things of the *Spirit*. They were not "spiritual" and were still "babes" in relation to growth in the Spirit (v. 1).

Paul should have been able to get into deeper truths with them by now, but he could not. The *milk* he talks about in verse 2 is the basic truths of the Christian life. In effect he was saying, "When you were first saved, I gave you "milk" – the basics truths. By now you should be able to handle "meat" – the deeper truths – but you are not."

As a result of their carnality, they were conflict-ridden. While having a favorite Bible teacher is not wrong, they were divided over who should be their *most important* teacher. Some said Paul and others said Apollos. Paul points out that all teachers are appointed by God. God is the one who brings forth salvation and growth, and He alone should get the glory.

Teachers should not be exalted or glorified; they are only tools God uses to bring glory to Him. In fact, Paul describes these teachers as "ministers" (v. 5) who "labor" (v. 8). We use the word *minister* to refer to an officer in a church but originally, as used here, the word referred to a "servant who labored," literally, a "dust runner"; that is, "one covered in road dust as he runs to carry out his master's assignments."

Life stEP — Are you growing in the Lord? If you have been saved for any period of time, you should be moving on to deeper things of the Word. Is the Spirit of God controlling your life? Stop right now and ask the Lord to search your heart and convict you of any areas in your life where you are still taking your first hesitant "baby steps" rather than walking skillfully!

1 Corinthians 3:9-15

What is the writer saying?

How can I apply this to my life?

pray — New Zealand – For continued transformation of lives through effective prison ministry.

All who serve the Lord are working together for the honor and glory of God. Paul likens the church to a cultivated field (v. 8) or to a building (v. 10). He said that God is the one who brings forth fruit (v. 7) and is the master builder (v. 10). God uses the ministers of the Gospel as general contractors, but it is God who is the wise builder.

The foundation upon which God builds the church is Jesus Christ (v. 11). Every life is to be built on the foundation of Christ. The Bible is the blueprint for each believer, and we are to be careful how we build our lives. They should be built with works that last for eternity; Paul describes these lasting works as "gold, silver, and precious stones." He describes works that don't last as "wood, hay, and stubble" (v. 12). When gold, silver, and precious stones are put into the fire, they are purified.

When wood, hay, and stubble are put in fire, they are burned up. All will stand before God someday and the fire of his glory and judgment will reveal whether a person has built wisely or unwisely (v. 13). This is talking about the judgment for works done during a Christian's life, not for sin. All sin was already judged on the Cross. The issue here is not our eternal destination, but our rewards in heaven (v. 14).

Paul said in Acts 20 that the Word of God builds us up. In Ephesians 4:11-14 he says that the church builds us up as well. Every church should be dedicated to teaching the Word so that people might grow.

Life stEP

We will all stand before God to give an account for our lives (2 Corinthians 5:10). Are you living your life as a Christian with that day in mind? Are you careful about how you are building your life, and what materials you are using to build it? What quality "building materials" can you use today as part of God's ongoing "construction project" in your life?

1 Corinthians 3:16-23

What is the writer saying?

How can I apply this to my life?

The Holy Spirit indwells the life of every believer (v. 16; Romans 8:9). Therefore, we are the *temples of God*, and we are to be *holy places* just as the Old Testament temple was holy. First the tabernacle and later the temple were built as special sanctuaries where God would "commune" (Exodus 25:22) with believers. The temple was to be a *holy place* (Psalms 65:4) since God would dwell there. Thus, the priests were to keep very specific regulations to ensure the purity of this *holy sanctuary* so that God's holiness would be honored.

Every Christian needs to recognize that the temple is a picture or pattern that our bodies and our lives ought to model. When we understand that we are the caretakers of the *holy sanctuary* where God comes to commune with us, then we will be careful to maintain the purity of our bodies and our lives. After all, God lives there!

The person who believes in the Lord is to be wise according to the Bible, not according to the wisdom of this world (v. 18). When compared to the true wisdom of God, the wisdom of the world is just *foolish* (v. 19) philosophy and speculations, for it rejects the truth of God.

The world says that our bodies belong to us and we can do whatever we want. God desires that we treat our bodies as the *temples* that they are. The primary concept is that we are to live so that we might reflect God's holiness, which is what it means to glorify Him. God's glory is who He is; He is glorious. Each Christian in his body and life is to radiate God's glory, which means to choose to live in a biblical way.

When people watch you, do they see a *holy place* of God? Are you committed to being a *holy temple to God*? Or are you allowing things to come into your body that are not pure and holy? How about doing a spiritual inspection to see what is *tracking dirt* into your *temple-body*? What needs to be done so that your body stays pure and holy?

1 Corinthians 4:1-13

What is the writer saying?

How can I apply this to my life?

pray *Taiwan – For believers to accept a more active and committed role in their local church bodies.*

Paul gives us a humble perspective of himself when he uses the word *minister* (v. 1). This compound Greek word is very graphic, meaning *under + rower*. It pictures oarsman under a ship's deck, carrying out the captain's orders. It came to be used of freemen, soldiers, or slaves who acted on the orders of their superiors. Thus we have Paul's perspective of himself and his *stewardship* (*assigned duties*) for God. He viewed himself as *God's subordinate* who was assigned the responsibility of declaring the "mysteries" of God (v. 1) made known to us in God's Word.

In verse 2, he says he must be a *faithful steward* of God's Word. A *steward* was a trusted worker on a large plantation. When the landowner needed to leave for a time, he would turn the affairs of the plantation over to his *stewards*. While the landowner trusted his stewards to *faithfully carry out* their assigned responsibilities, he would also require them to give an account of their actions upon his return.

Thus Paul knew he was to *faithfully carry out* his responsibilities on God's *plantation* (i.e., God's spiritual workings in the world) and that he would be judged by "the Lord" (v. 4) as to the faithfulness of his service. As a result, the judgments of men did not affect him (vv. 4-5).

In verse 6, Paul says that he uses this picture of a humble steward in order that the Corinthians "might learn" not to get "puffed up" about their teachers. He and Apollos are merely God's humble stewards; their works will be approved or disapproved by God, not by the people of the church.

After all, every Christian at Corinth had received their various spiritual gifts and ministries from the Lord (v. 7), so they, too, should be humble and not proud in their service.

Do you have a *ministry* for our Lord Jesus; perhaps an important and visible responsibility? Then be sure to learn Paul's lesson of humility. Don't be proud in your personal success and popularity! Rather, recognize that you are to be the Lord's faithful steward. Perhaps you could write out a short *statement of assignment* to define what stewardship the Lord has granted to you.

1 Corinthians 4:14-21

What is the writer saying?

How can I apply this to my life?

The words that Paul wrote here were hard, but he was writing out of love so that the Christians at Corinth might be *warned* (v. 14). There are many influences in our lives, but only a few are godly influences that really build up our lives spiritually (v. 15). Paul reminds them that he had "begotten" them "through the Gospel" (v. 15) – i.e., they had been saved through his preaching. Therefore Paul urges them to be "followers" of him (v. 16), and to remember his "ways which be in Christ" (v. 17).

The word *followers* is the Greek word from which we get *mimic*. It means "an imitator; one who follows the example of another" (see Hebrews 13:7; 2 Thessalonians 3:7). Paul is asking them to *mimic* him; that is, *to follow his example*.

Timothy was being sent to them to remind them of the basic truths which Paul had taught them (v. 17). Paul said that he would come to them "shortly" (v. 19). In verse 21, he asks: if he were to come immediately, would they want him to come "in the spirit of meekness" or with hard rebuke ("with a rod")? There are times when both types of response are necessary. Most of us, however, would want the love and meekness, not the rebuke. The point is, if they repented and started to act biblically, then when he came, he would come with love and meekness. However, if they did not get things straight, he would have to come in harsh rebuke.

Life stEP

How do you take spiritual correction? Has your life been changed by a godly Christian who confronted you about sin in your life so that you were encouraged to *change*? Most of us have been blessed with humble, godly people who have helped build up our lives. Take time this week to thank one such person who has had a positive role in your life.

1 Corinthians 5:1-13

What is the writer saying?

How can I apply this to my life?

pray — *Philippines – For effective outreach to youth through evangelistic sporting events.*

The Corinthian church had previously received a letter from Paul (nicknamed "*O Corinthians*"!) in which he had told them that they should not have fellowship with people who were living in known sin, particularly fornication (vv. 9-11). They had applied this only to those who were "without" the church (v. 12), i.e., *non-believers*. Paul points out that this principle of separation applies to those who say they are "brothers" (v. 11) and thus are "within" the body of the church.

There was a man living with his stepmother in a sinful relationship (v. 1), and Paul rebukes the church for not confronting the couple about their sin. Rather than being sorrowful (v. 2) over the sin in their midst, they were proud (vv. 2, 6) of their accepting these people into their fellowship.

The New Testament teaches that, after confronting someone in sin, if he is not willing to repent, we are to bring another witness with us and confront him again.

If he refuses to repent, then we are to bring it to the whole church so that the wayward believer may be confronted in love (Matthew 18:15-17). If he still refuses to repent, he is to be delivered over to Satan (v. 5) and the church is to separate themselves from him (v. 2b).

If such discipline does not occur, the "leaven" of their sin will affect the whole congregation (vv. 7-8), like yeast affects a loaf of dough! If a person who says he is a Christian is living in unrepentant sin, we are not to have normal fellowship with him, even to the point of not sharing a meal (v. 11). This may seem harsh, but such a response will cause the people involved in sinful conduct to consider the seriousness of the sin.

However, if an unbeliever is living like that, we are not to withdraw from him. He is simply doing what comes naturally. Rather, we are to seek to reach him with the Gospel.

Since our individual conduct affects our whole church, it is important to ask: are you living a life that seeks to be separate from sin? Is there a Christian friend of yours who is choosing to live in sin? According to Paul (see also Galatians 6:1), this "brother" needs you to confront him, with meekness and brotherly love, concerning his sin! Your responsibility is to go to him personally, not to gossip about it.

1 Corinthians 6:1-11

What is the writer saying?

How can I apply this to my life?

It is inevitable that civil disagreements will arise between brothers and sisters in Christ. How do we handle these disagreements? Are we to take them to court (v. 1)? Not according to Paul in this passage. The principle given here is that if we have a legal matter against a brother or sister in Christ, which is not dealing with a criminal issue, we are to seek to get other Christians to arbitrate for us (vv. 1-4). If we take other Christians to the civil courts, it is a terrible testimony concerning the unity of the body of Christ, which is the church (v. 7).

Our passage today deals with *civil issues*. If a person has committed a crime, then we must turn elsewhere in Scripture to learn a parallel principle: that God has established civil governments to be the *higher authorities* that deal with such "evil" doings (Romans 13:1-6).

Today's passage (v. 7) says that we should be *willing to take the wrong* done to us (note again this applies to civil issues of business or personal quarrels) rather than take the matter to the civil courts. We should be willing to take the wrong for the sake of the testimony of Christ.

Paul then reminds them that people who are living in continual sin will not go to heaven (vv. 9-11). Does this mean that we have to live without sinning in order to go to heaven? No, of course not. Rather, if a person calls himself a Christian, yet persists in a sinful lifestyle, they are lying and are not really saved (1 John 2:1-6). He points out that they used to live in sin like that (v. 11), but now that they are saved, they no longer live in such immoral conditions. When the Lord saves a person, He changes his life. A person who has been saved is in the process of being changed to be like Him (Philippians 1:6; 2 Corinthians 5:17).

Life Step Are you willing to *take a wrong* so that God and His Church would be honored? Commit to God today to never take your quarrel with another believer before others before you first deal with the issue with them face to face. If you are unable to resolve the *wrong* done to you face to face, you must also be committed to the principle of taking the issue to some mature believers to help you solve the crisis.

1 Corinthians 6:12-20

What is the writer saying?

How can I apply this to my life?

In today's passage, Paul states a vital *principle of Christian liberty*: In the gray areas of life, all things are lawful, but not all things build a person up to be like Jesus (v. 12). It seems that the Corinthians were treating a sexual problem in their church as a *gray* issue. Paul points out that any sexual relationship outside the bonds of marriage is wrong (v. 18).

They had reasoned that sex was similar to food (v. 13) in that it was just a physical activity meant for the fulfillment of the body. As a result, some were engaging in sexual immorality with harlots (vv. 15-16) and justifying the activity as inconsequential. Paul shows that this reasoning is faulty and that the body is to be used as a vehicle to honor God and Him alone (v. 17). We should never take that which is meant to glorify God and pollute it with a prostitute or sexual perversions (vv. 16-18).

The sin of fornication is a serious sin, for it defiles the temple in which God lives, which is our body. Paul encourages them to "flee fornication" (v. 18). The English word *pornography* is derived from the Greek word used here. It means *any sexual sin*, such as adultery, as well as any lewd sexual act or conduct. The command here is in the present tense, which means that we must *keep on fleeing* such things. It is not a one-time thing, but a continual attitude that we are to cultivate in our hearts.

The reason Paul gives for us for choosing sexual purity is powerful: God has bought us and we belong to Him, therefore we should use our bodies for His glory alone (vv. 19-20). To glorify God means to put Him on display in our lives. God is holy and pure and to glorify Him with our bodies means to be holy and pure in our sexual lives.

Life stEP As you consider your relationship with someone of the opposite sex, plan ahead so as to be sure you stay as far away from situations that might lead to sexual temptation. Now consider other kinds of sexual uncleanness: what are you doing to stay away from sexual things that pollute your mind and heart? Are there things you watch on TV or look at on the computer that are *pornography*? How about asking God to give you the "power" (v. 14) to maintain a pure body and mind?

1 Corinthians 7:1-9

What is the writer saying?

How can I apply this to my life?

In this chapter, Paul answers a question the Corinthians had asked him about *celibacy* (v. 1), i.e., *the single life*; that is, *remaining unmarried*. In his answer, Paul points out that:

1. Celibacy, for some Christians, is a "good" choice (v. 1);
2. The celibate person faces the temptation of *sexual sin* (v. 2);
3. It is wrong for married people (vv. 3-5) to be celibate, i.e., to not *come together* sexually;
4. As marriage is the expected state of life (see Genesis 2:18, 22-24), celibacy is a special gift from God (vv. 6-7);
5. If a life of celibacy is too tempting for a Christian, then that Christian should get married (vv. 8-9).

In verse 1, Paul uses the word *touch* as a euphemism for the sexual relationship. It is good for a man or woman not to have sexual relationships with one another. Therefore, in order not to give in to sexual impurity, people should marry. Marriage is the only context for sexual relationships that God blesses. The husband and wife are intended for each other's sexual needs (vv. 3-4). The only exception to this is if they both consent to abstain temporarily for spiritual reasons (v. 5).

Paul states that some people have the *gift* of singleness (v. 7, *a special enablement from God*) and some do not. The gift of singleness is that of being single and loving it. God grants this gift to some, but He does not choose this for many! The reality is that God intends most people to marry. Paul saw celibacy as a great asset for service to the church, especially during times of "distress" or persecution (v. 26).

Is it possible that you have the gift of celibacy (singleness)? If so, trust God for grace to enjoy singleness. If you are married, are you serving the Lord *together*? If you are dating, you need to be sure to stay pure until you are married.

1 Corinthians 7:10-24

What is the writer saying?

How can I apply this to my life?

pray *Portugal – For God to burden hearts with a passion to evangelize other Portuguese–speaking nations.*

To understand this text, we must first understand the historical situation. These people had recently come to know Christ. They understood marriage to be spiritually important, but they had many questions. "Now that I am saved," they might have thought, "what am I to do? Should I stay with my spouse even though they do not know the Lord? What if my spouse is unsaved and leaves me, what do I do then?"

Here Paul seeks to answer these questions. He states that it is wrong for a believer to divorce his spouse (vv. 10-11). Even if there is separation, there shouldn't be divorce; rather, they should seek "reconciliation" (v. 11).

In verse 12, Paul says that there is no other revelation on this in the Bible, so he would comment on it. If you are married to a non-Christian, stay in the relationship. God will use this *mixed marriage* of a saved person and an unsaved person to expose the unsaved spouse to the Gospel. Thus, the unsaved spouse is said to be "sanctified" (v. 14) by the saved spouse. In other words, the unsaved person has come under a *special influence of the Holy Spirit.* And *who knows*, perhaps the Christian spouse will have the opportunity to "save" his partner (v. 16).

Be sure to live for the Lord and put Him first. If your spouse can live with that, then great, stay with him or her. However, if the spouse decides he won't live with a Christian and chooses to leave, you are to let him go (v. 15).

Another question they asked was, "What if I am saved and now married to my third wife? What should I do?" Paul answers this in verses 17-24. The principle he shares is simple: stay in the same marital situation you were in when you were saved (v. 20).

Life stEP

If you are married to a non-believer, how can you show your spouse the love of God? How can you work in harmony with the Holy Spirit to commend the Christian life to your spouse? If you are single, don't marry a non-believer. This would dishonor God and make your life miserable. Since you were "bought with a price" (v. 23), remain "free" (v. 22) from one who is still *bound to sin*!

1 Corinthians 7:25-40

What is the writer saying?

How can I apply this to my life?

In this passage, Paul is sharing words of wisdom with those who are not married (thus assumed to still be "virgins," v. 25). There was some distress going on at this time that caused Paul to say that if you were single, it is probably better to stay so because of the present situation.

Some say that it was the rise of persecution of Christians, while others say that it was the poor view of marriage in the culture of Corinth. Whatever it was, Paul's encouragement was to stay single (v. 26). Nevertheless, if you do marry, Paul says, you have not sinned (v. 28).

Paul adds that there are some advantages to being single. If you are married, you have to be concerned with meeting the needs of another person; if single, you can just concern yourself with what God wants (vv. 32-33). If you are married, when making decisions, you have to come to an agreement with your spouse; if you are single, you do not (vv. 33-35).

The last part of the passage is difficult to understand. Likely he is talking to older men considering marriage. The Corinthians may have asked, "What if a person is getting on in age and wants to be married?" Paul says to go ahead and get married; he was not forbidding that (v. 36). Moreover, if you decide not to marry, that is fine as well (v. 37).

Finally, Paul reminds them that marriage can be a good thing if the parties involved know that when they marry it is *for life* (v. 39a) and then with the condition that the marriage is *"only in the Lord"* (i.e., only between two Christians, v. 39b). People in our culture (which has a 50% divorce rate!) obviously need to take this counsel to heart!

Life stEP

Have you considered singleness as an option for your future? Are you willing to pray about it? Singleness is not, as we often think, *a runner-up prize* for those Christians who can't find a mate. Rather, let's remember that Paul says those who remain single "do better" (v. 38). If you do not think you have the gift of celibacy and desire to marry, are you committed to marrying *for life* and then *"only in the Lord"*?

1 Corinthians 8:1-13

What is the writer saying?

How can I apply this to my life?

pray Pray for those that work with the youth of your church to have love, wisdom, and perseverance.

In Chapters 8-10 Paul discusses *gray issues*. A *gray issue* is something that is not specifically addressed in Scripture, such as clothing styles, music styles, what things you do on Sunday, etc. Discussions about these issues often lead to angry arguments and can divide churches.

One issue in particular was affecting the unity of the church at Corinth: Christians were divided over whether or not to eat meat offered to idols or to eat in the temple restaurant. Animals were sacrificed to the gods in the pagan temples. Part of the meat was burned, part was served in the temple restaurant, and the rest was sold in the temple market. People saved from this background were offended when they saw Christians eating in the restaurant or serving meat that had been offered to idols. They believed that demons somehow affected that food and Christians should not eat it. Who was right?

In the first six verses, Paul states that there is nothing wrong with the meat or with eating the meat. All things are clean and there is nothing wrong at all in eating the meat. Then was it okay to eat in the temple restaurant? Not necessarily. If eating in the temple or serving the meat at home would offend a weaker Christian brother, then it should not be done (vv. 8-13). A weaker brother is someone whose faith has not yet been strengthened and who is still very "young" in biblical knowledge. They need to be loved, encouraged, and taught. If we exercise our liberty and it negatively affects them, then we sin against the Lord (v. 13). This is the principle of love: we are willing to not exercise our liberty because we love our brothers in Christ.

Are you willing to give up the right to do something that could negatively affect another Christian? If your music, your dress, or anything else causes a weaker brother to stumble, you must be willing to not exercise that liberty around them.

1 Corinthians 9:1-10

What is the writer saying?

How can I apply this to my life?

In Chapter 9 verses 1-18, Paul illustrates his willingness to give up his own liberty for the cause of Christ. In our passage today, he gives a number of reasons why he has the right to be paid for the Gospel ministry. In tomorrow's passage he then will give reasons why he gives up this right to a salary!

First Paul argues that his apostolic office deserves payment for services rendered (vv. 1-6). The word *apostle* means "one who has been sent." Paul was sent by the Lord Himself to the Gentiles to reach them with the Gospel. It seems some may have doubted his apostleship, so he shares with them the evidence that he is indeed an apostle: mainly, that he has seen Jesus (v. 1) and that he was instrumental in the founding of their church (v. 2).

Paul's second argument is that it is the usual custom to receive payment for labors. He gives examples of a soldier and a farmer (v. 7). The third argument is that the Old Testament taught that laborers should be compensated for their work (vv. 8-10).

The point he is making here is that a person's sustenance should come from their work. Thus, if a person gives themselves to the gospel ministry, then they should be taken care of by the people who are benefiting from the ministry. Could you imagine at the end of your next work week your boss coming to you and saying, "Well, I know your first priority is not the money you earn here, but rather God's glory, so I am not going to pay you this week." What would your response be? We are to make sure that we are taking care of those who invest their lives in the ministry of the Word. They should be freed from the cares of this world so they can concentrate on ministry for the honor and glory of God.

Life stEP   Pray for your church that they might generously take care of the needs of your pastors, missionaries, and others in Gospel ministries. Pray for those who are in ministry that their financial needs would be met so that they could give themselves wholly to the ministry of the Gospel. Also, take a minute and consider how you personally could be used by the Lord to meet a financial need of someone in the Lord's ministry.

1 Corinthians 9:11-18

What is the writer saying?

How can I apply this to my life?

pray *Papua New Guinea – Effectiveness of literacy ministries that enable nationals to study God's Word.*

In verses 11-14, Paul states that those who minister the Word of God should have their physical needs met by the people of God. This is how it was in the Old Testament (v. 13). Many of the animal sacrifices at the temple were only partially burned, and the rest of the meat was given to the priests who *ministered* at the temple. This becomes a pattern for Christians who are *ministers* of the gospel.

However, Paul gave up this right so that people would not think that he was in ministry for the money (vv. 15-18). This is another illustration of being willing to give up a liberty for a higher good, which is the topic of Chapters 8-10.

This is one of the reasons we support missionaries from our local churches. We send them out with their financial needs met, so that when they preach in other countries, they don't need to ask for money from the people they're ministering to. If our missionaries are seen as being in ministry for the money, the gospel message could be "hindered" (v. 12). So then we see that Paul also did not take money from the people to whom he ministered when he was in a missionary setting. However, he did accept money from mature churches that gladly accepted the responsibility to take care of the needs of missionaries.

Paul then makes a stunning transitional statement in verse 16: he did not want any glory for preaching the Gospel. One of the reasons he preached was that he realized that God would hold him responsible if he was not obedient (v. 16). Another motivation was that the Lord would reward him if he was faithful to the task (v. 17). Paul realized that his most important payday was the one coming when he stood before the Lord. He also realized his most important *job* was faithfully sharing the gospel of Christ with others – and that "without charge"! (v. 18)

Life **stEP** Why do you share the gospel? Why should you? Are you looking for creative ways to reach people for Christ? Here is a challenge: get an index card and write the names of ten people that you want to be saved. Call it *My Top Ten List*, and commit to pray for those people every day. Ask God to open opportunities for you to share Christ with these people. When one gets saved, add another to your list.

1 Corinthians 9:19-27

What is the writer saying?

How can I apply this to my life?

There are two crucial principles Paul shares here that are vital in reaching people for Jesus Christ: *self-denial* and *self-control*.

First, we are encouraged to exercise *self-denial* (vv. 19-23). In self-denial, we give up the right to do what we want in order to reach others. Paul says (v. 22) that he adapted to various people's customs in order to reach them. While he did not violate biblical principles, Paul ordered his life so that he did not unnecessarily offend others. He adopted new customs so that he would be pleasing to those he desired to influence with the Gospel. For example, if we were going to reach in-line skaters for Christ, we might have to buy some skates and go skating! Paul was willing to change his ways in order to share the Gospel. That takes *self-denial* (v. 23). Next, he shares that it takes *self-control* (vv. 24-27) to be willing to lay aside your freedom to reach others. He illustrates with athletes. Athletes have the right to eat cake and cookies but instead they watch what they eat and drink. They train hard and long. The great marathon runner, Bill Rogers, would wake up at 2:00 a.m. so he could run ten miles in the morning and ten more in the evening. He did this so he could reach his goal. Do we have to give up our comforts? Only if we want to reach our goal of winning the lost! If an athlete is willing to do all that for temporal gains, what more should we be willing to do for the glory of God?

In verse 27, Paul writes that the biggest enemy to being able to do this is US! We have to "*keep under*" our bodies, which means to *keep control* of our bodies. We are not to give into our fleshy desires, but to be committed to doing what is right and godly.

Remember the *My Top Ten List* from yesterday? Let's extend the list by adding a *My Top Two Commitments*. Write out your commitment response to the following: (1) *Self-denial*: What things in my life am I willing to set aside so that I can reach these ten people for Christ? (2) *Self-control*: What things do I have to do to achieve my goal of reaching these friends for Christ?

1 Corinthians 10:1-11

What is the writer saying?

How can I apply this to my life?

pray   *Ecuador – Pray for God to call more laborers to reach the impoverished of Quito and Guayaquil.*

Paul talks about the danger of taking God for granted. The Israelites enjoyed the blessings of God. They had regular guidance from the Lord (v. 2). All of their needs were taken care of in miraculous ways (vv. 3-4). In spite of all these benefits, they still did not live in a pure manner before God. He gave them great blessings, yet instead of praising Him, they took Him for granted. Worse than that, they began to lust after evil things (v. 6). They got involved in idolatry, which, at its root, is putting anyone or anything in the place of God. In verse 7, it says the Israelites got drunk and were involved in sexual uncleanness (the implication of "*play*" – see Exodus 32). As a result, God judged them harshly.

Two times in this text Paul says that these things are written for our benefit (vv. 6, 11). When things in life are going smoothly, it is very easy to forget the Lord and be drawn toward evil. The Israelites were often complainers (v. 10), and we must be careful not to follow their bad example. When we complain, we are saying either (1) God is not in control or (2) we don't like (or trust) what God is doing!

This is a grave danger for us who have enjoyed spiritual privilege for extended periods of time, especially for us who are *second generation* Christians. Many of us have grown up in Christian homes and good churches. We have enjoyed all the extras like youth groups and summer camp. The danger is we get so used to God's blessing that we, too, tend to take Him for granted! When a few *rough* waves rock the *boat* of our lives then we, like Israel, begin to complain. Next we stop being careful about staying pure in conduct and we begin doing ungodly things.

So then, what must you do to be careful? How can you keep your fellowship with God a top priority in your life? How can you guard against questioning God by complaining? How can you keep your life pure so as to honor the Lord? When you do experience some of those *rough waves*, be sure to stop and ask yourself, "What does God want to teach me through this trial?" (See James 1:2-4)

1 Corinthians 10:12-22

What is the writer saying?

How can I apply this to my life?

pray   *Spain – For the youth of Spain to embrace the claims of Christ and the relevancy of God's word.*

In today's passage, Paul gives the Christians at Corinth warnings in response to his previous examination of the failures of Israel to act in accordance with God's many abundant blessings (vv. 1-11).

First Paul points out their over-confidence (v. 12). Some believed they were so strong that they were above temptation. We, too, tend to think we are a lot stronger than we really are, and that we don't need God to keep us from sin.

Next, Paul presents the opposite extreme: *to despair* (v. 13). After all, if Israel failed to keep a right walk with God, how could a Christian living in Corinth, a sin-filled city, expect to do any better? Paul used the word *temptation* here to describe the trying conditions which God allowed them to face. *Temptation* could be translated *test*, and it means "to analyze the quality of a thing by testing." It is speaking of God using difficult external circumstances in our lives to test the strength of our faith. When we

begin to lust or long for some thing, some circumstance, or some person, it becomes a *testing of our character*. In this verse, Paul is declaring that with every trying circumstance in which you find yourself, you can trust that God is faithful to provide you with the wisdom to handle it biblically and with purity.

One of the biggest temptations is *idolatry*, which is putting something in the place of God (vv. 14-15). God will not tolerate any rivals taking His place in our lives. We are to live for Him and for Him alone. Our fellowship with God cannot be right when we make other people or things our top priority.

In verses 16-22, Paul talks about the fellowship of the Lord's Table, or communion. Since the Corinthians were involved in idolatry, they were not having true fellowship with God (v. 19). This was an affront to God (vv. 21-22). God demands total holiness and commitment in worship.

Life stEP

Paul defines *covetousness* as *idolatry*. That means having a stronger desire for things than for God. That puts idolatry in a different light, doesn't it? What can you do throughout the day to make God the *top priority* in your life? How might you fellowship with Him?

1 Corinthians 10:23-33

What is the writer saying?

How can I apply this to my life?

pray   *Romania – Outreach to thousands of street children and orphans who possess Europe's highest HIV rates.*

Paul wraps up his discussion of *gray area issues*. He again states that *all things* are lawful (v. 23, see 6:12; 8:9). That means that *all things* that are not clearly forbidden in the Bible are lawful for us to do. Of course that does not mean we *should* do them! How then do we cultivate conviction in these areas? That is Paul's purpose here. He gives us some clear questions to ask that will guide our own personal convictions:

— Is this *prohibited* in the Scriptures? v. 23
— Will it *build me up* to be more like Christ? v. 23
— Will it help me *build others up* to be like Christ? v. 24
— Am I doing this solely because *I want to*? v. 24
— Will it enhance or hinder *my testimony* to the lost? vv. 25-30
— Will it *glorify God*? v. 31
— Will it *offend* anyone? v. 32

From elsewhere in 1 Corinthians we could add:
— Would I want others to *imitate me* in this? 11:1
— Will it cause a young believer to *stumble*? 8:13

Paul had four guiding principles:
• He was not willing to do anything that would make another Christian stumble.
• He was not willing to do anything that would hinder his being able to share the Gospel to a lost person.
• He was not willing to do anything that did not build him up in Christ.
• He was not willing to do anything that was not pleasing to God!

Yes, we are free, but to do what God wants us to do! Before we knew the Lord, we were bound by our sin nature. Now that the Holy Spirit lives in us, we have the power to obey God and are free to do so!

 Life stEp

So, take a *gray issue* that you encounter and process it through this list. For instance, since the Bible does not forbid watching R-rated videos (they had not been invented!), is it OK to watch them? *What would Jesus do* (WWJD) must be the determining factor!

1 Corinthians 11:1-10

What is the writer saying?

How can I apply this to my life?

Paul discusses the chain of command in marriage. God has set the man to be the leader in the home (v. 3). Paul points out that in all relationships in life there has to be some type of submission.

The authority of the man in the home has nothing to do with being better than women; it has to do with the role that God has assigned to each.

We are all equal in essence, that is, in our *persons*, but we have different roles. God the Father and God the Son are equal in essence, yet the Father is the head over Christ (v. 3). That is a great illustration. In the home, man is to be the head over the wife, but they are equal persons.

In the Greek and Roman world at this time, there was a powerful women's liberation movement. The sign of submission in this culture had been for a wife to have her head "covered" (vv. 5-6) with a veil or with a draping of their outer garment over their head, like a hood. To show their rebellion against submitting to their husbands, the women were taking off their veils. Paul basically says, *Keep your veils on!* (vv. 5-10)

Similarly, women were shaving their heads (vv. 5-6), which was the hairstyle of prostitutes. Christian women were not to display their bodies as if they were prostitutes. God created the "woman for the man" (v. 9, i.e., a wife for her husband); therefore, a woman should not present herself in public as if she were *for sale*! When a woman is fulfilling her God-ordained role, she will be fulfilled and God will be honored. This was not happening in Corinth.

To apply this passage we must ask, "How does a Christian woman show respect to her husband's leadership in the home?" It will be different from place to place, but we should be sensitive to maintaining God's clear distinction between the roles of men and women.

1 Corinthians 11:11-22

What is the writer saying?

How can I apply this to my life?

pray   *South Korea – Complete renewing of the mind for South Koreans saved out of Buddhism and Confucianism.*

This passage continues the discussion on the roles of men and women. God designed gender roles for a purpose (v. 12). In the Corinthian culture, prostitutes shaved their heads, or wore the hair closely cropped. Therefore, if Christian women took off their veils and cut their hair short, they would be associated with prostitutes.

Notice also that Paul says that men were not to have "long hair"; such a hairstyle was *unnatural* and *shameful* (v. 14). Paul's point here was not primarily the length of a man's hair. For instance, Spartan warriors wore their shoulder-length hair tied up in a kind of pony-tail. No one ever thought them effeminate! Paul is pointing out that a man should be *manly* or distinctive in his appearance, and thus he should not have a hair style that would appear *feminine*. The conclusion is that a woman's hairstyle should be distinguishable from a prostitute's and also from a man's hairstyle (v. 15).

Paul then moves on to a discussion about some of their meetings. Their practice was to enjoy a kind of "potluck" dinner before they shared in the "Lord's Supper" (v. 20, i.e., communion). But these dinners had gotten out of hand: while some were going without food, others were over-indulging and even getting drunk (v. 21). Apparently the rich Christians were eating only with other rich people, shaming (v. 22) the poor who had come without food! So Paul asks, "What? ...do you despise [hold in disrespect] the Church of God?" Paul rebukes them for not sharing in an *unselfish* manner. After all, the entire point of the Lord's Supper was to celebrate the Lord's great *unselfish* act of dying as a sacrifice and substitute for others! (See v. 24.)

So then, we have two questions to consider: First, how about your appearance? Do you have a hair-style and clothing that is distinctive to your sex, whether male or female? Are you bringing glory to God by how you will present yourself today? Second, are you striving to be *unselfish* in your conduct at church and with Christian friends? Are you seeking to follow the example of Christ?

1 Corinthians 11:23-34

What is the writer saying?

How can I apply this to my life?

pray   *Uruguay – For God to save and call a witness among the upper middle-class, which is estimated to be the largest un-evangelized group.*

This passage describes the *Lord's Supper*, which we often call *Communion*. It is referring back to the Christ's last meal with His disciples. It was a *Passover Meal*, which had been an annual celebration of the Jewish people since the night the Death-Angel *passed over* them as the Lord prepared to bring them out of their slavery in Egypt. (See Exodus 12.) But on this night, before His crucifixion, Jesus transformed the *Passover Meal* into the *first Communion Service*. (See Matthew 26:26-28.)

The *Lord's Supper* and the two *elements* used are to stimulate us to remember Jesus (vv. 24-25). The *bread* reminds us of the sin-free life of Jesus Christ. The bread was unleavened bread. Leaven is an illustration of sin in the Bible. Jesus was tempted in every way "as we are, yet without sin" (Hebrews 4:15). The *cup* reminds us of the death of Jesus, as signified by the shedding of His blood. The cup represents the wrath of God's judgment of sin, and Jesus drank it for us! The "new testament" (v. 25) refers to the new *covenant* or *contract* that Jesus purchased for us with His own blood. Under this *new contract*, we have a relationship with God through faith in Jesus Christ as our Savior.

Before we partake of the Lord's Supper, Paul instructs us *to examine ourselves* (v. 28). As a matter of fact, the Corinthians were celebrating the Lord's Supper with unconfessed sin in their lives. As a result, God was chastising them – some even to the point of death (v. 30).

When we come to the Lord's Supper, we must examine ourselves and then partake only after we have confessed any known sin to the Lord (v. 28). God chastens us so that we will be brought back in right relationship with Him. God loves us enough to discipline us; not to hurt us, but to bring us back into a right relationship with Him (v. 32). That is how much He loves us!

Life stEP

An important part of our quiet time with God is spiritual examination, just as we should do before taking part in a Communion Service. Take a minute to look *inside*. Is your daily communion or fellowship with God being disrupted because of sin in your life? Examine your own heart and confess any known sin to God your Father!

1 Corinthians 12:1-11

What is the writer saying?

How can I apply this to my life?

pray *Pray for those in your church who are seeking employment.*

This section begins a three-chapter discussion on *spiritual gifts*. It is obvious that the Corinthians misunderstood spiritual gifts. Our text corrects this misunderstanding. Paul states that when they were unsaved, they were "carried away" into idolatry (v. 2). The phrase implies irrational activity. The Corinthians apparently were seeking an exciting experience, but that is not how the Spirit of God works. So then, how do the gifts function?

1. In verse 4, the Greek word used for *gifts* is *charismata*, from which we get the word *charismatic*. It means *a gift that is bestowed to show that a person is favored*. These are literally *grace-gifts* from God!

2. In verse 5, they are called *administrations*. This word is related to our word *deacon* (a nickname for *servants*, i.e., *dust-runners*). Thus God has given us gifts as an aid in our service for other Christians.

3. In verse 6, spiritual gifts are called *operations*. This Greek word is a form of our word *energy*. It emphasizes God has given *the power needed to put our gifts to work in His service*.

Notice we have three times in these verses the phrase *differences* (or *diversities*)...*but the same*. This is a great truth; *unity* in a church comes from the workings of a *diversity* of grace-gifted people. All have different gifts to enable each to provide different services. Then all are *energized* by God to serve His people.

In verse 11, three additional elements are added:

1. We see that the "*same Spirit*" directs the workings of all the gifts.

2. Moreover, it is the Spirit of God who gives gifts "*as He wills.*" This means we do not choose a gift, nor do we pray to get certain gifts.

3. Thirdly, He gives gifts to "*every man.*" This means you are specially gifted by the Spirit of God to serve the people of God!

Do you know what gifts God has given you? More importantly, how are you using those gifts for His glory? Today, what could you purposefully do to serve someone in your church?

1 Corinthians 12:12-20

What is the writer saying?

How can I apply this to my life?

pray — *Praise God that He supplies all our needs according to His riches in glory by Christ Jesus (Philippians 4:19).*

The illustration of the *body* is used here to show that all believers have an *interdependence* on one another. In the first part of the passage, Paul stresses the unity we have in Christ (v. 12).

In verse 13, he states that the Holy Spirit has *baptized* us all into the body of Christ. We refer to this as *Spirit-baptism* to distinguish it from *water-baptism*. The word *baptize* simply means *to dip, or to place into*. In *water-baptism*, we go through a ceremony were we are dipped into water and taken up out of the water as a picture that testifies that we were saved by the death, burial, and resurrection of Jesus Christ.

It is important to note that the Spirit-baptism mentioned here is a different *placing into* than water-baptism. Spirit-baptism occurs at salvation when the Spirit *places us into* the body of Jesus Christ. This is not an experience that we feel or do; it is accomplished by the Spirit at the time of our salvation. That is why there is no place in the Bible where we are commanded to be baptized by the Spirit, because it happens automatically at salvation. We know this because it says that *all* are baptized (v. 13), not just the people who have received a *second blessing* (as some teach).

Not only does the Spirit of God place us into the body of Christ (another name for His Church), He places us as the exact *part* of the body which He has chosen for us (v. 13). It is according to His own purposes that He selects which part of the body of Christ He wants us to be. God is the One who sets the members in their place (v. 18). We are all different by design and we are all needed. In the physical body, all the members are needed to function effectively, and all cannot be the same body part, or there would be no effective function. So it is in the body of Christ; we are all different (vv. 4-6), yet we are all needed.

Life stEP — You are needed in the body of Christ. Are you functioning the way you should? Imagine what it would be like if your legs suddenly decided not to work. What effect would that have on you? So then, what should you be doing this week to be a functioning part of your local church?

1 Corinthians 12:21-31

What is the writer saying?

How can I apply this to my life?

pray *Columbia – For an end to violence and widespread corruption within the government.*

Today's passage continues the illustration of a body with all of its parts that was introduced in yesterday's passage.

We have a tendency to think that certain people are more important in the church than others. For instance, if you are a youth leader, it would be very easy to think that you are more important than, say, a member of the choir. But is that true? Paul says here that *every* member of the body is equally important – even those parts of the body that we think are not as presentable. For instance, take our toes. They are not the best looking part of the body. But if you are a girl, you pedicure them, paint the toenails, and do whatever you can to make them presentable.

What is the spiritual point being made here? We are to respect all parts of the body (vv. 23-26). Each member of a church is vital to that church being successful in glorifying God. As in the physical body, when one member of the body hurts, it affects the whole body. Have you ever hit your thumb with a hammer? Does it affect your whole body?

We are to regard each member of the body of Christ as valuable and necessary, not just those who are most popular or have the most visible positions. We are all needed in the fellowship of the saints. In addition, we are all made differently by God (vv. 28-30) so that we might serve different needs in our churches. We are not all the same and that is by God's design. According to verse 28, God is the one who has set us in the body with the gifts that He has chosen for each of us.

Life sTEP

Do you have a tendency to look at others in the church and wish you had their gifts? Or do you look down on others in the body because they do not seem as gifted as you are? God is the one who made people the way they are, and we are to appreciate each person in the body. Also, we are to love and serve them equally. So then, who is like a *hurt thumb* in your church and how can you come to their aid today?

1 Corinthians 13:1-13

What is the writer saying?

How can I apply this to my life?

This chapter is known as the *Love Chapter*. Paul is showing that all spiritual gifts need to operate in the context of *love* (vv. 1-3), which is to say, *a desire to actively and selflessly serve others*. No matter how wonderful our gifts are, if they are not used in an attitude of love, then they matter little (vv. 1-3).

Love is not defined in this passage as much as it is described. We are shown how love acts in a practical manner. Paul makes sixteen statements here about *love*. The emphasis of these is how we treat people. Love is patient with people (v. 4). Love does not try to exalt self, but others (vv. 4-5). Love does not get easily upset, because it is primarily concerned with others, not with its own feelings (v. 5). The point is that love is *others-oriented* not *self-oriented*. When we love, we are more concerned about doing what is best for the other person, not what is best for ourselves.

As a result, love is positive, encouraging, and enduring (v. 7). For all of eternity, we will love God and love others. The spiritual gifts to which the Corinthian people were giving all of their attention, howbeit in a self-oriented manner, will one day pass away (vv. 8-10), but love will never pass away. As vital as gifts are, love is much more vital for it is eternal.

In verses 10-13, Paul states that when we get to Heaven there will be no more need for those spiritual gifts we hold so dear now, so we need to keep them in their proper perspective. There are three virtues that he exalts in verse 13. *Faith* is vital; it is by faith we have been saved. *Hope* is important, for we have a confident expectation that Jesus is coming back. And as important as those two are, *love* is the greatest, for love exemplifies the character of God (1 John 4:8).

Make a list of the sixteen characteristics of love from this chapter; "love is ....". Then substitute your name for *love* in each of its various descriptions. Ask yourself: how well do I fit this description? Finally, ask God to show you how you could be others-oriented in your demonstration of this self-giving love.

1 Corinthians 14:1-9

What is the writer saying?

How can I apply this to my life?

pray   *Ukraine – Christian camps. For God to give youth a passion to live for Him and reach their land.*

The Corinthian Church had exalted the *gift of tongues* above all other gifts. The *gift of tongues* was the ability to speak in an unlearned foreign language. Some people today teach that speaking in tongues is *angel talk* or an *ecstatic utterance*. However, the Bible clearly teaches that it is simply being able to speak in another language you did not previously learn (Acts 2:1-21). It was a *showy gift* (one could show others that he was extra-special!). It was also mysterious and supernatural as well. Thus, it seems that many, for selfish reasons, wanted to be able to have this gift. We saw earlier that not all people have the same gifts; some have one and some have another. Yet today, some teach that everyone should speak in tongues. But that teaching contradicts what Paul taught in chapter 12. Now Paul states that *speaking in tongues* has its place, but *prophecy* is more needed. *Prophecy* is *speaking forth God's Word* (v. 3-4), and its purpose is to:
• *Edify*, which means *to build up other Christians in the faith*;
• *Exhort*, which means *to encourage spiritual progress*; and
• *Comfort*, which means *to console those who are losing heart.*

Tongues will not edify the whole body if there is not an interpreter, and it seems that this is how they were practicing this gift (vv. 5-6, 9).

In verse 6, Paul states that if he came to Corinth speaking in tongues as they were, it would not benefit the body, for they would not understand what he said. But if he came speaking God's Word clearly (like a pastor who *speaks forth* the meaning of God's Word, as an Old Testament *prophet*) then all will understand and will be built up.

The goal of spiritual gifts is to build up the whole body, and tongues cannot do that if they are not used correctly, which they weren't in this assembly. The key in public ministry is seen in verse 9, that what is spoken should be able to be understood by all who are there.

Life **stEP**   Ask God to help you clearly share His message. Make a commitment to know the Word of God so that you can share it with others. How could you edify, exhort, or comfort a fellow Christian today?

1 Corinthians 14:10-17

What is the writer saying?

How can I apply this to my life?

pray *Thailand – For courage to accept Christ in a land where patriotism and Buddhism are seen as one entity.*

In today's passage Paul is continuing his explanation of why the "*edifying of the church*" (v. 12) by means of the *clear declaration of the Word of God* (meaning of *prophecy*, v. 4) is a church's highest priority. At the same time, he explains why *speaking in tongues* is not a priority. There are many "voices" saying many things but this is only *noise* (v. 10, the meaning of "*voices*" here), if people don't know what they are saying (v. 11). So, Paul advises, since you are eager to exalt spiritual gifts, excel in the ones that edify the church (v. 12). The word *edify* was used of building a home or a temple. Thus, we are to use our spiritual gifts in a manner so that we are building up the church, not tearing it apart.

One must ask, "In the early Church, could *speaking in tongues* build up?" Yes, but only if there was an *interpreter* (v. 13). What about praying in tongues? Paul says it makes no sense at all to pray or worship in a language you do not know (v. 15). This is instructive, because many today say that they are able to worship and pray in tongues. They will even say that it is the best worship and prayer. Yet Paul states just the opposite of that here. God is most honored when we worship Him according to knowledge and not just in an emotional experience! Emotions (such as fervency) have a place, as long as we pray with understanding as well (v. 15).

As a result of the above, we conclude by noting that there was a time and place for tongues, along with some strict rules for using them (which we will see in the next passage). The Corinthians were misusing the gift of tongues and they had wrongly exalted this gift above all other gifts. Unfortunately, the same error is taking place in some churches today.

Life **step** You should speak and sing to God with full understanding of what you are communicating. Since Paul links together *praying in the Spirit* with *understanding* (v. 15), why not ask the Holy Spirit to give you the name of a missionary that you will get to know so that you can pray for them with understanding? Then send them a letter or e-mail requesting information concerning their prayer needs!

1 Corinthians 14:18-26

What is the writer saying?

How can I apply this to my life?

Paul states he would rather speak five words that people understand than speak 10,000 words in "an unknown tongue" (v. 19). Paul's point was that the emphasis needs to be on how people use their gifts to serve their church, not on how personally exciting a gift seems to be.

We also see here the main reason why tongues have passed off the scene today. According to verses 21-22, tongues were a sign to the Jews. What was the purpose of this sign? Paul quotes from Isaiah 28:11-12, where Isaiah prophesied that tongues would be a sign of God's impending judgment on Israel for their rejection of Jesus as their Messiah. God says that He would speak to Israel with people of other nationalities (v. 21), yet they would still not listen.

This, then, was the major reason for tongues during the time of the early Church: a sign to unsaved Jews of the judgment that God was about to bring upon them. This prophecy was fulfilled in A.D. 70 when Titus of Rome attacked and destroyed Jerusalem. After this the *warning-sign* was no longer needed. So we see that in Paul's day (he is writing here at around A.D. 55), the gift was still functioning and he was trying to get them to use it in a biblically restricted way.

Also notice that tongues, without an interpreter, will never help the lost come to Christ. In fact, those without Christ will think people who speak in tongues are "mad" or *out of their minds* (v. 23). It is much more effective to *speak forth in a clear manner* the Word of God (meaning of *prophesy*, vv. 4, 24) which God will use to win the lost (v. 25).

Are you able to clearly explain the Gospel message to lost friends? Be sure to stick to the Word of God! It is God's intended tool for evangelism. Have you marked key *salvation verses* in your Bible? An important and helpful string of verses to know is called the *Roman's Road*. It begins at Romans 3:23 then progresses on to 6:23, 5:8, 10:9 and ends with 10:13. Take a minute and, beginning at 3:23, underline each verse and then, in the margin next to it, carefully write: #2-6:23. Continue to 6:23, underline, write: #3-5:8, and so on.

Friday 48

1 Corinthians 14:27-40

What is the writer saying?

How can I apply this to my life?

pray *Nicaragua – For godly politicians with the credibility and wisdom to end divisive disputes.*

The gift of tongues was given to the Church by God and was to be used according to God's principles. Paul closes the chapter by listing guidelines for the use of tongues in the body. We saw yesterday that tongues are no longer in use today, but when tongues were still in use, there were some important limitations:

• Because tongues were a sign to unsaved Jews concerning impending judgment, there should be unsaved Jews present (v. 22)!

• No more than three people should speak in tongues at any service (v. 27). Also, these are to speak sequentially, not all together. Again, the emphasis is on orderliness to permit understanding.

• There had to be an interpreter present (v. 28). Otherwise, the tongue speakers should be silent; tongues could not be used. Thus each must have known their gifts as well as the gifts of others.

• Women were not to speak in tongues in the assembly (v. 34).

• If the first four principles were kept, then they were not to forbid tongues in the service.

As we compare this list with the conduct of churches today, we see a big gap. In many churches that practice speaking in tongues, women are commonly the major speakers, which violates this passage. Another violation is churches allowing simultaneous speaking by dozens of tongue-speakers, with no interpreters (and, thus, no edifying of the church)!

Paul's main point concerning the use of tongues was that all be done in a *decent and orderly* manner (v. 40) so people would understand what was happening. If not used correctly, tongues would bring "confusion" (v. 33) to the church; not *edification* (v. 26) and *comfort* (v. 31).

Are you using your spiritual gifts to *edify* or build others up in the Lord? Are you helping others discover what their gifts are so they can learn how to use them in service for the Lord Jesus? How can you have a more significant role of serving others in your church?

1 Corinthians 15:1-11

What is the writer saying?

How can I apply this to my life?

pray *Spain – For missionaries to be humble, loving, and culturally sensitive as they seek to minister.*

In this chapter, Paul clearly teaches the truth of the resurrection of Jesus Christ from the dead. Some were teaching that Christ did not rise bodily from the dead. In verse 1, Paul says that he had preached the gospel to them when he was with them. The word *gospel* means *good news*. The key to this gospel which Paul preached was that one must believe that Jesus has risen from the dead to be saved (vv. 3-4).

He defines the four central truths of the gospel in verses 3-4. These are: (1) Christ died for our sins, (2) He was buried, (3) He rose again, and (4) all of this happened as prescribed by Old Testament "Scriptures." Paul points this out to show that the Resurrection is a vital part of what we must believe to be saved from our sin.

In the Old Testament, in order for a truth to be established, you needed two witnesses. In verses 5-8, Paul goes beyond that minimum requirement to establish the truth of the Resurrection. After His Resurrection, Jesus was seen by Peter first and then by all the Disciples. Later He was seen by over 500 believers at the same time. Lastly, Jesus was seen by His brother James, and then by Paul himself!

Paul defines himself in verse 9 as the least of all the apostles. He was amazed that God had called him – a man who had previously devoted his life to persecuting the Church. As a result, Paul says, "I am what I am" totally "by the grace of God" (v. 10). Grace is God's *undeserved favored attention*. It is God withholding from us what we do deserve (often called *mercy*), and pouring out on us multiple blessings we do not deserve! Paul realized he did not deserve all the great blessings of his salvation, let alone the privilege of preaching the Gospel. As a result, Paul was extremely thankful, and to show his gratitude, he desired to minister as hard as he could for the glory of God (vv. 10-11).

Life stEp When you share the Gospel, make sure you include the teaching about Jesus rising from the dead. Along with Paul, we can say that *we are who we are* only by the grace of God. How about making a list of God's blessings in your life? Also take time to thank God for saving you from your deserved judgment!

Sunday 49

1 Corinthians 15:12-19

What is the writer saying?

How can I apply this to my life?

pray Peru – For a softening of hearts among the 700,000 unusually resistant, university students.

Again in today's passage we find Paul arguing against an insidious doctrine that was being spread by "some among you" at Corinth (v. 12).

To argue for the truth of the Resurrection, Paul starts out by showing what happens if there is *no resurrection* from the dead (v. 12) as presented by those who were teaching this doctrine:

• If there is no resurrection, then Jesus is not alive but still dead (v. 13)!

• If He is not risen from the dead, then Paul was lying (v. 15), since he claimed to be one of the "*witnesses*." Paul, then, is worthy of death.

• If the Resurrection is not true, their faith in Christ is useless (v. 14).

• If salvation is by faith in the Lord's resurrection, then that faith is in vain (v. 17a); therefore, all Christianity is to no avail.

• If that is true, then we have not been saved from our "*sins*" (v. 17b) and are still dead spiritually and on our way to hell (vv. 16-18).

• If Christ is not raised, then all of the believers who have died previously have "*perished*" and will never be heard from again (v. 18).

• If all this is true, then we are to be pitied above all people, for we have lived a lie (v. 19). As a matter of fact, we should be "*miserable*."

The point he is making is that the Resurrection is a fundamental teaching of Christianity. It is not an optional, secondary belief; it is essential to everything else. If you do not believe in the Resurrection, then you are not saved. You cannot be a Christian and deny the Resurrection. It is the bedrock of our faith. If Jesus is not alive, then we do not have salvation in Him.

Life sTEP

Since Israel in the Old Testament worshipped God on Saturday, why does the church meet on Sunday? It is to remember that Jesus rose again on the first day of the week. The Lord's resurrection was so important that the Church moved the day of worship! Therefore, do not allow a Sunday to go by where you forget to praise the RISEN SAVIOR! Since Jesus is alive, why not thank Him now for giving you victory over sin and death by His resurrection?!

Monday 49

1 Corinthians 15:20-28

What is the writer saying?

How can I apply this to my life?

pray *Bahamas – For Christians to guard themselves from materialism.*

In verse 20, we have one of the most victorious statements in the entire Bible: "Now is Christ risen from the dead." In the Greek, it can be translated that *Christ is risen from among the dead ones*. Jesus was buried with the dead ones, but unlike them, He rose from the grave!

Seeing that Christ is risen from the dead, Paul goes on to state the implications of His resurrection:

• All who are born are born dead (v. 22a, "in Adam," therefore corrupted by sin).

• But all who are "in Christ" (v. 22b) will be resurrected; will live again! Why? Because Jesus was the "firstfruits" (v. 23). This is a picture of a wheat field where some grain ripened early and was harvested. The farmer would rejoice for he then had hope that the rest of his grain would soon be ready for harvesting. *We* are the rest of the grain in God's field! We can rejoice for we know that we shall likewise be *harvested* soon by God's work of resurrection in our lives!

When we are resurrected, we will reign with Jesus (vv. 24-26) because we are in Him. Because Jesus is alive, the "last enemy" (*death*, v. 26) is doomed. The point of all redemptive history is that God might be honored and glorified (v. 28). God is glorified in the resurrection of Jesus Christ. Jesus said we live because He lives! The guarantee we have that we too shall rise again from the dead is that Jesus rose again.

Since we have been "*made alive*" (v. 22) when we were "*saved*" by faith in the death, burial, and resurrection of Jesus (vv. 2-4), we will never die spiritually. Our assurance of this is based on the resurrection of Jesus Christ. Christ has indeed been raised from the dead!

 Life STEP Just as surely as Jesus rose and went to heaven, so you also will rise and go to heaven. If you are a believer, you are "in Christ" (v. 22), and He is alive, so you will be alive forever and ever! Since this is true, how should you start conducting yourself as an eternal child of God?

1 Corinthians 15:29-38

What is the writer saying?

How can I apply this to my life?

pray

Serbia – For genuine forgiveness between ethnic groups that have been at war for so long. Pray that people would be able to rebuild trust and cooperation.

Our passage today begins with a widely misunderstood verse! To understand it, we need to notice two key words. In verse 29, Paul uses the pronoun *they* (who were being "baptized for the dead"). Then in verse 30, Paul switches to the pronoun *we* (who endanger ourselves). So then, Paul is telling us that he was not one of those people who practiced "baptism for the dead," nor was he encouraging Christians to follow their example. He is only identifying what this group was doing. We know from other writings that this group did not even believe in resurrection! Paul, therefore, argues that their practice of baptism for the dead makes no sense; why baptize a living person on behalf of a dead person if you say the dead have no possibility of being resurrected?

Another argument for the resurrection is that Paul and the other apostles were continually persecuted for their faith, and if there is no rising from the dead, then their suffering is in vain as well (v. 30). If this life is all there is, then why not just enjoy it (v. 32)?

Paul encourages them not to spend too much time with those who reject the resurrection (vv. 33-34). This *"evil"* company was *corrupting* them! They had started listening to the teaching that there was no resurrection, and that, in turn, had led them to a sinful lifestyle (v. 34). The warning for us is that when we spend lots of time with people who reject the truths of Christianity, it won't be long before we start to live like them. Yes, we need to reach the lost for Christ, but we must be careful not to get too close to their ways or beliefs, lest they will corrupt our morals (v. 33).

Paul also says there were some who reject the resurrection because the body dies and then decays (v. 35). Our mortal, sinful bodies *must* die, so that our glorified bodies can be raised up (vv. 35-37). God is all-powerful and is able to give us a new body ready for eternity (v. 38).

Life stEP

Who do you spend time with? Are you influencing them for Christ? Or are they affecting you for the world? Choose wisely those who have input into your life. Ask the Lord to show you if you have been corrupted by "evil" friends! *"Awake"* (v. 34) to the damage they have done!

1 Corinthians 15:39-50

What is the writer saying?

How can I apply this to my life?

pray   China – Special need for study Bibles and children's Bibles and safety for those transporting them.

Paul continues to answer questions about the doctrine of the resurrection of the dead (v. 35). The first was *"How are the dead raised up?"* That is, by what means is a dead body put back together? Since putting a decomposed body back together was a seemingly impossible task, both Greek philosophers and Jewish Sadducees believed it was beyond the power of the gods (or God) to *revive dead men and make them immortal.* Even the gods do not have such unimaginable power!

Others were asking, *"With what body do they come?"* (v. 35) That is, will it be with the same body or will it be changed somehow? Paul illustrates his answer by pointing out that there are many different kinds of "bodies" in the world now (vv. 39-41). Humans, land animals, fish and birds have different kinds of *glorious* bodies. The same is seen in the glorious *heavenly bodies*: sun, moon, and stars. *Glorious* is used to emphasize that God, by His Creation, has demonstrated that He *does have* the *unimaginable power* to do *seemingly impossible things.*

All this points out the reasonableness of the Christian belief in the resurrection; i.e., God is again going to do something *glorious* because He has the necessary power to raise dead bodies and change them into *spirit-bodies outfitted for an eternal, heavenly existence* (vv. 41-44)! We now live in a *natural body,* but we will be given an *eternal spiritual body.* Our heavenly bodies will no longer be *corruptible;* but instead will be *incorruptible* bodies that can live in heaven (v. 50). When a Christian dies physically, he is still alive spiritually. God takes the elements of his earthly body and makes from them a heavenly body that will be outfitted for eternity in Heaven (v. 50)!

Since, as a Christian, you have God's promise that you are going to Heaven with a heavenly body, now is the time to start living by the truth that you will become a person outfitted for Heaven! So then, while still in your earthy body, do you already "bear the image" (v. 49) of Jesus Christ, the Lord from Heaven (v. 47)? What aspect of your character needs some reshaping by God's unimaginable power?

1 Corinthians 15:51-58

What is the writer saying?

How can I apply this to my life?

pray — Slovakia – God to mobilize broadcasters committed to producing programming in the Roma language.

The next question that may have been on the readers' minds was, "What about those who are alive when the Lord returns? What will happen to their bodies?" Paul answers these questions in today's passage.

A *mystery* (v. 51) in Scripture refers to something that had been previously hidden, but is now divinely revealed. Paul is revealing here that, whether we die or not, *all* of our bodies will be changed. We get the English word *metamorphosis* from the Greek word Paul uses here. It means to *totally change form*. It will happen quickly, in the "twinkling of an eye" (v. 52). The bodies we presently have will be changed into bodies that are ready for Heaven. Our present bodies are "mortal" bodies, which is to say, *a body that is going to die*, but we will get immortal bodies – that is, a body that will last forever. And what bodies they will be! The result of having an immortal body is that it will never die. Death will have been totally defeated and *life* will win! We will never fear death again (v. 55). All of the thanks and glory goes to the Lord for giving us this victory (v. 57).

As a result of this great truth, we should *stand firm in the faith*, which is the meaning of the word *steadfast* (v. 58).

Paul then makes a climatic statement: "always abounding in the work of the Lord" (v. 58). This is to say, *In light of the reality that we will spend eternity with the Lord, we should not be swayed from serving the Lord with all of our hearts while on this earth.*

Paul reinforces his climatic conclusion with the related truth that our labor for Christ is *not in vain* (v. 58). That means that such work will not be empty or useless; not only does Christ reward faithful laborers, but others will become Christians and join us for an eternity in Heaven!

Life stEP

All of the above will happen when the Lord returns. He could return at any time. Are you ready for the Lord Jesus to come back? Are there things in your life that would embarrass you if the Lord came back now? If so, repent and get right with the Lord today! Then ask yourself, how can I live today like the godly resident of Heaven I will become?

1 Corinthians 16:1-12

What is the writer saying?

How can I apply this to my life?

Paul now gives some closing instructions. First, he talks about a special offering for the church in Jerusalem (v. 3). He tells them to take the offering on the first day of the week (v. 2; i.e., Sunday) which was when the early church met for worship. The sum that they should give is not specified here. All Paul says is that they should give that which is in keeping with how "God hath prospered him" (v. 2b). To some people, ten percent might be a huge sacrifice; to others, even fifty percent would not be a hardship. We should give as the Lord has moved us to in our hearts. Our primary giving should go to our local church, but, as illustrated here, it is also good to give to other worthy ministries as the Lord leads.

In verse 5, Paul says that he would come to them (in Corinth, a city in southern Greece) after he finished his work in Macedonia (a region in northern Greece). He hoped that he could stay the winter there. This shows that the apostle, as a result of his eighteen months of hard work in their midst (See Acts 18), had a special link with these people and would love to be able to renew his relationships with them.

Notice Paul's submission to God's will when he discusses his plans; in all of his plans, Paul follows the principle, "if the Lord permit" (v. 7; see James 4:15). It is not our right to insist that our plans be carried out; rather all our plans are subject to God's power, permission, and providence (God's benevolent care and guidance).

Paul gives some instructions concerning a potential visit by Timothy (vv. 10-11). Paul wants them to receive Timothy as a worthy servant of the Lord. He then says he had encouraged Apollos to go immediately to Corinth, but Apollos did not think it was the right time. Apollos had determined that he would come at a later date as the Lord directed him.

Are you giving faithfully to the work of the Lord? Maybe you do not have a lot of money. Give a portion of what you have! Don't wait until you can afford to give. Be faithful to the Lord in the present time. Are you subordinating your plans to the overriding providence of God? After all, it is His prerogative to set His plan and timing in your life!

Saturday 49

1 Corinthians 16:13-24

What is the writer saying?

How can I apply this to my life?

pray Papua New Guinea – For Christian youth camps to see significant salvation and consecration decisions.

In this last section, Paul gives some general exhortations and greetings. In verses 13-14, he reminds them of five basic principles:

• He encourages them to be on their guard, to watch out for evil teaching and evil people.

• He tells them to be steadfast, or firm, in their faith. It means not to waver, but to hold to the fundamentals of the faith with all of their might.

• He instructs them to be courageous and *act like men* (KJV, "*quit you like men*"). This reminds us of the words of the Lord to Joshua in Joshua 1:6-9, "Be strong and of good courage." We need people of courage who are willing to stand firm in a day of wickedness.

• He encourages them to be strong. It takes strength to stand firm for the Lord.

• He reminds them to do all in an attitude of love. Since the Greek word

agape is used here, it means, *Be sure to put other people's needs before your own.* He then encourages the people to support Stephanas in the work of the ministry there (v. 17). It is most likely that Stephanas was a pastor there, or perhaps the church met in his home.

Finally, Paul sends them greetings (vv. 19-20) from the churches in Asia (a Roman province in today's Turkey) and from the people that were ministering with Paul. Paul always remembered people. He realized that ministry is all about people, and he was never too busy or too important for people. He closes the letter with a warning (v. 22) and a loving farewell (vv. 23-24).

In this epistle, we see that Paul loved people enough to tell them the truth. We need to follow that example. At times, we are tempted to tell people what they want to hear as opposed to what they need to hear. Commit yourself today to be willing to tell people what they need to hear from the Word of God. Thank God today for the example of the Apostle Paul.

Second Timothy is one of three books known as the Pastoral Epistles. The other two include 1 Timothy and Titus. The older apostle Paul wrote these books (in his 60s) to two younger men, Timothy and Titus (probably in their 30s). These young men were both serving in pastoral-like roles; Timothy in Ephesus and Titus in Crete. Paul wanted to tell them how to "behave" themselves "in the house of God, which is the church of the living God..." (1 Timothy 3:15).

Helpful to the understanding of the books individually is to take them collectively. Three themes resonate throughout all three: (1) church organization, (2) sound doctrine, and (3) consistent Christian living. While all three books touch on all three themes, each book has its particular emphasis, and those three themes follow the order in which they have been placed in most Bibles (though not written in that order). 1 Timothy emphasizes church organization; 2 Timothy, sound doctrine; and Titus, consistent Christian living. Charles Erdman, in writing of these three books early in the twentieth century, offered this summation of these three themes: "Church government is not an end in itself; it is of value only as it secures sound doctrine; and doctrine is of value only as it applies to real life." The point is this: you *organize* (1 Timothy) so that you can teach *sound doctrine* (2 Timothy), and you teach *sound doctrine* so that *consistent Christian living* (Titus) can result.

As Paul writes, Timothy is serving as his representative to the church in Ephesus. During Paul's first missionary journey (Acts 13-14), he and Barnabas preached the Gospel in the cities of Lystra and Derbe (Acts 14:1-20). Timothy, who had a Greek father and Jewish mother, responded to the message, leading Paul to address him as "my own son in the faith" – "my dearly beloved son" (1 Timothy 1:2; 2 Timothy 1:2). The book of Acts, as well as Paul's own letters, make it clear that Timothy was a capable, trustworthy individual. He could be sent ahead or left behind to carry on the apostle's work (Acts 19:22; 20:4). As to personality, there is some indication that he was somewhat timid in nature (2 Timothy 1:6-7), easily discouraged or frightened (1 Corinthians 16:10-11; 2 Timothy 1:8), and prone to sickness (1 Timothy 5:23). Yet, with all that being said, there is no question that Paul placed great trust in him. His recommendation to the Philippian Church makes that crystal clear: "I have no man likeminded" (Philippians 2:20).

As to 2 Timothy itself, it is written from prison where Paul is awaiting execution. This book is the last known writing we have from the great apostle's pen, and in effect it is his *last will and testament,* the most personal of all his letters (with the possible exception of the short letter written to Philemon). It is believed by many that Paul was arrested and placed in prison when Nero began his campaign of persecution shortly after Rome burned down in A.D. 64. Nero blamed the Christians for starting the fire. (After all, had they not predicted the world would come to an end in a great fire?) He also executed many of them in extremely cruel fashion, including Peter, who, according to one of the early church fathers, was crucified upside down. As Paul authors this second letter to his son-in-the-faith, Timothy, he was very much aware of his apparently soon-to-come death (by beheading).

Even more so than the other Pastoral Epistles, the open sharing of feelings and thoughts marks this letter. The major emphases of the book would include:

(1) *Encouragement to be faithful...* Timothy was somewhat timid and Paul, reminded of his *tears* (1:4), used this letter to challenge him to *hang in there*. Paul was well aware that the Christian life is not played out on a ball field, but lived out on a battlefield, and that one of the essential characteristics of a faithful servant of Jesus Christ would be endurance in the midst of difficulties.

(2) *To turn over leadership to Timothy...* generations come and go, and knowing his time was short Paul wanted to be sure that leadership for the next generation was in place. Jack Wyrtzen, founder of Word of Life Fellowship, often remarked, "It is the responsibility of each generation to reach its generation for Christ."

(3) *Paul's final and definitive testimony...* a reminder to Timothy that he (Paul) had finished well, and an underlying, not-so-gentle hint that he (Timothy) too, should desire a similar finish. Major theological emphases would include:

(1) The coming apostasy of the last days, detailed in chapter 3. Paul warns Timothy that there will be difficult days ahead for believers, and so he passes on instruction as to how Christians are to behave and respond. Jesus had predicted such times would come (John 15:18-25; 16:33; 17:15-18). Paul himself had written earlier of those coming days (1 Thessalonians 3:1-8), and warned the Ephesian elders of them (Acts 20:29).

(2) The importance, value, and application of Scripture, scattered throughout the book, including 1:13; 2:2,15; 3:14-17; 4:2-4. Paul was encouraging Timothy not only to pass on the truths of Scripture to the generations that follow, but also to pass on the basis of those truths, the inspired (God-breathed) Word of God. It is, as many conservative local church constitutions state: *The final authority (the supreme standard) for all faith (what we believe) and practice (how we behave).*

2 Timothy 1:1-7

What is the writer saying?

How can I apply this to my life?

Paul, as in his earlier letter to Timothy, introduces himself as *an apostle of Jesus Christ*, a title unnecessary if this letter was for Timothy's eyes only, for Timothy certainly knew Paul's position. Nevertheless, as in his other *pastorals*, Paul was providing Timothy with the credentials necessary to carry out his task of leading the church of Ephesus. While some might choose to downplay the words of their young pastor, they could hardly do the same with the words of one who was clearly recognized as *one sent from God*, with a message to deliver. Adding the words *by the will of God*, Paul makes it clear that he understood his apostleship was an assignment from God.

This letter, with the possible exception of Philemon, is the most personal of all that Paul wrote. Written from a Roman dungeon, it is often looked upon as Paul's *last will and testament*, and was the final book from his pen. He addresses

Timothy as his *dearly beloved son* (or his own born-one), and in that designation makes it clear that he and Timothy had a very special relationship, that of father and son *in the faith* (see 1 Timothy 1:2). The relationship engendered both deep concern as well as thanksgiving in Paul's heart for his young protégé (vv. 3-4).

Concerned that Timothy's apparently timid nature could curtail his ministry (see *tears*, v. 4), Paul reminded him of *his faith* (found first in his mother and grandmother, v. 5) and of *his gifting* (v. 6). That gifting was the enabling resource that Timothy was to use to carry out his ministry; it was already present, not something to be added to his character, and was to be *rekindled*. Broadening the thought of gifting, Paul challenges Timothy to remember that neither he nor Paul (*us* in verse 7) had been given "the spirit of fear; but of *power...love*, and of a *sound mind*" (v. 7).

Life stEP   Timothy had Paul's letters; we have much more, the entire Word of God. He was gifted; so are we. Let us see to it that we use what we have been given (and it is not *fear*) to perform our service for the Lord.

2 Timothy 1:8-12

What is the writer saying?

How can I apply this to my life?

pray

Costa Rica – That the church's vitality will not be sapped by secularism, materialism, and the influence of the New Age mindset.

Aware that Timothy's timidity could cause enough shame for him to back away from an effective ministry, as well as from Paul (as a prisoner) himself, the apostle encourages his young follower to be a "partaker of the afflictions of the gospel" (v. 8). Suffering is part of the believer's calling and when it comes, should be accepted as part of God's will. Furthermore, when it comes, it will be accompanied by the *power of God*, always available for encouragement and strength.

Verse 8, which ends with *God*, is followed by the work of God in salvation, ("hath saved…and called us"). He does so "not according to our works, but according to his own purpose and grace" (v. 9). That purpose, once hidden, is now revealed through Paul. God did not eliminate death through the cross, but He did disarm it. For the believer, its sting is gone (cf. 1 Corinthians 15:55-57) and Christ has brought "life and immortality" (v. 10)…the condition of never dying, to light (they were in the shadows in the Old Testament).

The believer is called to holiness (v. 9; 1 Peter 1:15-16). Writing to persecuted believers, Peter advocated holy living… lives consecrated to God, and lives befitting our true identity and position in Christ (1 Peter 2:10-11). Paul's challenge to Timothy is similar, using himself as an example. He had suffered many things for the cause of the Gospel (vv. 11-12) but was never ashamed. Why? Because: "I know whom I have believed (a continuing attitude of belief with trust), and am persuaded that he is able to keep that which I have committed unto him" (his very being) (v. 12)…and that which God committed to both he and Timothy, (v. 14), God had committed the Gospel to Paul (1 Timothy 1:11); he was passing it on to Timothy (1 Timothy 6:20; 2 Timothy 4:7), who was to pass it on to faithful men…(and) others also (2 Timothy 2:2).

Life stEP

The believer has a choice when suffering comes: to back away in shame from his commitment to Christ hoping to avoid pain; or to accept it as part of God's purpose in his life and meet it head on with the provided power of God.

2 Timothy 1:13-18

What is the writer saying?

How can I apply this to my life?

pray — Romania – For building materials and skilled laborers to meet the demand for new church construction.

In verse 12, we found Paul using himself as one who steadfastly remained faithful to his commitment. In verses 13-14, Timothy is exhorted to maintain a similar commitment. He is to "hold fast the form of sound words." *Form* can mean *example* or *pattern* (1 Timothy 1:16). Paul both preached and lived the Gospel, establishing a pattern for others to follow (1 Corinthians 11:1). *Sound* comes from a Greek word that gives us our English word *hygiene*, meaning *healthy*. *Words* means *teaching* (in Titus 1:9 it is "sound doctrine," also 1 Timothy 1:10). Taken together the challenge is to provide *healthy teaching*, for the opposite (cf. 2 Timothy, 2:17) could result in a crippling disease.

"That good thing which was committed unto thee" (v. 14), is a clear reference to the Gospel (1 Timothy 6:20). Having received it, Timothy was to *keep* it, and was reminded that only by the power of the Spirit could he do so. *Keep* means *to guard*, and coupled with 1 Timothy 6:20 ("keep that which is committed to thy trust") means the Gospel has been placed on deposit with Timothy (a banking analogy). It is to be guarded, kept, and available for use on demand.

Remember, this letter is being written from a prison dungeon where Paul awaits trial and subsequent beheading. Circumstances are dire. Desertion among believers has escalated. The *some* of 1 Timothy (1:6; 1:19; 5:15; 6:10; 6:21) have become the hyperbolic "all" of 2 Timothy (1:15; 4:16), many being led by two deserters named *Phygellus* and *Hermogenes*. Yet even in troubled times God provides relief, and He does so here in the person of *Onesiphorus* (*one who brings profit or benefit*). This godly man was probably a deacon in Ephesus when Paul was there, for verse 18 can be translated: "...and in how many things he fully played the deacon..." He came to Rome, searched hard for Paul, found him and served him without fear or shame (vv. 16-17).

Life STEP — Onesiphorus was unashamed to serve Christ and his fellow believers. We should do likewise.

2 Timothy 2:1-7

What is the writer saying?

How can I apply this to my life?

"Thou therefore, my son (an expression of strong affection), be strong in the grace (undeserved divine help) that is in Christ Jesus" (v. 1). With these words Paul both exhorts and challenges Timothy to be faithful to his calling, while at the same time drawing a contrast between that which he desires for his young *son-in-the-faith*, and the defectors of the previous chapter (1:15). They had turned their backs upon Paul and the Gospel ministry, but by depending on *the grace that is in Christ Jesus* and its accompanying power, and not upon his own power, Timothy would not have to repeat their error nor experience their fate.

Then begins a series of pictures demonstrating the characteristics of a faithful servant of Jesus Christ. He is to first be faithful as a *teacher* (v. 2). That which he has heard he is to pass on to others. In fact, Timothy is to be part of an endless chain of passing on truth to succeeding generations (i.e., God to Paul to Timothy to faithful men to others also). This is the same procedure laid out by Christ in the Great Commission (Matthew 28:19-20), that of making disciples (discipleship).

In vv. 3-6 Paul gives three additional illustrations of faithfulness to demonstrate to Timothy the seriousness of his task. The *first* is that of a *soldier*, and as such he is to (a) endure hardness; (b) not entangle himself with the affairs of this life (not that they are wrong – just don't get caught up in them); and (c) seek to please his commander. For the believer, that commander is Jesus Christ. The *second* illustration is that of an *athlete*. He is to "strive for masteries" (contend in the games), but to do so lawfully. To receive the victor's crown, his life and ministry must follow biblical directives. The *third* illustration is that of a hardworking *farmer*. Only through strenuous, diligent effort will a bountiful harvest result.

 Life **stEP** We should follow Paul's example and ask the Lord to give us understanding to please Him.

Thursday 50

2 Timothy 2:8-14

What is the writer saying?

How can I apply this to my life?

pray — *United Kingdom – Wisdom for those ministering among the 900,000 college and university students.*

Here Paul directs the readers' thoughts, as well as ours, to Jesus Christ and His resurrection. *Of the seed of David* points to His *humanity* and the fulfillment of the promises God made to David (cf. 2 Samuel 7:16). *Raised from the dead* focuses attention on the *deity* of Christ, and the power of God demonstrated in the resurrection (cf. Romans 1:1-4). To Paul, the paramount truth of the Gospel (he called it *my Gospel* – Romans 2:16; 16:25) was the resurrection.

That Gospel of his (v. 8) is what brought about his present distress (v. 9). He is chained like a common criminal, because he preached it. Yet "the word of God is not bound" (v. 9). In fact, in prison he could still preach the Word. In fact, as many have pointed out, he often had a *captive audience*; the Roman soldiers to whom he was chained. That being the case, he was able to "endure all the things for the elect's sakes." (v. 10) He wanted to see

the salvation resulting in these who believed, culminating in eternal glory, salvation's final state (v. 10).

In verses 11-13 we have the longest of the five *faithful sayings* contained in the pastorals (1 Timothy 1:15; 3:1; 4:9; 2 Timothy 2:11-13; Titus 3:8). Thought to be *prophetic sayings* by the New Testament prophets in the early church, they summarized their beliefs in a pre-canon age. The theme here is Christ's death and resurrection, and our union with Christ in those significant historical events (v. 11). "If we suffer (better: endure), we shall also reign with him," but, "if we deny (fail to endure) him, he also will deny us (the reign or reward that could have been)" (v. 12). Then comes a contrast of God's faithfulness versus man's unfaithfulness (v. 13). The latter can never abrogate the former. For Christ to abandon His own would be contrary to His nature (cf. John 10:27-30; Hebrews 10:23; 13:5).

 Life STEP — God faithfully fulfilled His promise by sending the Redeemer. Pause now to thank Him for His faithfulness and recommit yourself to be faithful to Him.

2 Timothy 2:15-19

What is the writer saying?

How can I apply this to my life?

Paul's charge to Timothy continues, *don't get caught up in fighting over words!* The result is *no profit* and *the subverting (turning upside down) of the hearers.* Positively, however, (v. 15) "study (be eager, zealous, diligent) to shew (present oneself for service) thyself approved (accepted after testing) unto God, a workman that needeth not to be ashamed, rightly dividing (cutting straight) the word of truth." Proper preaching, says Paul, goes straight ahead, never veering left or right, always *correctly handling* the Word, never twisting or changing the truth.

Having been attacked by false teachers, Timothy was warned to: (a) *Stick to the essentials.* Don't argue over empty words and philosophies (v. 16) (b) *Rightly divide the Word.* Failing to do so gives room to false teachers to promote false doctrines, which unchecked eat like a gangrene (Greek- *gangraina,* i.e., a malignant sore that eats away healthy tissue) (v. 17). These false teachers (two are named) *erred* (wandered away) *concerning the truth* (v. 18), probably teaching there was no bodily resurrection, that the resurrection of believers had already occurred. Early Gnosticism emphasized a spiritual resurrection over a future bodily resurrection. Unchecked, this sort of *spiritualization* will destroy weaker believers, because the resurrection is central to the Gospel, hence the need for proper exegesis.

"Nevertheless" (v. 19)...in spite of the efforts of the false teachers..."the foundation of God standeth sure." Exchanging his negative tone for a note of encouragement, Paul...based on the tense of the verb...indicates that he saw the truth of God standing firm, not only in the past, but also in the present (cf. Isaiah 40:8). Armed with that truth, and knowing to whom we belong, the challenge is to live a life of purity.

Life stEP   Pray for those whose job it is to preach the Word of God. The souls of their listeners may be dependent upon their rightly dividing the Word of Truth.

2 Timothy 2:20-26

What is the writer saying?

How can I apply this to my life?

pray — India – For God to save and call to homeland missions many of the 22 million Indians living abroad.

Verse 20 employs the phrase *a great house*. This is a reference to the church, *the household of God* (1 Timothy 3:15), in which are two general types of vessels: those of honor and much value (*gold and silver*), and those of dishonor and little value (*wood and earth* – pottery). The emphasis is not on the usefulness of the vessels (for the latter are probably more useful than the former that are saved for special occasions), but the value or quality of the vessel. Wood and pottery will eventually chip and break and must be replaced (a picture of false teachers whose worthlessness is recognized and leads to removal). This is not true with gold or silver. Their value is retained.

The honored vessel is to purge himself from those who are dishonored (v. 21). Contamination must be avoided. The results of doing so: (1) he is *sanctified* – set apart for a holy purpose; (2) he is *meet* – profitable for the master's use (*master* – Greek despot – strong term denoting God's total authority);

and (3) *prepared (ready) for every good work*. Having avoided contamination, the honored vessel is to maintain his value by staying clean. This is a two-step process. *Negatively – Flee*: avoid, shun *youthful lusts* (more than simply sexual, but also pride, ego, power, love of money, etc.) *Positively – Follow*: pursue after, *righteousness, faith, charity, peace* (1 Timothy 6:11). Both steps are vital. To fail in either will render one's ministry valueless.

Paul then cautions Timothy to *avoid* "foolish and unlearned (stupid) questions (arguments)…they do gender (breed) strifes (quarrels)." He had given similar instructions earlier (1 Timothy 1:4,7; 4:7; 6:20; 2 Timothy 2:16). He then calls Timothy the *servant (doulos)* of the Lord, and as such he has no will of his own. He is to be governed by his master in every respect. The chapter's latter verses (vv. 23-26) explain how to deal with problems in God's house so that strife and contention are avoided.

Life STEP — Let us also *flee*, *follow*, and *avoid*.

2 Timothy 3:1-7

What is the writer saying?

How can I apply this to my life?

pray   *Taiwan – For revival in the one Han Chinese nation that remains resistant to the Gospel.*

Here we see the necessity of chapter two's exhortation. The theme is "the last days" (v. 1) and the character of men in those days. Those *last days* began with the life and ministry of Christ (Hebrews 1:2), and will continue until Christ returns. They will be difficult days marked by *apostasy* (a falling away – the act of professed Christians who deliberately reject the revealed truth of the deity of Christ and the effectiveness of His cross work). As Christ's return draws closer, man's evil characteristics (vv. 2-5, 8) will intensify (v. 13). Civilized behavior will completely break down.

Numbered among those characteristics are *lovers of their own selves* and *covetous*, the *twin sins* from which all the others flow. That such is the case can be seen in such characteristics as *unthankful, unholy, high-minded* (conceited), and *lovers of pleasure more than lovers of God. Without natural affection* and *disobedient to parents* suggest the breaking up of society as God intended it to be. Striking one's father was as bad as murder in Roman law; abusing a parent in Greek culture caused disinheritance; and honoring parents was the fifth of the Jews' Ten Commandments. Today's divorce statistics show how rapidly we are moving away from God's standards and how rapidly we seem to be moving to the end of the age. All of the age-end characteristics can be found on the pages of today's newspapers, further indication that Christ's return is drawing near.

Accompanying all of the above is a *form of godliness,* but that is all that it is…a form…for the true power of godliness is denied. The apostate religionists of the last days go through the motions and maintain their external forms, but they have not experienced the dynamic power of true Christianity that results in changed lives. From such, *turn* away.

Life stEP   The dark days in which we live have only one remedy: the Gospel of Jesus Christ.

2 Timothy 3:8-12

What is the writer saying?

How can I apply this to my life?

Paul uses Jannes and Jambres (not mentioned in the Old Testament, but found in Jewish tradition opposing Moses) as examples of men in the past that resisted God's truth. They were *men of corrupt minds*, similar to the apostates of Paul's day (and ours) who cannot understand truth (cf. Romans 1:21- 22; Ephesians 4:17-18; 1 Timothy 6:5), and *reprobate concerning the faith* (v. 8). Like Jannes and Jambres, this new group of truth-deniers will not get very far for "their folly shall be manifest unto all" (v. 9). Truth always triumphs in the end.

Verse 10 begins a new section of what can be considered Paul's final advice to Timothy. To encourage him to *hang in there*, he gives a strong word of personal testimony. He begins with "But thou...," demonstrating the difference between Timothy and the men Paul just referenced and continues: "hast fully known (you've observed)"...and notes that which his observation revealed: a life-style (that of Paul's) worth emulating. It begins with doctrine (teaching), goes on to *manner of life* (conduct), *purpose* (chief aim), and *faith* (the Gospel). To underscore that none of the above came easily, he mentions some personal characteristics that are vital when persecution comes to those who desire to live godly lives (v. 12): "longsuffering, charity, patience (endurance) (v. 10)." He reminds Timothy that he had endured numerous persecutions, but out of them all, the Lord delivered him (v. 11; cf. Acts 14:19-20; Psalm 34:17).

Paul moves from his own experiences to a word of encouragement by noting that persecution, in some sense at least, is the lot of all non-compromising believers. God does not always deliver His children from persecution but, as Paul has demonstrated and as Scripture testifies, He promises to be with them as they go through it (Matthew 28:20b).

Life STEP Endurance demonstrates the seriousness of our commitment to Christ. Keep on keeping on!

Tuesday 51

2 Timothy 3:13-17

What is the writer saying?

How can I apply this to my life?

pray *Aruba – Pray that the gospel radio broadcasts going out in the Papiamento language will yield fruit.*

Verse 13 is a transitional verse linking Paul's charge to Timothy (v. 14ff), and the importance behind it to the offenders described earlier in the chapter. *Therefore, Timothy, remember what you've learned, and who taught you* (your mother, grandmother, and Paul). The ladies taught him the Old Testament and pointed him to the Messiah. Paul comes along and provides the information that Christ indeed was the Messiah, and Timothy responded in faith.

Verses 14-17 are the key verses in 2 Timothy, demonstrating the unparalleled value of the Scriptures. Its words bring about salvation (v. 15) and equip us for productive Christian living (v. 17). Its effectiveness is because "all Scripture is given by inspiration of God" (one word in the Greek: God-breathed). Inspiration...the out-breathing of God...was the process that produced the product: the Word of God. Because

it is God's Word, it is *profitable* (v. 16). It takes the believer and guides all his footsteps, from start to finish. One writer (Guy King) describes those steps this way: (1) FORWARD STEPS – *doctrine*, teaching. How to move ahead in the Christian life. (2) FALSE STEPS – *reproof*. The pointing out of one's faults. (3) FALTERING STEPS – *correction*. Learning not only how we have gone wrong, but how to get right. (Cf. Psalm 119:9). (4) FIRST STEPS – *instruction*. This is a word that would be used for the training of a child. That training is to be *in righteousness*. For all these purposes, the Holy Scriptures are both highly profitable and highly effective. *By faith* Timothy became *a child (teknon – born one) of God* (1 Timothy 1:2). Now, by utilizing the Scriptures, he has grown into a *"man of God."* The result is *"good works"* (v. 17).

 Life stEP The title *man of God* usually reserved for prophets in the Old Testament can today belong to all believers. Let's live up to it!

2 Timothy 4:1-4

What is the writer saying?

How can I apply this to my life?

pray   *Ukraine – For believers willing to translate biblical resource material into the Ukrainian language.*

Be reminded as we work our way through this fourth and final chapter of the book that this is the last chapter we have from the pen of the Apostle Paul. As he begins to bring this letter to a close, Paul's appeal to Timothy to *hang in there* comes into clear focus. To support his appeal he reminds Timothy that Jesus will one day return in judgment (v. 1) and he is answerable to the Lord as to how he carries out his ministry. This idea of judgment is a primary theme of the apostle, especially as it relates to the life and ministry of believers (cf. 1 Corinthians 3:11-17; 5:11-12).

The ministry Timothy is to have is spelled out in verse 2 where five exhortations are given. The final four flow quite naturally out of the first, which is: (1) "Preach the Word," for the Word is the foundation of any ministry. It is to be done (2) with urgency: "instant in season, out of season..." Whether the time is convenient or inconvenient, or circumstances favorable or unfavorable...just do it!

(3) Included should be reproof (*to correct, convince*) – show them how they have done wrong. (4) Rebuke – show them how wrong they were to do wrong. Finally, (5) exhort – show them that they must right the wrong and not repeat it. There is an implication in this *Preach the Word* command. It is not preach about the Word, or even from the Word, but preach the Word, which implies knowledge. This makes study (remember 2:15) of the Word vital. All of these exhortations are to be accompanied with *long-suffering* (great patience) and *doctrine* (careful instruction) (v. 2).

Why the command? Because the time will come (v. 3) when men will not want the Word. They will want to hear what makes them feel good, (*having itching ears*). Given time those *itching ears*, which are satisfied with shallow religious entertainment, will soon become deaf ears, as they turn away from the truth to man-made fables (v. 4).

Preach the Word. The instruction is to Timothy, but applies to us as well. Faithfully pass on the Word of God.

2 Timothy 4:5-8

What is the writer saying?

How can I apply this to my life?

Earlier (v. 2) Timothy is told to "preach the Word." Why? "...the time will come" when men will not want "sound doctrine" (v. 3) or "truth," but will turn to "fables" (v. 4). In light of that, Timothy is given four instructions in verse 5: "*Watch*" – be sober in judgment. "*Endure afflictions*" – the work of the ministry is not without its price. "*Do the work of an evangelist*" – remember to evangelize the lost (a difficult, but still required, task for someone timid). "*Make full proof of thy ministry*" – accomplish the purpose to which you've been called. Those instructions are valid not only for Timothy, but for all of God's children.

In verses 6-8, Paul makes it clear it is time for him to move on and pass the torch to others. His reflective words form perhaps the greatest *exit testimony* ever recorded. He has come to the end of his life with no regrets. He goes on (v. 6) to illustrate in two ways his victorious view of death. First, "I am now ready to be offered" (poured out like a drink offering). He considered his life and ministry an offering to God (Romans 15:16; Philippians 2:17). Second, "the time of my departure is at hand." It is time to set sail, take down the tent and move on (cf. 2 Peter 1:14-15).

He then uses three illustrations (v. 7) that demonstrate his finishing well. "I have fought a good fight," i.e., the act of a soldier (2:3-4). "I have finished my course," i.e., the goal of an athlete (2:5). "I have kept the faith," i.e., the responsibility of a steward of the Gospel (1 Timothy 1:11). Having done so, Paul expects the same from Timothy (1 Timothy 6:20, 2 Timothy 1:14).

"Henceforth," (v. 8) a reward is waiting, the end result of a lifetime of faithful service to Christ the *righteous judge*, who when He returns, would bring with Him rewards for those who served God faithfully during their earthly sojourn (Matthew 5:10-12).

Life stEP   What a joy to have no regrets and to know that you have done what God asked of you. Follow Paul's example!

2 Timothy 4:9-15

What is the writer saying?

How can I apply this to my life?

pray · Columbia – For the need for quality teachers to train young leaders among the 20 theological schools.

Following his *exit* testimony (vv. 6-8), Paul requests Timothy to: "come shortly unto me (v. 9)," and "come before winter" (v. 21) implying that when winter comes, travel will be more difficult, so an early arrival would be preferable. "The cloak that I left at Troas with Carpus, when thou comest, bring with thee" (v. 13), indicates it will provide some comfort in the cold surroundings of his prison cell.

Paul then begins to list some of his co-workers (he always recognized their importance and was grateful for their assistance). The first one mentioned, however, triggered unpleasant memories. *Demas*, who at one time had been one of Paul's trusted co-workers (cf. Colossians 4:14; Philemon 24), had deserted him for what the world had to offer (v. 10) and, apparently when he was most needed. *Crescens* was off to Galatia on ministry and *Titus* to Dalmatia as Paul's emissary. "Only Luke is with me" (v. 11), but for one afflicted with some physical problem as was Paul (2 Corinthians 12:7-9), who better to have as a companion than a medical doctor? "Take Mark, and bring him with thee." This was the young man who had earlier deserted Paul but had since proved himself (Colossians 4:10). He was now *profitable* for the ministry (v. 11).

Besides the cloak, Paul requests his *books* and *parchments*. The *books* may have been some of Paul's own writings, and *parchments* Paul's personal copies of Old Testament Scriptures. In verses 14-15 Paul refers to an *Alexander*, who in some way did Paul *evil*. Regardless of how it was done, Paul shows no bitterness or *get-even* attitude. At the same time, Paul cautions Timothy to be on guard against him.

Life stEP · The ministry of one's co-workers can make or break the ministry being performed. Thank God for those who serve faithfully with you, and pray that like John Mark, you also will be *ministry-profitable*.

2 Timothy 4:16-22

What is the writer saying?

How can I apply this to my life?

pray   *Korea – Protection and perseverance of nearly 100,000 believers confined in North Korean camps.*

In this passage, the forgiving attitude of Christ is seen in Paul. Although many had abandoned him, he asked the Lord not to hold them accountable for their actions (v. 16). He writes, "At my first answer" (defense)–the preliminary hearing prior to trial–"no man stood with me." No one appeared to serve as defense attorney, though that was a common practice. Furthermore, "all men forsook me." Those who could have testified for him were also absent. Yet Paul, in spite of their abandonment, like Christ (Luke 23:34) and Stephen (Acts 7:60) before him, exhibits the grace of God he himself had experienced (1 Timothy 1:12-15). Left alone (but not alone – "the Lord stood with me," v. 17), Paul conducted his own defense and took the opportunity to preach the Gospel… "that by me the preaching might be fully known." He left nothing out. Even as he said to the Ephesian elders in Acts 20:27, "I…declare unto you all the counsel of God," he used this opportunity to preach the complete Gospel about which he had written (1 Corinthians 15:1-4). His defense was unusual; it said little about him, but much about the Lord, "that all the Gentiles might hear." The Lord again (2 Corinthians 11:16-33), delivered him "out of the mouth of the lion," a metaphoric expression in Paul's day to express deliverance from extreme danger and a biblical image Paul was familiar with (cf. Psalm 22:21; Daniel 6:22).

Paul extends final greetings (vv. 19-22), naming nine of his co-workers. His benediction (v. 22) is two-fold. *Personal* to Timothy: "The Lord Jesus Christ be with thy spirit." *Corporately* to all believers: "Grace be with you (all). Amen."

Life stEP   Grace… the watchword of Paul's life. He had experienced it, and he passed it along to others. May the forgiving Spirit that prevailed in him permeate our lives as well.

Jonah means "Dove" and is spelled "Jonas" in the New Testament.

He lived during the long reign of wicked King Jeroboam II (793-753 BC) in the Northern Kingdom of Israel. His story probably takes place around 760 BC. (There are no dates in the book but this would be the general time of Assyria's dominance in the Middle East during which time the Northern Kingdom of Israel still existed. It was destroyed in 722 BC). Jonah lived near Nazareth which is interesting since in John 7:52 the Pharisees mockingly say, "Search, and look: for out of Galilee ariseth no prophet."

The story has been dismissed as a fairy tale by liberal thinkers. However, Christ Himself refers to the story in Matthew 12:39 and states that what happened to Jonah was a picture of Christ's own death, burial and resurrection. Well-meaning Christians have tried to defend the story by recounting tales of whalers washed over board, swallowed by whales and recovered days later but these stories have been researched and demonstrated to be "tall tales" of over-imaginative New England sailors. God does not need our help in performing miracles as, by definition, a miracle is something contrary to the laws of physics.

It is interesting to note that in the Assyrian historical records, while not mentioning this spiritual revival, there nevertheless was a period of quiet about the time of Jonah's revival. There also seems to be some "heart preparation" by God in that during the reign of the Assyrian king Assurdan III (771-754 BC) the city of Nineveh was devastated by the plague in 765 BC and 759 BC and experienced a total eclipse of the sun on June 15, 763 BC.

The theme of his book is "International, Cross-cultural Missions." God calls him to be such a missionary but Jonah needed an attitude adjustment first. In chapter one, Jonah rejects the mission. In chapter two he reconsiders the mission. In chapter three he completes the mission and in chapter four he regrets the success of his mission.

While Jonah lost the joy of being an evangelistic tool in the hand of God, he does illustrate the fact that God always intended the Jewish people to be an evangelistic force to the gentile world as expressed in Exodus 19:6, Isaiah 61:6 and Zechariah 8:23.

In Jewish history, legend has it that Jonah went on his trip during the Feast of Tabernacles. During this week-long holiday 70 bulls were sacrificed every year (Numbers 29). These 70 bulls supposedly represent God's provision of salvation for the 70 gentile nations in the known world. The Book of Jonah is also read on the afternoon of Yom Kippur (The Day of Atonement) as a reminder of God's mercy and humans' need to repent.

Jonah 1:1-17

What is the writer saying?

How can I apply this to my life?

pray *Venezuela – For the despair caused by poverty, crime, and violence to cause people to seek Christ.*

Jonah was the first man commissioned to go to a foreign field. He was also a reluctant prophet. God said "Go" (v. 2); Jonah said "No" (v. 3); and God said: "Oh?" The point is clear. When we say no to God, we will certainly be the object of the correcting hand of God. It is interesting that Jonah went the opposite way "from the presence of the Lord." This was foolishness because it can't be done. (See Psalm 139:7-12.) He probably tried to rationalize his disobedience. After all, he "found a ship going to Tarshish." Did he assume this to be God's second choice? He walked down to the dock, and there, on time, a ship showed up to the very place he had in mind. Remember that the Lord never leads us contrary to His Word, even if the circumstances appear to work out. When we decide to go against God's commandments in the wrong direction, Satan will always supply the transportation. Note that he even paid the fare. While he was honest toward man, he certainly wasn't honest to the Lord. God sent a great storm. Great storms follow great disobedience. Jonah even becomes the *hero* in the situation, claiming the storm was his fault and volunteering to be thrown overboard.

 Is there a bit of Jonah in you? Are there times when you too have a double standard; one for man and one for God? Be assured that one sign that we belong to Him is His dealing with us in our disobedience.

Jonah 2:1-10

What is the writer saying?

How can I apply this to my life?

A great fish swallowed Jonah. Should we take this as a literal account? Absolutely, Christ did. (See Matthew 12:40.) Jonah was disobedient to the Lord's command, and we find him alive in the belly of the whale. Yes, God sent him to *whale seminary* for a postgraduate course in obedience. If you count the personal pronouns in this chapter, you will discover that Jonah is still learning. We should not be so concerned about who is in the whale, but what is in Jonah. He is a stubborn prophet to be sure. It's almost as though he is in the belly of the whale, looks around and wonders how he is going to *fix this place up*. If that seems far-fetched, look at verse nine where it says, "But I will sacrifice unto thee with the voice of thanksgiving; I will pay that which I have vowed!" Think of it, he decided to tithe! He is going to fulfill his obligation. He has *personal pronoun—it is* which can be devastating for any child of God.

Finally, in desperation, he turns from *self* and exclaims, "Salvation is of the Lord" (v. 9). That did it! When we come to the end of ourselves and recognize Him and His Lordship, we are on the way to recovery. Immediately, the Lord responds, "And the LORD spake unto the fish, and it vomited out Jonah upon the dry land" (v. 10). Note, he didn't just tell the whale to cast him out, but also specified "on the dry land." He could have said, *Swim Jonah! The rest is up to you*. No, when God does something it is a complete work. Praise God for that!

Don't forget the words of Christ when He said, "For as Jonas was three days and three nights in the whale's belly; so shall the Son of man be three days and three nights in the heart of the earth" (Matthew 12:40). Thank Him for His death and resurrection.

Jonah 3:1-10

What is the writer saying?

How can I apply this to my life?

pray   *China – For the failure of all government attempts to impose false doctrine on registered churches.*

Finally, we find Jonah conforming to the will of God. Verse three is refreshing. We are told that the Word of the Lord came to Jonah "the second time" (3:1). How thankful we should be that the Lord is in the business of giving second chances. It was so with Peter, with John Mark, with me and with you. I imagine that you are grateful—I certainly am!

Now we see this once rebellious prophet as an obedient prophet, preaching the gospel to the whole city of Nineveh. Historians tell us that the city had about 600,000 people. The message was short and succinct. In Luke 11:29-30, we are told that Jonah was a sign to Nineveh. Note that the whole city turned to God. It was, without a doubt, the greatest example of conversion ever recorded. They were not brought to the Lord by a gimmick but by the clear, unmistakable message of judgment. Sometimes we hear people saying that God can't work in a great way today – citing the wickedness of the people and their indifference to the things of God. But you must remember that this city was known for its cruelty and sinfulness. It was so bad the Lord threatened to judge it. But thankfully, they repented and turned to God. Let us pray for revival in our land – that there would be a turning to the Lord in repentance and faith. We must remember that in the Great Commission, Christ said: "Lo, I am with you always, even to the end of the age" (Matthew 28:20).

Life stEP   As we think of evangelism and outreach, we need to remember that "indeed a greater than Jonah is here" (Matthew 12:41). Are there people for whom you are burdened? Does their conversion seem impossible? Don't give up. God is able! Keep praying!

Jonah 4:1-11

What is the writer saying?

How can I apply this to my life?

pray — Ecuador – Praise for effective Christian radio ministry that encourages believers and spreads the Gospel.

If the book of Jonah had ended in chapter three, it would have been *a happily ever after* conclusion. But, such is not the case. The Prophet Jonah is found reacting to the mercy of the Lord in sparing the city of Nineveh. Several questions are in order here.

1. What made Jonah angry (vv. 1-4)? He was hurt because he felt his reputation would be damaged. He was more interested in his good name than in the souls to whom he preached.

2. Why was Jonah apathetic (v. 5)? We find him sitting on the east side of the city waiting to see what the Lord would do. So there he is sitting in the heat of the day and the Lord prepared a gourd to come over his head to shelter him from the heat. Jonah was glad!

3. What pleased Jonah (v. 6)? Does it surprise you that the first sign of joy and happiness in this whole book is found when Jonah's head is sheltered? Jonah was delivered from the belly of the whale and is used mightily so a whole city is converted, but the real joy comes when his body is protected. You can tell a great deal about a person when you discover what makes them angry – or glad. God allows the gourd to be smitten, the gourd so cherished by Jonah. It withered. Then the sun and the wind fell on Jonah and he wanted to die. What a commentary on Jonah's attitude.

4. What lessons can we learn from this (v. 11)? The answer is clear. We get a true understanding of a compassionate God in contrast with a man who had no compassion.

Life stEP

Do we have the mind of Christ? Do we see the world as He sees it? Can we look through the eyes of the Lord compassionately? Let us pray that God will burden us today for a lost and dying world and to act on it.

There are twelve *Minor Prophets*, so called, not because they are unimportant, but because they are smaller than the *Former Prophets* (Moses, Joshua, Judges, 1 & 2 Samuel and 1&2 Kings) and the *Major Prophets* (Isaiah, Jeremiah, Ezekiel, and Daniel). The Minor Prophets cover some of the same themes as the other prophets, but in addition, they emphasize social justice and true worship. Nine of the books of the Minor Prophets were written before the destruction of the Temple in 586 B.C. while the last three were written after the return from the Babylonian Exile (the *Post-Exilic Prophets*— Haggai, Zechariah, and Malachi). One is written against the country of Edom (Obadiah). Two are written about Nineveh (Jonah and Nahum). Two condemn the Northern Kingdom or "Israel" (Hosea and Amos). Seven are directed to the Southern Kingdom or "Judah" (Joel, Micah, Habakkuk, Zephaniah, Haggai, Zechariah, and Malachi).

Micah's name means, *Who is Like Jehovah*. He came from Moresheth, about twenty-three miles southwest of Jerusalem. He was a younger contemporary of Isaiah who preached to the common people of Judah while Isaiah ministered in the capital city of Jerusalem and Hosea ministered in the Northern Kingdom. His ministry is dated 730-700 BC. The theme of his book is: *Judgment Followed by Blessing*. The outline of Micah is:

Judgment Announced	1-3
Deliverance Announced	4-5
Israel's Destruction Predicted	6
Thy Kingdom Come	7

Isaiah and Micah ministered through the period of time when Israel tried to force Judah to join in a coalition against the Assyrians. The ungodly kings of Judah (such as Ahaz and Manasseh) displeased the Lord by trying to protect themselves through military might and treaties made with Assyria and Egypt. These human efforts were doomed to fail and by 701 BC, the erstwhile allies, the Assyrians, had conquered every city of Judah except Jerusalem. In the Assyrian chronicles King Sennacherib bragged that he had "shut up King Hezekiah like a bird in a cage." Fortunately, Hezekiah was a godly king and when he called upon the Lord with Isaiah and Micah's encouragement, God delivered Jerusalem from the Assyrians.

While Isaiah ministered to the leaders and aristocracy in Jerusalem, Micah ministered to the common folk. He condemned the idle rich (chap. 2), oppressive government (chap. 3), and hypocritical, ritualistic state religion (chap. 3). Even though Micah was younger, Isaiah shows his support and appreciation of Micah by quoting material from Micah 4 in Isaiah 2 (Jeremiah attributes the quote to Micah in Jeremiah 26:18).

Jeremiah also quoted Micah, which God used to save Jeremiah's life from evil King Jehoiakim! (3:12 in Jeremiah 26:18). In Matthew 2:5, the religious rulers quote Micah 5:2 identifying Bethlehem as the birthplace of the Messiah in response to Herod the Great's questioning. In Matthew 10:21, 35, 36, Christ quotes Micah 7:6 as He prepares the disciples for the hardships of their ministry. Important predictions in Micah include the 722 BC destruction and exile of the northern 10 tribes (1:6), the 701 BC attack by Assyria on Judah (1:9), and the 586 BC destruction of Jerusalem and deportation by the Babylonians (3:12, 4:10, 7:13).

Micah 4:1-8; 5:2-4

What is the writer saying?

How can I apply this to my life?

pray *South Africa – For national churches to commit financial aid to those seeking to attend Bible school.*

Someday Christ will come to the earth and establish His kingdom. The first few verses of this passage deal with that. The "mountain" should be taken literally; it is a reference to the Mount of Olives where Christ will someday return (Zechariah 14:4). The Golden Age of the Kingdom is described. Of course, the rapture of the church comes first, followed by the Tribulation, and lastly, the Kingdom. We see that the Kingdom is universal (v. 2). It is peaceful (v. 3). Also, inflexible righteousness and justice will characterize it. Verse three is often quoted as something of a goal for the United Nations. We must leave the passage in the context. Only when the King of King comes will we have such peace.

Now as we approach chapter five we have verses that speak of both His first and second comings. As you study your Bible, you will find similarities between Isaiah and Micah. (Isaiah is Micah enlarged.) Both speak of the birth of Christ; Isaiah tells us the manner of his birth, while Micah gives the place (Bethlehem). "Bethlehem" means *house of bread* and "Ephratah" is from the Hebrew meaning *fruitful*. Both point to Christ the Bread of Life (John 6:35) and the vine (John 15:1). Isn't it interesting that in one verse we have both the first and second comings of the Lord? Peter must have had passages like this in mind when he said the prophets searched regarding the sufferings of Christ (His first coming) and the glory that was to follow (His second coming).

Just as the Word of God was literally fulfilled at Christ's first coming, so it will be with respect to His second coming. How wonderful to know that the Lord is in full control and will be good to His precious promises.

Micah 6:1-8

What is the writer saying?

How can I apply this to my life?

pray | *Uganda – For churches to make a commitment to educate, nurture, and disciple their young people.*

Here we find the Lord beseeching both nature and man. The mountains are called as silent witness of all that God has done for Israel in past days. In verses 4 and 5, we see Him calling Israel to remember what He had done for them. How easily they had forgotten His miraculous hand on their behalf. The reply of Israel is seen in verses 6-7. What we read here is heartbreaking. They seemed so willing to do something, but it was so very short of full obedience. There was a *hands-off* policy and a partial commitment. How foolish to offer God their things and yet hold back their hearts' affections and their obedient living.

Note in verse eight what the Lord requires. Can man meet God's standard? Man in himself cannot meet God's standard; only when he is born again. Then the Holy Spirit can do in and through him what he could never have done in himself. (See Romans 8:1-3.)

There are both outward and inward requirements. It has been said that this verse is the epitome of the whole law. The liberal often uses this verse to show that this is religion in which he believes and that it is sufficient for him. Indeed, this could well be called the *Standard of the Kingdom*. But the requirement of God must be coupled with the redemption in grace and shared righteousness. This is followed by practical righteousness in the power of the Lord.

Life **STEP** | While we cannot perform the morality of the law, it can indeed be displayed in us. This is the secret of the victorious Christian life.

Micah 7:7-20

What is the writer saying?

How can I apply this to my life?

pray — *Jamaica – For quality staff and increased enrollment among Jamaica's Bible schools and seminaries.*

Note the "I wills" of verse seven and nine. Here we have a trusting remnant in the last days. Their confidence is in the Lord. There is a bearing of indignation followed by a restoration referred to in verse nine. Verses 11-12 indicate a later and final fulfillment of the prophecy. The walls are to be built in that future day after the Tribulation. Verse 13 shows, however, that first the land would be desolate. In verse 14, we have a prayer. It is answered in the next three verses (vv. 15-17) depicting the Millennium. Verse 18 predicts the conversion of Israel.

Verses 18 and 19 are beautiful. Still God's justice is seen in clothing Israel with the righteousness of God. It must be remembered that all salvation, whether in the Old Testament, in our present day or in the Tribulation is based on Christ's finished work and the applied righteousness of God through Christ. So, in a real sense, we have in this chapter the divine pardon in justice, the salvation of Israel and the eventual Messianic Kingdom.

These verses are read, along with Jonah, in the synagogue on the afternoon of the Day of Atonement. On the afternoon of the New Year, the Orthodox Jew can be found going to a running stream and symbolically emptying his pockets of his sins as he recites verses 18-20.

Life STEP — Every believer knows that all such rituals cannot avail for man's sin. Our sins are only cast in the *sea of God's forgetfulness* when we enter into the provision God has made through His blessed Son.

The following chart is provided to enable everyone using Word of Life Quiet Times to stay on the same passages. This list also aligns with the daily radio broadcasts.

Week 1	Aug 30 – Sep 5	Psalms 77:1-79:13
Week 2	Sep 6 – Sep 12	Psalms 80:1-86:17
Week 3	Sep 13 – Sep 19	Psalms 87:1-91:16
Week 4	Sep 20 – Sep 26	Psalms 92:1-97:12
Week 5	Sep 27 – Oct 3	Psalms 98:1-103:22
Week 6	Oct 4 – Oct 10	Ephesians 1:1-2:22
Week 7	Oct 11 – Oct 17	Ephesians 3:1-4:32
Week 8	Oct 18 – Oct 24	Ephesians 5:1-6:24
Week 9	Oct 25 – Oct 31	Joshua 1:1-5:15
Week 10	Nov 1 – Nov 7	Joshua 6:1-14:15
Week 11	Nov 8 – Nov 14	Joshua 20:1-24:33
Week 12	Nov 15 – Nov 21	Titus 1:1 - Philemon 25
Week 13	Nov 22 – Nov 28	Revelation 1:1-2:29
Week 14	Nov 29 – Dec 5	Revelation 3:1-6:8
Week 15	Dec 6 – Dec 12	Revelation 6:9-10:11
Week 16	Dec 13 – Dec 19	Revelation 11:1-14:7
Week 17	Dec 20 – Dec 26	Revelation 14:8-17:18
Week 18	Dec 27 – Jan 2	Revelation 18:1-20:6
Week 19	Jan 3 – Jan 9	Revelation 20:7-22:21
Week 20	Jan 10 – Jan 16	Judges 2:1-7:25
Week 21	Jan 17 – Jan 23	Judges 8:22-17:6
Week 22	Jan 24 – Jan 30	Amos 1:1 - Obadiah 21
Week 23	Jan 31 – Feb 6	John 1:1-3:12
Week 24	Feb 7 – Feb 13	John 3:13-5:14
Week 25	Feb 14 – Feb 20	John 5:15-6:58
Week 26	Feb 21 – Feb 27	John 6:59-8:24

Week 27	Feb 28 – Mar 6	John 8:25-10:13
Week 28	Mar 7 – Mar 13	John 10:14-12:11
Week 29	Mar 14 – Mar 20	John 12:12-14:14
Week 30	Mar 21 – Mar 27	John 14:15-16:33
Week 31	Mar 28 – Apr 3	John 17:1-19:22
Week 32	Apr 4 – Apr 10	John 19:23-21:25
Week 33	Apr 11 – Apr 17	Proverbs 16:1-18:12
Week 34	Apr 18 – Apr 24	Proverbs 18:13-20:30
Week 35	Apr 25 – May 1	Zechariah 1:1-5:11
Week 36	May 2 – May 8	Zechariah 6:1-9:17
Week 37	May 9 – May 15	Zechariah 10:1-14:21
Week 38	May 16 – May 22	Hebrews 1:1-3:19
Week 39	May 23 – May 29	Hebrews 4:1-6:20
Week 40	May 30 – Jun 5	Hebrews 7:1-9:10
Week 41	Jun 6 – Jun 12	Hebrews 9:11-10:31
Week 42	Jun 13 – Jun 19	Hebrews 10:32-11:40
Week 43	Jun 20 – Jun 26	Hebrews 12:1-13:25
Week 44	Jun 27 – Jul 3	1 Corinthians 1:1-3:15
Week 45	Jul 4 – Jul 10	1 Corinthians 3:16-7:9
Week 46	Jul 11 – Jul 17	1 Corinthians 7:10-10:11
Week 47	Jul 18 – Jul 24	1 Corinthians 10:12-12:20
Week 48	Jul 25 – Jul 31	1 Corinthians 12:21-15:11
Week 49	Aug 1 – Aug 7	1 Corinthians 15:12-16:24
Week 50	Aug 8 – Aug 14	2 Timothy 1:1-2:26
Week 51	Aug 15 – Aug 21	2 Timothy 3:1-4:22
Week 52	Aug 22 – Aug 28	Jonah 1:1 - Micah 7:20